Vocation

studies in vocational and continuing education

vol. 15

edited by
philipp gonon & anja heikkinen

peter lang
bern · bruxelles · frankfurt am main · new york · oxford · warszawa · wien

Fernando Marhuenda-Fluixá (ed.)

Vocational Education beyond Skill Formation

Vet between Civic, Industrial and Market Tensions

peter lang

bern · bruxelles · frankfurt am main · new york · oxford · warszawa · wien

Bibliographic information published by Die Deutsche Bibliothek
Die Deutsche Nationalbibliothek lists this publication in the Deutsche
Nationalbibliografie; detailed bibliographic data is available on the
Internet at <http://dnb.d-nb.de>.

British Library Cataloguing-in-Publication Data: A catalogue record
for this book is available from The British Library, Great Britain

Library of Congress Control Number: 2017937982

ISSN 1660-3443 pb.   ISSN 2235-7327 eBook
ISBN 978-3-0343-2806-7 pb.   ISBN 978-3-0343-2807-4 eBook
ISBN 978-3-0343-2809-8 MOBI ISBN 978-3-0343-2808-1 EPUB

This publication has been peer reviewed.

The author acknowledges the support of the series editors, Anja Heikinnen
and Philipp Gonon, as well as the financial support provided by the latter.
The author acknowledges the generous and anonymous reviews by more
than 30 scholars all over the world, who have provided useful feedback
for authors to improve their chapters.

© Peter Lang AG, International Academic Publishers, Bern 2017
Wabernstrasse 40, CH-3007 Bern, Switzerland
info@peterlang.com, www.peterlang.com

Printed in Switzerland

Table of Contents

Section 3. Tensions between the Global and the Local: Adoptions, Rejections and Reactions to Standardization of VET Traditions

Fernando Marhuenda-Fluixá

Vocational Education, Labor and Citizenship: The Working Class, the Workforce and the Provision of Qualifications from Early to Contemporary Capitalism[1]

1. Conflicting roles of vocational education and training (VET), past and present

This book is part of the Peter Lang Series on Studies in Vocational and Continuing Education and it intends to contribute to the dialogue initiated in some of the previous volumes. Like previous books, this one compiles a variety of contributions from academics across the world, namely America (South and North), Africa and Europe.

In doing so, the book takes into account historical and comparative research with the focus set upon the contribution of VET policies and practices to the development of citizenship in at least three different domains: The first dimension is national identity, given that VET policies were developed, as part of educational policies, to contribute to the establishment of the nation-state; the second dimension is working class identity in a different way, because VET was considered originally, and it remains so to a large extent still, as the education provided for the lower classes; while academic secondary education, particularly at the post-compulsory level, was reserved for the elites; the third dimension is again working class identity, yet with an empowering meaning, as the

1   I want to acknowledge the generous reviews to this chapter contributed by Dr. Mary Jane Curry and students at her Doctoral Seminar at the Warner School of Education at the University of Rochester. This introduction was written while the author enjoyed a research stay at the University of Rochester, NY, USA, sponsored by the University of Valencia (UV-IN-EPDI16-382923).

education of the working class by the working class members themselves, therefore as the raising of a class consciousness proud of itself, with its own set of values and with a clear determination to become an autonomous class and not being dependent from the decisions of the elites.

Through this approach, the book maintains the critical perspective that is embedded in the series, for it takes into account not only pedagogical perspectives but also economic and cultural ones, alongside the history of VET, mostly developed in section 1. The book also does so by addressing current developments that address the tensions around the construction of citizenship at a time of various challenges and identities, as portrayed in sections 2 and 3, that focus upon present VET developments around the world. Some of these may seem new, while other challenges reenact past episodes in history and show ongoing and open on unresolved disputes among classes and regions. While previous books in the series have attempted to look at historical approaches to VET (Molzberger and Wahle 2015; Berner and Gonon 2016) and others have looked at social issues (Mjelde and Daly 2006; Gonon *et al.* 2009; Weil, Koski and Mjelde 2009; Stolz and Gonon 2011; Deissinger *et al.* 2013), none has focused on the theme that this book addresses.

Similarly to other books in the series, there is a large presence of women contributing to the volume. When it comes to chapters drawing on the history of VET and its relation to the labor movement, the presence of women is sometimes neglected while with others it has to do with the role they were assigned at the time. When it comes to chapters on contemporary affairs, the best example in the book is the chapter by Heikkinen, Kalimasi, Opit and Sjelvgren, on VET and the health care professions, which shows how gender differences are still consistent in terms of labor conditions as well as vocational qualifications. Further work is needed in this regard as well as work that stresses the gender dimension in issues like sustainability, disability, accreditation or local development. If VET is to deal with citizenship and contribute to a liberating and emancipated workforce, women must be a driving force. Their neglect in the past two centuries has brought us to the current situation, to show how domestic justifications are still often disguised as civic ones, to use the framework provided by Boltanski and Chiapello (2002) which supports discussions in some of the chapters in this book.

Again, like some of the previous books in the series, the idea for this volume was set in 2014, as the call for the international research network VET and Culture (Vocational Education and Training and Culture; <www.peda.net/veraja/uta/vetculture>) conference in Valencia, Spain, was initially launched and afterwards held in July 2015. At that time, as is still the case nowadays, Spain, like other Southern European countries (some of them represented in this volume, like Greece and Italy) was suffering the pressure of austerity policies enacted since the beginning of the political and economic crisis that followed the Lehman Brothers crisis and the financial storm that followed in 2008. European policies, both at EU level as well as at the country level, particularly in the South, forced severe budget cuts in terms of funding education, as well as other public services, in addition to other citizen rights and traditions of the welfare system that had characterized most Western European countries since the end of WWII.

In this sense, both VET as well as other education policies have been under siege ever since. On one side, a global trend towards privatization of education has been identified (Apple 2006; Ball 2013) in recent decades, particularly since the turn of the century. On the other side, when it comes to VET policies, there is a growing demand that they be *more responsive* to the demands of the labor market, as if it were not responsive enough or as if the labor market were ready to recognize the contribution of VET to increased productivity, competitiveness and innovation in the world of work as most VET systems have proved to be sensitive to the calls made by industry and services. Third, if VET was in its origin a truly educational option for those who were not considered to deserve another educational opportunity, in recent times, once compulsory education became universal in most Northern countries and extended to the majority of the population in most Southern countries, if one may generalize, VET has been deprived of its educational dimension. Indeed, attempts have been made to reduce VET to a training scheme/provision that focuses mainly upon skills development, forging the skills that are demanded by industry.

In this sense, debates about curriculum design and development (Marhuenda and Ros 2015) may also be applied to VET, opening discussions from technical to political. That is the intention of this book, to deal with VET as we do with other educational policies and practices. This means to acknowledge its educational worth, while recognizing its distinctiveness. VET is about the preparation of the workforce, but it is also about providing alternative, non-academic pathways for young people in order to further their education and to fulfill their vocational expectations in the sense of responding to a call or vocation.

But the book also deals with the education of adult people, of people in their teens, in transition into adulthood and into the world of work. As some have recently shown (Harju and Heikkinen 2016), the understanding of adult education has significantly changed since it received attention in the 1960s, and it cannot be reduced to continuing education nor to updating the skills needed by the workforce, as some policies would like it to become. Work-related adult education is an issue that cannot be ignored in adult education, but it is only one shape of the many that experiential education can take. This is an issue that we are currently researching in the context of Work Integration Enterprises (EDU2013-45919-R)[2] where we are trying to identify the social and personal dimensions that go aside the technical competences achieved in the workplace and necessary for an integrated life as active participants of civil society (Marhuenda, 2017).

2. Looking at VET from a taken for granted viewpoint

The idea for this volume came up at the 22nd conference of the VET& Culture Network held in Valencia in July 2015. Some of the chapters in this book are elaborations of papers presented to that conference, while more than half of them are new chapters, authored by scholars who did not attend that conference but who submitted contributions in response to the call.

The call for papers for that conference, written by Germán Gil and Fernando Marhuenda, attempted to reflect upon VET policies and practices, taking into account their educational dimension and its contribution to the formation not just of the individual worker/person but also of the responsible free citizen. This call required a socio-cultural and historical perspective able to move beyond a mere skills approach, without neglecting the need to promote capacity building.

2   Educational, accompanying, qualification and developmental processes in work integration companies: innovating social inclusion through employment.

There is a clear explanation for why such call was made from scholars in Spain in the autumn of 2014. The country, like others in Southern Europe, as well as in other regions of the world, has been severely hit by the confrontations between the center and the margins of the current economic developments. Spain has been displaced from the center, which it started approaching in the mid 1980s, to a marginal position, with both internal and external justifications for the austerity policies that are being implemented by the economic and political powers in worldwide institutions as well as in European ones. Such policies are imposing not only budgetary restrictions, but also a certain disrespect for civil rights, particularly those related to labor relations, which took a long time and many fights to achieve. Industrial work is under siege, and trade unions are being monitored if not demonized.

The current financial crisis has been used to widen the gap between capital and the workers. Data show how wealth has grown and is being distributed differentially, as an increasing number of scholars explain (Navarro and López 2012; Martínez 2013; Ariño and Romero 2016). This is a global trend, however, that manifests in diverse ways in different countries and regions throughout the world and that we intend to show in this book, with contributions from different regions at different levels of economic and social development, with different welfare regimes, as well as with chapters on how these trends, claims and pressures have been dealt with during the history of certain successful regions. That is the case of Switzerland, for example, which is very well covered in the book with three different contributions.

Across the different chapters in the book, we discuss *whether* and *how* vocational education can keep its educational value and *whether* and *how* vocational education is able to contribute in a proactive way to the demands, neither merely nor necessarily of the market, of citizenship and of the increasing participation of the large majority of the working force in economic and industrial decisions. We consider this plea particularly current at a time when workers' rights are being undermined across the world: in European countries, as a response to the ageing of the population and the need for human resources able to support the pension system developed as part of the welfare system; in other countries because the role of informal work (Bacchetta et al. 2009) has been much larger than that of formally recognized forms of work.

The labor market has undergone continual changes that have accelerated in the past decades. Some of the countries discussed in this book, in Southern European – Greece, Spain – or in South America – Brazil, Ecuador – have been used as experimental sites for new developments in terms of labor relations and production policies internationally, often through the intermediation of international funding bodies. While the labor market demands a skilled workforce, working conditions are increasingly precarious (Castel 1997; Standing 2011) and some international institutions claim for decent work (International Labor Office 2013; European Economic and Social Committee 2016; Comisión Europea 2014). The old divide between blue and white collar workers is now taking different shapes.

Across the past four decades, vocational education has contributed to the improvement of general education as a whole and helped it meet demands of the world such as greater application of content or the reduction of the academic weight through the introduction of work experience of various kinds. Apprenticeship has been strongly recommended by authors worldwide (Hamilton 1990; Marhuenda 2016) and the debate over dual systems and dual approaches to VET is heated in many countries worldwide, as one of the symposiums held at the Valencia conference showed (examples in Canada, México, the United States of America and Spain were debated) and it is discussed in the final section of this book.

It may be the right time to consider whether despite these efforts, vocational education is an independent educational offering, with its own identity; or perhaps it continues to be considered a subaltern educational offer, reserved for those not willing to pursue academic work. If this is the case, we wonder whether vocational education is ready to accept the challenge of merely serving the needs of the industry or whether it is ready to play a role in the formation of a strong working class consciousness about its role in political and economic discussions. The examples from different times and countries presented in the book show that the latter can be the case, which is a relevant contribution to the overall discussion from sections 1 and 2. This is a question behind many of the chapters of this book and clearly stated in the discussions held at the conference in Valencia.

All of these transformations happen parallel to and within the framework of the revision of the social contract of the welfare state that has ruled continental Europe since WWII. The European social protection system seems to be witnessing the end of its days, which is having a huge impact upon the workforce and working culture. The social contract that was part of the post WWII way of living in Northern and Western countries is being questioned and upheld (Castel 1997; Bauman 2000; Sennett 2000; Standing 2011).

Will vocational education nowadays be able to educate the workforce in terms of cooperation, political consciousness? Can we identify practices or policies with a clear determination to look for collective solutions and to share common problems instead of searching for individual alternatives to the current difficulties of the labor market? These are central questions that the contributors to the book were invited to address, from different historical, national, regional and theoretical perspectives. All contributions have been arranged in three sections, in which we intend to provide some answers for these questions, as well as to assess whether there is hope or whether our questions may not make sense any longer but rather pertain to a different era, one that has already passed. The reader of the volume must answer these questions. My belief is that most of the contributions provide a basis for worry as well as hope.

We expect the debates raised and addressed in this book to enlighten our present. We expect historical and contemporary considerations to inspire and challenge the reader's approach towards vocational education and citizen-related issues like the transitions between education and work, old and new forms of labor-market precariousness, low-quality employment and different forms of unemployment. Those are the issues that have been discussed along the years by networks such as VET&Culture or SUPI (Hepp et al. 2016).

3. Structure and content of the book

Section 1 covers how the central debates in the book relate to the origins of vocational education as well as the working class, as these two fields have strong connections and interdependencies. During the 19th century, European nationalisms ended with the establishment of the nation-state and the guarantee of basic compulsory education, which had three aims: first, to provide equal educational chances to the young generations, inspired by the principles of Enlightenment; second, to assure the consolidation of the modern state with the teaching of a common history, geography and language conducive to creating a national identity; third, to give those willing to learn beyond compulsory education the chance to develop their knowledge and skills. The end goal was to improve the productivity and competitiveness of the workplace, whether through the teaching of scientific disciplines or the development of vocational education emerging from a context where medieval guilds were not able to meet the fast-changing needs of the Industrial Revolution.

The relations between national citizenship and vocational education are addressed in the cases of Switzerland, Denmark and Italy, focusing upon the transformation of the guild training system into the apprenticeships that will be the basis for the development of a system of vocational education that fell far behind the expectations of the States themselves, yet contributed to its consolidation and differentiation.

Lorenzo Bonoli contends that although apprenticeship took a long while to be settled as a national educational policy, it contributed to developing a national identity during the time that the reforms took to be introduced. These issues can be traced anew in Esther Berner's chapter, which approaches the issue in terms of the justifications of policymakers in order to maintain and update the apprenticeship system. There are clear connections between Bonoli's chapter and Chiara Martinelli's, which deals with the debates over the role of apprenticeship and the modernization of VET at the birth of Italy as a nation-state.

Focusing on the same period of time, the contribution of Ida Juul points to a different and critical dimension of the struggles over apprenticeship in terms of national definition and of working class definition. Juul provides details of the tensions between Denmark and Germany and attempts to introduce national borders that would differentiate the quality of apprenticeships, challenging the previous distinctiveness of global journeymen. But Juul also points to internal power struggles in Denmark among the growing power of the bourgeoisie based on free trade, the craft power of the guilds, and the aristocracy as represented by the king. In this sense, Juul's paper makes a seminal contribution to the book, for it highlights the beginning of the capitalist state and describes tensions behind today's professional and class struggles, even if there have been changes in the power imbalances.

Berner's chapter can be better understood in relation to the debates that Lea Zehnder and Philipp Gonon present (in the third section, as explained below), as both chapters refer to contemporary time, that of the reconstruction of VET systems after the years of wealth that followed the reconstruction of Europe after WWII. Furthermore, Berner points to the need to reconsider the industrial system after the first oil crisis of the early 1970s, which set the scene for the new developments that came at the end of the 20th century and the first two decades of the 21st. Berner tackles the main role that civic justification has played in the process of keeping and modernizing apprenticeship within modern Swiss educational policies.

While the focus of these first five chapters is on the relations between vocational education and national identity, the two remaining chapters advance the issues presented by Juul and give us different insights into class struggles: those of the development of a worker's identity and the role of education in the developing class consciousness and an alternative view to citizenship. This viewpoint strengthens the weight of social class, the relation of humankind to work, in order to empower a large majority of the population who did not see themselves properly acknowledged nor represented by the powers that took over democratic institutions in both America and Europe. In this sense, the internationalist approach towards citizenship raised by the working class as an alternative to national citizenship was a relevant issue in debates not only in the second half of the 19th century but also very vividly during the troubling times around WWI. While colonialism played a relevant role in strengthening the power of the economic elites, the peace movement was also an invitation to the working class not to embark on a fight that was not its own but which served the interests of different social groups.

Within this context, Kenneth Teitelbaum provides insightful views on the development of an education of its own for the working class in the United States between 1900 and 1930, with implications not only for the education of the young generations but also for the development of adult education. Similarly, Germán Gil portrays the contribution of the anarchist movement to education debates in Spain as the country was facing the loss of all of its colonies, suffering a great depression and the reconsideration of its national identity. While the 19th century powers wanted to keep its dominance over a growing working class that was starting to claim freedom and rights, the Enlightenment principles arrived to Spain so late and so distant from the rest of Europe. We must not forget that these were the issues behind the Civil War in Spain in the mid 1930s, which was also an experimentation camp for WWII and the Cold War that followed it.

Here, I would like to point out that both Teitelbaum and Gil are aware of sources that could provide rich examples of the role of women within the practices they portray.

Also relevant is the fact that in both chapters, the role of workers as a class that is able to develop self-awareness and to establish its own aims gives profound hope to the current times: There is the possibility to collectively and autonomously face challenges that pose a risk to a social group. Whether done at regional, national or international levels, even if it has not happened in the past without much effort, these two examples show the possibilities of action taken by the actors themselves, what we might now call collective agency.

Seen as a whole, section 1 allows us to think two of parallel and intertwined developments: On the one side, the education of the working class provided by the nation-state in order to satisfy the need to be comfortable with the universal claim to education while preparing the workforce of the nation for the global competition. On the other hand, the education of the working class provided by itself, in the attempt to construct a class perspective of its own, respectful of humankind and attempting to be freed of the powers that control it and that are under control of other social groups. These are not simple issues, but rather require the understanding of both outer as well as inner confrontations in the struggle to set free and to achieve full status of autonomy, speech, vote, power and control, hence freedom. In both cases shown for Spain and the US, even if Marxism played a role as an ideology to facilitate the struggle against oppression, we can also find the attempts of different groups to achieve the aim of liberation while at the same time escaping from new forms of oppression that may arise from Marxism itself.

As a whole, section 1 equips the reader with a wide historical perspective where the Northern and Western societies were those allowing for such developments, as most other regions in the world were still severely suffering exploitation through colonialism, mainly by European countries.

Section 2 turns to present times and is more de-centered than the precedent section, insofar it provides examples from different regions, in both Western (Germany) and Southern Europe (one chapter focusing on Greece, two on Spain) as well as in South America (one chapter dealing with Brazil, one with Ecuador). Chapters in this section cover the different attempts by state institutions as well as by civic promotion or free citizens' initiatives to make VET more comprehensive and more educational, as well as to make it an offer as appealing, appreciated and valuable as academic pathways.

That is the case of the chapters addressing wider concerns that have come to VET debates recently, such as the introduction of sustainability into the curriculum, as Burkhard Vollmers and Werner Kuhlmeier describe and, to a certain extent, also advocate for the efforts conducted by the German administration towards this aim. This attempt cannot be described without criticism, yet they acknowledge its contribution to the fulfillment of what is required nowadays from education in terms of global awareness of environmental issues worldwide.

Patricia Olmos, for her part, offers the problems but also the benefits of adapting VET to an educated audience of young people with different forms of disability, providing a twofold understanding of what VET is able to provide as well as advocating for the contribution of a fully trained and skilled workforce with disability able to actively participate as equals with the rest of the workforce from the perspective of producers as well as consumers.

Both chapters bring a more thorough understanding of citizenship and how VET can contribute to increase awareness of it and contributing to a better future for citizenship. It can be seen as a late consequence of the ideas of Enlightenment being brought to all of the population but also as an effect of the second and third generation of human rights, which expand to include environmental issues and a diverse society, both in cultural terms as well as the different capabilities that each person is able to activate. Therefore, VET can provide a significant contribution to the expansion of the idea of citizenship. It is also worth noting that both approaches come from very different positions: While the German government's push toward providing space for sustainability is a top-down attempt, which seems to have been well received by those in charge of applying it, the story described by Olmos is the result of a bottom-up approach, where citizens go well ahead of governments. The provision of VET for people with disability as a chance to bring their education pathways further as well as to improve their individual skills is the result of the advocacy of people with disabilities, together with their families and support associations. They have claimed and struggled for this to happen, within wider approaches such as person-centered planning and independent living movements.

None of these neglects the possibilities embedded by the other, and both approaches are portrayed as equally valid and respected. Citizenship can be advocated for and improved from both strands. The story behind the chapter written by Vollmers and Kuhlmeier shows us that we should not reject all initiatives that arise from governmental institutions and that the official democratic representatives and powers can also be honest in their attempts to improve working and living conditions. This is relevant if we consider we are at a time of severe retreat and loss of credibility of the political institutions and the people in office.

That is what one might tend to believe by reading what Katerina Arkoudi-Vafea has to tell us in her chapter. She gives us data and her interpretations of the impact of the austerity policies and budgetary cuts imposed upon Greece by European politicians as well as by international financial institutions, as an example of how a country has submitted a relevant part of its national autonomy to external powers. Much has been written about Greece, in terms of the Greeks' responsibility, their standing up against foreign impositions, and their acting as a model for other countries to be aware of what might happen to them. The Greek population has suffered and is still suffering from the extreme conditions that different and successive Greek governments had created to arrive at such great economic troubles, as well as what they were ready to accept in order to be able to receive economic aid. Those effects can be perceived *also* in VET as well as in many other areas of social life.

This chapter is the first evidence provided for how vocational education providers, vocational education teachers, and vocational education students have been affected by the financial crisis, and it debates ways in which this situation can be confronted and responded.

Section 2 also includes two chapters that illustrate well how the global and the local are intertwined and how VET has contributed and can contribute not only to economic development but also to local and community development, an additional value added by work-related education and that make these examples particularly relevant in terms of the social and educational contribution of VET. These chapters show that vocational education cannot only be responsive to the demands of the labor market, but is also able to serve the needs of the communities in which it is located and of the people living in those communities, be they urban or rural, whatever its degree of development has been so far. And, certainly, letting people take lead on the direction they want to give to their VET system, is the main suggestion that Tania Brabo offers when referring to the educational practices of the *Movimento dos Trabalhadores Rurais Sem Terra* (MST) in Brazil. And that perspective is equally taken by Vicente Palop, who focuses on the grassroots level to understand the dimensions behind the possibilities for full local sustainable development, where people and communities are empowered, as is the case of the community of Marcabelí in Ecuador.

Nevertheless, these examples also hint at how citizenship is often at stake, thus it is good to take the historical perspective into account and see how advancements are the result of ongoing struggles. There is no system, policy, nor practice that is able to escape these tensions, not even the seemingly well-consolidated apprenticeship system in central European countries.

The chapters in section 3 deal with concrete examples in current VET practices around the world, from Canada to Tanzania, Uganda, Finland, Norway, Spain and Switzerland. All of these examples are specific: Some deal with certain regions, some with particular occupational fields like health and home care, a highly feminized occupation; others have to do with the target populations of VET programs, some with the risk of segregation. All of these chapters address some of the latest trends and developments that VET is taking in those particular fields or areas. This section portrays a diversity of issues currently part of the VET debates, and the disputes about the role, the aim, the control and the autonomy of VET institutions, practitioners and administrators. That is why this section pays attention to the tensions between the global and the local, for what happens in one of those areas cannot be detached from what is going on in other VET related fields. Most of these developments, despite their concreteness, are part of a larger landscape in which what happens at one place has an impact and is being affected by what is going on elsewhere.

Indeed, VET today is subject to the effect of the economic movements worldwide and global competition. This is reflected in many ways: The international mobility of workers, the recognition of qualifications acquired elsewhere, occupational definitions that have a local embeddedness but also wider resonance. Furthermore, we can recognize that the winners and the losers in the global competition face similar problems and challenges in different parts of the world.

Citizenship is no longer just a national issue; it is neither only occupational nor class-related as it might once have been. The quest for one's identity is a claim, perhaps even a necessity, in the postmodern era, and the construction of the self has to be done with the tools provided, both at education and in the world of work. Bottom-down policies are spreading all over the world; experiments are being conducted in some regions, funded and promoted by international or non-national institutions of both economic, political or cultural domains. And people in charge of applying these policies and recommendations, in order to test new programs and schemes, apply them with trust or fear, they welcome them or they suspect them, they apply them or they adapt and transform them, some resist them as well. Section 3 deals with these practices, how alternatives are constructed, and how they are able to confront, subvert, and reproduce mandates and external pressures.

These processes speak about the current ways by which people and groups affirm their identities as well as their citizenship, claiming an active role in deciding on their work, how to do it, how to define and handle it, and the power to focus on the areas that most demand their attention.

Those are the claims addressed in the paper by Lea Zehnder and Philipp Gonnon, as they hold that the role of the civic justification has been the largest one in the most recent debates and reforms behind the Swiss apprenticeship system, far beyond the weight of other competing rationales like the industrial or, to a lesser extent, the market. Their use of Boltanski, Thevenaut and Chiapello, which others have also applied to the study of education (Derouet 2005, 2009) and particularly to the case of vocational education (Molpeceres 2004; Martínez *et al.* 2015) proves to be a relevant tool to better understand the complex interrelations that affect institutions nowadays, where there is a constant attempt to redefine and reinterpret the position in which one finds him/herself. The authors stress on the civic justification is particularly significant as a way to counteract the other demands, particularly market ones, posed upon VET. It is even more relevant to put this discussion at the core of one of the most reliable and accepted dual systems in the world, the Swiss one.

Thomas Deissinger and Daniela Gremm also engage in an analysis of the dual system, but from a different perspective: The adoption of the German dual system in a country as far and as different as Canada. This is only an example of the wider trend that can be traced in the last decade of countries with certain disposition to export their VET models and other countries open to change to adopt a foreign model, particularly dual systems or apprenticeships. There has been a wealth of literature about these issues in the past years, some from a national-political approach, from stakeholders and from theoretical perspectives on education reform and comparative education (Busemeyer and Trampusch 2012; Euler 2013; Valiente *et al.* 2015; Marhuenda et al. 2016). Deissinger and Gremm enrich our understanding here by questioning whether Canada's VET system needs to look at the German system in order to make improvements to its VET provision, even if there is a need in Canada to reform a system that seems to be responding effectively enough to the current demands it faces.

A different approach to a worldwide extended VET related practice nowadays is that of the accreditation of knowledge acquired in different contexts, be they formal VET institutions, the world of work or experiential learning. María José Chisvert and Ana Córdoba go deep into these processes, how they have landed in the context of Spain, what expectations they have raised for those with less education and how the guarantees established around the process, within a civic convention, have hindered the possibilities that such a process was promising to offer. It is a good example of how a policy may create the opposite effects to those expected.

Again in the Spanish context, referring to the lower levels of qualification as in the previous chapter, Míriam Abiétar, Almudena Navas and Fernando Marhuenda address what happens to the vocational training provided to young people who have dropped out of the educational system, those who might be at risk of being potential end-users of VET provision with hardly any recognition in terms of qualification achieved. This chapter also deals with issues addressed elsewhere in the book, like the moral dimension of VET or its disciplinary character, together with the compensatory role it plays, or as a form of education provided for the lower classes, those who do not seem to deserve highly valued academic education. In their analysis, they contend that current basic VET policies are refurbishing previous ones, fruits of the movement of conservative modernization worldwide as it has been received in Spain in the past two decades.

Again, the disputes between the global and the local, policy and practice, teachers and trainers and young people can be better understood here, and it can also be confronted by the data and explanations provided by Lorenz Lassnig and Stefan Vogtenhuber in the last chapter in this book, where they contend the role of VET in the context of an increasing merging with higher education and as the value of different educational levels is being reshaped within a global context. They discuss and challenge common sense views on the worth of VET.

In the same context of Abiétar, Marhuenda and Navas, of VET provided for the young people categorized as the least able or the most problematic, both factors implying an obstacle for them to engage in further academic studies, Liv Mjelde contributes in her paper. She addresses such forms of training provision in Norway in the past decades while bringing the debate to a different realm. This realm is that of the possibilities that Vigotskyan learning theories have on the introduction of alternative educational practices that may prove particularly effective in the case of VET, for they take into account the relations between practice and theory in a much more comprehensive way than academic educational systems tend to consider. Mjelde's paper is hence a theoretical contribution, illustrated with examples of practices discussed elsewhere in this book.

The remaining chapter in this section raises our awareness of how several of the issues tackled in the section, like basic VET provision, the accreditation of knowledge and the connections between theory and practice are being debated in the North and the South, the West and the East, and how women are at high risk of suffering what we might call educational as well as labor violence. Anja Heikkinen, Perpetua

Kalimasi, Elisabeth Opit and Jesse Sjelvgren write about the work that women perform in the health and home care in countries as different as Finland, Tanzania and Uganda. They debate the connections between working and living conditions and educational and accreditation practices. They deal with the role of professional bodies, employer-employee relations, and trade unions, while at the same time connecting these to discussions on curriculum design.

In summary, the volume raises concerns about the risks and the hopes, the problems and the challenges, that citizenship and vocational education face nowadays. By providing illustrations from recent research where alternative and empowering practices can be identified, embedding both educational relations and working class solidarity, the authors in this volume alert us to the challenges that these practices face, how limited they are in scope and how current political discourses of employability and entrepreneurship are trying to reshape the role of VET. These problems and contradictions are present all throughout the book. Therefore, the book ends without a clear response to the contribution of VET to citizenship, while at the same time questioning the formation of citizenship without the contribution of VET.

References

Apple, M. W. 2006. Educating the 'Right' Way. Markets, Standards, God and Inequality. New York, Routledge.

Ariño, A. and Romero, J. 2016. La secesión de las élites. Barcelona, Galaxia.

Bacchetta, M., Ernst, E. and Bustamante, J.P. 2009. La globalización y el empleo informal en los países en desarrollo. Ginebra, Organización Mundial del Comercio y OIT.

Ball, S. 2013. The Education Debate. Bristol, Policy Press.

Bauman, Z. 2000. Trabajo, consumismo y nuevos pobres. Barcelona, Gedisa.

Berner, E. and Gonon, P. (eds.) 2016. History of Vocational Education and Training. Bern, Peter Lang.

Boltanski, L and Chiapello, E. 2002. El nuevo espíritu del capitalismo. Madrid, Akal.

Busemeyer, M. and Trampusch, C. (eds.) 2012. The Political Economy of Collective Skill Formation. Oxford, Oxford University Press.

Castel, R. 1997. La metamorfosis de la cuestión social. Buenos Aires, Paidós.

Comisión Europea 2014. Comprender las políticas de la Unión Europea. Empleo y Asuntos Sociales. Luxemburgo, Oficina de Publicaciones de la Unión Europea.

Deissinger, T., Aff, J., Fuller, A. and Jorgensen, C.H. (eds.) 2013. Hybrid Qualifications: Structures and Problems in the Context of European VET Policies. Bern, Peter Lang.

Derouet, J.L. 2005. Repenser la justice en education. Éducation et Sociétés 16: 29–40.

Derouet, J.L. 2009. La place des établissements scolaires en France sous la Ve République: une recomposition parallèle des formes de la justice et des formes de l'État (1959–2009). Revista Portuguesa de Educação, 22(2): 7–34.

Euler, D. 2013. German's Dual Vocational Training System: a Model for Other Countries? Bielefeld, Bertelsmann.

European Economic and Social Committe 2016. Opinion of the European Economic and Social Committee on Decent work in global supply chains. REX/462, Brussels, 25 May 2016.

Gonon, P., Kraus, K., Oelkers, J. and Stolz, S. (ed.) 2009. Work, Education and Employability. Bern, Peter Lang.

Hamilton, S. 1990. Apprenticeship for Adulthood. Preparing Youth for the Future. New York, Free Press.

Harju, A. and Heikkinen, A. (eds.) 2016. Adult education and the planetary condition. Tampere, Finnish Association of Adult Education.

ILO 2013. Decent work indicators. Geneva, ILO.

Marhuenda, F. 2016. Becoming Precarious? Education and Social Inclusion Beyond Employability. Pedagogy, Culture and Society. DOI: 10.1080/14681366.2016.1160680.

Marhuenda, F. 2017. Learning at work: Researching personal development and competence building in work integration companies. Educar, in press, 1–19.

Marhuenda, F. and Ros, A. 2015. What Sense Can We Make of the Possibility of Vocational Didactics? An Approach from the Spanish School-Based System Complemented by Non-Formal Vocational Training. International Journal for Research in Vocational Education and Training, vol 2, n. 3, DOI. <http://dx.doi.org/10.13152/IJRVET.2.3.3>.

Marhuenda, F.; Chisvert, M.J., and Palomares, D. 2016. La formación profesional dual en España. Revista internacional de organizaciones, 17, 43–63.

Martínez, I. *et al.* 2015. Comprehensive Education Boundaries and Remedies on the Edges of the Spanish Educational System. European Educational Research Journal, vol. 14 (2–3), 293–311. DOI: 10.1177/1474904115590043.

Martínez, M. 2013. Educación, neoliberalismo y justicia social. Madrid, Pirámide.

Mjelde, L and Daly, R. (eds.) 2006. Working Knowledge in a Globalizing World. Bern, Peter Lang.

Molpeceres, M.A. (coord.) 2004. Identidades y formación para el trabajo en los márgenes del sistema educativo. Montevideo, OIT-Cinterfor.

Molzberger, G. and Wahle, M. (eds.) 2015. Shaping the Futures of (Vocational) Education and Work. Bern, Peter Lang.

Navarro, V. and López, J. 2012. Los amos del mundo. Las armas del terrorismo financiero. Madrid, Espasa.

Hepp, R., Riesinger, R. and Kergel, D (eds.) 2016. Verunsicherte Gesellschaft. Dordrecht, Springer.

Sennett, R. 2000. La corrosión del carácter. Barcelona, Anagrama.

Standing, G. 2011. The Precariat. The New Dangerous Class. London, Bloomsbury.

Stolz, S. and Gonon, P. (eds.) 2012. Challenges and Reforms in Vocational Education. Bern, Peter Lang.

Valiente, O., Scandurra, R., Zancajo, A., and Brown, C. 2015. Un model de formació professional dual per a Catalunya? Reptes en el disseny i implementació de la reforma. Barcelona, Fundacio Jaume Bofill.

Weil, M., Koski, L. and Mjelde, L (eds.) 2009. Knowing Work. Bern, Peter Lang.

Section 1.
Nation, Work, Class and Identity: Vocational
Education and the Formation of Citizenship

LORENZO BONOLI

An Ambiguous Identity: The Figure of the Apprentice from the XIX Century up to Today in Switzerland

1. Introduction

One of the main features of the Swiss Vocational Education and Training (VET) system is the high rate of young people choosing after obligatory schooling a dual-track apprenticeship, organized partly in a training company and partly in a vocational school. The percentage of young people choosing this kind of education is 61%, as against a European average of 14% (OECD 2012). This type of vocational education is well established in Switzerland, with a long history, good employment opportunities and social recognition.

In Switzerland, as in other European countries, the current model of dual-track apprenticeship comes directly from the traditional apprenticeship that developed in the context of the medieval guilds. After the abolition of the guilds and the development of industrialization, this model of on-the-job training evolves during the last decade of the XIX century and the first decades of the XX century into the modern dual-track model that combines, under state control, on-the-job training in the company (3–4 days per week) with school classes at school (1–2 days per week).

Even though this model of VET seems to be successful in Switzerland and has such a long tradition, it is surprising to observe that the figure of the apprentice remains highly ambiguous.

What is an apprentice? A learner, a worker or something else?

The aim of this contribution is thus to understand when and how the ambiguous identity of the apprentice appears and develops.

Basing my research on a discourse analysis approach, I will try to describe what kind of identity emerges from official documents, such as laws, reports, official statistics, etc. written from 1880 to 1930.[1] As a theoretical and methodological approach, "Discourse analysis"[2] focuses on the discourses produced, in this case, by the principal actors of the VET domain at that time, in order to highlight the forms and the conditions of discourse production and reception. The analysis focuses, first of all, on *what was said* about apprentices, and, secondly, on the reasons explaining *why this could be said*. In other words, it underlines which statements about apprentices were possible and largely accepted at that time and, on the other hand, which socio-cultural and political reasons can explain this possibility and this acceptance. The identity of the apprentices will emerge from this analysis as a regularity in the way the sources speak about them and, therefore, categorize them. This analysis will show how, in Switzerland, the ambiguity of the identity of the apprentice develops from the end of the XIX century and subsists through the process of institutionalization of the domain during the first decades of the XX century.

Finally, a glance to the present will reveal that this ambiguity remains an issue with little variation until today.

2. The three dimensions of the identity of the apprentice

If we observe the way official texts and public debate refer to the apprentice today, it appears that he or she presents at least three dimensions, working like three poles to constitute a composite identity.

---

1   The period 1880–1930, as we will see, covers the entire process of institutionalization of the VET system in Switzerland, from the first official initiatives at a federal and cantonal level until the first federal act on VET, adopted in 1930, which introduced a nation-wide system.
2   For an introduction to this approach, see Maingueneau (1991). The work of Michel Foucault (especially 1966/1969) represents an important model of the constitution of this approach, which has undergone recent development in the domain of social sciences, see Power (2011), Keller (2011), Jäger (2012) and Füssel & Neu (2014).

The apprentice is today at the same time a worker, a learner and a minor.

The apprentice is a *worker*. He or she signs a work contract, he or she has to respect work hours, he or she has to work on productive activities and receives a salary.

But at the same time, the apprentice is a *learner*. His or her salary is lower than a normal worker's salary, his or her productive activities must be directly related to the profession being learnt, he or she is coached by a trainer, he or she has to follow complementary classes in vocational schools and pass exams at the end of the apprenticeship[3].

And finally the apprentice is a *minor*: a person demanding special protection and coaching. Work hours and work conditions are adapted to his or her age, he or she can receive vocational guidance and special coaching and, furthermore, complementary school classes include courses on general knowledge, citizenship education and sport, fostering his or her physical and psychological development and social integration.

Considering the complexity of the combination of these three dimensions, it is pertinent to raise the question of their origins. How do these three dimensions come together to construct the ambiguous identity of the apprentice? When do they appear historically? And what kind of socio-economic and political conditions do or did they reflect?

As I will demonstrate, an analysis of the history of the Swiss VET system shows that the modern figure of the apprentice develops from the beginning of the XIX century as that of a worker. Only progressively, with the process of institutionalization of the domain, does the figure of the apprentice begin to incorporate the other two dimensions. And only at the beginning of the XX century does a balance between these three dimensions seem to be found; a balance that is still present today.

---

3   These first two dimensions refer directly to a tension that characterizes all dual models of training between "production" and "education", between, on the one hand, the obligation for the apprentice to produce, like all the other workers, and on the other hand, his or her commitment to learn the profession. On this tension, see the sociological studies of Gilles Moreau (2003) or Nadia Lamamra (2013).

3. At the origin of the modern figure of the apprentice

Originating in the medieval guilds system, the figure of the apprentice finds a new identity during the XIX century, particularly after the radical socio-economic changes caused by the French Revolution and the Industrial Revolution, which determined the progressive decline of the guilds and of their traditional training system[4]. The result of this decline is that during the entire XIX century, traditional apprenticeship undergoes a severe crisis, as witnessed in the following quotation from Robert Comtesse, Swiss politician, future Swiss president: "Today, as everyone admits, apprenticeship is suffering from the worst crisis ever. Apprenticeship is dying! Good apprentices are no longer being trained. This is the general cry". (Comtesse 1890, p. 19–21)

This crisis pushes public collectivities such as the Confederation, the central power, and the Cantons, the regional powers, to take the first measures to relaunch the initiation of young people into professions. In 1884, the Swiss Federal Government will adopt the first national disposition in the domain: a federal decree on vocational education that assures public funding to VET institutions (mainly vocational schools or Sunday or evening classes). In 1890 the canton of Neuchâtel is the first canton to pass a law on apprenticeship, aiming at the protection of young apprentices and at the assurance of the quality of the training. In the following years, 23 out of 25 cantons will also adopt such legal dispositions. But it is only in 1930 that a federal act on vocational education and training is accepted in Parliament. This act sets the bases of the current Swiss VET system, with some key points such as the regulation of dual track apprenticeship (written contract, combination of training in the work place and classes at school, final exams and protected diplomas) and the attribution of the organization of the domain to three main actors: the Confederation, the Cantons and the professional organisations[5].

---

4   On the guilds system and its decline see Krebs (1933) and Savoy (1910). For a
     contemporary analysis, see Gonon 1998.
5   For a general historical reconstruction of the development of the Swiss VET
     system, see Wettstein & Gonon (2009), Bonoli (2012) and Berner (2013).

4. The apprentice as a worker

Although, from the last decades of the XIX century, the debate on the crisis of the traditional apprenticeship is launched, the figure of the apprentice still appears only rarely in official documents such as laws, government reports or official statistics. And when it does appear, it appears mainly as a worker (see the setting of the picture in Fig. 1), but a specific kind of worker: a young and unskilled worker, possessing no profession, often abandoned to him or herself, exploited and facing an uncertain future.

Figure 1: "Particularly strongly built apprentices" (Hottinger 1920, p. 9).

This situation is often criticized in public debates, where it is considered as a negative consequence of the new industrial working conditions, which, in the case of apprentices, emphasize the dimension of profit rather than the dimension of education, as in the columns of the *Journal de Genève* in 1891:

The apprentice is no longer considered as a pupil, but as a novice worker, who has to be exploited. Parents ask that their child get a salary as soon as possible and, on his side, the master tries to take advantage of his work. He does not give him the time needed for his instruction. […] What one seeks here is to find the cheapest manpower. (The question of the apprentices, *Journal de Genève,* 28.05.1891)

4.1 From a legal point of view

From a legal point of view, at the time in question, there were no general dispositions concerning apprentices and apprenticeship. The apprentice was commonly considered as a worker, and the apprentice contract as a work contract. Questioned on the status of apprenticeship in 1890, the Federal Government confirmed this vision by underlining explicitly that the apprentice contract, "even though it is not explicitly named in the Code of Obligations […] is regulated by this code under chapter eleven of the service agreement. The contract of apprentice is nothing but a reciprocal service agreement"[6] like any other work contract. We will see later the implications of this decision that officially assigns the apprentices to the legal category of workers.

4.2 In statistics

Examples of the worker-oriented identity of the apprentice are abundant, for example in the domain of statistics. Official statistics on apprentices are very rare before 1900 and the few available data come from statistics in the domain of work and not from statistics in the domain of public education[7].

An excellent example of this comes from the report on Swiss factories established in 1873 by Victor Böhmert. In this report, some scattered data on apprentices appear, as in Fig. 2, where the number of apprentices [*Lehrknaben*] of the steam engine factory Escher, Wyss

6   Louis Ruchonnet, President of the Swiss Confederation, in Departement de l'Agriculture et de l'industrie, Canton Neuchâtel (1896, p. 12).
7   On the development of the Swiss VET statistics, see Bonoli (2016).

& Co is reported in the same column as the other workers, with no apparent distinction except lower wages.

This example also shows the categorical problems raised by apprentices. They are here considered as an apparently homogeneous group distinct from all other workers of different professions (such as painters, joiners, locksmiths, tinsmiths, cutters, etc.), and this even though the group of apprentices is composed of young adults being trained for different specific professions. It appears that the status of the apprentice was not clearly established: on the one hand, he was considered as a worker and received a wage, but on the other hand, he did not *yet* have a "profession", so that he could not be attributed to a specific professional group.

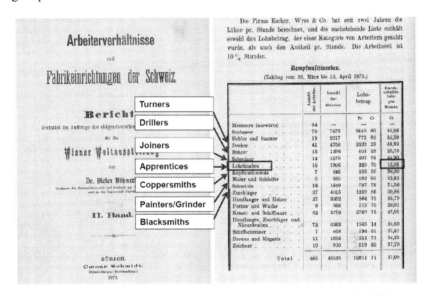

Figure 2: Workers (and apprentices) in the Escher, Wyss & Co company, in 1873, from Böhmert (1873).

It is helpful to specify that around 1900 the concept of "profession" (*Beruf, profession, professione*) signified more than a simple technical activity aimed at earning enough money to live. It was considered as the condition of social integration, the way to find one's place in society and to contribute to its functioning[8]. From this perspective, the ambiguity of the figure of the apprentice also came from its "in progress" status of not being yet completely in a determined profession but in a transitional situation and still depending on the family for a living.

A solution to this ambiguity was proposed in the Federal Census of the Population of 1900, which offers the first national data on apprentices, counting them as members of the professions they were learning. The introductions to the Federal Censuses of 1888 and of 1900 reflect the long discussions held on this issue before this solution was found[9]. Several aspects were highlighted. One of these refers to the fact that other young people also shared the transitional status of the apprentice, for instant university students, but the categorization of the latter was different. In particular, the debates raised the comparison with students of medicine. Why should apprentices be counted as *workers* in the profession they were learning while students of medicine were considered as *learners* dependent on the profession of their parents, and not belonging to the category of doctors? In this case, the productive activity of apprentices and the fact that they received a wage, i.e. two preeminent worker characteristics, were determinant to explain the choice of considering apprentices as members of the professions they were learning.

4.3 Institutional attribution of apprenticeship

A further example of the worker-oriented identity comes from the institutional attribution of apprenticeship to cantonal departments of work or the economy.

If we consider the *Guides of Public Instruction* published around 1900 in the Canton of Geneva (see fig. 3), we are quite surprised to discover that apprenticeship does not appear in these Guides as an educational track. And this, even though the percentage of apprentices in

8   As Giuseppe Ambrogini pointed out in a book on vocational guidance written on 1926: "The moral personality of the individual develops positively only through the melting pot of the profession, because only professional activities assure the full social value of a man"(1926, p. 6). For an analysis of the concept of profession (*Beruf*) see Schriewer and Harney (1999).

9   On these discussions, see Bonoli (2016).

Geneva, according to the Federal Census of 1900, was more than 30% of the age class 15/18, by far the largest percentage concerning upper secondary level.

Apprenticeship was a way to be at work rather than a way to be in the world of education. Thus it was consistent that apprenticeship was not part of public instruction. It was under the control of the cantonal *Department of Trade and Industry* and not under the control of the *Department of Public Instruction*, who published these brochures. The case of Geneva is not isolated: we find this same attribution of apprenticeship to departments of trade or industry or to departments of public economy rather than to departments of public instruction in a number of other cantons.

Figure 3: *Guides of public instruction*, Canton of Geneva, 1890, 1896, 1900.

5. The first changes: towards a composite identity

Toward the end of the XIX century, this work-oriented identity is also strongly criticized, as in the quotation from the Geneva journal quoted above. In the same article, some lines below, we already find the idea of the apprentice as a composite figure: not only worker but something more: a minor, needing special work conditions and special coaching, and a learner, needing good and complete training:

> All these facts are contrary to the two principles which have to found every apprenticeship: 1 – The master has to behave with his apprentice like a good father of a family; 2 – He has to teach him his profession in all its elements, in the same way he practices it himself without hiding anything from him. (The question of the apprentices, *JdG*. 28.05.1891)

The first official documents explicitly integrating these two dimensions are the cantonal laws on apprenticeship that appear progressively from 1890 on. These laws are above all laws for the protection of young apprentices. This protection focuses on three levels: first of all, on the physical integrity of the apprentice, with measures to assure acceptable hygienic and safety conditions and tolerable working hours, and to ban physical punishments or mistreatment. But the protection offered by these first laws also considered the moral and civic development of the young apprentice as a future member of society. In this respect, in almost all the cantonal laws, we find articles specifying that the master has to behave with the apprentice not only like a "good father of a family", as mentioned in the previous quotation, but also control his moral behavior, as appears in article 5 of the Law on the Protection of Apprentices and Workers of the Canton of Obwald, passed in 1901:

> Art. 5. The master must behave with the apprentice like a good father of a family. He has to control the behavior of the apprentice and to inform his guardian in case of serious errors or bad inclinations. He has to protect the apprentice from bad examples, incitation to vulgarity, exuberance and alcoholism. He has to exercise the best possible influence on the moral evolution and character construction of the apprentice. (Canton of Obwald 1901)

These elements clearly underline the fact that the apprentice was not considered as an ordinary worker, but a "working minor" needing special conditions of work and special coaching.

At the same time, it is important to notice that in these first cantonal laws the protection of apprentices comprehended also protection against possible abuses in the process of teaching a profession. These laws introduced the compulsory written contract, where the profession being taught, the length of the apprenticeship, the costs, etc. had to be explicitly mentioned. Moreover, they introduced control of the real competencies of the master and the obligation for him to effectively train the apprentice in the profession mentioned in the contract, prohibiting the occupation of the apprentice in working activities not directly in relation to the profession.

Besides, these cantonal laws comprehend also articles on the complementary vocational schools and final exams as measures to improve the quality of apprenticeship, as in the Law of the Canton of Bern passed in 1905:

> Art. 13. In locations where industrial or commercial vocational schools are available, the master is obliged to enroll the apprentice and to accord to him the necessary time to frequent them, even during work time for at least three hours per week. [...]
> Art. 17. The apprentice has to pass an exam, at the end of his apprenticeship period, on the competence and knowledge necessary for practicing the profession. (Canton of Bern 1905)

The introduction of these last elements underlines the *learner* dimension of the apprentice: he or she has not only to work, but to learn a profession in the workplace, attend classes in a school and take final exams.

5.1 Philanthropy and social political preoccupations

The appearance of these other dimensions in the cantonal laws arises for several reasons

First of all, it responds to a general "philanthropic" movement that develops at the end of the XIX century in Switzerland, as in other countries, promoting the protection and the instruction of children and young adults. This movement in the context of VET can be seen as a reaction to the extremely poor working and living conditions of the lower classes of the population, but it can also be considered as an extension of the debates defending the importance of education that had characterized the introduction of compulsory primary school in Switzerland at the beginning of the XIX century[10].

---

10   See Forster (2008), for the introduction of compulsory primary school in Switzerland.

Secondly, the appearance of these other two dimensions arises for socio-political reasons

Around 1900, like other European countries, Switzerland faces a very unstable political situation with strikes and lock-outs. In the public debate, the "social question" was at the center of preoccupations. This expression refers to the extremely poor living conditions of the lower classes of the society and to the social and political instability generated by the workers movements that culminated in a number of strike movements[11].

In this context, VET is asked to contribute to reducing social tensions at three levels. First, improving living conditions of the lower classes thanks to better technical instruction and better integration in the world of work; second, assuring better social and moral integration into Swiss society of young people coming from the lower classes; third, contributing to the socio-political stability of Swiss society, reducing the number of young people following the protest movements[12].

The preoccupation of the elites of the time in relation to these three levels emerges clearly in this quotation from Louis Albert Roulet, a state counselor of the Canton of Neuchâtel, who said: "A good worker [a worker with a good professional instruction] is never a bad citizen. He knows how to earn his living honorably and he will not augment the army of nihilists and communists [*partageux*]" (Louis Albert Roulet, State Counselor Canton Neuchâtel, cité in *Journal de Genève* 02.08.1882)

With respect to these considerations, it appears that the political elites of the time also had socio-political reasons for driving the young apprentice from his or her exclusively worker-oriented identity to a composite identity, minor/learner/worker.

The minor/learner dimension justified the moral and political control and education of young adults coming from the lower classes of the population. This control and this education was exercised concretely in the company, under the supervision of the master, as mentioned in

---

11 As shown by Hirter (1983, p. 847), between 1880 and 1914, there were 2624 strikes and lock-outs in Switzerland. The pick was reached in 1906 and 1906 with 264 and 282 strikes and lock-outs.

12 The role attributed to VET in response to the problems raised by the social question is analyzed in Bonoli 2015.

the Cantonal Law of Obwald quoted above, and in vocational schools, especially through general and citizenship education, whose task was to "achieve the intellectual and technical instruction of the worker, develop the feeling of his personality, inculcate in young people the feelings of order and of duty, which our worker population needs above all" (Genoud 1903, p. 5).

5.2 Legal authority reasons

But the appearance in the first cantonal laws of these two other dimensions is not only the reflection of this "philanthropic" vision or of socio-political preoccupations, it responds also to legal and political issues, because, as we will see, cantonal governments will put the accent on these two dimensions in order to defend their authority on the domain of the apprenticeship.

In fact, the cantonal laws on apprenticeship raised a problem of legal authority between the federal authority and the cantonal authority, a kind of contrast quite common in Swiss history.

The problem was to know if the cantons had the authority to regulate apprenticeship or if this authority resided only within the Confederation. To put it simply[13], at the time, the cantons had the authority over everything concerning public instruction and public safety, while the Confederation had the authority over the domain of work obligations and working conditions in factories. So the problem was the following: if the apprentice was considered as a worker, only the Confederation could intervene and introduce measures to regulate a particular work contract. But if the apprentice was considered more as a minor or as a learner the cantons had the right to regulate apprenticeship.

In this complex situation, cantons wanting to pass laws on the domain were driven to underline these two latter dimensions. A good example comes from the Cantonal Law of Fribourg passed in 1895, where it is clearly specified that this law would regulate the contract of apprenticeship from the point of view of the protection and of the instruction of the "minor":

13   For a more detailed explication see Uldry (1979) and Berner, Gonon & Ritter (2011).

First article

The contract of apprenticeship, considered from the point of view of the protection of the minor and of his vocational instruction, is the contract through which a person practicing an industrial or commercial profession engages to teach this profession to another person, who, in return, has to assure determined services. (Canton of Fribourg 1895)

But even though the cantons tended to put forward these two dimensions, the validity of these cantonal laws was often contested, considering that the apprentice contract was a worker contract and for this reason was under the authority of the Confederation.

This complex legal situation will find a definitive solution only in 1930 when the Swiss parliament will pass the first federal law in the domain.

6. The first federal law, 1930

The composite identity of the apprentices was confirmed in the first federal law of 1930, which introduced for the first time nation-wide regulations for apprenticeship.

The federal law of 1930 was based largely on previous cantonal laws and borrowed the most successful measures from different cantonal legislation. Like the cantonal laws, it included measures oriented to the worker, to the minor and to the learner. It proposed a balance between the three dimensions, or at least an official recognition of the composite identity of the apprentice.

It must be said that the composite nature of these measures facilitated the political acceptance of the law, since all the political groups of the time could find some articles defending their interests. The law was proposed by the milieu of handicrafts, which wanted state intervention to improve the quality of VET, and the left and the trade unions did not oppose the law, because it also comprehended measures for the protection of young workers[14].

---

14   Concerning the parliamentary debates on the first federal VET act, see Bauder 2008.

7. Conclusion

The law of 1930 set the basis of the current Swiss VET system. No essential changes have occurred in the legal status of the apprenticeship since then and the ambiguity of the identity of the apprentice remains with little variation until today. If current official documents as well as public debates are considered, the three different dimensions mentioned above will be easily found.

In some research coming from the economics of education, the apprentice is first of all considered as a non-qualified worker, whose productivity is low in the first year of the apprenticeship, but augments progressively in the following years to reach the productivity of a qualified worker[15]. In other official documents concerning youth unemployment or drop-out problems in the domain, apprentices are often described as young adults demanding special coaching, vocational guidance and ad hoc internships[16]. And finally in the context of flexibility and mobility in the world of work, the learner dimension is underlined by stressing, on the one hand, the importance of general knowledge (languages, bookkeeping or ICT tools, etc.), acquired at school as a necessity for developing good professional opportunities in the work market, and on the other hand, the importance of continuing the educational path up to tertiary level education[17].

Finally, then, what is an apprentice in Switzerland?

He or she is a composite figure, presenting at least three different dimensions that can be underlined according to the perspective adopted.

It can be said, however, that this composite identity may be one of the keys to the success of apprenticeship in Switzerland, because it responds to different demands coming from different horizons: from the world of work, from social and educational positions, and finally from the young adults themselves and their families.

---

15 See for example Strupler and Wolter (2012).
16 See in particular Häfeli and Schellenberg (2009).
17 See on this the declaration of intentions on the theme "transitions" of the main stakeholders of the Swiss VET system signed on March 2015, on line: <www.edk.ch/dyn/11473.php>.

References

Sources

Ambrogini, G. 1926. Dal Popolo al popolo. Intorno al grave problema dell'istruzione professionale, della scelta professionale e del tirocinio. Mendrisio, Tipografia & Libreria Moderna.

Boehmert, V. 1873. Arbeitsverhältnisse und Fabrikeinrichtungen der Schweiz: Bericht erstattet im Auftrage der Eidgenössische Generalcommission für die Wiener Ausstellung (Band I/II). Zürich, C. Schmidt.

Département de l'agriculture et de l'industrie, Canton de Neuchâtel. 1896. Notice sur les examens professionnels et la surveillance des apprentissages dans le canton de Neuchâtel. Neuchâtel, Paul Seiler.

Département de l'instruction publique, Canton de Genève. 1890/ 1896/1900. Guide de l'instruction publique. Genève, Association des intérêts de Genève.

Comtesse R. 1890. La question des apprentissages. Neuchâtel, Borel.

Genoud, L. 1903. L'organisation des cours professionnels pour apprentis des métiers en Suisse. Lausanne, Payot & Cie.

Hottinger, M. 1920. Die Lehrlingsführsorge bei der Firma Gebruder Sulzer. Zürich, Gebrüder Fretz.

Krebs, W. 1933. Alte Handwerkersbräuche. Basel, Gesellschaft für Volkskunde / Helbing & Lichthahn.

Journal de Genève (JdG), 1880–1930. (Archive on line <www.letempsa rchives.ch>).

Savoy, E. (1910). L'Apprentissage en Suisse. Louvain, Peeters.

Statistische bureau des eidg. Departements des Innern. 1894. Die Ergebnisse der Eidgenössischen Volkszählung vom 1. Dezember 1888. Bern, Orell Füssli.

Statistische bureau des eidg. Departements des Innern. 1907. Die Ergebnisse der Eidgenössischen Volkszählung vom 1, Dezember 1900, Dritter Band. Bern, Gustav Grunau.

Laws

Canton Fribourg. 1895. Loi sur la protection des apprentis et des ouvriers (14 novembre). Landmann (ed.), Die Arbeitsschutzgesetzgebung in der Schweiz. Basel, Helbing & Lichthahn, 257–261.

Kanton Obwald. 1901. Gesetz betreffend Förderung des Handwerkes (28 April). Landmann (ed.), Die Arbeitsschutzgesetzgebung in der Schweiz Basel. Helbing & Lichthahn, 237–242.

Kanton Bern. 1905. Gesetz über gewerbliche und kaufmännische Berufslehre von 19 März 1905. Gesetze, Dekrete und Verordnungen des Kantons Bern. Bern, (5. bd.), 40–53.

Secondary literature

Bauder, T. 2008. Der Entwicklungsprozess des ersten eidgenössischen Berufsbildungsgesetzes. Unterschiedliche Interessen, gemeinsames Ziel. Bauder & Osterwalder (eds.), 75 Jahre eidgenössisches Berufsbildungsgesetz. Bern, Hep.

Berner, E. 2013. Verbundpartnerschaft – Schlagwort oder Erfolgsrezept? Zur Steuerung der schweizerischen Berufsbildung. In M. Maurer & P. Gonon (eds.), Herausforderungen für die Berufsbildung in der Schweiz. Bern, Hep.

Berner, E, Gonon, P., & Ritter, H.J. 2011. Zwischen Gewerbeförderung, Sozialpolitik und liberalen Bildungsbestrebungen. Zur "Vor"-Geschichte der dualen Berufsbildung in der Schweiz (1870–1930). Zeitschrift für Berufs- und Wirtschaftspädagogik, (107): 14–32.

Bonoli, L. 2016. The development of statistics in the VET domain in Switzerland: Issues and difficulties between 1880 and 1930. In E. Berner & P. Gonon (eds.), History of VET – Cases, Concepts and Challenges. Bern, Peter Lang.

Bonoli, L. 2015. Formation professionnelle et question sociale. A l'origine de la "vocation sociale" de la formation professionnelle suisse. Revue suisse des sciences de l'éducation, (37): 383–398.

Bonoli, L. 2012. La Naissance de la formation professionnelle en Suisse: entre compétences techniques et éducation morale. Education permanente, (192) : 209–221.

Foucault, M. 1966. Les mots et les choses. Paris, Gallimard.

Foucault M. 1969. L'archéologie du savoir. Paris, Gallimard.

Forster, S. 2008. L'école et ses réformes. Lausanne, Presses universitaires et polytechniques.

Fuessel, M. and Neu, T. 2014. Diskursforschung in der Geschichtswissenschaft. Angermueller & *et alii* (eds.), Diskursforschung. Ein interdisziplinäres Handbuch (Vol. 1, pp. 146–161). Bielefeld, transcript Verlag.

Gonon, Ph. 1998, Berufliche Bildung zwischen Zunft, Handelsfreiheit und Demokratie. Schweizerische Zeitschrift für Erziehungswissenschaft, (3): 419–429.

Haefeli, K. & Schellenberg, C. 2009. Facteurs de réussite dans la formation professionnelle des jeunes à risque. Berne, EDK-CDIP.

Jaeger, S. 2012. Kritische Diskuranalyse. Eine Einführung. Münster, Unrast-Verlag.

Keller, R. 2011, Diskursforschung. Eine Einführung für SozialwissenschaftlerInnen. Wiesbaden, VS Verlag.

Lamamra, N. 2013. Entre produire et former : Tension entre éducation générale et préparation à l'entrée sur le marché du travail dans la formation professionnelle suisse. Questions d'orientation, 4. Actes du congrès international d'orientation de Montpellier. Montpellier. 74–82.

Maingueneau, D. 1991. L'analyse du Discours. Introduction aux lectures de l'archive. Paris, Hachette.

Moreau, G. 2003. Le monde apprenti. Paris, La dispute.

OECD, (Organisation for economic co-operation and development). 2012. Education at a Glance. Paris, OCDE.

Power, M. 2011. Foucault and Sociology. Annual Review of Sociology, (37): 35–56.

Schriewer, J. & Harney, K. 1999. Beruflichkeit versus culture technique. Contribution à la sémantique du travail en France et en Allemagne. In B. Zimmermann, C. Didry, & P. Wagner (eds.), Le travail et la nation. Histoire croisée de la France et de l'Allemagne Paris, Maison des sciences de l'Homme.

Strupler, M. & Wolter, S. 2012. Die duale Lehre: eine Erfolgs-geschichte – auch für die Betriebe. Ergebnisse aus der dritten Kosten-Nutzen-Erhebung der Lehrlingsausbildung aus der Sicht der Betriebe. Glarus/Chur, Ruegger Verlag.

Uldry, R. 1979. 75 ans de formation professionnelle 1904–1979. Genève, Conférence des offices cantonaux de formation profes-sionnelle de la Suisse Romande et du Tessin

Wettstein, E. & Gonon, Ph. 2009. Kapitel 4: Die Entwicklung der Berufsbildung im Rahmen der gewerblichen Frage. Berufsbildung in der Schweiz. Bern, Hep.

Chiara Martinelli

A School for the Many but Attended by the Few: Industrial and Artistic Industrial Schools in Regional and National Data

1. The evolution of Industrial and Artistic Industrial Schools: from the "engine of progress" to the cauldron of good citizens

Until 1907 industrial and artistic industrial schools were not ruled by the State and they were considered as a sort of low-quality kind of schools (Conti 2000, unp. PhD thesis and Morcaldi 2004). They were not assessed by the Law Casati in 1859, even though few of them were already established. Furthermore, they were not managed by the Minister of Public Education as the other kinds of schools, but by the Minister of Agriculture, Industry and Commerce (hereafter MAIC) (Soldani 1981 and Fumi 2015). The official letter with whom the Ministry Benedetto Cairoli in 1878 established these institutes gave them an ancillary role.

The role Casati formerly gave to technical education can explain the eventual marginalization industrial and artistic industrial schools suffered. In Casati and his officials' minds technical education should have trained pupils to factory works: however, after five reforms in barely fifteen years, technical education became a modern lyceum without Latin. The scant demands of vocational training were not fulfilled until 1869, when the Paris Exposition highlighted the close relationship between workers' education and industrialization (Colombo 1984, Bolchini 1986 and Misiti 1996). Before the Exposition, liberalist common thought that industrialization was reserved only to natural resources-gifted countries was assumed as true in Italy. The evidence that also countries like Prussia, Belgium and France could have reached the UK thanks to improvement in workers' training undermined the adamant liberalist beliefs (Sanderson 1999).

Evidence gained from the international event prompted the Ministry of Agriculture, Industry and Commerce in considering more carefully industrial education. Since the 1870s the Italian state showed its interest in vocational education establishing several daily industrial schools all throughout the country. Curricula and subject taught were decided by the government itself. After few years their failure was patent. Only the industrial schools in Biella (Piedmont) continued to work as planned; the schools in Foggia (Apulia), Savona (Liguria), Carrara (Tuscany), Fabriano and Fano (The Marches) must have reformed deeply; the one in Colle Val d'Elsa (near Siena) was closed few years between the 80s and the 90s; the institute in Palermo was closed after five years (*Annali dell'industria e del commercio*, 1880, 6).

A real, pivotal shift occurred only in 1878, when Benedetto Cairoli issued an official letter to prefects, provinces, municipalities and trade unions. He assessed two kinds of vocational schools: the industrial and the artistic industrial ones. The first should have trained perspective technicians and foremen; the second one artisans and manual workers for little factories. After the state schools failure he demanded the establishment and the management of such schools were relocated to private citizens and local administrations: previous events made him to assume only decentralized institutions could know industrial demands. The State should have been relegated in a secondary role: he could encourage and give a little fund to the new institutes – up to the 2/5 of the whole outlay – but not more (*Annali dell'industria e del commercio*, n° 13, 1880).

Industrial and artistic industrial schools started to emancipate from their role only during the first years of XX century, thanks to their increase in enrolment. Pupils were 25673 in 1896, 32474 in 1906 and 56024 in 1914. Since 1908, their number overcome the one attained by the elitist general high schools (the so-called *ginnasi-licei*). Whilst between 1861 and 1900 76 new industrial and artistic industrial schools were established, during the first fifteen years of XX century the number arose to 31 (*Annuario Statistico Italiano,* 1900, 1917 and *Notiziario sull'insegnamento commercial e industriale* 1910).

The expansion made patent a few issues concerning industrial and artistic industrial role and status. The most important debated topics dealt with industrial and artistic industrial teachers' juridical status and the legal value of graduates' certificates. On the first side, teachers were paid lower than colleagues employed in technical schools and *ginnasi-licei*: they were hired by the single school-board which could decide their salary and their retirement allowance. On the other side, graduates' certificates did not allow them to apply for public job vacancies. Conversely, graduates from technical schools received a legal diploma who allowed them to do it.

The increasing number of industrial and artistic industrial schools made the discussion around the first topic to emerge. After teachers gathered themselves in an association – the Association of vocational teachers – in 1899 and after three conferences where they claimed a state law on their minimum wage and on their retirement salary, in 1904 MAIC allowed them to access to a national retirement fund (*L'istruz-ione industriale* 1931). Therefore, in 1908, their status was compared to the one attained by their Minister of Public Education's (hereafter MPE) colleagues. Conversely, notwithstanding pupils' uprisings, industrial and artistic industrial graduates' certificates persisted to not to give them the access to public competitions and to Engineering studies.

The legitimisation of industrial and artistic industrial schools reached a pivotal shift thanks to Law Cocco-Ortu in June 1908. The law introduced a threefold reform. Firstly, it assessed on a national level vocational schools and it divided them in five kinds of schools: the industrial schools, the artistic industrial, the feminine professional, the agrarian and the commercial ones. Secondly, it assessed on a national basis the years vocational courses should last and the subject to be taught, even though the law left this task to the national guidelines the Minister Francesco Nitti emanated in 1913 ("Gazzetta Ufficiale del Regno d'Italia", n° 128, 1908 and Istruzione professionale [industriale e commerciale], 1913).

Trends in vocational schools were not an exception though. In the very first years of XX century Italian post-elementary education went through a remarkable process of enrolment increase. It occurred mostly in technical education: pupils attending *scuole tecniche* and *isti-tuti tecnici* triplicated. Even during their period of expansion, industrial and artistic industrial schools were considered as a sort of technical institutes for less gifted pupils. Whilst technical schools were managed by the State and each of them was established thanks to a state law, industrial and artistic industrial schools depended on local administrations and private citizens' decisions. Not only they run the risk to be closed every year due to financial constraints. As a MAIC's official letter complained in 1904, they were so little known that perspective pupils' families wrote to the Minister asking information about vocational education[1].

However, thanks to their expansion, industrial and artistic industrial schools became the new topic of the ongoing political and intellectual debate. The new trend in post-elementary enrolment rate made scholars, politicians and schools policy-makers scared. The increase did not modify the tight dimension of post-elementary attendance in Italy: it was extremely low in 1901 – just 3% of 10-to-19 year-old people who could be enrolled – and even though the absolute increase was remarkable, attendance percentage remained around 6% in 1913 (Checchi 1997)[2]. It was a disappointing achievement, almost of all if compared to the ones attained by other countries: in the same years, pupils enrolled in post-elementary courses were the 20% of 10-to-19 year-old people in Sweden and USA and the 12% in Austria-Hungary (Goldin 1998, Cvcerk and Zajnek 2013).

What actually was a limited growth was perceived as a sort of creepy flood due to the previous stagnation. This wrong perception led the ongoing debates to search feverishly for a school which could absorb the new enrolment wave diverting it to technical schools and universities. Such a *Weltanschaung* is well documented by the Italian cultural reviews published during that time, as for example *Il Marzocco* and *La Voce* (Castelnuovo Frigessi 1964, Cingari S., 2012). The "spostato" (literally: the diverted one) – i.e., a low- or middle-rank young adult who, even though his social roots, attended high schools and University – became the main

---

1   Archive of the Mutual Aid Society in Viggiù, *Fondo scuola di disegno* cit., Corrispondenza, *Lettera del Ministro di Agricoltura, Industria e Commercio, Dei programmi e dei regolamenti delle Scuole industriali e commerciali alle scuole private e secondarie del Regno*, Rome, 5th november 1902.

2   My calculation. Data is retrieved from: *Annuario Statistico Italiano* 1878–1915, MAIC's enquiries 1868–1911.

character of articles about the topic. Leftist politicians as well as right-ist ones strived to define a new kind of post-elementary school which could divert lower-ranked pupils to prosecute their studies. "When afflu-ent classes don't show their concerns on lower-classes' schools" warned the socialist journalist Gaetano Salvemini in 1903 "the latter will invade elite's schools and they will divert them to attain their aims"[3].

Industrial and artistic industrial schools became soon to politicians and intellectuals' eyes the most suited institutes for such a task. In their opinion, they would assume a salvific role as they would train skilled foremen who wouldn't pursue social mobility. Not only reviews and journals, but also teachers' and headmasters' booklets insisted on this point. It was a pivotal shift as, before shift in enrolment rate, their essays focused on links nurtured by industrial and artistic industrial schools with industrialization and the economic development.

The social functions of vocational education were stressed also in other European countries. In 1869 the same opinion was backed by John Scott Russell, who was taken in charge by the government to investigate on ongoing developments in European and not-European vocational education. "If I have heretofore insisted" he wrote

> more on the value of systematic national education for moral purposes than an instrument of material and pecuniary personal and national wealth, I have done so because [...] the wealth and greatness consist, to my mind, much more in the multitude of good citizens than in the multitude of good dollars (Scott Russell 1869).

In the newly-born Germany the so-called Trade Regulation enacted in 1871 obliged 14-to-20 year-old apprentices to attend an evening indus-trial course (Gessler and Howe 2004). The guidelines was not only due to higher skills demands, but it was also aimed at taming a potential youth radicalization.

"We won't never train *spostati*: this is our pride and our merit" wrote a few teachers in the first issue of *La scuola industriale*. From 1906 to 1912 the review hosted articles and proposals about the reform of industrial and artistic industrial schools.

---

3   "quando le classi agiate [...] non si preoccupano se non delle proprie scuole, e trascurano le scuole del popolo, questo invade in mancanza di istituzioni più adatte le scuole dei ricchi, e le perturba".

Twofold directions were pursued by *La Scuola industriale*'s edi-
torial board. Firstly, the persisting contrast between vocational and
technical education, where the latter one was presented as an unfairly
"privileged" stepbrother. Secondly, the peroration of the social and economic advantages Italy could have attained thanks to a broader diffusion
of industrial and artistic industrial schools. These institutes, claimed
Oreste Forte in one of his articles, embodied actually Gabrio Casati's
technical schools (Forte 1906a).

Forte's predicament mirrored headmasters and vocational teachers'
booklets. Making the most of the inauguration of the Arts and Crafts
School in Pausula (The Marches) in 1911, the headmaster gave a speech
about the economic and working opportunities vocational education could
give to students. His address intermingled economic and social topics:

> Government's decision was well planned. The establishment of these industrial
> schools allowed working classes' offspring to pursue their studies after primary
> school and to apply for a good job (*Regia scuola di arti e mestieri Luigi Lanzi in
> Pausula*, 1911)[4].

Headmasters' address at the industrial school in Alessandria was even
more patent:

> Looking at the necessity to preserve social order, industrial and artistic industrial
> schools are extremely useful. They will divert from technical and general high
> schools pupils who are unable to pursue such studies. Their happiness is sacrificed
> by the petty middle classes' aspirations. Parents rejected the possibility their son
> would be hired as a foremen and they preferred to see them as lowly, low-paid
> clerks (Burbi 1901)[5].

---

4   "il governo […] ben provvide allorquando, con la istituzione ed il consolidamento
    delle scuole professionali, aprì una via larga e sicura a quei figli del popolo che si
    sarebbero sentiti troppo umiliati se costretti a dedicarsi ad un mestiere dopo aver
    compiuto soltanto il corso obbligatorio nelle scuole elementari".
5   "Le scuole d'arti e mestieri in genere […] producono un gran bene sociale. Esse
    sono destinate a sfollare un po' alla volta le scuole tecniche e i ginnasi dei non
    atti o non inclinati allo studio, sacrificati dal vieto pregiudizio di genitori della
    borghesia spicciola, che tengono le arti manuali, le meccaniche, le industriali, da
    meno dell'*impieguccio d'ordine* – senza carriera, senza ideali, senza una mercede
    che permetta giorni non angosciosi al buon padre preoccupato del domani della
    sua famigliola".

Even the Real Commission appointed by the MPE Leonardo Bianchi in 1905 in order to assess a new reform of secondary education was influenced by these debates. Even though its competencies were limited to MPE's schools, it encompassed in its reform plan also industrial and artistic industrial schools. Indeed commissioners conceived their consolidation and their nationalization as the best way to tackle middle classes' tendencies to attend general and technical high schools: "the establishment of industrial schools" they wrote in their final survey

> makes pupils' natural selection possible. Hence, it will remove from general high schools all the students who are unable to pursue studies further because of their economic status or to their attitude (*Commissione reale per l'ordinamento degli studi secondari in Italia*, 1909)[6].

2. Popular school?

Summing up, the establishment of industrial and artistic industrial schools was prompted not only for their economic and industrial outcomes, but also because of their presumptive role in the context of a social containment policy. However, were industrial and artistic industrial schools actually attended by the perspective working class?

That's a gruelling issue. Unavailability of reliable, thorough enquiries is patent. That's not a MAIC's fault – ministerial repeated attempts to carry on surveys about the topic are well documented. The reason of such a failure lies in difficulties for scholastic administrations to maintain the contact with past pupils and graduates. As they were used to migrate, to obtain information about their job history became difficult.

Notwithstanding all these difficulties, MAIC's funds at the Central National Archives in Rome preserve a survey about graduates' career in industrial and artistic industrial schools[7]. It was recorded in 1882,

---

6   "L'istituzione delle scuole capaci di soddisfare ai bisogni svariati della produzione ha per immediata conseguenza la selezione naturale della scolaresca e quindi la liberazione della scuola di cultura da tutti gli elementi non destinati, per condizioni economico – sociali e per attitudini speciali, a seguire le vie dell'istruzione superiore".

7   National Central Archive, *Fondo MAIC*, bundle 261.

when MAIC's top aides tried to elucidate what working opportunities Cairoli's schools made possible. As only sixteen of the seventy-six state funded schools answered to the enquiry form, MAIC's officials decided to not include findings in the 1885 publication.

Even though lacks in representativeness, only this data could document whether industrial and artistic industrial education matched factories' demands in human capital.

Data about the following schools is provided: artistic industrial schools in Padua, Monza (Lombardy) and Aversa (Campania); drafting schools in Luino (Lombardy), Murano (close to Venice), Seravezza (Tuscany), Soncino (Lombardy), Terni (Umbria) and Bari; industrial schools in Foggia (Apulia), Fossano and Biella (Piedmont), Belluno (Veneto), Rome, Colle Val d'Elsa (Tuscany).

Figure 1 and 2 describe territorial mobility for artistic industrial and industrial schools graduates. Migration is the first relevant proxy for assessing the correspondence between scholastic courses and factories' demands. A close analysis to each single school can highlight the mystifying potential of a mere overall look. The straight majority of graduates (especially the one from artistic industrial schools) was able to remain in their hometown or in its surroundings, but situation may have changed regarding the single context.

For example, in comparison to the other case-studies, artistic industrial schools in Luino and Aversa show low rates in graduates' abilities to find a job close to their home. However, Luino was a small town near national borders; dwellers were used to seasonal migration in France and Swiss and, as it happened in other vocational schools close to national borders (as the ones in Udine, in Veneto, or Viggiù, in Lombardy), institutes were envisaged by perspective migrants as a viable way to improve their skills. Secondly, the Istituto artistico in Aversa was an orphanage which hosted male adolescents coming from all the Campania region. After graduation, pupils were used to search for a job close to their hometowns – hence they moved on a regional-wide dimension. Figures about graduates' career perspective confirmed such a trends – no former pupil moved abroad or in other Italian regions, but all of them worked within the same region the school was hosted.

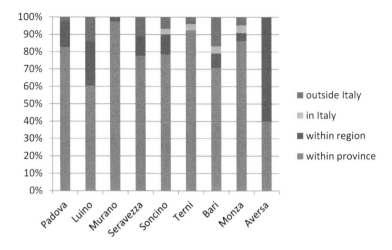

Figure 1: Artistic industrial graduates' territorial mobility, 1882.
Source: MAIC's fund, National Central Archive, Rome.

A closer look to figures about industrial graduates' highlights contrasting evidences. Schools in Fossano and Roma were characterized by graduates' full employment within province borders. Also figures of graduates from Foggia and Belluno outlined a situation where former pupils could easily found a job close to their towns. However, figures from schools in Biella and Colle Val d'Elsa notices a different situation. Roughly 75% of graduates from Biella 60% from Colle worked outside the provinces of Novara and Siena in 1882. Again, it is necessary to turn to micro-historical surveys for understanding why such trends occurred and for grasping differences among the two institutes.

The three-year industrial school in Biella (close to Novara and to the French border) was one of the first vocational schools ever established in Italy. It was inaugurated by the former Minister of Economic Affairs and right-wing politician Quintino Sella in 1869 and it aimed at training high-ranking technicians, factory directors and manager (Audenino 1995). Entry requirements confirmed this task. The main part of industrial and artistic industrial schools demanded a three or four primary classes attendance certificate; the industrial school in Biella required a technical school diploma, which pupils received after four years of primary schools and three years of *scuola* tecnica, a secondary general school without Latin which mirrored Prussian *Realschulen*.

Matching territorial mobility figures with career survey confirms Biella institute high-ranking but not at all. 56% of overall graduates were employed as foremen, managers or worked as entrepreneurs. However, among the other 44% who worked as artisans or common workers, the 55% of them was living in an other regions or abroad (in Germany or in Serbia).

Situation was even more complicated for the school in Colle Val d'Elsa. School-related figures indicate that people who moved outside Colle found a job as a worker or as a foremen. They didn't move as they obtained a high-ranked post massively like students from Biella: they moved because it was difficult to find a suitable job in their hometown, headmaster confirmed in a report written in 1881 (*Annali dell'industria e del commercio*, 1879, 10).

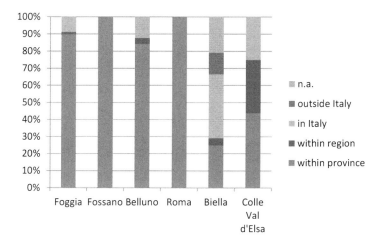

Figure 2: Industrial schools' graduates territorial mobility, 1882.
Source: MAIC's fund, National Central Archive, Rome.

Case-study analysis casted a grimmer light on evidences about graduates' career perspective, even though an overall look shows a different situation. Figure 3 elucidates differences in industrial and artistic industrial schools. Artistic industrial schools graduates worked in lower-ranked positions: more than 50% found a job as decorators (the 23%), bricklayer (roughly the 10%) carpenters and smiths. Most of them, we should underline, just continued the job they did during their evening or Sunday courses. Conversely, only the 9,74% of them was able to attain middle-high ranked jobs (managers, clerks, foremen, dealer). It's interesting to notice that no one was registered as foremen, whilst some of them are traceable among industrial schools graduates' list.

On the other side, graduates from industrial schools were more able to achieve higher-ranking jobs. Roughly, 35% of them worked as teachers, managers, dealers and clerks, figure claims. However, evidence shows part of them is employed in manual jobs as carpenters (15%) or smith (13%). Ironically, only 3% of them is registered as foremen – i.e., the job headmasters and politicians indicated as the most suited for industrial schools graduates.

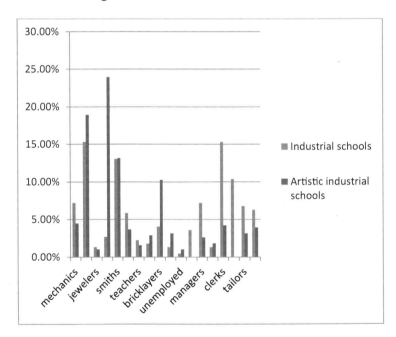

Figure 3: Graduates' career perspective, 1882.
Source: MAIC's fund, National Central Archive, Rome.

Summing up, public opinion's perception about industrial and artistic-industrial schools differed soundly from what actually they looked like. Political predicament alleged these schools as designed for popular classes, but the capacity to reach these aims depended from school to school. School boards independence (up to 1908) made them differ each school also on the ground of which was the public courses were aimed at. Whilst artistic industrial schools were generally aimed at training perspective factory workers and artisans, the aims of industrial schools changed soundly. Their tougher curriculum and the relatively considerable amount of school years they required before being enrolled made one risk patent, as it is signalled in some cases: to train pupils overqualified for local industries' demands. We can assume this conclusion only where is patently discussed, e.g. in Colle Val d'Elsa. Schools which were not endowed with a sound network could made former pupils to obtain a suitable job – like it occurred at the institute in Biella.

References

Commissione reale per l'ordinamento degli studi secondari in Italia, 1909 – Roma, Cecchini.

L'istruzione industriale in Italia 1931. Roma, Poliglotta.

Istruzione professionale (industriale e commerciale). Legge 14 Luglio 1912, n 854. Regolamento generale 22 giugno 1913, n 1014, e programmi generali d'insegnamento (Ministero di agricoltura, Industria e commercio) 1913. Roma, Bertero.

Notizie sulle condizioni dell'insegnamento agrario, industriale e commerciale in Italia 1910. Annuario per il 1910. Roma, Berterio.

Audenino P. 1995. Cosmopolitismo e ideologia industrialista all'origine dell'istituto tecnico industriale di Biella. In E. Decleva, C.G. Lacaita and A. Ventura (eds.) Innovazione e modernizzazione in Italia fra Otto e Novecento. Milano, Franco Angeli.

Bolchini P. 1986. L'esposizione internazionale di Londra del 1862 e l'Italia. La scelta e il trasferimento delle tecnich. Rivista di storia economica, 1.

Burbi G. 1901. La scuola d'arti e mestieri di Alessandria. Alessandria, Gazzotti.

Castelnuovo Frigessi D. (ed.) 1964. La cultura del '900 attraverso le riviste: La Voce (1908–1914). Torino, Einaudi.

Checchi D. 1997. L'efficacia del sistema scolastico italiano in prospettiva storica. In N. Rossi (ed.), L'istruzione in Italia: solo un pezzo di carta. Bologna, il Mulino.

Cingari S. 2012. Un'ideologia per il ceto dirigente dell'Italia unita. Pensiero e politica al liceo Dante di Firenze (1843–1945). Firenze, Olschki.

Conti E. 2000, Istruzione tecnica e professionale e sviluppo economico italiano (1859–1940): dottorato di ricerca in storia economica, 13 ciclo, unp. PhD thesis.

Colombo G. 1984 Industria e politica nella storia d'Italia. Scritti scelti. Milano, FrancoAngeli.

Cvcerk T. e Zajcek M. 2013. School, what is it good for? Useful Human Capital and the History of Public Education in Central Europe, NBER Working Papers.

Forte O. 1906. Lo stato giuridico delle scuole in Italia, La scuola industriale, 2: 4–5.

Fumi G. 2015. L'insegnamento delle materie economico-commerciali negli istituti tecnici. In C.G. Lacaita and M.C. Fugazza (eds.), L'istruzione secondaria nell'Italia unita. 1861–1901, Milano, FrancoAngeli.

Gessler M. and Howe R. 2004. The German dual vocational training system–the origin of the current architecture. [retrieved from: <http://ir.nul.nagoya–u.ac.jp/jspui/bitstream/2237/19014/1/3%E3%80%90Gessler&Howe%E3%80%91.pdf> – May, 14th 2016].

Goldin, 1998. America's graduation from High school: the Evolution and Spread of Secondary Schooling in the Twentieth Century, The Journal of Economic History, LVII, 2: 348.

Misiti M. 1996. L'Italia in mostra e la costruzione dello stato nazionale, Passato e presente, 3: 33–54.

Morcaldi M. 2004. Le scuole industriali: 1880–1930: formazione e capitale umano. Milano, Franco Angeli.

Regia scuola di arti e mestieri Luigi Lanzi in Pausula 1991. Macerata, Giorgetti.

Salvemini G. 1903. Per la scuola e per gl'insegnanti. Messina, Muglia.

Sanderson M. 1999. Education and economic decline in Britain, 1870 to 1990. Cambridge, Cambridge University Press.

Scott Russell J. 1869. Systematic Technical Education for the English people. Bradbury, Evans & Company.

Soldani S. 1981. L'istruzione tecnica: 1861–1900, Studi storici, 4.

Esther Berner

Citizenship and Participation: Apprenticeship as a Political Issue in the Swiss VET-Debate of the 1970s / 80s

1. Introduction

The post-obligatory educational offers in Switzerland are characterised by a strong focus on professional qualifications. Even today, three out of four diplomas awarded at this level are vocational certificates (Cortesi & Imdorf 2013). Thereby, the vocational education in the company and in the vocational school is of significant importance. In 2014, 90% of all learners in vocational education in Switzerland began their basic vocational training in a programme that took place simultaneously in the company and in the vocational school (Swiss Federal Statistical Office 2016a).

This dual model of vocational education and training (VET) enjoys high esteem in Switzerland. In retrospect, there were just two occasions when the advantages of this model were seriously questioned and alternative forms of organization of VET were brought into play: once in the late 19th century, i.e. in the early stage of the institutionalization of VET, the second time in the 1970s and 80s on the backdrop of a broader emancipatory-critical discourse (Gonon & Müller 1982; Berner 2012). As a counter-model served each time the training in (public) apprenticeship workshops. The proponents argued that this type of training was superior because it facilitated a systematic training under educational criteria and without productivity constraints. In both cases technological changes in the wake of the Second Industrial Revolution or the Third Industrial Revolution, respectively, represented important triggers for the reform discussions. Apart from questioning the quality of skill formation, apprenticeship was also criticized for the misuse of trainees as cheap labour by many employers. Uniquely, however, is the fact that the apprentices themselves emerged as a protest group in the 1970s and took part in the debate (Eigenmann & Geiss 2015). The venture for the introduction of public apprenticeship workshops culminated in a Swiss popular initiative in 1982. With a share of 81.6% no-votes in the referendum held four years later it was clearly defeated. Similar projects, which were at the time launched in several Swiss cantons, failed as well.

The article turns to the debate on apprenticeship preceding the vote. In the climate after the 68 movement the question of a proper organization of training had become, as hardly ever before and thereafter, a political-ideological issue. The low proportion of general education in VET, the neglect of a modern civic education and the lack of any connectivity to the academic education were considered by some as discriminatory; others judged the Swiss VET-tradition to be an important pillar of prosperity and social order.

Against this background, the contribution examines which actors, maintaining what positions, were involved in the dispute and, specially, how they justified their particular standpoint. Moreover, an answer to the question of why the initiative failed so clearly will be sought. As a theoretical framework I am using the so called *Économie des convention*, developed during the last three decades in context of the new French economic sociology. Yet, the reception of the approach has intensified in historical research and has also gained foothold in the sphere of educational research, especially in comparative studies. The next section (2) provides an introduction to that theoretical programme. Section 3 informs about the discourse-relevant political context and the involved actors. Part 4 is dedicated to the proper analysis on the basis of representative source material. In the summarizing conclusions (5) outstanding features of the debate under investigation – with a quick look at more recent VET-debates in Switzerland – will be presented.

2. Theoretical framework: *Économie des convention* and Justification Theory

As Rainer Diaz-Bone (2015) mentioned in a recent overall presentation of the *Économie des convention*, this approach does not represent a specific new paradigm, but a basic theory for transdisciplinary empirical analysis of economic institutions. It can be described as an application-oriented approach based on a pragmatic turn taking place in the French social sciences since the 1980s. It is import to note that the term *convention* does not stand for standards or customs, but for culturally established logics of coordination. Thereby, conventions are fundamental for the construction of evaluations, values and qualities, namely of objects, persons, acts and categories. Relating to conventions the question is to be answered, how radical uncertainties of economically relevant qualities in situations can be solved for the coordinating actors (*ibid.*).

Most fundamental in the development of the *Économie des convention* was the monograph *De la justification. Les économies de la grandeur* (engl. *On Justification. Economies of Worth* 2006) publishes by Luc Boltanski and Laurent Thévenot in 1991. Using the term *justification*, the authors point to the need of actors involved in a dispute to legitimate their arguments by moving beyond stating a particular or personal viewpoint toward proving that the statement is generalizable and relevant for a *common good*. In doing so, actors refer to different orders of worth regarded as particularly legitimate. Thereby, "[e]ach order of worth offers a different basis for justification and involves a different mode of evaluating what is good for a common humanity (in terms of market worth, or efficient technique and method, for instance)" (Thévenot *et al.* 2000, p. 236).

Justifications can involve positive arguments, claims, or position statements, but might also be critical denunciations of opposing views in the dynamic of public disputes: "The critique of justification from one order usually rests on the evaluative basis of another order (such as the denunciation of bureaucratic planning from a market flexibility perspective, for instance)" (*ibid.*, p. 237).

Originally, Boltanski and Thévenot had described six orders of worth[1]:

Table 1: Orders of worth by Boltanski & Thévenot (1991) (*cf.* Thévenot *et al.* 2000).

	1. Market	*2. Industrial*	*3. Civic*	*4. Domestic*	*(5). Inspired*	*(6). Opinion*
Mode of evalu-ation (worth)	Price, cost	Technical efficiency	Collective welfare	Esteem, reputation	Grace, singularity, creative-ness	Renown, fame
Test	Market com-petitiveness (short-term)	Competence, reliability, planning (long-term)	Equality and soli-darity	Trustworthi-ness	Passion, enthusiasm	Popularity, audience, recognition
Form of relevant proof	Monetary	Measurable; criteria, statistics	Formal, official	Oral, exemplary, personally warranted	Emotional involve-ment & expression	Semiotic (through signs, media)
Classical manifes-tation	A. Smith: *An Inquiry into the Nature and Causes of the* Wealth of Nations (1776)	Saint-Simon: *L'Industrie* (1817) bzw. *Du système industriel* (1819)	Rousseau: *Du contract social* (1762)	e.g. La Bruyère: *Les caractères ou les Mœurs de ce siècle* (1688)	Augusti-nus: *De civitate dei* (413–426)	Hobbes: *Leviathan* (1651)

2.1 The market *world of worth*

Arguments involving market justifications evaluate worth based on the price or economic value of goods and services in a competitive market. Relevant pieces or evidence brought in support of these arguments only qualify for market justification as long as they can be treated as exchangeable goods or services. These justifications consider the worth

1   In their book *Le nouvel Ésprit du Capitalisme* (1999) (engl. *The New Spirit of Cap-italism* 2005) Luc Boltanski and Ève Chiapello have added the project-based order of worth as a seventh justification principle. While important in recently introduced forms of flexible work organisation and corresponding learning arrangement, this principle has, yet, hardly any importance in the case examined here.

of things only in terms of price and support a very short-term construction of time in which the market competition test is the basis for evaluation (Thévenot *et al.* 2000).

2.2 *The* industrial *world of worth*

These justifications include arguments where evaluations depend on technical efficiency and professionalism, planning and long-term investment in infrastructure. The term "industrial" is here not limited to the industrial economic sector. While market justifications place value based on the competitive price of goods, technical competency justifications place value based on the efficiency of investments, professional planning and expertise and long-term growth. In addition, the form of proof involved in market justifications is short-term profitability, while the form of proof for planning justifications is long-term investment and technical or scientific competency (*ibid.*).

2.3 *The* civic *world of worth*

These justifications refer to the collective welfare as the standard of evaluation and propose or oppose projects based on such goals as equal access and protection of civil rights. In this world of worth human beings are part of a (enlightened, bourgeois) collective, such as parties, the state, associations, social movements, initiatives etc. By sacrificing the satisfaction of particular interests on behalf of solidarity and equality, separations, which impede collective action, can be overcome (*ibid.*).

2.4 *The* domestic *world of worth*

In the domestic order of worth the claim of a general value is warranted by personal tie or local attachment, so that personal character or proximity are considered the source of building blocks of universal goods. Traditions are valued and are constantly being revisited in making judgements about the present. Evaluations of this type support hierarchies of reputation and trustworthiness. The basic model of this world is the *family*. This model and the respective coordination principles can easily be transferred to family business or small and medium-sized enterprises (*ibid.*).

2.5 *The* inspired *world of worth*

This category of justifications involves judgements based on inspiration, passion and emotion and points often to the singularity or creativity of a person, object or action, which is the source of inspiration. Frequently, these sorts of arguments lead to the critique that they are unable to be discussed or challenged as general claims and that they are irrational or unreasonable (*ibid.*).

2.6 *The* renown *world of worth* (opinion)

This order of justification relates to arguments and evaluations, which point to the importance of fame and public knowledge for determining the worth of a cause. Thus, it differs from the other orders of justification which involve arguments to garner public support, but where the standard for judgement and evaluation of arguments is not the extent of public knowledge or renown itself (*ibid.*).

The concept of orders of worth and justification proposed by Boltanski and Thévenot (1991) allows to capture theoretically the model of vocational education deemed as adequate in a specific historic context. This faciliates the distinction of important principles of social ordering in the process of coordination and legitimation and, thereby, in the long-term social bond that develop between organisations – in our particular case between work and educational organisations (Berner *et al.* 2015). In contemporary or recent reform-disputes concerning vocational education we normally will find that statements often combine different orders of worth and thus build a compromise. Like the justifications themselves, these combinations differ from one case to another and bring about distinctions between different repertoires.

3. Context and actors

The economic context of the 1970s, when the traditional apprentice-ship model came under pressure, was characterized by the fear of a loss of apprenticeship positions caused by the recession following the oil crisis (1973). Microelectronics and information technology had begun to play a major role in many workplaces and led to a debate on necessary VET-reforms. Apart from these technical reasons other arguments in favour of fundamental reforms of the prevailing apprenticeship model were put forward, namely by accusing its paternalistic structure and its domination by economic utility. Whereas all actors acknowledged the necessity to react to the challenges caused by the economic and technical development, the second objection was expressed exclusively by the political left. Generally accepted was also the view that VET suffered from discrimination with respect to financial state support and was normatively devalued in comparison to higher secondary and university education. Indeed, compared to upper secondary education apprenticeship had lost attractiveness for many young people.

The debate led to an amendment of the Federal Vocational and Professional Education and Training Act of 1963. The legislation process and the final law of 1978 were clearly dominated by the conservative bourgeois parties and employers' interests. Progressive claims from the trade unions, left wing parties and student and apprentices' organisations were hardly integrated into the law. Nevertheless, in terms of a compromise it introduced a range of measures to assure the quality of training and by this means to increase the attractiveness of dual VET, namely:

- introduction of mandatory inter-company training courses as a complement to in-company training and vocational school;
- systematization and coordination of school-based education and company-based training;
- mandatory courses for masters and instructors in charge of apprenticeship training;

- differentiation of the apprenticeship by introducing a short-track apprenticeship for the weaker on the one hand and the enactment of the vocational secondary school (*Berufsmittelschule*)[2] for the talented young people on the other hand. In the highly selective Swiss education system[3] the former addressed, in concrete terms, school leavers with a basic certificate, including those with learning difficulties, the later addressed merely the best 2% (!) of those who entered vocational education after compulsory school.

When a Committee of the Socialist Labour Party (Sozialistische Arbeiterpartei) submitted in June 1982 a nationwide popular initiative under the title *Initiative for an ensured vocational education and retraining*, this was also a reaction to the poor impact that the left forces had on the amendment of the new law. The initiative requested the establishment of public apprenticeship workshops with at least 10'000 places to guarantee the right to undergo a full vocational education of 3 years for everybody, especially discriminated groups of immigrants, invalids and women. 75% of the costs were to bear by the employers, the remaining 25% by the federal state, the cantons and the unemployment insurance fund.

In the debate of the run-up to the vote the initiative received little support. Even representatives of the political left like the Swiss Federation of Trade Unions (Schweizerischer Gewerkschaftsbund) or the Social Democratic Party (Sozialdemokratische Partei) were reluctant or divided. It seems that both learnt their lessons from the 70s, when their more radical claims were rejected. Although they were still supportive of reforms, they chose another, moderate strategy. In the meantime, the apprentice's protest movement, anchored in the unionist youth organisation and very active in the 70s, had died away, too.

---

2   The *Berufsmittelschule* offered an extra school day per week to the gifted apprentices of some professions, provided the consent of the employer.
3   Lower secondary school (about 11- to 15-year-olds) of most of the 26 Swiss cantons was usually divided into three performance levels, the most demanding of them leading to Gymnasium. Notably, in 1980 little more than 10% of the Swiss 19-year-olds obtained a baccalaureate (Swiss Federal Statistical Office 2016b).

To depict the whole range of arguments and their alignment with different orders of worth, the following key actors and stakeholders must be taken into account:

1. Socialist Labour Party (Sozialistische Arbeiterpartei)[4].
2. Swiss Federation of Trade Unions (Schweizerischer Gewerkschaftsbund).
3. Swiss Industry and Trade Association (Schweizerischer Gewerbeverband)[5].
4. Swiss Association of Vocational Education (Schweizerischer Verband für beruflichen Unterricht).
5. Government / political parties.

In the following section, the principal positions of these interest groups and parties and the corresponding justifications are presented in a condensed manner. As a basis serve position statements in brochures, reports and parliamentary debates, which were published or held during the voting campaign and thus had to offer convincing arguments in favour of the own point of view.

---

4   The Socialist Labour Party, until 1980 named Revolutionist Marxist League (Revolutionäre Marxistische Liga), emerged in 1969 from the Labour Party (Partei der Arbeit) and represented the Swiss section of the Trotskyist Fourth International.

5   The Swiss Industry and Trade Association represents small and medium-sized companies (crafts- and businessmen) and is politically connected to the conservative Swiss People's Party (see section 4.5). The other important employers' association is the Federation of Swiss Employers' Organizations (Zentralverband Schweizerischer Arbeitgeber-Organisationen). Unlike the former, the Federation was not much involved in the debate of the 80s, quite in contrast to its participation in the negotiation of the new law of 1978. Strongly associated with market liberalism, it was opposed to any kind of state interventionism in VET-policy. The Federation of Swiss Employers' Organizations is tied to the Free Democratic Party (see section 4.5) and representative of larger (export-oriented) enterprises.

4. Dual or workshop-based apprenticeship: Actors and justifications

4.1 Socialist Labour Party

The Revolutionist Marxist League (Revolutionäre Marxistische Liga) – which changed its name in 1980 to Socialist Labour Party – started its campaign in favour of progressive VET-reforms in 1979, right after the adoption of the new law. Contrary to other critics of the current VET the Socialist Labour Party clearly rejected the existing apprenticeship model (Revolutionäre Marxistische Liga 1980). With their initiative in favour of public apprenticeship workshops the representatives of the party aimed to put apprenticeship, which was deeply rooted in the Swiss corporatist tradition, under the control of the workers and thus to break the employers' monopole in VET. To gather and train the apprentices together in big numbers in public workshops was also a measure to gain more influence on them. Providing the apprentices with an education that was more general and broader in terms of the acquired skills and competences, meant to ensure the autonomy of the future workforce and to make employees less dependent of the training firm.

The Socialist Labour Party estimated the training conditions in crafts and small industry as worst. These companies were important because, at that time, 75% of the apprentices were trained in such enterprises (*ibid.*). Considered better were big enterprises with own training workshops and a rotation system, which provided the trainees experience with various workplaces and brought them in contact with different technologies. While this ought to ensure systematic training and learning according to universalistic principles of rationality and efficiency as well as a supra-individual relationship between trainees and instructors, the domestic environment in crafts and small business was rather characterised by intimacy and personal relationships, which were prone to arbitrariness.

Apart from the industrial convention, which is reminiscent in those statements as a starting point for an anti-domestic critique, the civic convention was present, too. Vocational education ought to become a public affair, independent from business interests.

4.2 Swiss Federation of Trade Unions

The Swiss Federation of Trade Unions was the leading leftist actor in the debate about VET-reform preceding the new law of 1978 and supportive of the establishment of apprenticeship workshops, but did not join the initiative, except its women's and youth committees. Instead, the union released its own recommendation for a future-oriented vocational education in 1985 (Schweizerischer Gewerkschaftsbund 1985). The report stressed that the own proposal built upon the existing structures and was not meant to play off one model against the other. Obviously in contrast to the initiative, the strong relation between economy and vocational education was by now recognised, along with a market regulation of training opportunities and career choice. On the other hand, the union called for some counteractions against the domination of VET by the business and against a dehumanization of working conditions due to the technological progress. To guarantee mobility in the light of an increasing frequency of career shifts the union favoured process-independent qualifications and key competencies. Also in order to allow a broad education and training, including general education, the proportion of time spent in the company should be shortened in favour of the time spent at vocational school and inter-company training courses. Along with the strengthening of these newly introduced courses the union saw a need for establishing some additional apprenticeship workshops, but without proposing a break with the dual VET-tradition.

The proposals built upon a compromise between the civic and industrial orders of justification, which formed the basis for a critique on the domestic world. Great quality differences concerning apprenticeship between the companies were considered as major problem of the dual model, whereas the size of the company was a deciding factor (Häfeli *et al.* 1981). The Swiss Federation of Trade Unions, too, generally preferred training conditions of big enterprises, among other things because they were considered to be equipped with up-to-date technology.

Only when it came to subjects like personal development (*Persön-lichkeitsbildung*) or the cultivation of professional pride (*Berufsstolz*), some positive allusions to the domestic world can be found on this side. Other votes, for example in favour of a better coordination of in-company training and vocational school or in favour of the institutionalisation of VET-research, referred to the industrial order of justification.

4.3 Swiss Industry and Trade Association

The association of crafts and small industries was the leading advocate of dual apprenticeship. Its report on vocational education and training of the year 1986, released midst in the referendum campaign, marked an explicit statement in support of the corporatist model. Here, as a first principle, the association claimed that Swiss education policy was to realize within the regulative framework of a free market economy. The sixth and last principle stipulated that education policy had to refrain from any kind of experimentation and accused the initiative to be ideologically motivated.

The adherence to the dual apprenticeship was justified by the following arguments, whereas the domestic justification played a key role:

• The fact that this model has proven its worth in the past and, in connection to this,
• its appropriateness to the Swiss economic singularities like localism, the economy's tight structures etc.
• The orientation on the labour market, which contributed to a smooth transition to work and thus low youth unemployment rates.
• As a fourth argument, the report specified:

> Undergoing an apprenticeship, the young person not only acquires vocational skills, but the contact with the supervising master and the customers, the necessity to observe deadlines, the contact with machines and tools *etc.* are encouraging capacities like fair-mindedness, responsibility, punctuality and autonomous thinking and working (Schweizerischer Gewerbeverband 1986, p. 5).

Both, the Swiss Industry and Trade Association and the Socialist Labour Party, sustained the introduction of economics as a teaching subject for pupils and apprentices. Whereas the latter underlined the emancipatory character of this knowledge, it provided for the former an appropriate means to prevent the pupils from considering "the world to be a self-service store, where everybody can choose the job of his dreams and get a vocational education at taxpayers' expense" (*ibid.*, p. 9).

4.4 Swiss Association of Vocational Education

The association of the Swiss vocational school teachers and principals was one of the predominant actors in the reform discourse since the early 70s. The association stood in for moderate reforms of the current system. The introduction of public apprenticeship workshops was a matter of discussion in its journal for several times. All in all, the articles sought to give the reader balanced informations about already existing apprenticeship workshops. These workshops for singular professions were valued successful and regarded as an important supplement especially for the training of a highly skilled workforce. However, the association clearly rejected a generalization of the workshop-model at the expense of dual apprenticeship.

In a statement immediately before the vote of September 27/28, 1986 the association sharpened its position in favour of dual apprenticeship and against the initiative by highlighting the improvements achieved by the new law (Ganz 1986). These included, in the first place, a certain differentiation of VET-programmes according to ambition levels (see section 3), which the association – contrary to the left groups – advocated strongly. From the association's point of view, the coordination of VET with market principles was essential for the allocation and regulation of training.

All stakeholders agreed that the technological changes placed new demands on VET. Concerning the question, how the new skills were to define and at what training setting they were to acquire, they disagreed. The Socialist Labour Party and the Swiss Federation of Trade Unions approved that in times of increasing specialization a depletion of work was to counteract. The structuring of VET-professions by comprehensive professional fields should ensure a broad basic education and increase the horizontal permeability. On the other hand, both, the Swiss Federation of Trade Unions and the Swiss Association of Vocational Education favoured the development of abstract, process-independent qualifications. The claims of the Swiss Industry and Trade Association show that the transition from transferable key competences as logical thinking or quick perception to adaptation skills such as flexibility and mobility, which, as some critical authors (e.g. Offe 1970; Lenhardt 1974) noted, served to maintain power relations at the workplace, was fluid.

4.5 *The Swiss Federal Council and the Parliament*

Before proceeding to the popular referendum, the Federal Council and the parliament had to deliberate on the initiative. The former gave its opinion on the matter in a message to the parliament, dated August 22, 1984, and suggested to refuse the initiative. It stated that the proposed measures were unnecessary and ineffective. Public apprenticeship workshops, which allow everybody to choose a job independently from the job market, would violate the market principles and create unemployment. The expenses for the public as well as for the business would exceed the available resources and affect the enterprises' willingness to provide training. All in all, the Federal Council found that, due to its close coordination with economic demands and its touch to real working life, firm-based apprenticeship had proven to be most successful.

Subsequently, the parliament was invited to deliberate on the initiative. In both chambers and the respective commissions the large majority joined the Federal Council in its rejection on the basis of market arguments. The representatives of the conservative and liberal parties, and also the Green Party (Grüne Partei), were in strong support of the apprenticeship, thereby advocating the close cooperation between business and the state underlying this model. The Social Democratic Party (Sozialdemokratische Partei) was split into, but acknowledged in total the advantages of the dual system. Only the Labour Party (Partei der Arbeit) decried it for pedagogical shortcomings and its patriarchal and capitalist basis. The Labour Party justified its position with reference to civic as well as industrial justifications. Interesting to note are arguments brought in by the conservatives and liberal conservatives relating to the domestic mode of evaluation. A representative of the right-wing conservative Swiss People's Party (Schweizerische Volkspartei), yet president of the Industry and Trade Association of the Canton of Zurich, defended the apprenticeship-model by stating that "the daily collaboration of apprentice and master was more valuable than any theoretical instruction" (Amtliches Bulletin der Bundesversammlung, 26.9.1985, p. 1610). By taking a domestic viewpoint to criticize the civic world of worth, a representative of the Christian Democratic People's Party (Christlichdemokratische Volkspartei) made a similar statement. Against tendencies towards humanization in the sphere of education he set learning in the hierarchical relationship of master and apprentice. "It is fulfilling to see a young man passing through the rigorous school of a brave, respectable and understanding master to get prepared for professional life" (*ibid.*, p. 1615). Another member of the parliament, representative of the Free Democratic Party (Freisinnig-Demokratische Partei), argued:

> The good contact, mutual confidence that develops between master and young man or woman is the basis for a successful professional education. Firm-based education is beneficial for the apprentice. He is permanently in contact with professional people and not only gets technical qualifications, but has also the occasion to develop a sense of collaboration, discipline and teamwork. At the end of the apprenticeship he is already a recognized personality in his professional milieu (*ibid.*, p. 1617).

As expected, the liberals aligned their votes readily with the market world of worth. But it was still possible to compromise such arguments with a domestic tenor, as another representative of the Free Democrats demonstrated by praising dual VET as an "organically grown" system, which facilitates a "natural governance" (*ibid.*, p. 1616).

5. Conclusion

By raising the question of the didactically adequate training setting, the debate on apprenticeship workshops of the 1970s and 80s touched on the overarching problem of the *common good*. The existing positions on how to define and how to promote that wider goal were analysed in this contribution by drawing on the theoretical framework of the Économie *des convention*. In this way, differences that transcend the traditional left-right-scheme as well as specific argumentation patterns negotiated on various compromises became apparent. Since apprenticeship had a long tradition in Switzerland, adherence to it could be justified by arguments from the market *and* the domestic world of worth. The domestic justification was used by the conservatives (Swiss People's Party, Christian Democratic People's Party and the economically import Swiss Industry and Trade Association) and by the liberals (Free Democratic

Party). The clear failure of the apprenticeship workshop-initiative can be explained by the fact that the market justification has almost universally – i.e. with the exception of the radical left – been accepted as well as by its peculiar, case specific compatibility with the domestic world of worth.

With respect to the workshop-model, on the other hand, not only the civic, but also the industrial world of worth played an import role. Representatives of the left resorted to the industrial justification to distance themselves from the domestic order of worth. Yet, in the then emerging key competences-discourse the industrial world of worth was omnipresent, too. Mainly the Swiss Federation of Trade Unions and the Swiss Association of Vocational Education jumped on this bandwagon. That new concept promised the union side training that was oriented towards mobility and autonomy. Thus, a link to the civic world of worth was quite possible. The Swiss Association of Vocational Education acknowledged it as a necessary response to new demands on learning brought about by technological change. Still, between the two actors existed fundamental differences regarding the need for differentiation of basic vocational training and thus regarding the role of selection mechanisms. While the left, including the unions, contested such measures, the Swiss Association of Vocational Education saw this as a means to enhance the attractiveness of basic VET for the talented young school leavers. Turning to the system level, a blurring of the boundaries between the academic and the vocational track was not intended by this widely recognized policy. Interestingly, but to elaborate elsewhere, at this point the introduction of the vocational secondary school (see section 3) did *not* aim at making the school system more permeable (*cf.* Jörg 1973).

In this regard, the situation has gradually changed now. The reforms of the 1990s led to the development of the sector of higher vocational education (introduction of the vocational and the specialized baccalaureate as well as universities of applied science etc.), which opens new career paths. In 2015, 16% of the 19-year-olds obtained a vocational or specialized baccalaureate (20% an academic baccalaureate after Gymnasium) – a tendency that is viewed particularly positive. The starting point as well as the aim of the recent VET-reforms are comparable to the situation in the 80s: loss of attraction and decrease in supply of apprenticeship positions and the will to keep the ratio of academic baccalaureates at low level. Yet, to valorize vocational education, a *gradual* permeability between vocational and academic education was introduced. The reform process of the 90s led in 2002 to the latest revision of the Federal Vocational and Professional Education and Training Act. Interestingly and in contrast to the historical case examined, by then there was no longer any dissent about the primacy of the dual apprenticeship model among the different groups and parties (Berner 2013). In this regard, further analyses would be of interest. A plausible hypothesis might be that the economic downturn of the 90s made market justifications even more acceptable, whereas the launched reforms neutralized, to some extent, the civic critique.

References

Amtliches Bulletin der Bundesversammlung. Verhandlungen des Nationalrates und des Ständerates. 84.062 Gesicherte Berufsbildung. Volksinitiative. [retrieved from: <https://www.parlament.ch/de/services/volksabstimmungen/verhandlungshefte> February, 29th 2016].

Berner, E. 2012. Rationalisierung der beruflichen Bildung im Zeichen der Industrialisierung in der Schweiz. In Rationalisierung in Handwerksberufen – Beiträge des XXX. Gesprächskreises für Technikgeschichte vom 2. bis 4. Juni 2011 im LWL-Freilichtmuseum Hagen / LWL-Freilichtmuseum Hagen – Westfälisches Landesmuseum für Handwerk und Technik.

Berner, E. 2013. Verbundpartnerschaft' als steuerungspolitischer Slogan. In Maurer, M. & Gonon Ph. (eds.). Herausforderungen für die Berufsbildung in der Schweiz. Bern, hep.

Berner, E.; Gonon, Ph. & Imdorf, Ch. 2015. The Genesis of Vocational Education in Switzerland from a Justification-Theoretical Perspective: The Cases of Geneva and Lucerne. In Berner, E. & Gonon, Ph. (eds.). History of Vocational Education and Training in Europe – Cases, Concepts and Challenges. Bern, Peter Lang.

Boltanski, L. & Chiapello, E. 2005. The New Spirit of Capitalism. London, Verso.

Boltanski, L. & Thévenot, L. 1991. De la justification. Les economies de la grandeur. Paris, Gallimard.

Cortesi, S. & Imdorf, C. 2013. Le certificat fédéral de capacité en Suisse – Quelles significations sociales pour un diplôme hétérogène? In Cahiers de la Recherche sur l'Education et les Savoirs, Hors Série no. 4.

Diaz-Bone, R. 2015. Die "Economie des conventions". Grundlagen und Entwicklungen der neuen französischen Wirtschaftssoziologie. Wiesbaden, Springer VS.

Eigenmann, Ph. & Geiss, M. 2015. There Is No Outside to the System: Paternalism and Protest in Swiss Vocational Education and Training, 1950–1980. In Berner, E. & Gonon, Ph. (eds.). History of Vocational Education and Training in Europe. Cases, Concepts and Challenges. Bern, Peter Lang.

Ganz, P. 1986. Abstimmung über die Lehrwerkstätten-Initiative. In Schweizerische Blätter für beruflichen Unterricht 111, no. 8/9. 203–205.

Gonon, Ph. & Müller, A. 1982. Öffentliche Lehrwerkstätten im Berufsbildungssystem der Schweiz. Eine Erhebung über die Entstehung und die qualitative und quantitative Bedeutung der öffentlichen Lehrwerkstätten im industriell-gewerblichen Bereich. Luzern, Eigenverlag.

Häfeli, K.; Frischknecht, E. & Stoll, F. 1981. Schweizer Lehrlinge zwischen Ausbildung und Produktion. Muri b. Bern, Cosmos.

Jörg, R. 1973. Die Reform der gewerblich-industriellen Berufslehre aus der Sicht interessierter Verbände und Lehrlingsgruppen. Zürich, Eigenverlag.

Lenhardt, G. 1974. Berufliche Weiterbildung und Arbeitsteilung in der Industrieproduktion. Frankfurt, Cosmos.

Offe, C. 1970. Leistungsprinzip und industrielle Arbeit. Mechanismen der Statusverteilung in Arbeitsorganisationen der industriellen "Leistungsgesellschaft". Frankfurt, Europäische Verlagsanstalt.

Revolutionäre Marxistische Liga 1980. Berufsbildung im Kreuzverhör. Fragen und Antworten um einen Vorschlag für öffentliche Lehrwerkstätten.

Schweizerischer Gewerbeverband 1986. Berufsbildungsbericht des Schweizerischen Gewerbeverbandes. Verabschiedet an der Sitzung vom 30. April 1986 in Lausanne durch den Vorstand des Schweizerischen Gewerbeverbandes.

Schweizerischer Gewerkschaftsbund 1985. Grundzüge für eine zukunftsoffene Berufsbildung. In Gewerkschaftliche Rundschau: Vierteljahresschrift des Schweizerischen Gewerkschaftsbundes 77, no. 4. 100–115.

Swiss Federal Statistical Office (2016a). Entrance by profession, canton, type of education, gender and form of training. [retrieved from: <https://www.pxweb.bfs.admin.ch/Selection.aspx?px_language=de&px_db=px-x-1502020100_101&px_tableid=px-x-1502020100_101\px-x-1502020100_101.px&px_type=PX> February, 29th 2016].

Swiss Federal Statistical Office 2016b. Baccalaureate graduation quote by type and gender 1980–2015, table no. ind-d-405102_td2.

Thévenot, L.; Moody, M. & Lafaye, C. 2000. Forms of Valuing Nature: Arguments and Modes of Justification in French and American Environmental Disputes. In Lamont, M. & Thévenot, L. (eds.). Rethinking Comparative Cultural Sociology. Repertories of Evaluation in France and the United States. Cambridge, Harvard University Press.

Ida Juul

The Twin Aspiration of Danish Craftsmen to Maintain their Traditional Privileges and Be Accepted as Respectable Members of the Emerging Bourgeois Society

1. Introduction

The period from the mid-18th century to the passing of the Danish apprenticeship law in 1889 was a period of great turbulence and dramatic social change. The late 18th century was characterized by agricultural reforms and the rise of a new self-assertive class of farmers who began to make their voices heard politically. At the same time, the number of smallholders and the proportion of unpropertied people grew. An urban bourgeoisie inspired by the ideas of the enlightenment increasingly challenged the absolutistic state and its power base, the rural nobility. This urban bourgeoisie, consisting of the bureaucrats of the absolute state, intellectuals and industrialists, mainly located in the capital, began to organize in clubs and patriotic societies (Engelhardt 2010, p. 79; Clemmensen 1987, p. 34). This led to an institutionalization of public opinion which the absolute state was unable to ignore and, in the end, to the peaceful transition from absolutism to a constitutional monarchy based on the principles of a division of power, as advocated by Montesquieu, and the introduction of civic rights. Neither the agricultural reforms, the ideas of the enlightenment nor the clubs and the patriotic societies were of Danish origin (Habermas 1962, Juul 2013, pp. 60–61). They were products of ideas generated in other European societies, transplanted and transformed in order to fit into a Danish context typically with some delay – with the country, as it was, situated at the edge of Europe. Until the middle of the 19th century, the Kingdom of Denmark was a typical medium-sized European state with a mixed population speaking different languages and consisting of different nationalities. A Danish national identity was not yet fully developed and the different sectors of the kingdom had little in common apart from the fact that they were subjects to the same king, who resided in Copenhagen. The German influence was strong as a consequence of the German speaking residents in Slesvig and Holsten, who made up approximately one third of the population in the kingdom (Østergård 2001, pp. 19–20). The influence from Northern Germany was also a result of Danish craftsmen travelling to Germany for work as part of their training and, correspondingly, German craftsmen travelling to Denmark. In addition, there was a strong German element in the Danish administrative system. Many of the reforms in the late 18th century were carried out by officials born in either Germany or Holsten. As a consequence, both the nobility and the craftsmen were strongly influenced by German culture, although these influences stemmed from different sections of the German society, representing aristocratic and popular culture respectively. In the late 18th century, both cultures came under pressure as an anti-German Danish national identity began to evolve (Østergård 2001, pp. 42–43, Feldbæk 1992, pp. 167–186, Juul 2013, p. 61).The development of a national identity was primarily a project led by the educated bourgeoisie. Education and support for political and economic liberties became important markers distinguishing the bourgeoisie from the nobility, on the one hand, and the manual workers, including the craftsmen, on the other.

This paper discusses how the process of modernization influenced the education of Danish craftsmen and how these craftsmen reacted by adapting to some elements while resisting others. The general hypothesis guiding this paper is that, prior to the passing of the first apprenticeship law, Danish vocational education and training was strongly influenced by ideas from abroad. Until the beginning of the 19th century, this influence mainly came from the northern parts of Germany, but later the picture became more diverse, and later again a more specific Danish model for training and educating craftsmen began to evolve. The paper is divided into two parts. The first part analyses how the Danish guilds became influenced by German crafts culture. The second part analyses the sources of the growing criticism of the guilds and

the different attempts to minimize their role in controlling the education and training of apprentices. This criticism is analysed from two
perspectives: both a cultural and an economic perspective. Finally the
paper examines how first the state, then the enlightened bourgeoisie,
and later again the craftsmen themselves reacted to the criticism and
how the criticism resulted both in the abolishment of the control of the
guilds over training and education and in the establishment of a system
of technical schools laying the foundations for the Danish dual system
of today.

2. Education and training of craftsmen under the control of the guilds

Until the 19th century, the education and training of apprentices was
mainly practical and under the control of the guilds. The origin of the
Danish guilds dates back to the religious communities of the early
Middle Ages which in the 14th century were transformed into craft based
organizations. In the pre-modern towns of Denmark, as in most parts
of Europe, businesses were strictly regulated. In order to secure the citizens in the towns a living and a stable delivery of consumer goods,
retail was reserved for the citizens of the towns. Prices and the quality
of the products were controlled by the town councils. The guilds played
an important role in the regulation of both the economic and social life
of the towns as they supervised the quality of the product and monitored
the conduct of the craftsmen. They punished breaches of standard and
collective norms and functioned as courts in disputes among their members (Jacobsen 1982, pp. 49–50 and pp. 176–179, Nyrop 1893, p. 13).
    The guilds also represented an element of egalitarianism as they
ensured that every master had access to the labour force in the form
of apprentices and journeymen. There were restrictions on the number
of journeymen a master was allowed to employ. The limit was typically placed at two or three, implying that a master who had engaged
three journeymen would have to release the third journeyman if another
master was in need of labour. In addition, the guild made sure that

both the wealthier and poorer masters had access to raw materials and customers. The aim was not to secure equality among the masters, but instead to ensure that all masters were able to obtain a standard of living suitable for a master of a craft. Being member of a guild distinguished craftsmen from other residents of the town and constituted the social and cultural framework for their daily lives. In the early 15th and 16th century, the difference in wealth between the poorer and the richer craftsmen was not significant as there was limited access to the labour force as well as to customers (Degn & Dübeck 1983, p. 33). The members of the guilds were obliged to help fellow masters who were unable to earn a proper living, to pay for the sick and pay the customary respect to their colleagues when they died. Apart from preventing severe polarization among the masters, these restrictions and regulations resulted in a relatively fixed ratio between the numbers of apprentices, journeymen and masters, which meant that the prospect of becoming a master was a realistic possibility for a journeyman. The typical duration of an apprenticeship was four to five years, after which the journeyman was expected to travel abroad for a year or more. Returning to Denmark he was expected to perform a masterpiece after working a couple of years for a master (Degn & Dübeck 1983, p. 73, Nyrop 1893, pp. 6–9). The institutionalization of the travelling craftsmen not only served as a means to learn new skills and as a source of innovation, it also played a role in the regulation of labour supply and demand. The journeyman was not expected to marry before he was able to settle as a master. Married journeymen were rare at the time and were looked down upon. Later, in the late 18th century when married journeymen became more common, there were a number of disputes among masters and journeymen as the unmarried journeymen refused to work in the same workshops as those who were married. Some masters ended up settling such disputes by hiring separate locations in the town reserved for the married journeymen (Dybdahl & Dübeck 1983, p. 76). The growing number of married journeymen was a consequence of a process of polarization among the craftsmen, especially in the booming construction sector. Many impressive buildings and monuments were being erected in the late 18th century, especially in Copenhagen, as a sign of the power and glory of the absolute state and the success of the major merchants who, to a large extent owed their wealth to triangular trade.

Until the passing of the law of free trade in 1857, which was fully implemented in 1862, the training of apprentices underwent few changes. The apprentice was trained in the workshop of the master and the approval of the apprentice and the control of the training were in the hands of the guilds. This type of training was predominant in most parts of Europe. Control of the training of apprentices and the approval of masterpieces did not only function as a means to secure the quality of the products, but also as a means to control and limit access to trade. It is therefore no coincidence that the masterpiece was made compulsory before the journeyman's test became widespread. This illustrates the importance attributed to the control over access to the ranks of the masters. From the 16th century, the journeyman's licence, that is to say the masters' or the guilds' approval of the successful fulfilment of the apprenticeship, became widespread. In the 17th century, it became common for apprenticeships to be completed with a test, which underwent some standardization after 1622 as an effect of the Danish king's aspirations to centralize power and correspondingly limit the power of the guilds. The monopoly of the guilds was seen by the king as an obstacle to the growth of the craft sector and therefore as contrary to the economic doctrine of that time, which promoted a growth in national production in order to minimize imports and secure a positive balance of trade (Nyrop 1893, p. 5; Wittendorff 2003, p. 93).

Seen from a cultural and social perspective, the members of the guilds lived their lives relatively isolated from government interference. But the interests of the guilds did not always coincide with state policy. Especially after the Reformation, when the king and the central government grew more powerful, the self-regulating practices of the guilds became an object of scrutiny. The result was several, mostly unsuccessful, attempts to regulate or abolish the guilds (Berg 1919, 31–33, Degn og Dübeck 1983, p. 193, Klöcker-Larsen 1962, pp. 10–11).

One of the main reasons why the king was unsuccessful in his attempts to control the guilds was that the power of the Danish guild system was not only based on the guilds' position in Danish economic and social life but also on the influence of the German guild system. This influence was not just a strategic choice, from the guilds' perspective, but also a consequence of the power balance between the Danish and the German guild systems, which shifted strongly in favour of the latter during the 17th century. The background was the strong migration of journeymen from Germany to Denmark and vice versa. German journeymen were highly regarded in Denmark as they were thought to be better trained and educated than Danish journeymen. However, the German journeymen were unwilling to work for Danish masters unless these were willing to conform to German crafts culture and ceremonies called the "Zunft" and to adopt the statutes of the German guilds. The argument was that this was necessary as the German journeymen would otherwise be denounced as being "Geshimpft", that is to say unworthy or undignified, when they returned back home and would therefore have difficulties finding work as their journeymen colleagues would refuse to work with them. The same argument was used by the Danish journeymen who, as part of their training and preparation to become masters, were expected to travel abroad.

Until the end of the 19th century, both the apprentice and the journeyman normally formed part of the household of the master. They were under the strict surveillance of the master, who regulated their lives not only at the workshop, but also in the household. Seen from the perspective of the Danish journeymen, travelling abroad not only represented an opportunity to learn new skills and customs, it also gave access to a new form of freedom and independence which stood in contrast to the restrictions at home where the journeyman was subjugated to the authority of the master and subjected to the surveillance of the guilds. In addition, the "Zunft" functioned as a means to strengthen a collective cross-national identity among journeymen. As will be shown later in the paper, this collective identity could easily be transformed into a weapon which could be turned against the masters. Seen from the perspective of the masters, the adoption of German customs, the "Zunft", was a necessity in order to be able to hire both German and Danish journeymen. There is, however, evidence suggesting that the masters also approved of the "Zunft" as a means to distinguish themselves from the poorer and less educated population of the towns. The masters of the 17th and 18th centuries therefore did not look favourably on attempts from the absolute state to forbid the practice of ceremonies of the "Zunft". In one case, a master was sentenced to 13 years in jail for not obeying the orders of the king (Nyrop 1914, p. 37; Karmark 1989, pp. 48–55).

The growing independence and proletarization of the journeymen

In the 16th century, the journeymen began to establish their own organizations with the encouragement of the masters under whose supervision they remained. The separation of the journeymen from the masters began as a means to support the travelling journeymen and to regulate the hiring of journeymen coming either from other Danish towns or from abroad. In order to solve this problem, the masters initiated the establishment of special inns, often, but not always, housed in the respective guild. At the inn, which was marked by the signage of the guild in question, the travelling journeymen would receive a treat consisting of a meal and some beer and would be offered a place to sleep if no work was available. Next to the door hung a slate listing the names of masters in need of journeymen. The masters were listed on a turn taking basis. If no job was available, the travelling journeyman was expected to leave the town the next day with a little money collected by the journeymen in the hope that he was luckier in the next town he would visit. The system was more or less the same in the other Nordic countries and in northern Germany. However, the inns did not only function as a sort of labour exchange, but also as a meeting place for the journeymen. The social activities of the masters and journeymen thus became separated in time and space, but still under the surveillance of the masters. In the course of this process of separation, the journeymen transformed the rituals and norms of the guilds so that they became more elaborate and rigid and, in the end, the subject of criticism, both by the state and the evolving public opinion.

In the 17th century, it became common that, in addition to the journeyman's test supervised by the master and the guild, the prospective journeyman also had to be accepted by the journeymen's organization. This implied that the journeyman gave a barrel of beer to the journeymen gathered at the journeymen's inn and underwent a rite of passage, the specifics of which varied according to the different crafts. These rituals, which combined elements of Christianity with elements inspired by old crafts traditions, mainly mimicked similar rituals practised in Germany. The ceremony which symbolized the transition of an uncultivated and unworthy apprentice to a dignified journeyman could be quite brutal and there is evidence that at least one apprentice was hospitalized as a consequence of such a ceremony (Henningsen 1960, p. 16). The ceremony was completed with the instruction of the apprentice in the special greeting, usually in verse, which the journeyman needed to be able to perform on his travel abroad in order to identify himself as a "honest" journeyman and thereby distance himself from a simple beggar.

As the transition from apprentice to journeyman, and later to master of a craft, was relatively unproblematic in the 15th and 16th centuries, conflicts of interest between masters and journeymen were relatively rare and the relationships between the masters on the one side and journeymen and apprentices on the other were paternalistic in nature. Mobility within the various social strata was more common than mobility between the different strata. However, in the 17th century the masters began to use various means to restrict the entrance of journeymen to the ranks of the masters. One of the tactics used was to raise the cost connected to the performance of the masterpiece. These expenses consisted primarily in the many meals which were to be served to the masters supervising the performance. The expenses could also be raised by making the performance of the masterpiece more complicated and thus more time consuming. Yet another means was to raise the entrance fees to the guilds. The masters used a combination of these tactics and it became less of a given that an apprentice would be able to establish himself as an independent master when the time came to marry and have a family (Nyrop 1893, pp. 11–12, Dybdahl & Dübeck 1983, p. 131).

All these factors combined meant that the conditions of the craftsmen underwent dramatic changes. The paternalistic relationship between master and journeyman was weakened and conflicts between masters and journeymen became more frequent. The separation of the organizations of the masters and the journeymen and the role the "Zunft" played in the creation of a collective cross-national identity and solidarity among the journeymen were significant in these confrontations. The system of travelling journeymen made it possible to share information over long distances about the working conditions in the different workshops and to establish blockades of particular workshops, and in some cases even entire towns, if the masters did not live up to what was perceived to be decent treatment of their employees (Strømstad 1955, p. 20).

In the 18th century, journeymen received most of their salary in the form of accommodation and meals in the house of the master and only a minor part in money. For the journeymen, the freedom to leave the master for another job, the amount of holidays and the quality of the meals were more important issues than the sum of money they were paid. To be treated with respect and honour was also an important issue and violation of this was often the factor triggering a conflict (Ravn 1986, p. 48, Sørensen *et al.* 1992, pp. 86–109). Conflicts of interest between masters and journeymen reached their climax in the great carpenters' strike in 1794 when more than 400 journeymen went on strike in the city of Copenhagen (Sørensen *et al.* 1992, p. 77). The strike started as a dispute over the freedom for three journeymen to leave their masters in order to travel home to their families in Germany. Normally a contract between master and journeyman was for three months and the journeyman was allowed to leave on four special days a year. The dispute was about the interpretation of these rules. In reality the strike was the culmination of a dispute over payment which had not been resolved despite several requests from the journeymen. In order to settle the strike, a commission was set up with the mandate to investigate the factors triggering the strike and the many other conflicts that had occurred in the years before. The commission resulted in the act of 1800, which represented an attempt to reduce the power of the guilds and improve the conditions of the journeymen by making access to the rank of master easier and less costly. As a means to discipline the journeymen, the commission forbade the practice of foreign customs, meaning the German "Zunft". The latter was a consequence of the leading role played in the strike by the German journeymen living in Copenhagen. The regulation outraged the masters, who felt it threatened their privileges. However, as had been the case with so many other attempts to restrict the power of the guilds, the reform had no lasting effects and by the 1820s the guilds had regained much of their former power (Nyrop 1914, p. 141).

To sum up, the period from the middle of the 17th century to the end of the 18th century was characterized by a process which, on the one hand, strengthened the position and collective identity of the craftsmen as a group; the adoption of the German "Zunft" played an important role in this process. On the other hand, a process of polarization within the class of craftsmen accelerated in the late 18ᵗʰ century. In this process of transformation, the "Zunft" began to function as a cultural weapon which could be turned against the masters in disputes over working conditions and salaries.

3. The growing criticism of the guilds

In Denmark, the doctrines of economic liberalism were not directly linked to the process of industrialization in the same way as was the case in England. In spite of the low level of industrialization, however, the doctrines gained substantial support among enlightened circles in Denmark. The Danish proselytes of economic liberalism were primarily to be found among liberally minded merchants, academics and government employees. The Adam Smith's magnum opus: The Wealth of Nations, was translated into Danish only three years after its publication in English. Smith, who was a strong critic of the role played by the guilds, argued for economic freedom and a more developed division of labour (Smith 1776/199, 222 ff). However, the Danish supporters of the principles of economic liberalism were primarily concerned with the improvement and expansion of the crafts. There was no place for the guilds within their worldview. Accordingly, in 1761 it was decided that no new guilds were allowed in Denmark (Jensen, Knudsen & Stjernfelt 2006, pp. 913–4).

It was, however, characteristic for Denmark that the advocates for the guilds were also quite numerous and determined to fight for their interests. Although the guilds weren't seriously threatened until the middle of the 19ᵗʰ century, they were subject to growing public criticism. This criticism was inspired by ideas of knowledge as something which all individuals should have access to. In The Great French Encyclopedia from the early 18ᵗʰ century, a key publication within the Enlightenment movement, one of the ambitions was to systematically document, categorize and describe the different tools and procedures used by the different crafts. The underlying intention was to undermine the secret knowledge of the guilds and stimulate technological development. An example illustrating the opposing conceptions guiding the ideas of the Enlightenment movement and the tradition underlying the guilds was a dispute in 1773 between representatives of the Royal Academy of Arts of Copenhagen and the city's magistrate. The latter supported the interests of the guilds while the former argued that the Academy should approve the masterpieces for cabinet makers. The representative of the Academy, possibly the director, argued that the approbation should be in the hands of the Academy as this was the only way to ensure that the craft would in the future be able to compete with foreign products, the alternative being that the craft be left to the mercy of its "inherent barbarism". The intellectual superiority of the Academy was indiscreetly stressed by referring to the great work of André Jacques: L'art de Menusier, parts 1 and 2, published in 1769 and 1770. It was added that, should this work be unknown to the magistrate, he was advised to consult the French Encyclopedia of 1751 in order to acknowledge which skills were required in order to perform work of excellency (Bak Jensen 2004, p. 70, Juul 2013, p. 65).

In addition to the alleged negative effects it had on economic growth, there was strong criticism of the cultural norms linked to the guild system; a criticism which was directed towards the craftsmen in their capacity as citizens. The craftsmen, both masters and journeymen, were perceived as being out of touch with the changing times and as lagging behind other groups within society when it came to education. Part of this criticism was directed at the inns reserved for the travelling craftsmen, which were increasingly associated which a clientele of idle and drunken craftsmen who were not really looking for jobs. It was not only the cultural norms of the craftsmen which were the object of criticism, however, but also their work performance. There were several complaints that good craft traditions were in decline and lagging behind the advances made in other European countries. There were stories circulating claiming that the shoes produced by shoemakers seldom fitted the customers, even though they were produced on demand. Likewise, it was claimed that cabinetmakers used wood that hadn't been sufficiently dried (Nyrop 1914, pp. 30–36, Juul 2013, p. 65). The explanation given for this undesirable state of affair was that the training of apprentices was based solely on manual work and imitation. This meant that the crafts lacked a source as well as an incentive to innovate their procedures and develop their sense of taste. These unfortunate circumstances were aggravated by insufficient drawing skills among the craftsmen, which meant that the same patterns and drafts were used generation after generation. Seen in light of this criticism, it is not surprising that access to drawing lessons came to play an important role in the initiatives promoted by different sectors of society in order to educate the craftsmen. Moreover, there were complaints about the declining quality of the training of apprentices. The masters were accused of misusing the labour of the apprentice for tasks which had nothing to do with the craft the apprentices were supposed to learn. Opinion makers complained about the conditions under which the apprentices were trained. Apprentices were said to be exposed to the harsh physical and disciplinary conduct of the masters and the journeymen. The argument put forward was that this stopped men of wealth and education from pursuing an apprenticeship for their sons, despite the fact that the crafts represented the opportunity for a secure and prosperous living (Nyrop 1893, p. 21).

As mentioned above, the policy of the Danish absolute state was to secure that the crafts-sector grew and flourished so that imports could be restricted. This strategy was double-edged. On the one hand, the state made different attempts to prevent the guilds from abusing their control over the masterpieces to restrict the number of masters. On the other hand, the criticism led to the establishment of the Royal Danish Academy of Arts in 1754 with the explicit intention to improve the arts and crafts of the nation. The initiative was inspired by the French Academy of Arts, but it was not until the 1770s that the Academy began to play a major role in the education of craftsmen. From 1771, apprentices were given the right to attend drawing lessons at the Academy free of charge. These lessons were attended by hundreds of apprentices living in Copenhagen. The drawing lessons typically consisted in the study and copying of drawings of classical ornaments and sculptures and were not directed towards a specific craft. It was therefore not always easy to motive the apprentices. In addition, the Academy was assigned the task to control and approve the drafts and the masterpieces of the more artistic crafts. The number of rejected drafts and masterpieces illustrates the eagerness and commitment shown by the Academy in the fulfilment of their task. More than half of the masterpieces were rejected on the basis of both alleged imperfection and lack of fashion sense. The masters did not look favourably on the arrogance of the Academy. Furthermore, the masters were concerned that the Academy would undermine their control of the access to the different crafts as the statutes of the Academy stated that painters, sculptors, architects and engravers were allowed to practise without being members of a guild, provided that they were members of the Academy. An indication that the guilds were unwilling to accept this without a battle was the case in which a later royal landscape painter and former apprentice was summoned before the police court and sentenced to pay a daily fine until he accepted to enter the guild of painters (Bak Jensen 2004, p. 70, Berg 1919, p. 118 Meldahl & Johansen 1904, p. 93).

Contrary to the educational efforts of the absolute state, which formed part of an economic strategy, the initiatives taken by the educated bourgeoisie in the late 18th century were influenced by philanthropic ideas mainly spreading from different parts of Europe to Denmark. Some masters were involved in these movements, although they never played a decisive role (Clemmensen 1987, p. 62, Nyrop 1914, p. 89).

Among the initiatives directed towards the education of craftsmen were a series of lectures given in 1765 in Copenhagen by the Norwegian Ulrik Green (Norway was until 1814 under the sovereignty of the Danish king) and financed by a small donation from the king (Nyrop 1893, pp. 26–27). The inspiration came from Ulrik Green's visit to England in 1762 where he became acquainted with English craftsmen. According to his description, the English craftsmen were able to discuss philosophical questions and matters concerning their crafts in an engaged and highly reasonable way (Nyrop 1893, pp. 24–25). Ulrik Green decided to contribute to a similar level of education among Danish craftsmen. His lectures were extremely popular. Four masters kept watch at the entrance to the lecture hall. The reason for this was that there had been some incidents where students had interrupted the lectures arguing that "uneducated should not be allowed to listen to stuff like that" (Bauer 1893, p. 451).

Green was far from the only representative from the educated bourgeoisie who was concerned with the level of education among craftsmen. Another example was the German priest N.H. Massmann who set up a Sunday school in Copenhagen, inspiring similar initiatives in other parts of the country. N.H.Massmann himself was probably inspired by a similar school in Kiel, which, in turn, was inspired by the English Sunday school movement (Nyrop 1900, p. 13). The Sunday schools were mainly intended to compensate for the lack of adequate schooling of the craftsmen. The lessons consisted primarily of basic literacy and numeracy teaching. The philanthropic societies which contributed to the financing of the schools later required that the lessons were more explicitly directed towards the educational needs of the crafts and industry. As a result, drawing lessons were added to the curriculum (Nyrop 1900, p. 40).

The many initiatives aimed at the education of craftsmen, and the endorsement they received, reflect that the term citizen had gained a new meaning. In earlier times it was a legal concept which was related to those living in a certain town and performing a certain trade. As the educated bourgeoisie became more influential, the concept gained a broader meaning pointing to the economic as well as the cultural potentials of the citizen. Education became an important marker of citizenship (Juul 2013, p. 69). In the 1830s, an educated man was one who had gained an exam from one of the upper secondary schools and preferably also been educated at The University of Copenhagen. These requirements were quite exclusive as they implied parents of some wealth. The stress on education did not only imply that the bourgeoisie was itself differentiated upwardly towards the nobility, whose primary marker was inherited privileges, but also downwardly towards the working-class. Education created a division between those who had it and those who did not (Engberg 2005, pp. 284–86).

Parallel to this development, a process of social differentiation had taken place within the class of craftsmen. At the beginning of the 19th century, there were very few major industries in Denmark and there was a general scepticism towards the liability of an industrial future in Denmark, suggesting that Denmark should concentrate on the development of arts and crafts a leave industrial production to larger counties such as America, England and France (Berg 1919, pp. 135). It was only after 1830 that new, larger scale industries began to emerge. Several iron foundries were established and some of these later developed into engineering firms. These companies would typically hire a new type of blacksmith who was not part of the guild system and its ties to the German rituals and traditions. Married journeymen, who had previously been looked down upon by their unmarried colleagues, became more common. This indicated that masters and journeymen were being segregated into two different classes – the working class and the class of employers – and this placed the masters in an ambivalent situation. On the one hand, the masters struggled to protect the guild system and their privileges from the criticisms formulated by the liberal bourgeoisie who was generally in favour of free trade. On the other hand, they aspired to be recognized as part of the same liberal bourgeoisie. The masters used education as an important weapon in this struggle. As entry into the ranks of the masters still took place via an apprenticeship and a few years of work as a journeyman, it made perfect sense to concentrate on the education of these two groups in order to increase the prestige of the craftsmen as such.

As the pressure on the craftsmen was two-sided, so was their reaction. In the spring of 1840, a commission was set up in order to investigate the guilds and associations of Copenhagen. Modelled on English practice, the work of the committee was not restricted to an audit of written sources, but also included consulting all relevant partners (Nyrop 1914, p. 206). The masters' reaction to the setting up of the commission was to organize themselves across disciplinary boundaries, disregarding any former disputes. The same year, The Association of Craftsmen in Copenhagen (Kjøbenhavns Haandværkerforening) was established. According to the statutes of the association, the purpose was both to counter prejudice and misinterpretations related to the functioning of the guilds and to promote education, especially among younger craftsmen (Hassø 1940, p. 25).

The battle against the introduction of free trade

The battle for or against free trade was a question which engaged public opinion. Pamphlets arguing both for and against the abolishment of the guild system were published in great numbers and it was also a question subject to heated debates in the press (Nyrop 1814, p. 222). The proponents of the guilds stressed how the guilds contributed positively to society and pointed to the role they played in securing their members an appropriate source of living, how they looked after the sick and poor, and made reference to the role they played in the training and education of future craftsmen. The aim was to convince the public that the guilds were perfectly able to play a positive role in a society under moderniza-tion and that the image painted by public opinion of the guilds as being anchored in an outdated culture was not consistent with reality. The old ceremonies and traditions belonged to a past long abandoned and the contemporary guilds were comprised of educated and tolerant citizens (Hassø 1940, p. 19).

When the commission set up in 1840 in order to investigate the guilds of Copenhagen finally delivered their report in 1844, the con-clusion was that the guilds should continue to exist. They were to be evaluated a new in 20 years. Both the journeyman's certificate and the masterpiece should continue to exist, but in reformed versions. Especially the masterpieces were to be reformed so that they could be accomplished in shorter time and with fewer expenses, and possibly supplemented by a theoretical exam. In the future, a journeyman should be allowed to perform a masterpiece without having passed an appren-tice test. In addition, every journeyman who had worked eight years for a master should be allowed to obtain citizenship and a licence to prac-tise a trade without performing a masterpiece (Nyrop 1914, p. 232). These propositions resembled those put forward in the report from 1800 which, as mentioned earlier, did not have any lasting effects. The same was to be the case for the recommendations from 1844. But, whereas the failure to implement the recommendations from 1800 was due to the strength of the guilds, the failure of the 1844 recommendations was more alarming as they were the result of the aspirations of the Ministry for the Interior to regulate not only the guilds of Copenhagen but the guilds of the entire country.

The promise of free trade in the constitution

Debates about the advantages and disadvantages of economic liberal-ism were paralleled by discussions about political freedom which in Denmark resulted in the peaceful transition from absolutism to a con-stitutional monarchy in 1848. In the constitution of 1849, there was a paragraph indicating that political and economic freedoms were seen as interconnected: "Any restraint on the free and equal access to trade, which is not based on the interest of the general public, shall be abolished by statute" (§88).

The paragraph was interpreted as a step along the road to free trade. However, it was not until 1855 that an interpellation in parliament demanded the paragraph implemented. At this point the guilds realized that it was time to take action. Craftsmen from all over the country were mobilized to participate in a meeting about the future of the guilds. At this meeting a resolution was adopted stating that, in the future, the masterpieces should be supplemented by a theoretical exam as proposed by the commission of 1844. In addition, the masters were to pass an exam before being allowed to establish themselves as manufacturers. This was ridiculed in the liberal press, which sarcastically noted:

> Presumably we will end up with a request to establish a complete university for craft and manufacture covering the whole monarchy with Latin for joiners, philosophy for tailors and a certificate for brush maker and with master painter Tilly as Rector magnificus (Hassø 1940, p. 159).

Master and alderman C.C.Tilly, who was the initiator behind the meeting, retorted in another paper (Berlinske Tidende 23–24th January 1856). He accused the proponents of free trade representing people who combined a minimum of technical knowledge with a total lack of knowledge of practicalities and who had a naive belief that freedom and equality would solve all problems in society. This naivety, he believed, was a result of the fact that they had never lived and worked as craftsmen. He encouraged all craftsmen to engage in the public debate in order to counter those who based their views on the subject primarily on what they had read in books or who had an interest in transforming the craftsman into hired servants or simple jobbers in order to gather capital by exploiting the sweat of their brow. He also took the opportunity to make a complaint about the way the theatres and the press portrayed the craftsman as the antithesis of the educated citizen. He concluded that it was high time that the craftsmen freed themselves from the paternalism of the educated bourgeoisie and took matters into their own hands in order to secure their common interests (Hassø 1940, p. 144, Juul 2013, pp. 73–74).

Unfortunately the initiative came too late. 14 March 1856, a book written by Otto Müller was published which recommended that the guilds be dissolved within three years. Otto Müller had been appointed by the Minister for the Interior to conduct a referendum on the question of the guilds. The question of education played a central role in Müller's statement. According to him, the apprenticeship test and the masterpiece represented the most important shortcomings of the guild system as those in charge of the exams had an interest in using them as a means to restrict access to the various crafts. In addition, the masterpiece was not a guarantee that the master in question was qualified as a manager or had any knowledge of economics. This shows that, according to Otto Müller, a master craftsman was more an employer than a craftsman. He viewed the apprenticeship test more favourably as it ensured that the journeymen had the required technical qualifications. However, he saw no reason to make such tests mandatory. If the masters required such a test, the apprentices would voluntarily subject themselves to one. In addition, he emphasized that it was a great disadvantage for the growing industry and for some crafts that one had to get an authorization of approbation in order to start up a business. Another main restriction was the fact that even larger factories were not allowed to have more than one outlet in addition to the factory itself. However, Müller emphasized that the primary reason for introducing free trade was to defend the idea of individual freedom. The craftsmen's counter-measure was to organize a large deputation to the king's residence, but it was too late (Hassø 1940, p. 190).

18 December 1857, a bill was passed in Parliament with 62 votes for and 19 against. This bill was to a large extent based on the principles proposed in Otto Müller's book.

The act of free trade

The implementation of the act of free trade meant that everybody was allowed to settle down as master as long as they obtained a citizenship which allowed them access to the craft in question (Nørregaard 1943/1977, p. 70).

While free trade as such was implemented 1 April 1858, it was not until 1 January 1862 that the requirement that craftsmen should be members of a guild and the mandatory journeyman's test and master-pieces were forbidden. These measures seriously undermined the power of the guilds. But as the date approached for the full implementation of the bill, concerns grew that the economic freedom would not in itself be enough to solve the problems faced by the industry and craft sector. This uncertainty was mirrored in administrative circulars that the Ministry for the Interior circulated in 1862 and 1864. On the one hand, it was highlighted that the exams in the context of the guilds were no longer valid, and on the other hand, the circulars encouraged the craftsmen collectively to engage in the education of future craftsmen. The latter was to be secured by the building of technical schools, the arrangement of industrial exhibitions, financial support for journeymen travelling to foreign countries, and by promoting voluntary journeymen's tests (Boje & Fink 1990, pp. 130–133).

Although there had been some attempts at the beginning of the 19th century, it was not until the establishment of the Technical Institute in Copenhagen in 1843 that craftsmen began to engage seriously in the technical school movement. From then on, local masters' organizations and industrial organizations were the driving forces in a process that resulted in the establishment of technical schools in all major cities and nearly every provincial town in Denmark. The initiative and the financing were based almost entirely on private money (Boje & Fink 1990, p. 128).

The establishment of technical schools indicated, on the one hand, that the drawing lessons offered at the Academy no longer fulfilled the requirements of the crafts. On the other hand, they symbolized the will of the masters to take matters into their own hands in order to rescue the reputation of the craftsmen. However, the establishment of the technical schools was paralleled by a process of specialization and segregation in the Danish education system in general. The College of Advanced Technology established in 1829, was originally open to the sons of the educated bourgeoisie as well as to craftsmen seeking further education. However, both the College of Advanced Technology and the Academy restricted admission in the 1850s to those with an education in foreign languages and liberal arts, thus excluding the majority of the craftsmen.

Drawing lessons for craftsmen were now to take place at the Technical Institute, which also functioned as a preparatory school for future architects and artists wishing to enrol at the Academy (Engberg 2005, p. 396, Wagner 1999, pp. 193–199).

The guilds and the supporters of economic liberalism

As the mandatory membership of the guilds was abolished, apprenticeship contracts, farewell notes and the period of notice concerning hiring and firing disappeared, as did rules regulating training placements. Every industrious citizen was now allowed to hire who he pleased and traders without citizenship were allowed to hire assistants for unskilled work. The spirit of liberalism did not go so far as to formally abolish the severe punishment for illegal strikes, however (Nørregaard 1943 /1977, p. 70).

There was, nevertheless, a growing concern that apprentices risked exploitation as cheap labour instead of being educated in the craft in question. In 1875, the Minister for the Interior set up a workers' commission with the mandate to investigate working conditions in Denmark. The commission was a response to a situation characterized by growing unemployment and a rising trade union movement. A report addressing what was called the workers question was published three years later. Among its findings, it stated that the lack of regulation of apprenticeship risked causing a decline in the abilities of apprentices due to abuse of their working capacity and the neglect of their intellectual development. The conclusion was that this would seriously affect the prospects of apprentices to become masters (Arbeiderkommissionen 1878, Fode *et al.* 1984, pp. 58–59).

The report included a draft for an apprentice law. According to the draft, only employers who were able to offer adequate training in the trade concerned were to be allowed to hire apprentices, meaning employers who had themselves been educated in the respective trade or who employed skilled workers with the relevant qualifications. This represented a moderation of the position put forward by Müller in his book that the skills needed for a master were more based on an insight in to the logics of economics and business than into the craft in question. In addition, the commission recommended that the apprenticeship contract be signed by a competent authority. Finally, it was proposed that it become mandatory for apprentices to have access to the technical education which was available locally (Arbeiderkommissionen1878, Fode *et al.*1984, pp. 58–59). The report of the workers'commission served as an inspiration for the proposal put forward in parliament in 1880/81. However, the proposal was too radical to gain political support. Similar proposals were put forward in 1881/82, 1887/88 and 1888/89 and, at last, an apprenticeship law was passed in 1889 (Klöcker-Larsen 1962, p. 13). In this accepted version, the paragraph which stated that masters who only performed very specialized work operations should not be allowed to recruit apprentices was deleted (Arbeiderkommissionen 1878, pp. 25–28). In addition, the law emphasized the paternalistic relationship between master and apprentice which had also characterized the regulations of the guilds. It was stressed that the apprentice was to be loyal, obedient and behave respectfully towards his master, assisting him in all matters as far as his work capacity and skills permitted. The responsibility of the master concerning the moral education of the apprentice was underlined as the master was required to protect the apprentice "from exposure to immoral practices" (Law nr. 39, 1889 § 9). The most important paragraph in the new apprentice law was the requirement that there be a written contract when a person under 18 years of age entered into an apprenticeship. This paragraph reflected the interest of the masters who had experienced that their apprentices left the workshop when they had gained sufficient skills in order to obtain a better paid job elsewhere. The law included regulations concerning the length of the apprenticeship, which was to be maximum five years, working hours, which should not surpass 12 hours per day, including two hours lunch break, wages, accommodation and food, payment for attendance at the technical schools during the apprenticeship; and payments connected to a voluntary apprentice test. The journeymen's tests were not made mandatory until the passing of a revised apprentice law in 1937. Instead, a letter was to confirm the length of the apprenticeship and specify the qualifications of the journeyman. However, the act committed the masters to allowing the apprentice to attend lessons at the technical school if the voluntary apprentice test involved an exam in drawing (Law nr. 39, 1889).

The following years were characterized by a series of political struggles in parliament which resulted in the gradual restoration of many of the regulatory mechanisms which had characterized the period when apprenticeship was under the control of the guilds. The labour movement played a central part in these struggles and was in some cases supported by sections of the employers' movement. The main opponent and defender of the liberal principle was the liberal party in parliament (Venstre). By 1937, the influence of the social partners on the training and education of apprentices was institutionalized. This system still represents the backbone of the Danish VET system today.

4. Conclusion

The aim of this paper has been to illustrate how the development of the education and training of Danish craftsmen was to a large extent influenced by ideas coming from abroad. It shows how these ideas were used in power struggles between the different sectors of society. In the early period of the guilds, these struggles were primarily between the king and the guilds. Later, they were followed by power struggles between masters and journeymen. The German "Zunft" played an important role in these struggles. Later still, concepts of freedom and education were central in the cultural confrontations between the craftsmen and the enlightened bourgeoisie. These struggles resulted in the engagement of the craftsmen in the question of education and, as a result, in the building up of a system of technical schools covering the entire country, which later laid the ground for the Danish dual system.

References

Arbeiderkommissionen1878. Betænkning afgiven af den ifgl. resolution af 20 de September 1875 til Undersøgelse af Arbeiderforholdene I Danmark nedsatte Kommission.
Bak Jensen, P. B.2004. Kunstakademiet. København. Space Poetry.

Bauer, A. 1893. Haandværkerundervisningen i Danmark gennem 50 Aar. Nationaløkonomisk Tidsskrift, Bind 1, Hæfte 7, 449–487.

Berg, R. 1919. Det danske Haandværks Historie. Kjøbenhavn og Kristiania. Gyldendalske Boghandel – Nordisk Forlag.

Boje, P., & Fink, J. 1990. Mesterlære og teknisk uddannelse i Danmark 1850–1950. Erhvervshistorisk årbog, 125–147.

Clemmensen, N. 1987. Associationer og foreningsdannelse i Danmark 1780–1880. Periodisering og forskningsoversigt. Øvre Ervik: Alvheim & Eide. Akademisk forlag.

Degn, O., & Dübeck, I. 1983. Håndværket i fremgang. Perioden 1550–1700. København, Håndværksrådet.

Dybdahl, V., & Dübeck, I. 1983. Håndværket og statsmagten: perioden 1700–1862 (Vol. 3). København, Håndværksrådets Forlag.

Engberg, J. 2005. Magten og kulturen. Dansk kulturpolitik 1750–1999. Bind II, Mellem enevælde og grundlovsstyre. København, Gads Forlag.

Engelhardt, J. 2010. Borgerskab og fællesskab. De patriotiske selskaber i den danske helstat 1769–1814. København, Museum Tusculanums Forlag.

Feldbæk, O, 1992 (ed). Dansk Identitetshistorie. Fædreland og modersmål 1536–1789. Viborg, C.A. Reitzels Forlag.

Fode, H., Møller, J., & Hastrup, B. 1984. Håndværkets kulturhistorie: Perioden fra 1862–1980. København, Håndværksrådets forlag.

Habermas, J. 1962 Strukturwandel der Öffentlichkeit. Frankfurt am Main. Suhrkamp Verlag.

Hassø, A. G. 1940. Et Bidrag til Københavns Haandværks Historie i det sidste Hundred aar. København, Chr. Erichsens Forlag.

Henningsen, H. f.1960. Behøvling og hønsning: indvielses- og optagelsesskikke i håndværkerlav. Håndværkerrådets Forlag.

Jacobsen, G.1982. Håndværkets kulturhistorie. Håndværket kommer til Danmark. Tiden før 1550. København, Håndværksrådets Forlag.

Jensen H.S, Knudsen, O. and F.Stjernfelt, F. 2006. Tankens magt. København, Lindhardt & Ringhof.

Juul, I. 2013. De danske håndværkeruddannelser i krydsfeltet mellem det europæiske og det nationale. In Uddannelseshistorie. 47: 60–80.

Karmark, K. 1989. Laug og zünftighed: de tyske håndværkerskikke, deres ankomst, etablering og forsvinden belyst gennem det københavnske snedkerlaugs historie, 1577–1800. Århus, Aarhus Universitetsforlag.

Klöcker-Larsen, F. 1962. Lærlingeuddannelse i Danmark. København, Institut for organisation og arbejdssociologi.

Law nr. 39, 30 Marts 1889 19. november: Om Lærlingeforholdet. Indenrigsministeriet.

Meldahl, F. and Johansen, P. 1904. Det kongelige Akademi for de skjønne Kunster 1700–1904. København, Hagerup.

Nyrop, C. 1893: Biddrag til dansk Haandværkerundervisningens Historie. Kjøbenhavn, Nielsen og Lydiche.

Nyrop, C. 1900. De Massmannske søndagsskoler i hundrede aar: korte meddelelser. København, Nielsen & Lydiche.

Nyrop, C. 1914. Bidrag til vor Haandværkestands Historie i Tiden før 1857.

Nørregaard, G. 1977. Arbejdsforhold indenfor dansk Haandværk og Industri 1857–1899 (Reprografisk genudgivet ed.). Kbh.: Selskabet for Udgivelse af Kilder til Dansk Historie.

Ravn, T. B. 1986. Oprør, Spadserregange og lønstrejker i København før 1870. In F. f. Mikkelsen (ed.), Protest og oprør: kollektive aktioner i Danmark 1700–1985. Aarhus, Modtryk.

Smith, A. 1776/1999 The Wealth of Nations Books I–III. London, Penguin Classics.

Strømstad, P. 1955. Håndværkervandringer i lavstiden. In M. F. Møller (ed.). Den farende svend. Haderslev, Martin Winds Forlag.

Sørensen, P. H. Grelle og V. O. Nielsen 1992. Under herrer og mestre. Om arbejdsvilkår og Danmarks første storkonflikt i 1794. København, SFAH.

Wagner, F.M. 1999. Det polytekniske gennembrud: Romantikkens teknologiskekonstruktioner1780–1850. Århus, Aarhus Universitetsforlag.

Wittendorff, A. 2003. Gyldendal og Politikens Danmarkshistorie (2. udgave ed. Vol. 7). København, Gyldendal.

Østergård, U. 2001. Europas ansigter. København, Rosinante.

KENNETH TEITELBAUM

Citizenship, Workers' Education and Radical Activism in Early 20th Century United States[1]

1. Introduction

If vocational education can be taken to involve "preparing people to perform successfully in the workplace" (Bailey 2010b, p. 928), then it surely is the case that its roots can be traced back thousands of years, involving apprenticeships of various kinds. By the mid-19th century, however, more formal educational programming seemed necessary in the United States to prepare workers for the challenges of the new industrial order. Starting with the manual training movement, which was influenced by the work of Johann Heinrich Pestalozzi in Switzerland and Victor Della Vos in Russia, for well over a century educators, politicians and business leaders in the United States have debated the nature of vocational education and its place in the curriculum (Kliebard 1999, 2004). Put simply, to what extent should education for success in the workplace focus narrowly on the understandings and skills that prepare workers to adapt (adjust, fit in) most readily to the expectations (skills, understandings and dispositions) of their occupation? To what extent should current and prospective workers be provided with a more well-rounded education that includes critical thinking about their work and workplace and preparation to live meaningful, fulfilling lives as active (knowledgeable and skilled) participants in the larger (democratic) society? Indeed, should interests in citizenship and liberal education directly bear on what comprises vocational (or work, trade, or industrial) education, and if so, what approach to citizenship should be taken? Can a broader, more integrative approach be viewed as

---

1   In several places, material was adapted from two of the author's previous publications – see Teitelbaum (2009, 2011).

appropriate and even necessary for "preparing people to perform successfully in the workplace"?

Examinations of past practices can perhaps be useful in addressing these and related questions. A historical perspective can help to clarify not just the reasons that particular understandings and practices have come to dominate the landscape at particular periods of time, but also, with due recognition of the many and significant changes in ensuing years, other, alternative possibilities of viewpoints and experiences. This is perhaps particularly crucial during the last several decades that have seen the ascendance of neoliberalism, which has resulted in "economic mobility and national economic issues [as] the centerpiece of our thinking about schools" (Kliebard 1992, p. 199). Indeed, although the socializing function of schools has always included a focus on workplace preparation (Tyack 1974; Bills 2004), we are witnessing now an intensification of "vocationalization" in a broad sense (even as vocational education programs themselves have experienced a decline). As McCarthy, *et al.* (2009) put it, vocationalization has become "a ruling logic in curricular arrangements and the overall calculation of educational actors," so that increasingly in K-12 schools and on university campuses there is eroding support for humanities and social science learning goals, when in fact "it is precisely these courses that provide the best preparation for democratic citizenship and critical thinking" (p. 43). In other words, during a time when politicians, business leaders and many educators are touting the primary aim of schools and colleges as to produce workers who are effective in terms of skills and dispositions, when education for citizenship seems to have become overwhelmed by the development of human capital, alternative educational configurations and strategies that prioritize democratic citizenship, historically and currently, in formal and informal settings, might be especially critical to consider. At the least, they should be "kept alive" so that our options do not appear narrower than they are.

Historical studies of vocational education often focus on the debates within K-12 public education, particularly secondary schools, and traditional adult (and community college) education. But it is possible as well to attend to the efforts of community grass-roots groups that sought to provide an appropriate education for workers, in formal and informal settings, that, for example, would be appropriate in a society presumably guided by principles of democracy and social justice. This chapter takes up the question of vocational education as viewed by radical activists in the United States during the early years of the 20th century, with regard to the formal and informal educational and cultural activities they offered to members of the working-class community.

Specifically, the socialist movement in the United States during the early years of the 20th century sponsored supplemental activities for adults and children that embodied a relatively clear articulation of the intersection between education for workers and the ideology of citizenship. In the efforts of Socialist Party members and allied radical activists to address the needs of workers (and their children, who were assumed to be the next generation of workers), an essentially political movement set out to support current and future workers to be successful at their workplace in a world increasingly characterized by what was viewed as the tyranny of industrial capitalism. At the same time, significantly, these educators sought to encourage workers to become more knowledgeable about and to actively engage in the transformation of dominant economic and social relations, including in their work environment, in line with what were perceived (by radical activists) to be in their long-term interests. While the drudgery of some work could not perhaps be eliminated, the lives of workers, including at the workplace itself, could be enhanced by educational and cultural activities that addressed not just their occupational lives but more broadly their civic and personal lives as well.

To be sure, the educational efforts of radical activists in early 20th century United States were often downplayed by many of their own brethren, who insisted on an exclusive emphasis on direct political action and labor organizing. In addition, even when emphasizing civic participation and personal fulfillment, it was common for these radical educators to depart significantly from the kind of critical questioning and active engagement that John Dewey and more recent scholars such as Benjamin Barber, Michael Apple, Henry Giroux, Nel Noddings, Ira Shor, Joe Kincheloe, and others have considered to be the *sine qua non* of a strong democracy. Many at the time adopted the kind of direct instruction, "banking education" approach that Paulo Freire (1970) later critiqued in his seminal work, *Pedagogy of the Oppressed*, over-relying on lectures and rote learning about political and economic topics and more narrow vocational concerns. Still, there were in fact a number of educational initiatives during this period that did seek to encourage a broad, deliberative, imaginative and participatory approach to citizenship, workplace democracy, and personal fulfilment among workers and their children (Teitelbaum 1995). The uniqueness of the perspective embodied in these activities was perhaps well summed up by a young participant in Brooklyn at the time (*New York Call*, May 8, 1910): The supplementary education she received from working-class radical activists at the neighborhood Socialist Sunday School first and foremost "has taught me to be useful to all people, to be a useful member of the community, taking an absorbing interest in all things that concern the welfare of all its members."

2. Citizenship and U.S. public schooling

Citizenship education has generally been recognized as one of the essential goals of public schooling in the United States. From the start of the country's history, public education has been viewed as a bedrock of a democratic society. As Founding Father (and third President) Thomas Jefferson put it in his letters, "If a nation expected to be ignorant and free, in a state of civilization, it expects what never was and never will be… Whenever the people are well-informed, they can be trusted with their own government." He considered the future of republican government in part to be "absolutely hanging on the hook [of] public education" (Coates 1995). While Jefferson's views have been criticized for their limited, elitist view of the public, they served for many years as strong advocacy for the role of public schooling in the empowerment of democratic citizens (Wood 1998). As Benjamin Barber (1997) puts it, "public education […] [is] the very foundation of our democratic civic culture. Public schools are not merely schools for the public, but schools of publicness: institutions where we learn what it means to be a public and start down the road toward common national and civic identity. They are the forges of our citizenship and the bedrock of our democracy" (p. 22).

And yet, during the last half century, it can be argued that preparation for work (vocationalization) has in fact become the primary aim of public education (Kliebard 1999). Moreover, in recent years significant segments of the American populace, for both ideological and financial reasons, have downplayed (and even denied) the importance of learning about democratic citizenship in schools and colleges. Of course these developments need to be viewed within the frequent debates that have taken place during the last 100-plus years involving the nature of democracy, citizenship, citizenship education, and the extent to which education about and for democratic citizenship should be addressed in the curriculum of our elementary, middle and high schools. As David Warren Saxe (1999) puts it: "what constitutes citizenship in a free republic and what are the best means toward achieving that ideal continue to be hotly debated issues throughout the nation" (p. 78). As another social studies educator (Hamot 2008) suggests, controversies associated with these debates have involved a host of related critical issues, such as the role of free market capitalism, the nature and need for social reform, the character of pluralism, and the expectation of patriotism.

Generally speaking, the educational goals and pedagogical approaches regarding citizenship that prevailed in U.S. public schools in the late 19ᵗʰ century and early 20 century emphasized what has been referred to as weak, thin or protectionist democracy (Wood 1998), as compared to what might be considered a strong, robust, and actively engaged form. During a time of intensive immigration and urbanization and the rising fortunes of labor unions and radical activity, emphasis was placed on non-participatory approaches that involved rote learning about and appreciation for the presidents, the U.S. Constitution, how government works (*e.g.*, the bill-to-law process), and the like. As Saxe (1999) notes, in the nineteenth century "students simply memorized passages from textbooks." During the ensuing several decades there were attempts to instill a more active community-based approach to citizenship in the fledgling social studies movement, whereby students "were encouraged to identify and seek solutions to actual community problems" (p. 78) But generally, though prominent struggles over the curriculum among educators and political and business leaders have occurred often during the last century (Kliebard 2004; Teitelbaum 2008), narrow approaches to democratic participation have prevailed in the classroom, with more attention given to learning *about* the trappings of democracy (*e.g.*, voting in elections) than to instilling an understanding of and expectation for active civic participation (Teitelbaum 2011). John Dewey (1916) made a significant contribution when he famously posited democracy as "more than a form of government; it is primarily a mode of associated living, of conjoint communicated experience" (p. 87) – but there is little evidence such a perspective influenced the curriculum of most educators then and now (Cuban 1984). Indeed, as historian Ellen Condliffe Lagemann (1989) suggests, "One cannot understand the history of education in the United States in the twentieth century unless one realizes that [behavioral educational psychologist] E. L. Thorndike won and John Dewey lost" (p. 185), although it is certainly true (and significant) that "Thorndike's triumph was not complete" (Lagemann 2002, p. xi).

More specifically, the curriculum of 19th century American schools has been characterized as focused on "train[ing] citizens in character and proper principles" (Elson 1964, p. 1). Schoolteachers relied a great deal on the widespread use of memorization, copying from the board, and rote learning. Elementary education tended to stress moral training and personal character development along with the "three R's," as late 19th century educators and parents invested in the public schools some of the functions that had once been the primary province of the family and organized religion. Given the central role that schoolbooks played in schools during this time (Reese 1995), it is noteworthy that the general depiction of the United States in many texts was that it was the "land of opportunity" and that failure to get ahead was essentially the fault of the individual. Good character or hard work (or proper heredity) must have been lacking. On social and political questions, the tenor of the books was consistently conservative. When mentioned at all, socialism, like labor organizations in general, was identified only with "unscrupulous agitation and violence" (Elson 1964, p. 287) and as alien to American traditions and subversive to American government. With the increased immigrant population in the early 1900s, schools tended to place even more emphasis on respect for law, patriotism, and respect for private property. In 1918, the influential report of the National Education Association Commission on the Reorganization on Secondary Education offered support (though not as much as some business leaders and educators would have liked) for "fitting" school children to "their particular spheres in life," and to do this with as much efficiency, predictability and certainty as possible. An increased number of administrators and guidance counselors were hired, additional intelligence and other standardized testing was utilized, and the curriculum was more sharply and narrowly differentiated and stratified (especially in the high schools) so that children could be more effectively "scientifically measured" and "sorted" for their presumably appropriate occupations in life, all of which had the effect of legitimating an unequal social structure (see, *e.g.*, Callahan 1962; Krug 1969; Tyack 1976; Nasaw 1981; Kliebard 2004; Reese 2005).

The turn of the century was certainly a period of transition for U.S. public schooling. Besides construction programs for more schools, the first decades witnessed the widespread distribution of free textbooks to school children, hot lunches, medical exams, school libraries, smaller class sizes, extra-curricular activities, counseling services, the introduction of kindergarten as a part of public schools, the junior high school, truant and night schools, the comprehensive high school, playgrounds, better ventilation and lighting in buildings, and vocational training programs (Spring 1972; Reese 2005). These educational reforms were essentially viewed as part of the larger municipal reform movement of the time, as aspects of the larger attack on corruption in government and the need to educate and assimilate an expanding, more heterogeneous populace during a time of complex economic and social changes. Many of the reforms were actually initiated or at least supported by a host of local and national parent organizations, women's clubs, labor unions, and progressive and radical political movements (Reese 2002).

But while very supportive of the institution of public schooling as a democratic achievement, radical activists were increasingly concerned about the control of the institution by conservative government and business leaders who were primarily concerned with preserving the (unequal) American character and teaching middle-class virtues, in particular a kind of blind respect for private property, overreliance on professional expertise, and loyal adherence to authority. For them, the public school lent significant support to the rapid and problematic expansion of industrial capitalism by seeking to provide the needed training (in understandings, skills, habits and attitudes) to prospective workers and encouraging consumptive patterns that would help to fulfill the demands of mushrooming capitalist supplies (Bowles and Gintis 1976; Teitelbaum 1995). That is, public schools, as well as churches and the media, generally functioned as "guardians of tradition" (Elson 1964) during a time of intense, disruptive changes that seemed to be benefiting the few over the many. As Julie Mickenberg (2006) suggests about the mid-20th century, "mainstream civic education taught children to revere the American way of life as it was," in contrast to progressives and radicals who "made 'active opposition' to injustice and 'intelligent cooperation' hallmarks of good citizenship" (p. 271). Some radical activists sought to offset the messages being offered to workers and their children from the media, popular culture, the churches and the public schools by essentially creating their own counter-hegemonic educational institutions.

3. Radical activism and education for workers

On the title page of their volume on *Proletcult*, Eden and Cedar Paul (1921) quote from Henri de Man (later a controversial figure as a collaborator during World War II but at the time a leading Belgian socialist theoretician):

> When labour strikes, it says to its master:
>   I shall no longer work at your command.
> When it votes for a party of its own, it says:
>   I shall no longer vote at your command.
> When it creates its own classes and colleges, it says:
>   I shall no longer think at your command.
> Labour's challenge to education is the most
>   Fundamental of the three.

There is, in fact, a long history in the United States of formal and informal educational activities for workers (and their children) that would help them to "no longer think at your command." Critiques of public schooling and the development of alternative educational activities for workers date back at least to the early decades of the nineteenth century when, for example, women mill workers in Lowell, Massachusetts initiated circulating libraries and developed their own periodicals (Schaefer 1951). Around the same time, the followers of social reformer Robert Owen in the United States, who established utopian communities organized according to communitarian and cooperative principles, pinned their ultimate hopes on education reforms. They viewed formal education as the key to radical change, not reading and writing per se but the acquisition of progressive ideas. The various Workingmen's Parties of the late 1820s and early 1830s stressed the need for the expansion of the common school system at the same time that it critically assessed the quality of education being offered to the children of the working class. The New York Workingmen's Party, for example, complained about narrow pedagogy, overly strict discipline, and abstract lessons unrelated to current laws of the country (Buhle 1974). But at the same time, they viewed the new public school system as a means for workers to "protect themselves from economic and political exploitation," in essence "for gaining political and economic power" (Spring 2005, pp. 84–85). (Other reformers of the period advocated for the common schools for distinctly different reasons that had more to do with social control than with worker empowerment.)

It was during the late 1800s and early 1900s that the radical working-class movement in the United States garnered a significant level of support, not coincidentally at a time of increased immigration, urbanization, industrialization, and unionism (see, *e.g.*, Weinstein 1969; Stave 1975; Green 1978; Buhle 1981). Grassroots activists involved in educational work generally viewed this process of educating about and for radical social change as the province of the working class itself, or of those who strongly identified themselves with working-class interests, i.e., the organic intellectuals, disaffected bourgeois professional intellectuals, and professional intellectuals from the working class about which Antonio Gramsci (1971) wrote. (See also, *e.g.*, Boggs 1976; Carnoy 1982). As a placard at the Socialist Party's founding convention in Indianapolis in 1901 admonished: "*The emancipation of the working class* must be *the work of the working class itself.*" Socialists, anarchists, German and other ethnic radical groups, and labor and other activists provided networks of debating clubs, small libraries, singing societies, theater groups, newspapers, festivals, dance bands, street corner speeches, rallies, and the like for recruitment and socialization purposes but also to help educate workers, especially those who were immigrants, about the harmful effects of capitalist economic and cultural relations and the promise of the socialist or similar alternative (Teitelbaum 1995). Charles Leinenweber (1977) described these efforts as "flourish[ing] in the neighborhoods: in the streets, tenements, cafes, taverns, dance halls, theatres, barber shops, church basements, settlement houses and union halls" (p. 153). Even items such as "socialist playing cards" were available, reworking traditional images in an attempt to encourage a more critical understanding of current conditions. Advertised in the December 1908 issues of *International Socialist Review*, the cards included Kings that were the Trusts, Queens the Capitalist Virtues, and Jacks the Guardians of Society. Each card had a verse, as in the case of the King of Spades: "*Oil King*: I love to oil the college wheels, / And grease the pulpit stairs, / Where workmen learn to scorn the strike / And trust to Heaven and prayers."

More systematic educational activities for workers, serving as a kind of supplemental and essentially alternative, broadly-defined vocational education, were sponsored by local political party organizations and other groups of radical and labor activists. Indeed, as New York City Socialist Party politician and educator Algernon Lee stated, "Every branch [of the Party] was a little school of Social Science, much more than it was a political club" (Cornell 1976, p. 8). Lecture series targeted at the interests and needs of workers were common, as were literary societies, study clubs, and correspondence courses, often organized by women's clubs because Party leaders (most of whom were men) deemed the educational sphere as particularly "appropriate" for women activists (Buhle 1981).

In addition, more formal workers' schools and labor colleges were initiated during the first half of the twentieth century, although many lasted for a relatively brief period of time. Ruskin College, for example, was established in Oxford, England in 1899 for the specific purpose of educating workers to advance the cause of the British labor movement (Altenbaugh 1990). A short-lived Ruskin College was initiated in Florida as well, incorporated as a residential colony and adopting a more directly socialist-oriented curriculum that focused on occupational concerns and political and economic issues as well (Cornell 1976). The Finnish Working People's College of Smithville, Minnesota was organized by local radical labor activists in 1907 specifically to prepare editors, teachers, and agitators "in preparation for the advent of the socialist commonwealth." Those involved believed that the public schools were fostering an allegiance to bourgeois hegemony. In contrast, they sought to integrate the interests of their ethnic group and the concerns of working people by educating "to preserve Finnish culture, promote literacy, and instill socialist ideals" (Altenbaugh 1990, p. 65). By the end of the 1920s, the Finnish Working People's College had become more aligned with the Industrial Workers of the World and more explicit in highlighting the class struggle. The overt intention of the school was "to create 'a revolutionary working class' in order to generate radical social change and [...] to prepare workers to govern the new social order" (*Ibid.*, p. 69). The school continued to operate until 1941.

Another radical workers' school was the People's College in Fort Scott, Kansas, which remained as a correspondence school during its relatively short lifespan. Its basic approach was summed up in the July 1914 issue of the *Appeal to Reason* newspaper: "We are trying, as hard as possible, to blot out the ever present thought in the mind of man "What is there for me?" and to substitute therefor [*sic*] "What can I do to make this a better world to live in and to help my fellowmen [*sic*] on the road to happiness and contentment?"

Basic skills in such subjects as public speaking, short story writing, Spanish, advanced English, salesmanship, etc. were taught, in part for the roles students could play in fostering the coming socialist revolution but also no doubt to address the range of interests and needs of working people. As is the case today, education for workers could emphasize the vocational needs of workers or it could seek to expand their knowledge of (and allegiance to) the need for a critical (radical) transformation of society that, it was assumed, would lead to more equitable living and working conditions. Or, as in the case of the People's College, it could attempt to address the need for broader political understandings and advocacy along with instrumentalist concerns.

The Rand School of Social Science in New York City was one of the most successful adult schools established by American socialists.

Closely allied with the Party but not actually a part of the Party organization (for legal reasons), it was founded in 1906 and closed in 1956, long after its close affiliation with the Party had ended. During the height of its popularity in the second decade of the century, several thousand students were enrolled each year. The school was especially attractive to immigrant workers who could take basic courses as well as those more directly linked to the radical cause. In addition, because of the school's international human brotherhood character, they could feel not looked down upon, as might happen elsewhere (Cornell 1976). Well-known socialist and non-socialist radicals and liberals taught classes at the Rand School, for example ones in elementary and advanced socialism, U.S. history, English poetry, composition and rhetoric, economics, and union organizing, along with public speaking, shorthand, and other more occupation-oriented topics. During some of its existence it also offered correspondence courses, initiated extension sites in other parts of the New York City/New Jersey area, created a summer session (which was transferred in 1921 to Camp Tamiment in the Pocono Mountains of Pennsylvania) and sponsored a library, book store, and the Bureau of Labor Research (Teitelbaum 1995). In all these endeavors, the Rand School sought to address multiple areas of workers' lives, which also meant promoting the socialist cause to help in the improvement of their lives.

The Rand School served as a prototype for smaller, less successful efforts in communities throughout the United States, *e.g.*, in Newark, Boston, Philadelphia, Wausau, San Francisco, and Seattle. In addition, radical trade unions established their own labor colleges, the most well-known being Brookwood Labor College in Katonah, New York (established in 1921) and Commonwealth College in Mena, Arkansas (founded in 1923). These schools were founded on the premise that workers' education could play a significant role in promoting not only direct labor concerns but also critical understandings and participation in the radical reorganization of society. Those involved in these labor colleges viewed public schools as decidedly anti-labor and as fostering "passive acceptance and conformity to a bourgeois value system" (Altenbaugh 1990, p. 77). As labor leader James H. Maurer put it:

Our children are being trained like dogs and ponies, not developed as individuals. Such methods, together with the vicious propaganda on social and economic questions to which children are subjected, produce just the results that the conservative and reactionary elements of the country want, namely, uniformity of thought and conduct, no originality or self-reliance except for money-making schemes, a worshipful attitude toward those who have wealth and power, intolerance for anything that the business element condemns, and ignorance of the great social and economic forces that are shaping the destinies of all of us.

Maurer went on to assert that at Brookwood:

No dogma, whether originating among the employing class or in some labor or radical group, must be held sacred. Instead we must seek light and understanding everywhere in order that the individual may determine for himself or herself proper guidance and the ways of truth (Altenbaugh 1990, pp. 77–78).

Still, despite Maurer's last statement, it was clear that a primary goal of Brookwood was to serve the interests of the labor movement and, by doing so, help to usher in a new, more equitable social order.

Similarly, Commonwealth College was created to educate workers to be more knowledgeable about and motivated in agitating for radical social change. While the school described itself as experimental, autonomous, and non-dogmatic, one of the college's basic premises, according to two former students who were later teachers there, was that "the entire structure of society would have to be reformed and transformed to eliminate the disorders of an unplanned, competitive society." Moreover, while an education at Commonwealth might turn out individuals with differing views regarding the exact nature of the cooperative commonwealth and the means of social change, "it will turn out no strikebreakers" (Koch & Koch 1972, pp. 9–10 and 65). Like most of the other labor colleges, its curriculum was a mix of basic courses that would be of immediate, practical benefit to workers (including skills that enabled the college to continue functioning) and those courses that sought to arouse social consciousness, promote international worker solidarity, and enlist the aid of worker-students in the struggle for systematic and comprehensive social change (Cobb 2000).

Highlander Folk School (later the Highlander Research and Education Center), organized in 1932 near Monteagle, Tennessee and open until 1961, was another institution that provided what might be considered critical education for workers. While less overtly ideological than most of the other examples in this chapter, the school was noteworthy for its dedication to enabling local participants to help themselves, which included basing much of its educational program on the personal knowledge of the problems and experiences of the people involved. At the same time, the school was also clearly committed to the role that education could play in fostering fundamental economic and social change for a more equitable and humane society. Its co-founder and long-time director, Myles Horton, later participated in a "spoken book" with Paulo Freire (Horton & Freire 1990), in which he shared the intense passion for self-emancipation, radical social criticism, and transformative democratic change that inspired his work at Highlander. In its 30-year history, in a wide variety of residence, extension, and community programs, the school trained scores of activists who worked in the labor and civil rights movements in Appalachia and beyond. Glen (1988) describes the school's core curriculum as including "union problems, labor history and economics, public speaking and parliamentary law, dramatics, and labor journalism," which he suggests "continued to provide practical training in conducting the affairs of local unions" (p. 67). Later, starting in 1956, though still with leadership training in democratic civic participation in mind, Highlander sponsored "citizenship schools" in Johns Island, South Carolina that began by asking the local, mostly poor and black citizens what they wanted to learn. This started a literacy education program that "helped to accelerate the voter registration drive on Johns Island and in Charleston County during 1958 and 1959" (p. 163), even in the face of considerable white resistance. The success of these efforts led Highlander to expand the program to other Sea Islands and the city of Charleston, broadening its scope to include such topics as cooperatives, driver's education, health care and consumer education. "Singing schools" were also initiated not only to help teach reading and writing but also to promote a greater appreciation for the traditional music of the region. As occurred in many such efforts, Highlander held teacher-training workshops and "refresher" sessions to "help Citizenship School teachers adjust their work to fit the particular needs of their communities" (p. 168).

The Summer School for Women Workers was established in 1921 at Bryn Mawr College outside Philadelphia by the National Women's

Trade Union League. For the next 17 years, until it was forced to close in 1938, about 1,700 blue-collar students received an education that mixed the liberal arts with practical subjects, addressing both the "bread" and "roses" of students' desires (Hollis 2004). While the school started with a liberal humanist slant, it quickly became more explicitly leftist and feminist in its politics, progressive in its educational approach (in the Deweyan and social reconstructionist senses), affiliated with the burgeoning labor movement, and racially integrationist in its selection of students. Its curriculum increasingly took as its starting point that women's work and home experiences broached problems of industrial capitalism, and that there was a vital need for individuals to play an active role on behalf of the labor movement and radical social change in order to transform their own oppressive work environments. In other words, like the other examples cited in this section, this was an education intended to encourage working women to become not middle-class college students but, rather, on the local and national levels, labor organizers, educators, and impassioned activists for social-justice movements. In an article published in a 1934 issue of *Progressive* Education, the founder of the school, Hilda Worthington Smith, who had been dean at Bryn Mawr and later served in the federal government on related education programs, described worker education as decidedly not a narrow trade training for workers:

> In the broad interpretation of the term, workers' education offers to men and women workers in industry, business, commerce, domestic service and other occupations, an opportunity to train themselves in clear thinking through the study of those questions closely related to their daily lives as workers and as citizens. Its primary purpose is to stimulate an active and continued interest in the economic problems of our times and to develop a sense of responsibility for their solution.

She emphasized the need to focus on "current industrial and social problems of daily concern to workers," which would necessitate focus on the social sciences. Indeed,

> classes in economics, economic history, government, legislation, community problems, the history of the labor movement, current industrial situations, international affairs, social psychology, and other allied subjects are of great interest to those workers who are confused by changing industrial conditions, and who seek

to understand their own responsibilities as workers and as citizens (Gross, 2004, pp. 50–51).

Karyn Hollis (2004) describes the "materialist pedagogy" that was adopted at the Bryn Mawr summer school, one that provided a generally silenced population the opportunity to study, speak, and write publicly about their own experiences, in essence a chance to create their own discourse that was not "disembodied or dematerialized" (p. 5). Topics for essays, speeches, and plays included unemployment, housing problems, time work and piece work, government ownership of industries, and married women in industry, not as an attempt to prescribe solutions but to provide starting points for the study and public expression of what the students experienced under industrial capitalism. In this school, perhaps unusually so among these workers' schools (and probably influenced by the gendered nature of its student population), there was as much emphasis on personal development as social change. Still, the bottom line was the creation of a more just and egalitarian society. As one student at the time wrote:

> Here in Bryn Mawr we have found a voice with which to relate our individual experiences and we have found a wide common interest in the desire to bring humanity to a better basis… Social control and economic planning questions have not been confined to the classroom. Why are we so poor in a world of plenty? Why can't we make the things that people want when the material is at hand? Why should the workers of one country destroy the workers of another, and why, having made the world safe for democracy, should it be so difficult for the oppressed to make their voices heard? (Hollis 2004, p. 166).

These are the kinds of questions that informed many radical activist educators who provided learning opportunities for workers during the first half of the twentieth century in the United States, ones that, perhaps as part of an expanded social perspective and pedagogical approach, might seem quite relevant today.

Related initiatives by socialist and anarchist movement activists involved formal and informal, typically supplemental educational activities for workers' children that were intended to counteract the conservative and anti-working class orientation of the public schools. These efforts have been amply described elsewhere (Teitelbaum 1995, 2009) but an awareness of the extensive curriculum that was adopted can perhaps also be instructive when considering an education for workers. These educational settings during the first two decades of the twentieth century included Socialist Sunday Schools, Jewish Workmen's Circle (Arbeiter Ring) and other radical ethnic (German, Finnish, etc.) schools, and anarchist Modern Schools that were affiliated with the Francisco Ferrer Association. In the years that followed, communist-affiliated educational groups for workers and their children were also organized (Mishler 1999). Among the related themes emanating from the curriculum offered to workers' children in the Socialist Sunday Schools were the following ten (Teitelbaum 1995, 2009):

- Children from working class families were encouraged to reject the notion of the abstract individual, whereby the life of the individual, as an economic and social being, is set apart from (not situated within) the structural relations that play an influential role in determining, for example, the level of comfort one does or does not enjoy. The focus is placed instead on the individual in the context of the larger social world and, in particular, the interdependence and indebtedness of the individual to countless others, especially workers.
- Students are encouraged to be aware and proud of belonging to the community of workers. The dignity of labor was stressed and virtually every social issue or problem was viewed primarily from its effect on workers.
- Advocacy for economic and social relations that were cooperative and collectivist rather than intensely competitive and privatized was a major theme in these schools. Lessons addressed the nature and advantages of social ownership and management of large industries and services that were of benefit to an entire community.
- A fourth theme focused on instilling an internationalist (global) perspective, that is, the sense of viewing oneself as inextricably linked to the interests of workers in other nations. While the particular histories and social conditions of countries may be different, workers had similar needs and interests with regard to the exploitation of labor.
- As one educator put it, there was a need to teach students an awareness of "anti-sham patriotism." This was accompanied by anti-militarism, a sense that wars primarily hurt the lives of workers

(who did the fighting in such endeavors) and took attention and funding away from pressing domestic needs and benefited private capitalist interests.

- A revisionist interpretation of history and sociology was encouraged, so that the laboring class was perceived as an instrument of social progress, the plight of the poor was viewed not as the result of defective skills or character but as caused primarily by the exploitative nature of the capitalist organization of society, and different historical heroes were extolled. Among the individuals who were honored in lesson materials, youth newspapers, etc. were William Lloyd Garrison, Susan B. Anthony, "Mother" Jones, Eugene Debs, Karl Marx, and other national and international social critics and activists whose contributions typically were ignored, at best, in public schools.
- Advocacy for social justice and equality, with the differences between the few "haves" (with great wealth) and the many "have nots" (with needless suffering), was a consistent focus. This often involved discussions about adequate levels of food, clothing and shelter, the class struggle, and so forth.
- An awareness of serious social problems and the need not just to study them but to work together to agitate for their alleviation was another major theme. This often included an emphasis on poverty, unemployment, unhealthy and unsafe work conditions, child labor, alcoholism, poor housing and sanitary facilities, the destruction of nature, disease, etc. as endemic to industrial capitalism. Relatedly, workers needed to have more awareness of, and appreciation for, good hygiene, healthy diets, proper exercise, safety, and places for nature outings. This was a matter not just of the health of the individual but of the community at large as well.
- An emphasis on education (and self-education), not so much for students to rise out of the working class but more to gain a deeper understanding of the nature of capitalist America and the coming socialist society, was a key feature of the Socialist Sunday School curriculum.
- Deemed particularly important, especially in those schools that were guided by activists influenced by progressive ideas and practices, was a generally critical approach toward everyday social life,

dominated as it was in schools, the media, popular culture, the church, etc., sometimes insidiously, by capitalist influences. One prominent socialist educator urged teachers to "get them [the children] to asking WHY?" Alternative notions of everyday concepts were considered, so that success and justice, for example, were viewed critically from a more socially informed perspective.

While there were certainly different approaches and curricula employed by the different radical activists who worked to provide a supplemental education to the children of workers, for many the goal was not for children to become mindless followers of radical political doctrine when they reached adulthood but, rather, for them to comprehend the need for, and seek to enlist in, the struggle against the exploitation of workers and social inequality. As the Commonwealth College educators put it, at the least an education for workers (and their children) should "turn out no strikebreakers." And, as the young student quoted at the start of this chapter suggested, the intent was "to be a useful member of the community, taking an absorbing interest in all things that concern the welfare of all its members."

This section has examined examples of educational experiences for workers and their children that went well beyond the traditional emphasis on the tasks and dispositions deemed crucial by employers at the workplace. Socialist educators and allied activists were reacting in part to the predominant approach of scientific managers like Frederick W. Taylor and efficiency educators such as David Snedden, Franklin Bobbitt and Charles Prosser, who viewed anything but a narrow vocational curriculum for workers to be inefficient or irrelevant, given the current and expected future lives of those from the working class. Indeed, to them and to the employers, what workers perhaps needed to learn most of all besides new occupational skills was "obedience, punctuality, cleanliness, order, and an orientation toward work" (Bailey 2010b, p. 931). Among these efficiency educators, and given the troubling tumult of immigration, industrialization and urbanization that existed during this time, the emphasis was placed on the guarantee of social order rather than on the opportunities inherent in social change to bolster the benefits of democratic citizenship. The focus was essentially on preparing workers to contribute to common production goals in discrete and often minute ways, with as little disruption as possible. Simply put, personal fulfillment for workers, as Herbert Kliebard (1992) points out, was "not to be found in the workplace, but on the playing field, the sports arena, or even the neighborhood tavern" (p. 197).

Radical activists, on the other hand, viewed vocational education as a way to encourage meaningfulness at the workplace and at home and to prepare and encourage workers to advocate for more equitable social and economic conditions. It should be noted as well that their efforts also stood in contrast to those of mainstream organized labor, especially when that movement moved rightward in the 1920s. By that time, the labor movement was "cast[ing] a jaundiced eye toward any political utopianism that they had come to associate with their Communist rivals" and instead "skirted social issues" in all such educational ventures. As part of such a depoliticized education, where even the "unfettered exploration of ideas became taboo," mere training for union leadership and membership loyalty overrode other interests that workers themselves might benefit from (Altenbaugh 1990, pp. 44–45).

The approach of the socialist activists was much more similar to that of social reformer Jane Addams and John Dewey, who sought to humanize vocational (industrial) education so that it would have "a much broader purpose than simply trade training" (Kliebard 2004, p. 124). Addams, for instance, suggested courses geared especially to living healthier and more dignified lives (Bailey 2010a, pp. 932–933). In addition, from Addams' perspective the essential problem was that workers did not thoroughly enough understand the modern industrial system, that is, the character of work within a larger social context, and thus such knowledge should be a significant component of the educational activities provided to them. Similarly, Dewey emphasized the need for work life itself to be experienced in meaningful ways. (Noddings [2013] argues that Dewey perhaps downplayed the fact that some work will invariably be unpleasant.) In his usual effort to avoid dualisms, Dewey emphasized the need for an education that integrates the vocational with the academic, labor with leisure, and industrial intelligence with democratic values. It should foster in all schoolchildren, from all backgrounds, an understanding and appreciation of the varieties of work that comprise the world in which they live. While no doubt agreeing with Addams and Dewey on these issues, socialist activists sought to go beyond in particular ways, specifically to an education for workers (and their children) that would provide opportunities and encouragement to learn directly about politics and history, the labor movement and socialist principles, and public speaking and organizing, all in the service of the radical restructuring that they viewed as in workers' long-term interests. They sought to foster the critical questioning of everyday social, economic and political arrangements and to empower workers to join with others to actively address undemocratic and inequitable conditions and relationships. Like Addams and Dewey, they objected to vocational education that was intended merely to prepare workers for routinized and dehumanizing jobs and instead encouraged an approach that included a clear sense of being a knowledgeable and active citizen who seeks to change the world for the betterment of all, and most especially for the workers who were doing the dirty work of industrial capitalism. Whatever the results or lack of results that can be claimed for the educational activities of American socialists during the early years of the 20ᵗʰ century, they should not serve to obscure or eliminate from our collective memory the reasons for and nature of the efforts that were made. This may be especially important in efforts to contest what Michael Apple (1996) refers to as the ratification of "the neoliberal dream of reducing all education and training into simply one more adjunct to the industrial project" (p. 100).

4. Citizenship and education for workers

Like education, democracy, race, gender, skill, etc., work is an expansive concept that can be described as a "floating signifier" in that it seems to be readily understandable but in fact has multiple meanings for different people and in different contexts. In this chapter it has been used to connote "activities by which people gain their livelihood". This by definition refers to paid work (with the realization that this definition "leaves out an enormous range of demanding, time-consuming, and economically productive activity," including unpaid domestic labor and volunteerism) (Bills 2004, pp. 4–5). As such, dealing directly with one's livelihood, vocational programs would be remiss if they did not focus at all on what would help students to be successful at the workplace. The radical educators discussed in this chapter by and large understood this to be the case, especially for the programs and activities provided to adults, but they had an expansive view of what was meant by "successful." That is, they viewed it as their mission to help students "gain their livelihood" in the most meaningful, safe and non-exploitive environments possible, and in a society that honored their work and treated them fairly in terms of their basic needs and hopes for the future. These were connected concerns – successful occupational skills, empowerment at the workplace, and equitable social and economic conditions – and so they took the opportunity of the programs they offered to also focus on the benefits of active citizenship and liberal education, as well, it should be clear, of the advantages of aligning with the radical (socialist or anarchist) political movements of the time. It is the linkage between these concerns that points to the uniqueness of their efforts and the significant contribution that they made to our understanding of and approach to vocational education.

In addition, this historical discussion of workers' education and the ideology of citizenship should be viewed within the context of a central understanding partially alluded to above: the processes by which individuals come to see themselves as democratic citizens are varied and the conceptions of democratic citizenship that guide their lives are very different as well. What this points to is not necessarily a bad thing. As Diana Hess (2009) puts it, "multiple perspectives are an asset – not a hindrance – to democratic thinking, participation, and governance" (p. 77). Discussed openly and honestly, they can serve to enhance rather than weaken democratic life.

There have been many different attempts to identify conceptions of democratic citizenship and earlier I alluded to strong, robust and actively engaged forms in contrast to what has been referred to as weak, thin or protectionist. Realizing that any categorizations can conceal significant differences as much as clarify similarities, the work of Joel Westheimer and Joseph Kahne (2004) distinguishes three types of citizenship that perhaps can be helpful not only in our analysis of the activities described in this chapter but also with regard to current efforts to provide educational programs for current and prospective workers.

The first ideal type is the *Personally Responsible Citizen*. These are individuals who regularly vote, pay taxes on time, obey laws, give to charities, and follow current events. They may also help during times of serious need (*e.g.*, storms and floods), contribute to clothing and food drives, give blood, and pick up litter and recycle. This kind of citizenship has a lot to do with actions at the individual level and includes primarily limited involvement in the needs of the local community, with little focus on the larger social structures and institutions of which the local is ostensibly part. While not meant to disparage such an approach, in fact such a conception seems to function comfortably within neoliberalism, which Michael W. Apple (2013) succinctly characterizes as "a vision that sees every sector of society as subject to the logics of commodification, marketization, competition, and cost-benefit analysis" (p. 6) and Margaret Eisenhart (2009) describes as an ideology that "prizes individual accomplishments, distrusts government, and disparages the need to work across political, ethnic, and religious differences" (pp. 1–2). It is probably the case in the United States that most formal instruction in citizenship has, at best, adopted this conceptualization of what it means to be a citizen in a democracy.

The second kind of political identity is the *Participatory Citizen*. In this case, individuals are more actively involved in civic affairs, which could take place at the local, state and/or national levels. They do not just vote but they also campaign for chosen political candidates; do not just contribute to clothing and food drives but help to organize them; do not just give to charitable agencies but become actively involved on advisory boards; and do not just recycle at home but participate in neighborhood clean-up campaigns. This kind of citizenship includes greater engagement with collective efforts, joining with others in political and related activities to help shape the world in which we live.

The third category of citizenship referred to by Westheimer and Kahne is the *Justice-Oriented Citizen*. These individuals are particularly concerned with addressing systems of privilege and oppression and the root causes of social problems. They actively participate in collective strategies for change that challenge inequities related to issues of race, class, gender, and the like. While such individuals may be engaged in charity work and may volunteer for community-based organizations, they also identify with and advocate for larger social movements that seek to effect systemic change in support of the democratic ideal. They do not just help to organize clothing and food drives but also seek to address issues of hunger and homelessness in society; do not just engage in recycling but also organize with others to address the causes of environmental despoliation and climate change; and do not just vote or campaign for political candidates but actively work (and demonstrate) on behalf of policy and legislative changes that will insure the enhancement of democratic values and more equitable social conditions.

Two things seem clear: First, the radical activists in the United States during the early years of the 20th century described in this chapter believed that the education of workers should include more than just a narrow emphasis on the instrumentalities of their occupation. In the formal coursework they provided, as well as the extensive informal educational and cultural activities they sponsored, the practical skills and dispositions for succeeding in the workplace were studied and discussed alongside broader concerns related to leading meaningful and fulfilling lives, exploring significant content within what is typically thought of as liberal education, and becoming active citizens in/for a democratic society, which includes political advocacy and organizing. While the resources to support their initiatives and the actual extent of their efforts were both extremely modest, their approach to workers' education does provide a glimpse of an integrated curriculum that was guided substantially by interests in what Jean Anyon (2009) referred to as the need for a greater focus on "social justice, political participation, and the politicization of students" within conceptions and approaches to critical pedagogy and that I referred to elsewhere as "critical civic literacy" (Teitelbaum 2011).

And second, their conception of citizenship or political identity, emphasized to both adult workers and their children in educational and cultural activities, was decidedly more in line with the Justice-Oriented Citizen, as perhaps one might expect from those who identified so publicly with the radical political movement. Not aware at the time that many workers, and especially their children, would rise out of factory work in the years ahead, they sought not to assist their students to advance out of the working class but rather to transform what it meant to be a part of it. They sought to educate them in the best sense, not simply as a technical, instrumentalist endeavor but as an opportunity for growth, broadly defined, and as a vehicle for personal and social transformation. They understood that the "practical" could "never be divorced from historical, ethical, and political understanding without losing something in the process," that education should never be viewed as "simply training for industries' needs" (Apple 1996, p. 100).

These radical activists sought for their students to take the ideals of participatory citizenship seriously, to be active in the construction and reconstruction of political and economic life, and to do so with the best interests of other workers in mind. They sought to instill not so much a capability for individual advancement, but more so a commitment to democratic and equitable social relations for all, which for many of them essentially meant "clamoring for the eradication of capitalist society" (Altenbaugh 1990, pp. 46). They would no doubt have agreed with the central insight of Tyack and Cuban (1995), that "it's easier to provide vocational education than to remedy inequities in employment and gross disparities in wealth and income" (pp. 3–4). But at the same time, they viewed their educational efforts, constructed as they were with justice-oriented citizenship in mind, as in fact not separate from this more lofty and comprehensive goal but a necessary step to be taken to achieve it.

References

Altenbaugh, R. J. 1990. Education for struggle: The American labor colleges of the 1920s and 1930s. Philadelphia, Temple University Press.

Anyon, J. 2009. Critical pedagogy is not enough: Social justice education, political participation, and the politicization of students. In M. W. Apple, W. Au, & L. A. Gandin (eds.), The Routledge international handbook of critical education. New York, Routledge.

Apple M. W. 1996. Cultural politics and education. New York, Teachers College Press.

Apple, M. W. 2013. Can education change society? New York, Routledge.

Bailey, L.E. 2010a. History of vocational education curriculum. In C. Kridel (ed.), Encyclopedia of curriculum studies. Thousand Oaks, CA, SAGE.

Bailey, L. E. 2010b. Vocational education in curriculum. In C. Kridel (Ed.), Encyclopedia of curriculum studies. Thousand Oaks, CA, SAGE.

Barber, B. 1997. Public schooling: Education for democracy. In J. I. Goodlad & T. J. McMannon (eds.), The public purpose of education and schooling. San Francisco, Jossey-Bass.

Bills, D. B. 2004. The sociology of education and work. Malden, MA, Blackwell.

Boggs, C. 1976. Gramsci's Marxism. London, Pluto.

Bowles, S. & Gintis, H. 1976. Schooling in capitalist America: Educational reform and the contradictions of economic life. New York, Basic.

Buhle, M. J. 1974. Feminism and socialism in the United States, 1820–1920 (Unpublished doctoral dissertation). University of Wisconsin-Madison, Madison, WI.

Buhle, M. J. 1981. Women and American socialism, 1870–1920. Urbana, University of Illinois Press.

Callahan, R. E. 1962. Education and the cult of efficiency: A study of the social forces that have shaped the administration of the public schools. Chicago, University of Chicago Press.

Carnoy, M. 1982. Education, economy and the state. In M. W. Apple (ed.), Cultural and economic reproduction in education: Essays on class, ideology and the state. London, Routledge & Kegan Paul.

Coates, E. R. 1995. Thomas Jefferson on politics and government. In University of Virginia Library Thomas Jefferson digital archive. [retrieved from: <http://etext.virginia.edu/jefferson> September, 19th 2009].

Cobb, W. H. 2000. Radical education in the rural south: Commonwealth College, 1922–1940. Detroit, Wayne State University Press.

Cornell, F. 1976. A history of the Rand School of Social Science, 1906 to 1956 (Unpublished doctoral dissertation). Columbia University, New York, NY.

Cuban, L. 1984. How teachers taught: Constancy and change in American classrooms, 1890–1980. New York, Longman.

Dewey, J. 1916. Democracy and education: An introduction to the philosophy of education. New York, Macmillan.

Eisenhart, M. 2009. Civic engagement as history in person in the lives of high schools girls. Paper presented at the annual meeting of the American Educational Research Association, San Diego, CA.

Elson, R. M. 1964. Guardians of tradition: American schoolbooks of the nineteenth century. Lincoln, University of Nebraska Press.

Freire, P. 1970. Pedagogy of the oppressed. New York, Seabury.

Glen, J. M. 1988. Highlander: No ordinary school, 1932–1962. Lexington, The University Press of Kentucky.

Gramsci, A. 1971. Selections from the prison notebooks. New York, International Publishers.

Green, J. R. 1978. Grass-roots socialism: Radical movements in the southwest, 1895–1943. Baton Rouge, Louisiana State University Press.

Gross, S. J. 2004. Civic hands upon the land: Diverse patterns of social education in the Civilian Conservation Corps and its analogues, 1933–1942. In C. Woyshner, J. Watras, & M. S. Crocco (eds.), Social education in the twentieth century: Curriculum and context for citizenship. New York, Peter Lang.

Hamot, G. E. 2008. Citizenship education. In S. Mathison & E. W. Ross (eds.), Battleground schools, Vol. 1. Westport, CT, Greenwood.

Hess, D. 2009. Controversy in the classroom: The democratic power of discussion. New York, Routledge.

Hollis, K. L. 2004. Liberating voices: Writing at the Bryn Mawr Summer School for Women Workers. Carbondale, Southern Illinois University Press.

Horton, M. & Freire, P. 1990. We make the road by walking: Conversations on education and social change. Philadelphia, Temple University Press.

Kliebard, H.M. 1992. Forging the American curriculum: Essays in curriculum history and theory. New York, Routledge.

Kliebard, H. M. 1999. Schooled to work: Vocationalism and the American curriculum, 1876–1946. New York, Teachers College Press.

Kliebard, H.M. 2004. The struggle for the American curriculum, 1893–1958, 3rd ed. New York, Routledge Falmer.

Koch, R. & Koch, C. 1972. Educational commune: The story of Commonwealth College. New York, Schocken.

Krug, E. A. 1969. The shaping of the American high school, 1880–1920. Madison, University of Wisconsin Press.

Lagemann, E. C. 1989. The plural worlds of educational research. History of Education Quarterly, 29(2), 183–214.

Lagemann, E. C. 2002. An elusive science: The Troubling history of education research. Chicago, University of Chicago Press.

Leinenweber, C. 1977. Socialists in the streets: The New York City Socialist Party in working class neighborhoods, 1908–1918. Science and Society, 41(2), 152–171.

McCarthy, C., Pitton, V., Kim, S. & Monje, D. 2009. Movement and stasis in the neoliberal reorientation of schooling. In M. W. Apple, W. Au, & L. A. Gandin (eds.), The Routledge international handbook of critical education. New York, Routledge.

Mickenberg, J. L. 2006. Learning from the left: Children's literature, the Cold War, and radical politics in the United States. Oxford, Oxford University Press.

Mishler, P. C. 1999. Raising reds: The Young Pioneers, radical summer camps, and the communist political culture in the United States. New York, Columbia University Press.

Nasaw, D. 1981. Schooled to order: A social history of public schooling in the United States. Oxford, Oxford University Press.

Noddings, N. 2013. Education and democracy in the 21st century. New York, Teachers College Press.

Paul, E. & Paul, C. 1921. Proletcult (Proletarian culture). New York, Thomas Seltzer.

Reese, W. J. 1995. The origins of the American high school. New Haven, Yale University Press.

Reese, W. J. 2002. Power and the promise of school reform: Grassroots movements during the Progressive era. New York, Teachers College Press.

Reese, W. J. 2005. America's public schools: From the common school to "No Child Left Behind". Baltimore, Johns Hopkins University Press.

Saxe, D. W. 1999. Civic education. In R. J. Altenbaugh (ed.), Historical dictionary of American education. Westport, CT, Greenwood.

Schaefer, R. J. 1951. Educational activities of the garment unions, 1890–1948: A study in workers' education in the International Ladies' Garment Union and the Amalgamated Clothing Workers of America in New York City (Unpublished doctoral dissertation). University of Wisconsin-Madison, Madison, WI.

Spring, J. H. 1972. Education and the rise of the corporate state. Boston, Beacon.

Spring, J. H. 2005. The American school, 1642–2004, 6th ed. Boston, McGraw Hill.

Stave, B. (ed.) 1975. Socialism and the Cities. Port Washington, NY, Kennikat.

Teitelbaum, K. 1995. Schooling for "good rebels": Socialism, American education, and the search for radical curriculum. New York, Teachers College Press.

Teitelbaum, K. 2008. Curriculum. In S. Mathison & E. W. Ross (eds.), Battleground schools, Vol. 1. Westport, CT, Greenwood.

Teitelbaum, K. 2009. Restoring collective memory: The pasts of critical education. In M. W. Apple, W. Au, & L. A. Gandin (eds.), The Routledge international handbook of critical education. New York, Routledge.

Teitelbaum, K. 2011. Critical civic literacy in schools: Adolescents seeking to understand and improve the(ir) world. In J. L. DeVitis (ed.), Critical civic literacy: A reader. New York, Peter Lang.

Tyack, D. B. 1974. The one best system: A history of American urban education. Cambridge, Harvard University Press.

Tyack, D. & Cuban, L. 1995. Tinkering toward utopia: A century of public school reform. Cambridge, Harvard University Press.

Weinstein, J. 1969. The decline of American socialism in America, 1912–1925. New York, New Viewpoints.

Westheimer, J. & Kahne, J. 2004. What kind of citizen? The politics of educating for democracy. American Educational Research Journal, 41(2), 237–269.

Wood, G. H. 1998. Democracy and the curriculum. In L. E. Beyer and M. W. Apple (eds.), The curriculum: Problems, politics, and possibilities, 2nd ed. Albany, State University of New York Press.

GERMÁN GIL RODRÍGUEZ

Education and Work in the Libertarian Thinking of 19th and Early 20th Century Spain

> "There is no greater despot than the ignoramus"
> Anselmo Lorenzo

1. The proletarianisation of society and workers

Since the dawn of humanity, work has been the medium used to create a dialectical relationship between human beings and nature. By working, human beings have been able to use the limited resources provided by nature, and then transform them and produce goods and services to meet human needs. This relationship has not always been the same, it has changed over the course of history. "Work in order to eat and survive" had always been the basic approach of workers, but since the onset of the industrial age the vast majority of employees and workers came to believe that they should "work in order to live and be happy" (Tezanos, 2001, p. 12).

Work in the form of manual labour in which workers handle objects, gave rise to tools that made this activity easier. The close relationship between the object, manipulation by hand and brain development, led Engels to declare about work that, "It is the prime basic condition for all human existence, and this to such an extent that, in a sense, we have to say that labour created man himself" (Engels (1974, p. 59).

In Spain, the socialist movement and particularly libertarian socialism originated in enlightened thinking. It has the same global vision of manual labour as some enlightened thinkers, and the same view of the education, training and qualification that workers needed in order to master their trade. From the early Middle Ages until the late 18th and 19th centuries, this learning was controlled by guilds.

A variety of opinions about work and education/training[1] existed amongst enlightened thinkers. D'Alembert fought the contempt in which craftsmen and the mechanical arts were held, whilst Voltaire sought to salvage the inventors of the plough, the weaver's shuttle, the jack plane and the saw and define a life style based on the following premise: to work is to live. Whereas Locke demanded the right to work as an offshoot of the right to live and also declared work to be the basis of the principles of value, property and goods, Rousseau praised manual labour: "Of all the occupations that can offer sustenance to man, the one that brings him closest to the state of nature is work with his hands" (Rousseau 1985, p. 224).

Although Spanish enlightened thinkers were a minority, including particularly Benito Jerónimo Feijoo (1676–1764), Pedro Rodríguez Conde de Campomanes (1723–1803), José Moñino Redondo Conde de Floridablanca (1728–1808) and Gaspar Melchor de Jovellanos (1744–1811), they tried to renew life in Spain by means of education and work, amongst other things. As Sanchis said (2004), the Enlightenment demanded the recognition of the importance of manual labour and, by following different paths, discovered that work was a source of wealth. The net product included in goods means an increase in wealth that can only be achieved by labour.

The Spanish thinkers of the Enlightenment created an educational project which "believed wholeheartedly in the power of education as an instrument for achieving the desired happiness. The education-virtue-happiness equation upholds the educational utopia of enlightened thinkers and explains why they thought it was so important" (Ruiz Berrio 1998, p. 171). They believed that one way of solving Spain's problems would be to remedy the ignorance of the people by providing public education of a practical (utilitarian) nature including not only technical and scientific disciplines but also humanities, and that this would help overcome structural economic problems. To do so, these thinkers believed it was necessary to have qualified workers, middle management workers and a few experts capable of improving

1   In this article the concepts of education and training are regarded as synonymous, even though, strictly speaking, they are not.

techniques and developing useful sciences: "What is needed most is the study of exact sciences such as mathematics, astronomy, experimental physics, chemistry, natural history, mineralogy, hydraulics, machinery and other practical sciences" (Floridablanca, 1787, p. 224).

According to Ruiz Berrio (1998), middle management, i.e. engineers, needed the same sort of painstaking education as scientists, professors or managers in any realm. The children of day labourers, most craftsmen and small business owners could usually only aspire to a basic education, or at best, the professional training which was beginning to emerge at that time, for the training then provided by guilds was feared and rejected by those familiar with it or obliged to do it.

2. The mastery of a trade as an element of working-class identity

Following the victory of the bourgeoisie and their consolidation in power, this new social class proceeded to impose their global vision of society: liberalism, a new concept which introduced a new model of the organization of labour. Citing the freedom that took them into power, the bourgeoisie denied the growing proletariat access to economic and social assets, and proceeded to exploit the working class and exclude them from society for decades until the creation of an organized, militant proletariat that became engaged in the workers' struggle and achieved democratic rights for them.

The proletariat originated in the abolition of serfdom under the *Ancien Régime* and the dismantling of the trade guilds. The abolition of the guilds was one of the main aims of the bourgeoisie and provided the new labour market with a trained, qualified social group who mastered different trades. For these workers, their trade was the only thing they owned and their only means of making a living, and they managed to make it the core of their philosophy, transforming trades into professions and a source of livelihood.

Work well done was a source of pride and personal identity, and also the path towards personal development and the emancipation of the working class. Training and qualification took place in factories or workshops. The skills need to master a trade were passed down from one generation to the next and on the job. The link between being a good worker who mastered of a given trade, and political and trade union ideology was undeniable (Falaschi[2] 1936, Lafargue 1980, Sanchis 2004).

Anarchism did not regard work in the same way as capitalism. Whereas capitalism links work to salary and the worker's dependence on the capitalist, anarchism regards work as part of the core of the global vision of society. The great theorists of nineteenth-century anarchism defended economic systems such as mutualism (P.J. Proudhon), collectivism (Bakunin) and anarchist-communism (Kropotkin), and saw work as the core concept of their thinking.

In her article *Trabajo y Salario*, Leticia J. Vita (2007) describes five complementary trends in anarchism about the concept of work. Bakunin regarded work as a "human need" because human beings "need to work to remain in existence and develop themselves fully" (Bakunin 1997, p. 85). As an instrument of exploitation in a capitalist society, it was generally agreed by anarchists that "[…] those who collect the produce of land worked by others are merely exploiting their work. And those who increase the value of their capital through industry and commerce exploit the work of others" (Bakunin 1997, p. 216). Collective work was defended by Proudhon, who denounced that the force stemming from the collective labour of workers was an asset that was never acknowledged in salaries: "[…] that great force resulting from the union and harmony of workers, from their combined and simultaneous efforts is not paid" (Proudhon 1983, p. 108). Kropotkin defended work as a pleasant activity that meets physical, artistic and moral needs: "Work will always be the best incentive, the most beautiful and efficient ally of men in their emotional balance and physiological peace" (Andrés 1979,

---

2   In his essay El Trabajo Responsable, Falaschi praises the importance and purpose of work in social change. For example, "No matter how reactionary an individual may seem on account of his way of thinking, providing he is a skilled workman and willing to work he is a key element in the struggle for a free life. On the other hand, lazy and idle workers, even those with revolutionary thinking, are a serious problem for the new social experiment and increasingly so as general freedom grows" (p. 11).

p. 15). Work as a manual and intellectual activity has been defended by all anarchist thinkers and is the concept that underpins the pedagogical theories that do not distinguish between theory and practice, or between manual labour and intellectual labour. They believe that this division is at the heart of the power and hierarchy of the capitalist society, in which manual labour is reserved for the working class whilst "workers of thought" hold the positions of power. Peter Kropotkin[3] is one of the main representatives of this movement:

Until now, the political economy has insisted mainly on division. We believe in integration and maintain that the ideal of society, the state towards which it is moving, is a society of integral work, a society in which each individual produces both manual and intellectual labour. (Kropotkin 1972, p. 7)

This concept of labour is a far cry from the dominant discourse in post-modern societies in which, as André Gorz said:

Never has the "irreplaceable" or "indispensable" nature of work as a source of "social bonds", "social cohesion", "integration", "socialization" and "personal identity" been invoked so obsessively as since it became unable to fulfil any of these functions (Gorz 2000, p. 67).

For many people, work no longer enables social mobility, even for those with qualifications. Nor is it regarded as something that contributes to individual or collective development. It is simply seen a means of earning a living and not as a trait of one's identity or one's personal or collective development. Work well done has declined in social standing as opposed to the enormous quantities of mass consumption. At a time when what matters is salary as a means of subsistence rather than work as a source of satisfaction and personal well-being, it is essential to look upon work as a trait of identity and social development and as the core of social thinking, or work will run the risk of ceasing to be a trait of personal identity – with the ensuing decline in the prestige of trades, professions and even training.

---

3   For Kropotkin's concept of work, see particularly his Mutual Aid; Fields, Factories and Workshops; and The Conquest of Bread.

3. Education: a contributing factor to working-class identity

Workers always regarded training as essential because a lack of training was one of the main reasons they were defenceless against the bourgeoisie, so they quickly began to set up training centres, in order to, amongst other things, remedy their lack of schooling.

There was a long-standing tradition of practical education among Spanish workers, such as the school founded by the fourierist Antonio Ignacio Cervera[4] in Madrid for teenagers and adults which came to have more than 600 pupils within a few years of opening and teachers such as Pi y Margall[5] and Sixto Cámara[6].

Later, an ateneo or cultural centre[7] was established in Barcelona, inspired by Proudhonian thinking and also the Ateneo Catalán de la Clase Obrera (Catalan cultural centre for workers), of great importance in the second half of the 19th century in the realms of education and training for workers in Barcelona. This Ateneo was created in 1862 with the aim of fostering the education and training which the working class found so difficult to access. At first it provided a general education including language, mathematics, history and geography. Just one year later it had more than 200 pupils, although the numbers fell in the mid 1860s. Determined to be great philanthropists, the Ateneo's sponsors sought to improve the condition of the workers and this enabled the Ateneo to become a means of tempering working-class radicalism. The 1868 Revolution changed the philosophy of the Ateneo completely and it became a meeting place for the leaders of the working-class movement who

4   Antonio Ignacio Cervera was born in Palma de Mallorca in 1825 and died in Madrid in 1860. He was a working-class leader and journalist. In 1845 he created Escuela del Trabajador, a school for workers, in Madrid. He also founded El Trabajador, a bimonthly newspaper that supported working-class associations. He took part in the revolution of 1845 and was one of the founders of Falansterio Nacional (1858), a secret republican society that had 80,000 members.

5   President of the 1st Republic, June–July 1873.

6   Spanish utopian socialist (1825–1859).

7   These cultural centres were both schools and meeting places for the working classes and were managed by the workers themselves. They believed that emancipation could be achieved by effort and culture.

believed firmly in Bakuninism. It must also be said that the approach of the Ateneo shifted from a general education to one more focussed on science and technology due to the many engineers who taught there. Great emphasis was placed on mathematics, physics and chemistry, the basics of construction and sciences applied to arts and industry. Political economics was another major field. The humanities were not, however, neglected. It must also be emphasised that an elementary education was provided for female workers too. The Ateneo remained an example for many members of the working-class movement of Catalonia and in 1881, under the management of Manuel Bochons and Josep Pàmies, the Ateneu Obrer de Barcelona (working-class cultural centre of Barcelona) was founded.

Figure 1: Modernist certificate issued by the Workers' Cultural Association of Barcelona. 1918.

General Pavía's coup d'état in January of 1874 brought the First Republic to an end and abolished working-class organizations of any type, resulting in the closure of the Ateneo.

The working-class thinking[8] that took root in nineteenth-century Spain was a combination of three movements: Spain's mutualism; the anarchist or libertarian movement; and socialism-marxism. All three came together at the International Workingmen's Association (IWA), or First International, founded in 1864, and also at the 1870 Congress of Barcelona where they finally decided to join the IWA[9]. After joining the IWA, these working-class movements merged into two major trends: socialism (the PSOE was founded in 1879 and the UGT in 1888) and the libertarian anarchy that subsequently gave rise to the CNT in 1910. The socialist movement was strengthened by the presence of Paul Lafargue[10], and the anarchists had the support of Giuseppe Fanelli[11], Elisée Réclus and the Spaniard Fernando Garrido, among others.

The education of workers and their children was debated in practically all the main IWA congresses[12] in Geneva (1866), Lausanne (1867) and Brussels (1868). The 1866 Congress of Geneva in 1866 addressed two interwoven topics: work and education. The delegates sought to establish a working day of no more than 8 hours by law, to prohibit night shifts for women and children, and to have 18 declared the age of adulthood (Freimond 1973, pp. 80–81). As regards education, the congress declared:

For physiological reasons we believe it necessary to divide the children and young people of both genders into three classes. The first class for children aged 9 to 12, the second for those aged 12 to 15, and the third for young people aged 15 to 18. We also propose that work by the first group should be restricted by law to 2 hours a day, by the second group to 4 hours, and by the third group to 6.

The congress went on to say that, "It is desirable that elementary schools start teaching children before the age of 9", and voiced a demand:

Society cannot allow employers or parents to put children and young people to work unless such work is combined with education. By education

8   By working-class thinking, we mean the ideas and organisations that defend workers' interests, regardless of their ideology.
9   The first direct contact with Spanish working-class organisations was a message sent to the IWA Congress in Lausanne, Switzerland in 1867.
10 Son-in-law of Karl Marx who arrived in Spain in December 1871.
11 Arrived in Spain in October 1868.
12 The intention was to discuss this topic at the Basel congress (1868), but the question of education was not dealt with due to difficulties during the congress itself.

we understand three things: mental education, physical education entailing gymnastics and military exercises, and technical education including the general and scientific principles of any production, whilst also initiating children and young people in the use of the basic tools in every industry.

The declaration ended with the words,

Except perhaps for the first group, the cost of these polytechnical schools should be covered at least partly by the sale of their own products. This combination of paid productive work and mental education, physical exercise and technical learning will give the working class a standard of living far higher than that of the bourgeoisie and the aristocracy. (Freimond 1973, pp. 82–83).

4. Three ideas of education, or more

The anarchists soon realised how important the education of young people was in order to prepare the fighters of the future and change society. Although there was an ideological propagandist behind every anarchist, many schools for working, class adults were set up at the headquarters of trade unions and working-class associations, and also in cultural associations and cooperatives, an indication of the need to make culture available to the whole population. Workers took their children to rationalist schools and they themselves went to morning or night school, and even popular universities. The approach to teaching spread by Spanish anarchists was inspired by thinkers such as Paul Robin and James Guillaume[13], Fourier, Proudhon, Sebastian Faure[14], Bakunin, Kropotkin, Élisée Reclus, Tolstoi, etc. The three main styles of teaching

13 The education advocated was well-rounded and designed to develop moral, physical and intellectual attributes through scientific, professional and productive training in workshops, a type of institution that fulfils the requirements and interests of the working class.

14 In 1904, the anarchist Sebastian Faure created the libertarian school *La Ruche* for orphans and workers' children. It was called a "school of the future". The school closed in 1917.

which prevailed were the integral education[15] upheld by international-
ists, the neutral school advocated by Ricardo Mella, and the rationalist
school promoted by Francesc Ferrer i Guàrdia in his Modern School.

a) Integral education

The first conference about integral education was given at the Brussels
Congress of 1868, by Antonio Marsal Anglora[16] of the Brussels section
of the AIT. The integral education approach to teaching was accepted
by Spanish anarchists who subsequently championed it at the first Congress of the Spanish Regional Federation (FRE) held in Barcelona in
June 1870. A considerable part of that congress focused on the organization and education of the proletariat, i.e. "on their right to an integral
education in all fields of human knowledge".

As citizen Vergés said during the Barcelona Congress of 1870, "It
is necessary to provide an education for the working class; for them all
to be willing to learn and not devote themselves to worthless pleasures;
and for them to spend two hours learning because means for working
towards the common good are urgently needed." (Arbeloa 1972, p. 139).

The second FRE Congress, held in Zaragoza[17] in April 1872, championed the concept of integral education, defined as "the well-rounded
education that will equip the new generation with the latest scientific
knowledge and will produce people perfectly able to develop all their
physical and intellectual abilities" (VV.AA. 1872, p. 100).

Beginning at the Brussels Congress of 1868 (Freimond 1973,
pp. 430–443), the aim of integral education was "to bring men as close
as possible to perfection from those two points of view (p. 431) [...] a
well-rounded education that includes the study of science and the learning of a trade" (p. 438).

The underlying principle of an integral education is to develop a
person's abilities in preparation for the worlds of both thought and work.

---

15   *Integral education*, the term used in French and Spanish historiography, conveys
     the concept of a well-rounded education including the study of humanities, sci-
     ence and physical education.
16   Under the pseudonym "Sarro Magallán".
17   Second FRE Workers' Congress, Zaragoza, 1–11 April 1872.

This type of education is the same for everyone and is coeducational and secular, the belief being that workers guided by reason and science, and who are observant and not coerced, will acquire knowledge. This absolute faith in science and its approach based on observation and experimentation obviously bears the stamp of positivism.

Despite the extreme difficulties faced by the IWA, the anarchists, tireless propagandists that they were, published newspapers, magazines and pamphlets which they distributed among workers. They also created cultural associations to inform and educate workers. In this context and taking into account the need for women's emancipation, in 1872 the Barcelona federation of the IWA created a school for women at the Ateneu Català de la Classe Obrera (Catalan Cultural Association for the Working Class)[18].

The 19th session of the third Congress of the FRE in Córdoba from December 25 1872 to January 2 1873[19] included a discussion of "Means enabling international schools to be created", a report presented by Rafael Farga Pellicer, Severino Albarracín, Felipe Jané, Emmanuel Fournier, Manuel Bochons, José Pamies and Vicente Fombuena, which can be summarised as follows:

Our working class has an urgent need for education, having been driven by ignorance to misery and by misery to ignorance, a vicious circle imposed upon us by privilege and injustice. Although the exploitation of our class might excuse us for disregarding such an important matter, we are nevertheless convinced that only by our efforts can we escape from this scenario. It would be a crime if we did not look at this situation and focus some of our efforts on considering education, the revolutionary, socialist education of the working class. This is the trigger that will overturn and annihilate the old world, establish a complete revolution and cast off the yoke of ignorance, the trigger that will pave the way for a complete overhaul of society.

---

18   Yet another experiment staged in Spain to teach women on the basis of different ideologies. The relationship between the labour movement, education and feminism is extremely important, but lies beyond the scope of this paper. On the subject of education, mention must be made of the anarchist thinkers Teresa Claramunt (1862–1931), Soledad Gustavo (1865–1865), Isabel Vilà i Pujol (1843–1896), Antonia Rufina Maymón Giménez (1881–1959) and Josefa Martín Luengo (1944–2009).

19   Third FRE Workers' Congress held in Córdoba in 1873.

According to Tiana, the concept of integral education appealed to the emerging Spanish working-class movement on three counts:

Firstly, it attacked the basis of the ideological foundations of the division of work, thereby contributing to the final goal of emancipation which is the main aim of the working-class movement. Secondly, it proposed a polytechnical education which suited the needs and aspirations of the working class, and was able to train skilled, aware workers instead of idle, privileged beings. Thirdly, it was a proposal able to attract both the most radical and the most reformist movements and unite them in the ideological and propagandist struggle against the bourgeoisie (Tiana 1983, p. 119).

b) *The neutral school advocated by Ricardo Mella*

According to this movement, which emerged from Spanish anarchism in the early 20th century, education should have a neutral stance as regards values and content, and not convey any ideologies, not even anarchist ideology. The proponents of this movement believe that pupils who receive an unfettered education will choose the best road to emancipation by themselves.

The main proponent of neutral education was Ricardo Mella Cea (1861–1925). His ideas focus on the central role of the individual, because he considers that the State destroys the distinguishing features of individuals and prevents people from developing.

Ricardo Mella is one of the most important theorists of Spanish anarchism according to Federica Montseny, who describes him as "The deepest, sharpest and most clear-headed of all Spanish anarchist thinkers. His writings are all concise and short, but they set him on a par with the best theorists of international anarchism" (Rodriguez, 2014).

Mella was highly critical of the institutional education of his time for, "as long as the State controls education, as long as the Church is present in schools, as long as the conditions of social inequality are not eliminated, it is impossible for education to become universal and accessible to everyone" (Mella 1978, p. 35). Mella regarded education and non-institutionalised schooling as a means of social change because education meant "instilling in children a special way of behaving, seeing and thinking" (Mella 1968, p. 232).

The neutral education he championed was defined as:

Enabling young people, previously instructed in proven truths, to help advance all metaphysics, all theologies, all philosophical systems, all present, past and future forms of organization, all achievements and all ideals. It will be precisely the mandatory complement of schooling designed to arouse from within understanding, and not impose, a real approach to life; enabling each individual to react to this vast arsenal of ideas and rights to educate him/herself (Mella 1968, p. 209), [...] schools should not and must not be republican, masonic, socialist or anarchist, nor must they be religious". (Mella 1968, p. 208)

The distinguishing traits of neutral education were:

Ideological or methodological anti-dogmatism: "Just as no one has the right to suggest or impose a religious dogma on children, no one may lecture them on political opinions or social, economical or philosophical ideas". (Mella 1968, p. 208)

Individual freedom of thought. They agree entirely with libertarian thinking and in Mella's words: "Above all, we give priority to freedom, full freedom of thought and action, and we proclaim the real independence of the individual. We cannot recommend imposition or doctrinal methods of teaching for young people". (Mella 1968, p. 209)

A school that gives guidance.

Everything must be explained, but not imposed, no matter how true and fair we may think it is. (Mella 1968, p. 209), [...] School cannot and must not be anything more than a gym geared towards the full development of the individual. We must not, therefore, give young people any set ideas for they inevitably weaken and stunt the very faculties that we want to stimulate. (Mella 1968, p. 209)

Experience and science in response to Rationalism. According to Mella, the basis of education is science and experience, not rationalism. All experience is part of reality and all science is a part of experience:

Therefore, rationalism has failed as system, method or whatever to determine the truth, although it is still a powerful weapon against revelation, faith or the authority of dogma (Mella 1968, p. 133) [...] Many of the problems arising from human understanding are answered merely by well or poorly devised hypotheses, and it is clear that absolute neutrality is needed when expounding them because whilst one solution may seem logical and unquestionable to one person, it may seem absurd to some one else, therefore rationalism is an inadequate guideline for education. Once all subjects based on faith are eliminated, the education of young people would be reduced to teaching proven facts and explaining problems whose solutions are probably certain. (Mella 1968, p. 133)

Reason is not enough.

I'm not sure about Rationalism, whatever that means. I think this word always contains a touch of metaphysics or theology. Reasoning enables vast things of speculation to be built, but they are seldom solid or firm. Even then, many swear by the words rational, reason, etc. (Mella 1968, p. 97) […] Fewer reasons and more experiences; less rationalism and more realities; less gymnastics of feverish imagination and more positive knowledge and facts of nature, will make us more suited to and deserving of other civilizations. (Mella 1968, p. 98)

As Carmen Sobrino wrote in her introduction to Mella's study *Issues of Education*, Mella's pedagogical ideas can be defined as the continuation of that integral education which combines theory and practice; equality in terms of social classes; the abolition of rewards and punishments; coeducation and, above all, absolute freedom of pedagogy, making schools an instrument in preparing free, self-sufficient men and women able to think, reason and create for themselves, ridding schools of everything that makes them a means for perpetuating the established order. If we change education we will change humanity. (Mella 1979, p. 128).

In short, as Serra says, the neutral school is a free school in terms of content, methods and objectives, a school whose driving force is the value of experience and actions, a school that eradicates once and for all any vestiges that instil political, religious or social values, etc", (Serra 1984, p. 93) a school which, in essence, "provides access to experience in order to acquire knowledge, facts and realities. (Serra 1984, p. 93).

c) The rationalist school of Francesc Ferrer i Guàrdia

The pedagogical movement that influenced Spanish anarchism most was undoubtedly the rationalist Modern School[20] created by Francesc Ferrer i Guàrdia. Its influence crossed borders and contributed to Ferrer i Guàrdia being executed by firing squad on 13th October 1911. Its influence even eclipsed other libertarian experiments in education, causing some historians to regard the true libertarian school to be Ferrer i Guàrdia's rationalist school.

Rationalism was an educational paradigm that emerged in specific circumstances in the late 19th and early 20th centuries but despite its significant and persistent impact, it practically disappeared in the 1930s.

According to Lázaro Lorente (1992), this movement arose in Spain in a context characterised by a poor education system, a high level of illiteracy, an increase in secular movements, insufficient state schools, lip service to compulsory education[21], insufficient funding for the rationalist school movement, repression by the catholic Right, etc.

Figure 2: Modern school: Ferrer i Guardia.

20 The Modern School was created by the pedagogue and freethinker Francesc Ferrer i Guàrdia in August 1901 in Barcelona.
21 In 1857, schooling became compulsory from the age of 6 to 9, and was extended to the age of 12 in 1900.

The rationalist schools promoted by scientific movements received support from groups of masons, freethinkers and republicans who regarded experience as the basis of knowledge. These schools sought to provide an alternative to the teaching methods used in the state-run and private schools of that time.

Ferrer i Guàrdia was not a pure anarchist thinker as revealed by his transition from republican ideology[22] to anarchism. He created the Modern School following in the steps of pedagogues such as Paul Robin and Kropotkin, with financial support from Jean Ernestine Meunié and the help of university professors, masons, federal republicans and veteran anarchists such as Anselmo Lorenzo. The Modern School was active on and off in Barcelona between 1901 and 1909.

Ferrer i Guàrdia believed that

> The Modern School tries to fight all the prejudices that hinder the complete emancipation of the individual and so applies humanitarian rationalism which consists of instilling in children the desire to know the origin of all social injustices so that they can subsequently use their knowledge to fight and oppose such injustices. The Modern School is the study of everything that fosters the freedom of the individual and the harmony of society in a regime of peace, love and well being for everyone regardless of their class or gender[23].

The basic aims of the Modern School were: to enable all children to become educated, honest, fair, unprejudiced persons; to provide an education for children based on science and reasoning; to provide a secular education; and for there to be no segregation by gender or social class. Ferrer was against creating separate schools for poor children, he sought to educate children without fostering hatred amongst classes.

Ferrer's pedagogical practices became an educational model used by libertarians so the Confederación Nacional de Trabajadores (CNT) decided to spread the word about rationalist education at the congresses of 1910, 1919, 1931 and 1936.

---

22   He worked as secretary for the Spanish republican Manuel Ruiz Zorrilla during the reign of Amedeo I of Savoy.
23   Speech made in prison in 1906.

Teaching involved no tests or rewards or punishments. It encouraged children's natural curiosity and fostered learning in groups to achieve an education based on the principles of solidarity and universal equality.

This school was promoted by libertarian trade unions, although many anarchists regarded the Modern School as more freethinking than libertarian. Depending on where a school was set up, the subjects taught in class were closely linked to libertarian thinking.

The influence of the Modern School spread across all Spain and Portugal and became a cornerstone of the socialist movement in South America in the 20th century, resulting in several rationalist schools being built there.

The publication of a gazette and the creation of a publishing house helped boost its influence elsewhere in Catalonia and also in Valencia, Andalusia, the Balearic Islands, Murcia, etc. A number of rationalist newspapers also contributed to this expansion.

5. Epilogue – or what remains of libertarian, working-class culture

The influence of the anarchist or libertarian movement in Spain made a significant contribution to educating workers and their children by creating educational institutions and teaching methods that are not always acknowledged, partly because anarchism is usually regarded as synonymous with social disorder rather than as a defiant attitude to life which champions a humanity characterised by freedom, autonomy, non-conformity, and ethics, and also the transformation of individuals and society which had been prevented by capitalists who imposed a system that dehumanised and exploited workers economically. The anarchist social project clashed with the interests of groups in power intent on safeguarding their historical, personal and class privileges.

Their educational projects advocated universal education with no segregation by gender or social class (in a way similar to today's inclusive education), which paid particular attention to individual help and health, which encouraged students to work together and help each other rather than be competitive, which gave no rewards or punishments, and in which knowledge was based on science. These projects suffered constant political and economic meddling from the powers of the time who refused to relinquish the classist, segregationist education of yore.

The curricula of educational establishments (schools, cultural associations, etc) were drawn up, implemented and developed with help from pupils, parents and teachers, creating places where they could spend time together, places where some traits of the society of tomorrow were already beginning to take shape.

These educational experiments could not all be incorporated into or by the political system or by the educational authorities of that time, so they took place on the fringes of mandatory, mainstream education.

Anarchists believed that education and training were the cornerstones of personal and social change and should, therefore, be a constant, lifelong process. As a result, every anarchist was a focal point of cultural dissemination committed to on-going social change whose used trade unions, cultural associations, the press, theatres, discussions, the publication of books, etc, to create a constant climate of cultural creation and involvement.

This non-conformist attitude was precisely what caused many anarchists to reject, as early as the 19th century, structures of power, control and vested interest such as marriage. Anarchists were in favour of the free love and cohabitation practised by many people today.

In line with their all-encompassing view of life, anarchists also incorporated vegetarianism, naturism and animal protection into their essential social and political discourse. Ecologism and environmental protection were championed as roads to a balanced relationship between human beings and nature.

Figure 3: La Prosperidad school for adults. Madrid.

Likewise, their concept of education and the need for lifelong learning led them to establish day-time, evening and night schools for children, adults and workers including women, and also popular universities and cultural associations. Lifelong learning, a much vaunted concept today, is far from a recent invention.

Figure 4: Montseny, Federica. *Resurreción*.
Barcelona: Revista Blanca publications

Anarchists did not trumpet their struggle to liberate all humanity as a class ideology, they sought to change society as a whole and believed that this transformation required an internal change beforehand: education. With this approach it was logical that they aimed to better the education of the working classes, making a special effort to publish pamphlets, newspapers and journals about education. There are far too many libertarian newspapers and publishing houses to mention here (the list would be longer than this entire study), suffice to mention Solidaridad, La Revista Blanca, La Novela Ideal, Tierra y Libertad and El Luchador, by way of example.

Figure 5: Paideia Free School (Mérida).

From 1870 onwards, every libertarian working-class association that could afford one, had a school at their headquarters. Working-class organisations and societies were well aware that their social and working demands and the education of workers were inseparable parts of the same struggle. They also believed that the education of workers contributed to achieving universal solidarity. The valuable, profound and far-reaching experience gained in the field of education during Spain's 2nd Republic (1931–1939) was brought to an end by the fierce repression of teaching during the Franco period. Its influence did, however, persist in South America thanks to the exiled republicans who spread across the continent.

After democracy returned to Spain, some experiments/schools inspired by libertarian and other types of pedagogical principles emerged. The models championed by Ferrer i Guàrdia, Paulo Freire, Montesori, Ivan Illich, Freinet and others, have been incorporated into the methods adopted by state-run schools and private schools, and the education of children, young people and adults.

Finally, we would like to mention that there are currently several schools in Spain inspired by libertarian principles[24], including two in particular: La Prosperidad and La Escuela Paideia.

La Prosperidad is a school for adults established in 1973 as Escuela Popular la Prosperidad. It now teaches Spanish, computer sciences and Arabic, and organises discussion groups about gender issues, bicycle mechanics and economic alternatives. It has a club for disabled persons and a large library, screens films every Sunday and holds parties and outings. Its educational principles are based on the thinking of Ivan Illich and, above all, Paulo Freire.

Paideia, a school in Mérida (Badajoz) which opened more than 30 years ago, is regarded as a free, anti-authoritarian, anarchist school which has a regime of self-managed, free learning (from primary to secondary education) and a cooperative organisation based on the principles of freedom of the individual, anti-authoritarianism, empowerment of the individual, learning by playing and coeducation.

References

Andrés, T. 1979. Un amor truncado o el ideal que no muere. Barcelona, Autor.

Arbeloa, V M. 1972. I Congreso Obrero. Madrid, VM Arbeloa.

Bakunin, M. 1979. La Instrucción Integral. Mallorca, Editor José J de Olañeta.

---

24   For more information about libertarian alternative schools in Spain, see <http://www.nodo50.org.>

Bakunin, M., 1997. Escritos de filosofía política, tomo I. Barcelona, Altaya.

Campomanes, P. Discurso sobre la educación popular de los artesanos y su fomento. [retrieved from: <http://www.cervantesvirtual.com> January, 15th 2016].

D'Alembert, J. Discurso preliminar de la Enciclopedia. [retrieved from: <http://www.biblioteca.org> January, 15th 2016].

Delgado, B. 1982. La Escuela Moderna de Ferrer i Guàrdia. Barcelona, CEAC.

Engels, F. 1.974. Introducción a la dialéctica de la naturaleza. El papel del trabajo en la transformación del mono en hombre. Madrid, Ayuso.

Falaschi, F. 1936. El trabajo responsable. Barcelona, CNT.

Ferrer i Guàrdia, F. 1976. La Escuela Moderna. Madrid, Júcar.

Floridablanca. Estado General de la Población de España en el año de 1787. [retrieved from: <http://bibliotecadigital.rah.es> January, 15th 2016].

Freimond, J. 1973. La primera Internacional I, II. Madrid, Zero.

García Moriyón, F. 1982. Pensamiento anarquista español: individuo y colectividad. Madrid, Universidad Complutense.

García Moriyón, F. 1986. Escritos anarquistas sobre educación. Bakunin, Kropotkin, Mella, Robin, Faure y Pelloutier. Madrid, Zero.

Gil Rodríguez, G. 2006. Trabajo precario… futuro incierto. Valencia, Area.

Gorz, A. 2000. Miserias del presente, riqueza de lo posible. Buenos Aires, Paidós.

Jovellanos, M. G. 2012. Memorias sobre educación pública. Biblioteca Nueva, Madrid.

Kropotkin, P. 1972. Campos, Fábricas y Talleres. Madrid, Zero-ZYX.

Kropotkin, P. 1972. El Apoyo Mutuo. Madrid, Zero-ZYX.

Kropotkin, P. 1978. La Conquista del Pan. Madrid, Zero-ZYX.

Lafargue, P. 1980. El derecho a la Pereza. Madrid, Fundamentos.

Lázaro Lorente, L. M. 1992. La Escuela Racionalista en el País Valenciano (1906–1931). Valencia, Nau Llibres.

Lorenzo, A. 1913. Contra la ignorancia. [retrieved from: <http://www.anselmolorenzo.es> January, 15th 2016].

Lorenzo, A. 1947. El proletariado militante I, II. Toulouse, CNT.

Martín Luengo, J. 2006. Paideia. 25 años de Educación Libertaria. Madrid, Queimada.

Mella, R. 1968. Ideario. Barcelona, Producciones editoriales.

Mella, R. 1978. Forjando un mundo libre. Madrid, La Piqueta.

Mella, R. 1979. Cuestiones de enseñanza libertaria. Madrid, Zero-ZYX.

Paniagua, J. 2014. El Trabajo en la visión anarquista. [retrieved from: <http://estudios.cnt.es> January, 15th 2016].

Proudhon, P.-J. 1983. ¿Qué es la propiedad?, Buenos Aires, Orbis-Hyspamérica.

Rodriguez, S. 2014. La herencia de la familia Mella. [retrieved from: <http://www.farodevigo.es> January, 15th 2016].

Rousseau, J. 1985. El Emilio, Spanish translation of Emile. Madrid, Edaf.

Ruiz Berrio, J. 1998. La Educación del Pueblo Español en el proyecto de los Ilustrados. [retrieved from: < http://www.mecd.gob.es> January, 15th 2016].

Sanchis, E. 2004. Concepciones del trabajo: de las ambigüedades medievales a las paradojas actuales. Cuadernos de Relaciones Laborales, 22, 37–65.

Serra Pons, I. 1984. Presupuestos educativos de la pedagogía libertaria de Ricardo Mella Cea. Valencia, Universidad de Valencia.

Serra Pons, I.1986. Otro modelo de pedagogía española: la Escuela Neutral. Revista de Ciencias de la Educación, 128, 489–498.

Sola, P. 1978. Las escuelas racionalistas en Cataluña (1909–1939). Barcelona, Tusquets.

Sola, P. 2001. Francisco Ferrer i Guardia: la Escuela Moderna, entre las propuestas de educación anarquista. In J. Trilla (comp.), El legado pedagógico del siglo XX para la escuela del siglo XXI. Barcelona, Graó.

Tezanos, J. F. 2001. El trabajo perdido. ¿Hacia una civilización postlaboral? Madrid, Biblioteca Nueva.

Tiana Ferrer, Alejandro. 2010. Sobre la caracterización de la educación popular como campo de investigación histórica. Consejo Escolar de Estado, nº extraordinario, 8–24.

Tomasi, T. 1988. Breviario del pensamiento educativo libertario. Móstoles, Nossa y Jara.

Vita, L. 2007. Trabajo y Salario. El anarquismo frente al derecho. Lecturas sobre Propiedad, Familia, Estado y Justicia. Buenos Aires, Libros de Anarres.

VV.AA. Minutes of Second FRE Congress (Zaragoza 1872). [retrieved from: <http://anselmolorenzo.es> January, 15th 2016].

VV.AA. Minutes of Third FRE Congress (Córdoba 1872). [retrieved from: <http://memoriahistorica.cnt.es> January, 15th 2016].

Section 2.
Citizenship at Stake: Can VET
Practices Be Alternative?

BURKHARD VOLLMERS AND WERNER KUHLMEIER

Implementation of Sustainability into Germany's VET-System by Means of Model Projects: A Review on the Years 2005 to 2015

This contribution provides an overview about the strategies and instruments used in Germany to transform the complete VET-system according to principles of sustainability. Predominantly this happened by the realization of complex model projects involving practitioners and educational or vocational scientists. The following illustration focuses on the last 10 years and delivers a short insight into the future at the end. In Germany there is a big regulatory institution in the background of all strategies, techniques and achievements concerning the implementation of sustainability into Germany's VET-system. It is the Federal Institute for Vocational Education and Training, often referred to as the BIBB (German shortcut).

1. Institutional frameworks of the implementation of innovations into Germany's VET-system

The Federal Institute for Vocational Education and Training is the central control instance within Germany's VET-System. The BIBB operates on behalf of the Federal Government, first of all on behalf of the Federal Ministry of Education and Research (hereinafter referred to as BMBF, German shortcut). The implementation of structural innovations into Germany's VET-System, such as sustainability, usually is carried out by the BIBB at two levels: new definitions of regulatory instruments of vocational trainings in the dual system on the one hand and model projects combined with scientific research on the other hand.

The BIBB could be regarded as the central institution of Vocational Educational Governance in Germany. In general the four principles of governance in the public sphere are accountability, responsibility, transparency and fairness (Bevir 2013). The BIBB, operating as a largely independent government authority, puts these principles into practice by working in close contact with all stakeholders in Germany's VET-System. It is BIBB's aspiration to realize all forms of regulatory means and innovations with the participation of employers, unions, persons in charge within the educational systems and vocational and educational scientists. Specific boards of cooperation serve this purpose (for the example the "Hauptausschuss", Philippus 2010).

Mostly the BMBF decides which political and educational topics are the most important ones and should be promoted within the educational system in Germany. The BMBF provides funding to support model projects involving the targeted topics, both in the general educational system and in the VET-System. The BIBB receives the money to realize model projects in accordance with topics defined by the BMBF before. Via public tenders the BIBB acquires research partners. These scientists work at universities or in private research institutes. The practice of wide-span model projects has proven its value during the last four decades. In a review on 40 years of model projects in Germany VET-scientists wrote: "The objective of model projects is to support innovative developments within practice in VET. [...] Model projects combine innovative problem-solving with action-orientated research" (Dehnbostel *et. al.* 2010, p. 149).

Methods of model projects show continuity during the last 40 years. But BIBB has to react on some criticism concerning effectiveness (Jenewein 2007) and it has to react on new trends and topics in educational policy. Originally model projects tested new forms and methods of learning in a professional domain or within a specific target group, before implementation started on a broader level. Today model projects are created as big networks of different organizations within Germany's VET-system. Specific learning methods or didactical concepts are no longer starting points, but global educational or political ideas, such as sustainability (Dehnbostel *et al.* 2010, p. 157).

Moreover, the BIBB's model projects usually incorporate diverse Governance instruments that are discussed in Europe's education policy in order to enable learning outcomes on a broader level (see list in Ure 2015, p. 275). Instruments of national educational Governance that have been applied again and again in the last 40 years of model projects within Germany's VET-system are: experts groups, communities of practice, exchange of good practices and seminars or workshops of mutual learning.

In 2010 BIBB launched three domains of model projects:

• Sustainability in Vocational Education and Training (hereinafter referred to as BBnE, German shortcut),
• Quality assurance and development of vocational training in enterprises,
• Heterogeneity as a vehicle to obtain skilled staff.

The BIBB organized and supervised complex networks of model projects within these three domains which terminated in 2014. Final results were published by the BIBB (Kuhlmeier *et al.* 2014 on sustainability, Fischer 2014 on quality, Westhoff and Ernst 2016 on heterogeneity).

In the following passages the history of the implementation of sustainability into Germany's VET-system will be described. Not only the funding cluster BBnE that ran from 2011 to 2014 will be presented, but also its predecessors (the years 2005 to 2010) and its consequences (what was done after 2014 and what will be done in the years 2016 to 2019 in Germany's VET-system with special focus on sustainability).

2. The history of the implementation of sustainability: BIBB's model projects from 2005 to 2015

The implementation of sustainability into Germany's VET-system is guided by the BIBB in close cooperation with other political and educational organizations, mainly the BMBF and the German UNESCO. The UN-Decade of Sustainability in Education (2005 to 2014) is continued with the Global Action Program (GAP) Education for Sustainable Development (ESD) encompassing the years up to 2019. The UNESCO published a roadmap for implementing the GAP for ESD within the next four years (UNESCO 2014). It was translated into German (DUK 2014). This document is the basis for a specific German plan of actions. It is under development and has not been published yet. Currently the "Key issue paper" ("Eckpunktepapier" in German, BMBF 2015) defines the organizational structure of all initiatives to promote sustainability within the educational system in Germany. According to this paper six expert forums were launched. One forum is especially dedicated to VET.

Conceptual works of governance authorities related to sustainability within VET in Germany can be traced back to the year 2001. In that year the BIBB founded a specific organizational unit. Its task was to develop guidelines how to realize sustainability in apprenticeship and vocational training. In 2003 a paper was published by the BIBB. Its title was "Orientation framework for the integration of sustainability into vocational education" (Hahne and Kutt 2003). Six domains of work were listed in this paper:

- Identification of general vocational competencies related to sustainability,
- Identification of competencies related to sustainability that are of specific relevance in different professional domains,
- To find out areas of typical vocational activities requiring knowledge of sustainability and to create curricula for additional qualifications,
- To enlarge activities referring to sustainability within international cooperation,
- Creation of structures of sustainability within apprenticeships and professional work in enterprises,
- Creation of networks dealing with the topic of sustainability with focus on examples of best practice.

After the discussion of this paper on diverse conferences in 2003 and 2004 the BIBB set the main emphasis on model projects. In retrospect three phases can be differentiated. From 2005 to 2010 ten model projects were funded. They operated separately from each other. The years 2011 to 2014 were dominated by the big funding cluster BBnE. It was one huge network of model projects. The years 2014 to 2015 were dedicated to the discussion of the results of BBnE in order to develop a concept of continuing the transformation of Germany's VET-system according to the principles of sustainability.

2.1 The years 2005 to 2010: Ten different business-orientated model projects

These ten model projects were located within the branches of trade and commerce. The two main topics of all projects were resource efficiency and sustainable management strategies in industry and crafts. Moreover an interdisciplinary project was realized, called "sustainable forestry". Therein vocational training was connected to forestry and to research on environmental technologies (BIBB 2006). This project was part of the of a big research initiative organized and funded by the BMBF. It is called "research on sustainable development" (German shortcut is FONA = Forschung für nachhaltige Entwicklung). This research initiative continues to exist (www.fona.de). Essentially it consists of diverse environmental sciences.

BIBB's intern evaluations of all model projects lead to the conclusion that a stronger pooling of all activities was necessary. Moreover, the recommendation was to concentrate on classic professional work in those areas that have to deal with green topics in production and procurement. It was announced to exclude the business sector.

In 2010 the BIBB published a funding guideline calling for applications of interested and qualified persons within the four sectors metal and electro (with special focus on renewable energy), chemistry, construction sector and nutrition (BIBB 2010, p. 3). The model projects related to these sectors were integrated into one big funding cluster.

2.2 The years 2011 to 2014: The funding cluster BBnE

Six model projects were involved. They conduct their work mostly independently of each other. All of them developed special strategies of transfer and implementation. The six projects were supported by one scientific monitoring group consisting of scientists of the institute of vocational and economic education at the University of Hamburg and of consultants of the ICON-Institute in Cologne. The main task of the monitoring group was the evaluation of the funding cluster BBnE as a whole. Furthermore, each of the model projects was evaluated on its own according to summative and formative methods. The evaluation strategy was orientated towards strategies of the evaluation of hetero-geneous social networks of innovations in sociological and vocational research (Vollmers *et al.* 2014 with special reference to Deitmer 2004).

Three of the six model projects focused directly on renewable energy. These were "Technical Specialist for renewable Energies and of Energy Efficiency", "Offshore-Competence" and "BEE-Mobile". Branches involved were wind energy and electrically powered cars. The other three projects concentrated on the branches construction sector, "Sustainable Construction and Energy Efficiency", chemical industry, "Sustainable Careers in Education within the Chemical Industry" and nutrition and domestic service within community catering, "Frame-work of a Curriculum for Occupations in Nutrition and Housekeeping focused on Community Catering".

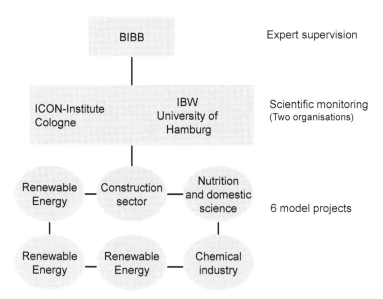

Illustration 1: Structure of funding-cluster BBnE (taken from Vollmers and Winzier 2013).

The model projects achieved different results and products. The majority conducted empirical research within their professional sector in order to identify new qualifications. Two of the projects developed curricula that found its way into VET-practice. The other four projects formulated recommendations how to implement their results into VET-practice or they constructed learning modules. The following table (taken from Vollmers and Winzier 2013) includes an overview about central results of BBnE.

Table 1: Results and products of model projects involved in funding-cluster BBnE.

Title of project	Main results
Technical specialist for renewable energies and energy efficiency	Curriculum approved by chamber of craft to provide additional qualifications.
Offshore-competence	Results of work-process-analysis; Guidelines how to implement proper skills into VET-regulatory-instruments.
BEE-mobile	Results of empirical research in the electric car sector; database of training offers on sustainability within industrial work.
Sustainable construction and energy efficiency	Interface-modules of learning; Courses for instructors; recommendations for sustainability within the construction sector.
Sustainable careers in education within the chemical industry	Implementation of sustainability into vocational trainings within the chemical industry.
Framework of a curriculum in nutrition and housekeeping focused on community catering	Worksheets for VET-teacher trainings at universities; worksheets for vocational education and training.

All six model projects and the scientific moderation group published their results in a research monography that was edited by the BIBB (Kuhlmeier *et al.* 2014). This publication rings in the third and final phase of the history of the implementation of sustainability up to the present. The conclusion of the BIBB was that a strong link between the participants in the funding cluster BBnE and experts that create general training regulations within Germany's VET-system are mandatory. Consequently the BIBB organized successive expert talks.

2.3 The years 2014 to 2015: Expert talks in the BIBB: How to connect regulatory instruments with results of model projects in BBnE

Participants of these regular expert talks were the BIBB-Department model projects, the BIBB-Department VET-regulations, scientists involved in the funding-cluster BBnE and the German social partners (employers' federation, trade unions). Results of the talks and recommendations for future steps of the implementation of sustainability were published in a "Discourse Paper" (BIBB 2015).

In retrospect the talks generated three discussion levels: principled discussions, strategy discussions and pragmatic discussions. The level of principled discussions was marked by skepticism. A lot of participants were of the opinion that sustainability would be a too abstract principle. No distinct consequences can be filtered out for efficient regulations of skilled work and apprenticeship (BIBB 2015, p. 20). On the strategic level a top-down-strategy can be differentiated from a bottom-up-strategy. Critics argued that the BIBB favors a top-down-strategy without concrete ideas how to secure an enthusiastic and continuous participation of skilled workers and apprentices. So top-down-strategies of the implementation of sustainability would fail in the long run (BIBB 2015, p. 22).

Nevertheless, on the pragmatic level of discussions a lot of propositions and recommendations were delivered how to integrate sustainability into the regulatory means of Germany's VET-system. An advanced organizer was created. It contains of all possible starting points of the implementation of sustainability into the regulatory instruments of VET in Germany.

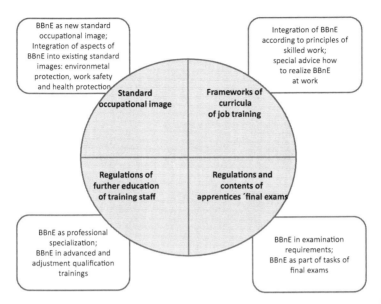

Illustration 2: Advanced Organizer – Implemention of BBnE into VET-regulations.

Translated illustration taken from Mohoric and Kuhlmeier 2015, p. 24 (© Andrea Mohoric).

So the BIBB's experts found out that structural reforms should be done within four areas of VET-regulations. Aspects of BBnE could already be found within two of them. Such aspects were already in frameworks of curricula of job training and in the standard occupational image "environmental protection". The remaining two areas of VET-regulations, further education of training staff and final exams of apprentices, such aspects of sustainability were missing.

After a systematic review of current VET-regulations Bretschneider (2015) concluded that sustainability is mentioned within frameworks of job trainings of apprentices explicitly, if professions are relatively new or if professions are located within domains of environment or installation engineering. Three examples are breeding and care of horses, agricultural laborant or plumbing and heating installer. Standard occupational image environment protection (as cross-sectional task) contains aspects of sustainability, but it is not comprehensive enough. Overall the author, who is occupied in the BIBB-Department of VET-regulations, states an operationalization gap (Bretschneider 2015, p. 4). Sustainability is a guiding principle in economy. But it is still an unsolved challenge to operationalize this principle in a concrete and obligatory manner if professional action on the job is concerned.

At the moment in Germany there is a standard occupational image called "environmental protection". It had been created 20 years ago and was referred to in a lot of regulatory instruments (overview in Kuhlmeier 2015a). An additional standard occupational image called "sustainability" would reflect newer tendencies of resource protection and efficiency within skilled work. Kuhlmeier (2015, p. 5) proposed the following table of contents for this new standard occupational image:

- To examine and to evaluate social, ecological and economical aspects of professional work with perceptions of contradictions and collisions of interests,
- To take into account regional and global effects of personal professional work.
- To consider future consequences, if things are produced and services are rendered,
- To use materials and energy in work processes and resulting applications under criteria of sufficiency, efficiency and consistency,
- To think of life cycles of products and processes if fabrication of products and rendering of services is concerned.

As stated above within two areas of VET-regulations there is a lack of nearly all aspects of sustainability. Most participants of the expert talks agreed on the point that it is very important to integrate the concept of sustainability into final exams of apprentices. That is the most relevant way to reach future skilled staff. As one example Kuhlmeier (2015, p. 7) proposed the following task during future final examinations of plasterers within the construction sector:

> Select materials appropriate for an additional insulation of a facade of a single-family house! Give special consideration to all aspects of resource protection, energetic amortization and disposal of waste!

The fourth and final area of VET-regulations is further education of trained staff. It seems promising to train future experts on sustainability. The will work as change agents and multipliers. Besides of the work on VET-regulations it will be necessary to address humans directly and convince them of the necessity of sustainability in VET. That's why the BIBB will launch further model projects.

3. The years 2016 to 2019: BIBB's new funding priority on sustainability

"From project to structure!" This BIBB-slogan is referring to the next steps of the implementation of sustainability. The BIBB's new funding priority (BIBB 2015a) spans the years 2016 to 2019 and contains of two different tenders:

Tender 1: Implementation of sustainability into the first phase of vocational education and training into the dual system in Germany: The domains trade and commerce are supported only because they were excluded from the first BBnE funding cluster from 2011 to 2014. So this tender can be regarded as an extension of the first funding cluster.

Tender 2: Configuration of sustainable learning locations within institutions of vocational education: This funding cluster refers to enterprises, vocational schools and inter-company training institutions delivering special concepts how to establish locations of sustainability within the VET-system. This tender addresses especially future change agents and multipliers that secure and spread the concept of sustainability. So this tender can be seen as continuation of the work on VET-regulations from 2014 to 2015.

The two funding cluster consists of six model projects each. BIBB will guide the two networks of model projects and will organize the external cooperation with persons and organizations. From the first funding cluster BBnE to the new tenders there is a continuity of experts on sustainability, both within the BIBB and within the scientific monitoring group. The scientific monitoring group of Tender 1 is located at the University of Hamburg again. Scientists involved are nearly the same as in the former funding cluster BBnE. Tender 2 will be monitored by the Research Institute of Vocational Education and Training (f-bb) in Nuremberg. Overall the two tenders include 27 alliance partners (listed in BIBB 2016).

4. Final remarks: Do the BIBB's model projects promote responsible citizenship?

Like a lot of similar institutions of administrative governance, the BIBB in Germany mainly tracks a top-down-strategy in order to establish technical and social innovations and new forms of cooperation between organizations and persons. Model projects in VET mentioned in this paper were planned and initiated on a high level of Germany's central federal administration. Grants were given to diverse organizations in different regions in Germany. Usually these organizations have differentiated expert knowledge concerning Germany's VET-system. Moreover, only management staff of these organizations participates directly in the model projects as partners of the BIBB. The question is if such a top-down approach touches individuals working on a low hierarchical level of organizations and enterprises such as temporary workers, unskilled workers or apprentices.

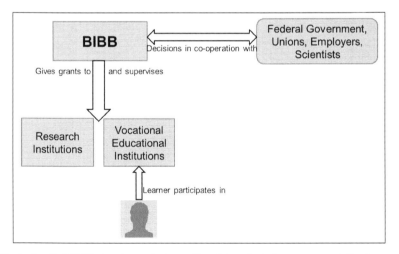

Illustration 3: BIBB's top-down-strategy of model projects (own representation).

The idea of a democratic and responsible citizenship has gained much support within politics of the European Union during the last 20 years (see for example Council of Europe 2010). Responsible citizenship means first of all a strong participation of citizens in the democratic development of their local community. To do so under aspects of sustainability means that individuals have to act according to this principle in daily life. This is to great extent their professional work. The question is how large model projects on sustainability in VET can support the participation of workers of low qualification or low position and of apprentices in a manner that these persons define sustainability as a major objective of daily work.

One fruitful strategy is to distribute easy to read brochures on model projects with examples of good practice to all kind of learners and workers. This is a significant part of BIBB's implementation strategy already. In cooperation with the BMBF the BIBB has designed diverse brochures concerning the funding cluster BBnE that address organizations and persons outside the funding cluster (see for example BMBF 2014). But a real bottom-up strategy would go on further. It has figure out how people being non-experts should be addressed already during the planning phase of model projects. It also has to reflect on possibilities how grants could be given to persons not being part of management staff of qualified organizations. And one has to consider how perspectives of these non-experts and beginners could be an essential part of scientific evaluation of future model projects.

Up to now it has been the problem that non-skilled workers and apprentices are not organized in unions or other pressure groups that could be potential partners of BIBB in talks and cooperation. Perhaps BIBB should reconsider if it opens official boards, committees and workshops to new groups and how to inform and invite these groups. This should be a vision for the next funding period of the BIBB after 2019.

References

Bevir, M. 2013. Governance: A very short introduction. Oxford, Oxford University Press.

BIBB – Federal Institute for Vocational Education and Training 2006. Berufsbildung im FONA-Programm. Ein Querschnittsprojekt des

BIBB zur Nachhaltigen Waldwirtschaft, Bonn. [retrieved from: <https://www.bibb.de/dokumente/pdf/fona_falter_a4_komplett_3. pdf> – September, 28th 2016].

BIBB – Federal Institute for Vocational Education and Training 2010. Förderrichtlinien zur Durchführung des Förderschwerpunktes „Berufliche Bildung für eine nachhaltige Entwicklung" in der zweiten Hälfte der UN-Dekade „Bildung für nachhaltige Entwicklung 2005–2014", Bonn. [retrieved from: <https://www2.bibb.de/bibbtools/dokumente/ pdf/FRL_NE_25_02_2010_4.pdf> – September, 28th 2016].

BIBB – Federal Institute for Vocational Education and Training 2015. Fachgespräche zur strukturellen Verankerung von nachhaltiger Entwicklung in der Berufsbildung unter dem Aspekt der Ordnungsmittel, Bonn. [retrieved from: <https://www.bibb.de/de/37287. php> – September, 28th 2016].

BIBB – Federal Institute for Vocational Education and Training 2015a. Förderrichtlinie zur Durchführung des Modellversuchsförderschwerpunkts „Berufsbildung für nachhaltige Entwicklung 2015–2019" vom 14. September 2015, Bonn. [retrieved from: <https://www2.bibb. de/bibbtools/dokumente/pdf/ab33_berufsbildung_fuer_nachh altige_entwicklung_2015-2019.pdf> – September, 28th 2016].

BIBB – Federal Institute for Vocational Education and Training 2016. Berufsbildung für nachhaltige Entwicklung – Modellversuche 2015–2019. Bonn. [retrieved from: <https://www2.bibb.de/bibbtools/doku mente/pdf/ab33_projektpartner_tabelle_2016.pdf> – September, 28th 2016].

BMBF – Bundesministerium für Bildung und Forschung 2014. Nachhaltigkeit im Berufsalltag. Berufsbildung für nachhaltige Entwicklung. Bonn, BMBF-Referat für Berufsorientierung. [retrieved from: <https://www.bibb.de/dokumente/pdf/23765_BIBB_Broschuere_ Gesichter_Geschichten_21x21_online.pdf> – September, 28th 2016].

BMBF – Bundesministerium für Bildung und Forschung 2015. Umsetzung des Weltaktionsprogramms „Bildung für eine nachhaltige Entwicklung" in Deutschland Eckpunkte für einen Aktionsplan, Bonn. [retrieved from: <https://www.bmbf.de/files/ WAP-Umsetzung_BNE.pdf> – September, 28th 2016].

Bretschneider, M. 2015. Das Konstrukt Nachhaltigkeit und seine Konkretisierung in Ausbildungsordnungen. BIBB – Federal Institute for Vocational Education and Training (ed.): Fachgespräche zur strukturellen Verankerung von nachhaltiger Entwicklung in der Berufsbildung unter dem Aspekt der Ordnungsmittel, Bonn. [retrieved from: <https://www.bibb.de/dokumente/pdf/5_Das_Konstrukt_ Nachhaltigkeit.pdf> – September, 28th 2016].

Council of Europe 2010. Council of Europe Charter on Education for Democratic Citizenship and Human Rights Education. Recommendation CM/Rec(2010)7 adopted by the Committee of Ministers of the Council of Europe on 11th May 2010 and explanatory memorandum. Council of Europe publishing, Strasbourg. [retrieved from: <http://www.coe.int/en/web/edc/charter-on-education-for-d emocratic-citizenship-and-human-rights-education> – September, 28th 2016].

Dehnbostel, P., Diettrich, A., Holz, H. 2010. Modellversuche im Spiegel der Zeit. In BIBB – Federal Institute for Vocational Education and Training (ed.), 40 Jahre Bundesinstitut für Berufsbildung. 40 Jahre Forschen – Beraten – Zukunft gestalten. Bonn, Bundesinstitut für Berufsbildung, Bielefeld, Bertelsmann. [retrieved from: <https:// www.bibb.de/veroeffentlichungen/de/bwp/show/id/6244> – September, 28th 2016].

Deitmer, L. 2004. Management regionaler Netzwerke. Evaluation als Ansatz zur Effizienzsteigerung regionaler Innovationsprozesse. Wiesbaden, Nomos.

DUK – Deutsche UNESCO Kommission 2014. UNESCO Roadmap zur Umsetzung des Weltaktionsprogramms „Bildung für nachhaltige Entwicklung", Bonn. [retrieved from: <https://www.bmbf.de/ files/2015_Roadmap_deutsch.pdf> – September, 28th 2016].

Fischer, M. (ed.) 2014. Qualität in der Berufsausbildung. Anspruch und Wirklichkeit. Bielefeld, BIBB und Bertelsmann.

Hahne, K. and Kutt, K. 2003. Entwurf für einen Orientierungsrahmen „Berufsbildung für eine nachhaltige Entwicklung" vorgelegt zur BIBB/BMBF Fachtagung am 26./27. März 2003 in Osnabrück, Bonn. [retrieved from: <https://www.bibb.de/dokumente/pdf/ft_ nachhalt_orientierungsrahmen.pdf> – September, 28th 2016].

Jenewein, K. 2007. Modellversuche und Entwicklungsprojekte in der Berufsbildung. Zum Selbstverständnis wissenschaftlicher Begleitforschung. Berufsbildung in Wissenschaft und Praxis, 36(1): 5–9.

Kuhlmeier, W. 2015. Strukturelle Verankerung der BBNE in Ausbildungsordnungen. Vortrag am 17. März 2015 auf der Tagung „ Zukunft gestalten – Verantwortung übernehmen. Berufsbildung für nachhaltige Entwicklung: Perspektiven und Strategien 2015+ in Osnabrück. Deutsche Bundesstiftung Umwelt (DBU). [retrieved from: <http://www.bibb.de/dokumente/pdf/Kuhlmeier_Forum1.pdf> – September, 28th 2016].

Kuhlmeier, W. 2015a. Was gibt es schon? Nachhaltigkeit in Ordnungsmitteln. BIBB – Federal Institute for Vocational Education and Training (ed.): Fachgespräche zur strukturellen Verankerung von nachhaltiger Entwicklung in der Berufsbildung unter dem Aspekt der Ordnungsmittel, Bonn. [retrieved from: <https://www.bibb.de/dokumente/pdf/4_Was_gibt_es_schon.pdf> – September, 28th 2016].

Kuhlmeier, W., Mohoric, A., Vollmer, T. (eds.) 2014. Berufsbildung für nachhaltige Entwicklung. Modellversuche 2010–2013: Erkenntnisse, Schlussfolgerungen und Ausblicke. BIBB und Bertelsmann, Bielefeld.

Mohoric, A., Kuhlmeier, W. 2015. Fachgespräche zu Ansatzpunkten für nachhaltige Entwicklung in Ordnungsmitteln, bei Betrieben und durch Instrumente. BIBB – Federal Institute for Vocational Education and Training (ed.) Fachgespräche zur strukturellen Verankerung von nachhaltiger Entwicklung in der Berufsbildung unter dem Aspekt der Ordnungsmittel, Bonn. [retrieved from: <https://www.bibb.de/dokumente/pdf/2_Doku_Fachgespraeche_Langfassung.pdf> – September, 28th 2016].

Philippus, U. 2010. 40 Jahre BIBB – der Hauptausschuss heute. In BIBB – Federal Institute for Vocational Education and Training (ed.), 40 Jahre Bundesinstitut für Berufsbildung. 40 Jahre Forschen – Beraten – Zukunft gestalten. Bonn, Bundesinstitut für Berufsbildung, Bielefeld, Bertelsmann. [retrieved from: <https://www.bibb.de/veroeffentlichungen/de/bwp/show/id/6244> – September, 28th 2016].

UNESO 2014. UNESCO Roadmap for Implementing the Global Action Programme on Education for Sustainable Development, Paris. [retrieved from: <http://unesdoc.unesco.org/imag es/0023/002305/230514e.pdf> – September, 28th 2016].

Ure, U.B. (2015): Governance for Learning Outcomes in European Policy-Making: Qualification Frameworks Pushed through the Open Method of Coordination. International Journal for Research in Vocational Education and Training (IJRVET), 2(4): 268–283. [retrieved from: <http://www.ijrvet.net/index.php/IJRVET/article/ view/116> – September, 28th 2016].

Vollmers, B., Reichwein, W., Effertz, P. 2014. Die wissenschaftliche Begleitung des Verbundes BBNE: Evaluation, Moderation und Dokumentation eines Innovationsnetzwerkes in der beruflichen Bildung. In W. Kuhlmeier, A. Mohoric, T. Vollmer (eds.), Berufs- bildung für nachhaltige Entwicklung. Modellversuche 2010–2013: Erkenntnisse, Schlussfolgerungen und Ausblicke. Bielefeld, BIBB und Bertelsmann, 119–134.

Vollmers, B. and Winzier, D. 2013. Sustainable Development (SD) in Technical Vocational Education and Training (TVET) – A Pilot Programme to Foster "Green" Business. In M. Gessler, L. Deitmer, S. Manning (eds.), Proceedings of the ECER VETNET Confer- ence 2013. Papers presented as part of the VETNET programme for ECER 2013 at Istanbul (10th to 13th September 2013). [retrieved from: <www.ecer-vetnet-2013.wifo-gate.org> – September, 28th 2016].

Westhoff, G. and Ernst, H. 2016. Heterogenität und Vielfalt in der beru- flichen Bildung. Konzepte, Handlungsansätze und Instrumente aus der Modellversuchsforschung. Bielefeld, BIBB und Bertelsmann.

Patricia Olmos-Rueda

The Role of VET into Social Participation and Self-determination of Disabled People as Full Citizens

1. Introduction

Traditionally, vocational education and training (VET) has been directly linked to the labour market in terms of qualification and qualified work-foce. However, this point of view is a very restrictive view because VET goes beyong the labour market. It is worth highlighting VET provides of personal and social benefits and makes possible to achieve not only labour but also personal and social outcomes (CEDEFOP 2011). In terms of McMahon (2009), VET provides the person with marketed and non-marketed benefits.

According to this perspective, it is worth noting that VET, as a form of education, supports social inclusion and develops a crucial role into the indivual's active participation in society. VET contributes to increase educational and labour participation, understood both education and work as forms of social and civic participation. In other words, VET contributes to the individual's capacity to participate in society as full citizens, therefore contributing to the well-being of the individual and society (CEDEFOP 2011; Meuronen, Moon and Patecka 2014).

Focusing, for example, on the current labour market which require high levels of qualification and new mediating concepts to cope with demands of working effectively (Guile and Griffiths 2010), people's difficulties for fulfilling these requirements prevent them from active participation and consequently they are at risk of exclusion so in many cases there are persistent patterns of social exclusion (Smith 2009). Generally, these difficulties are linked to the lack of qualification and a wider range of personal, social and labour skills that, at the same time, is consequence of barriers to vocational training and little chance of participating in successful educational and vocational training contexts. In many cases, VET is the pathway of these people for fostering training success, learning required skills and having the capacity to adapt in the changing labour market for their personal and social development. That is, to take part in VET contexts can open doors to possibilities in education and employment as well as encourages more active participation in society (Meuronen, Moon and Patecka 2014).

Within this framework of reference, VET is perceived as a pathway not only for acquiring skills for working, but also for people's personal and social development towards an autonomous, reponsible and participative adulthood as full citizens.

However, it is worth noting although training develops a crucial role into labour and social inclusion, it is not the only one element to be considered and it is worthwile noting training without adequate supports is insufficent. This fact has been taken into account by employment policies that since the seventies have considered training, and more concretely vocational training, as a key strategy in order to improve labour opportunities of all those who have special difficulties to access to the labour market (Comisión Europea 2000; Salvà and Nicolau 2000), taking into account this labour market as an important sphere of social participation and VET an important resource that develops a crucial role into social participation and self-determination of people with disability.

How VET develops this role and contributes to social participation and self-determination is the goal of this paper where elements such as social roles, social capital, identity capital and social, labour, cultural and personal development, among others, are going to be analyzed.

2. Social participation and self-determination of people with disability: VET challenges

In accordance with World Health Organisation (2011) dealing with disability is quite complex and controversial. On the one hand, disability as term is diverse, dynamic and multidimensional. On the other hand, the interaction of three factors has to be considered on its definition: health conditions, personal factors and environmental factors. In other words, the first barrier for dealing with disability is to be aware that disability is a part of the human condition, human rights issue and a social concern issue. For example, some disabled people are denied autonomy and self-determination for being full citizens when the condition of disability (especially intellectual disability) prevents those who are disabled from taking their own decisions about questions such as how they want to live their life as autonomous adults, what kind of job they want to get, or what kind of training they want to take, giving some examples.

Anyway, people with disability are one of the most vulnerable groups into the changing current social and labour contexts. Their disadvantage in relation to their participation into education, social contexts and labour market is well known. People with disabilities face more barriers than the rest of the population for accessing to these contexts of personal development, mainly to those that are related to disabled people as a workforce, although here we have to take into account the diversity of the disability; people with an intellectual disability are in more disadvantatge (Cavallaro, Foley, Saunders and Bowman 2005). As United Nations (1996) states they are the first who are dismissed and the latest who are contracted therefore disabled people's active participation in the society as full citizens is often questioned. In this event, disability becomes a social challenge. However, nowadays, employers sometimes prefer to hire people with tiny disabilities in order to get both the workforce and the tax reduction. So, in a way, disability is something that to a certain extent may have a profitable value as well.

3. VET benefits of people with disability: Social capital, identity capital and self-determination

Generally, disabled people have lower educational and training levels (Cavallaro *et al.* 2005; Nechvoglod and Griffin 2011) which leads them to unstable jobs and increases their permanent difficulties for accessing decent jobs; that is, to satisfactory jobs, with decent wages and sufficient in quality and quantity (CINTERFOR/OIT 2001). Lack of education and training of people with disability weakens their role in areas of social activity and leads them to stay out of personal, social and labour active participation processes (CEDEFOP 2011).

European Parliament (resolution of 16 September 1992 on the rights of mental handicapped), UNESCO (2000; article 14), European Commission (2010) and European Agency for Development in Special Needs Education (2012) claim that society is responsible of disabled people's integration in all the social participation spheres as full citizens. These social participation spheres involve education, training, work, rehabilitation, social assistance, civic rights, housing, to give some. In this way, one proposal is defined: ensuring the right to VET.

As we can see, training becomes a crucial tool for disabled people's social participation (Olmos 2009, 2013b) and VET becomes usually – but not always – the training pathway for them (Mavromaras and Polidano 2011).

Training contributes to social, labour, cultural and personal development of people with disability. Its main goal is they can develop a variety of social roles. VET, as a kind of training focused on people with disability as a key group, contributes to develop and improve both their education qualification and professional role as well as their employment chance and prospect (Callado 2008; Cavallaro *et al.* 2005; ILO 2000; Jones, Latreille and Sloane 2006; Kidd, Sloane and Ferko 2000; Mavromaras and Polidano 2011; UNESCO 2004).

In other words, people with disability become a challenge for VET; insofar it works for fostering disabled people's social participation and individual development (Rothman *et al.* 2013).

According to some authors and studies (CEDEFOP 2011; Colley 2003; Descy and Tessaring 2002; Field and Malcolm 2010; Hyland

2003; Preston and Green 2008; Schuller *et al.* 2002), benefits of VET for people with disability are understood in terms of identity capital and social capital; that is, these benefits are not only individual ones, but also both social and professional and contribute to their well-being and quality of life as citizens.

Social capital is a complex term that has been explored in relation to educational and training contexts among others such as economic, sociological and political (Millán and Gordon 2004). It is not a new idea but it is a new development of an old one (Ferragina 2009). The basis of social capital is social networks that make possible collective action in order to procure an advantage for the individual. This is the idea behind *it's not what you know, it's how you know* (Woolcock 2001; Woolcock and Narayad 2000).

Bourdieu (1986), Coleman (1988), Putnam (2000) and Côté (2005) state social capital is a resource that facilitates actions between actors and among actors within the social structure (*e.g.* cooperation, interaction, reciprocity, exchange which leads to achievement of individual goals). It is the aggregate of actual or potential resources that are linked to possession of a durable network based on unconditional trust and reciprocity among members; that is, on bonding relationships (dense ties to other networks or union ties) and bridging relationships (weak ties to other networks or bridge ties). For Forbes and McCartney (2010) these sorts of relationships are sub-types of social capital.

All these authors understand social capital entails the recognition of a person as a member of a group and this does not exist in isolation because it is the aggregate of many forms of capital such as physical, economic, educational, cultural or human capital interrelated (Jochum 2003). Someone can mobilize more resources as a member of a group than as an isolated individual in order to further his/her social, professional or educational development.

Social practices are developed in social structures. Training and work-related learning are forms of these social structures that provide people with disabilty with personal resources and tools such as particular knowledge, occupational and social skills, attitudes, and capacities to participate in civic life and in the labour market (Acar 2011; Colley, Hodkinsos and Malcolm 2002; Côté 2002, 2005; Helve and Bynner 2007; Jochum 2003). Therefore, training contexts as VET become pathways on bonding and bridging for becoming a full member of society. As CEDEFOP (2011) affirms, a full citizen as this allows establishing and improving social networks and develops a social role that can change the status of people with disability in society.

Nevertheless, although social capital is generated collectively, this can be used individually (Ferragina 2009). Here is where the concept of identity capital takes shape.

Identity capital is understood as a developmental-social psychological approach to identity formation (Côté and Schwartz 2002). Individuals form, validate and preserve their self-definition as members in social structures. Individuals need to nurture and develop personal resources to function effectively within these social structures (Côté 2005). This process of developing personal resources to function effectively within social structures (*e.g.* workplace) defines the concept of identity capital. How individuals score on identity capital acquisition depends on their social networks (connections) and on the resources which are acquired from those connections (Luyckx and Hans de Witte 2011; Weller 2009).

This approach of concepts of social capital and identity capital shows that individual identity cannot be understood without social identity. The individual's sense of identity (self-control and self-determination) is a consequence of individual's experiences in either training or working within social contexts (Guile and Griffiths 2010). For example, when people with disability is undertaking VET programmes, they enhance their identity, improve their self-control, change their perception of their own capabilities and feel they can continue their learning process in order to gain access to qualified employment. In this event, VET is a kind of social context; therefore, when disability condition prevents people to gain access to training contexts as VET, disabled people's access to social and individual benefits of VET are being denied. In other words, disability condition can deny disabled people's social interactions that determine their personal development, their capacity of self-determination and their possibilities to develop a social role as full citizens.

Within this perspective, it is possible to state VET becomes a good alternative for people with disability in supporting their social inclusion and participation (Nechvoglod and Griffin 2011) and obviously, in increasing their autonomy and control over their own choices; that is, in improving their self-determination.

According to some authors (Algozzine *et al.* 2001; Field, Sarver and Shaw 2003; Martin, Van Dycke, D'Ottavio and Nickerson 2007), self-determination is a key factor for disabled people in choosing their own choices for becoming full citizens, giving as an example the opportunity of taking their own decisions about their vocational pathways.

First of all, it is worth noting self-determination is an essential component of the well-being and a key variable of the quality of life what is a natural human tendency. People look for personal well-being and their active, responsible and autonomous participation not only in personal contexts, but also in social contexts for their development. It is why self-determination cannot be understood without quality of life.

Authors as Schalock and Verdugo (2003, 2007) and Schalock (2009) define an integral model of quality of life where different levels and dimensions are involved for a correct human functioning. According to these authors, for achieving an optimal level of quality of life the person has to successfully function in each defined level and dimension. Concretely, these authors identify a total of four levels where eight dimensions for the human functioning are identified for achieving optimal personal results of quality of life. In other words, this multidimensional model requires that the individual develops and improves his/her: 1) physical and 2) material well-being (health care, housing, employment, etc.); 3) personal development (education, functional skills, communicative skills, etc.) and 4) self-determination (autonomy, decision making, self-control, etc.); 5) social inclusion (participation, development of social roles, etc.), 6) interpersonal relationships (family, community, peers, etc.), and 7) rights (equality, respect, civic responsibilities, etc.); 8) emotional well-being (security, self-perception, stable environments, motivation, etc.).

Each one of above dimensions is involved in different levels of achievement. Dimensions 1 and 2 are the first one, dimensions 3 and 4 are the second one, dimensions 5, 6 and 7 are the third one, and dimension 8 is the fourth and last one. This model requires, on the one hand, the gradually achievement of these eight dimensions; that is, working from the first level to the fourth one and, on the other hand, a support system, understood as all those resources (human, material and functional resources) and personalized strategies that guide the individual in multiple development contexts.

As we can see, according to this model, social participation and self-determination are dimensions of quality of life. Now the question is how VET benefits these both dimensions social participation and self-determination.

It is true that training itself is not a sufficient condition for achieving successful personal and social development although it is necessary. Educational and training processes prepare people for developing those social roles that make possible social participation which implies responsibility, autonomy, personal initiative, independence, make decisions, capacity for controlling our own life or adaptability, to name a few. In other words, we are talking about self-determination understood as a personal process where the individual is the main responsible of his/her life choices without external influences (Whemeyer 1992).

Training in self-determination requires, among others, developing personal capacities and social skills, providing with chance for choosing or providing with adequate supports for overcoming the obstacles.

Working on self-determination also implies working people's capacity of self-control on their development contexts, being labour contexts one of the most critical for people with disability. According to Olmos (2011, 2013a, 2013b, 2014), work on key competencies or basic skills is needed into this training process for making possible disabled people's development in self-determination as one of the social dimensions of human functioning. Within this model framework, VET becomes a crucial factor to the extent that VET has as a goal to provide disabled people with resources for responding and adapting to social and labour requirements effectively. At the same time, this goal and requirement become a VET challenge that has to work for developing on people with disability the minimal mastery level of competencies that labour market requires as well as work for personal development and social participation of people with disability.

As we can see, training and employment are closely linked. One requires from the other. Related to people with disability, training is a crucial issue because it is one of the handicaps that they have in order to gain access to the job market. The low qualification of people with disability and the lack of professional training supply for them increase their barriers for participating in the society as full citizens.

Within this framework, VET becomes a crucial pathway for people with disability and it is necessary to focus on how to adapt VET for reponding disabled people's needs for becoming full citizens, who take their own decicions and develop active social roles, being their partici- pation in the job market one of these active social roles.

Authors as Nietupski (2007) or Schmidt and Smith (2007) state it is necessary to optimize work experience for people with disability through strong and adapted VET programmes that: 1) work with per- sonalised and intensive career support will maximise the possibility of entering employment, due to disabled peopole's increased vocational knowledge and interest; 2) work for independent living; 3) work for promoting disabled people's confidence to participate as part of society as a workforce.

In accordance with these authors' arguments, a study in 2009 (Olmos 2009) shows how social and labour agents, who work for integrating people with disability in social and labour contexts, argue VET has to work on behalf of people with disability for being full cit- izens (Olmos 2009). In other words, it is necessary that VET and the VET curriculum work on social participation through development of social skills and key skills for getting a workplace, that is, working on social and labour inclusion; on employability and adaptability; on self-determination; on providing disabled people with individual sup- ports of training and guiding where the role of a tutor or coach in train- ing and employment contexts is crucial; and, in collaboration between training and employment services.

4. Working on a shared model

Developing the role of VET into social participation and self-determination of people with disability as full citizens requires a shared responsi- bility. In accordance with Forbes and McCartney (2010) or Guile and Griffiths (2010), it would be necessary thinking about a connective and multi-systemic model where bonding and bridging relationships would be interrelated.

Within this perspective, Olmos (2009, 2011) suggest a model where three levels are identified. In each one some crucial factors are involved. The first one (macro-level) is the national on where family, community, society, economy and policy are the key factor. The second one (meso-level) is the practice level where labour market, entrepreneurs, tutors and integration services, where VET programmes for people with disability are developed, are the key factors. The third one (micro-level) is the individual level where people with disability as individual, their knowledge and skills are involved.

This model requires from these different levels and their integrated factors working in collaboration for guiding people with disability to gain access or returning to the job market and/or educational contexts; that is, to be involved in social participation contexts where they can take their own decisions supported by others.

In this way, this model works for examining disabled people's self-control and self-perception about their personal resources and for knowing what is what training and labour context require and expect from people with disability.

While the macro-level (society, economy, etc.) and meso-level (labour market, entrepreneurs, etc.) are who determine which are the minimal requirement that are expected from disabled people in training and labour context, the micro-level is who works the awareness process on disabled people's self-control and self-perception. Tutors and integration services have an important role as support for guiding disabled people in this process. They have to work with disabled people for awareness on their capacities and capabilities and training them in order to develop all those minimal competences that the job market requires from them. Nevertheless, tutors and integration services have to work in collaboration with families, who have to support tutors' actions, and with entrepreneurs, supporting and guiding them during the process of labour integration of people with disability into the workplace, offering supports and guiding them for introducing natural supports in this workplace in order to make possible a good integration process. It is possible due to training and development of training-based and work-based approaches that necessarily requires from this collaboration between training contexts (tutors, Integration services) and labour contexts (job market, entrepreneurs).

As we can see, this model works in order for people with disability to become aware of their weaknesses and lack of personal resources in order to make decisions. This process requires a formal and informal mentoring process (Colley, Hodkinson and Malcolm 2002) where people with disability, tutors, families and organisations collaborate to achieve outcomes in developing the social participation, social inclusion and self-determination: for example, they work together to identify disabled people's needs, to rectify their skill deficits, to develop their active citizenship, to educate them in social awareness, to allow them experiment with and create new identities, to change their dispositions in line with social norms and values, or to enhance their social capital ties, to name a few.

Training and guidance processes provide people with disability with personal resources for an effective social participation therefore VET, as training process, is a way to achieve these outcomes. Nevertheless, it is only possible if VET is understood within a social perspective where reciprocal social networks such as family, community, friends, institutions, peers, tutors, entrepreneurs and so on are crucial elements in supporting people with disability in acquiring key resources associated with optimal identity development and in guiding young people into their full social participation as full citizens (Côté 2002, 2005; Schwartz, Côté and Jensen 2005).

5. Conclusions

As we have seen before, to deny the access to successful vocational education and training of people with disability prevents them of real opportunities for choosing and leads them to be excluded of contexts of social participation, such as workplace, as well as for being part of society as full citizens. As CEDEFOP (2003) and ILO (2008) state, in the practice the range of training options open to people with disability is limited to training programmes oriented to low skills, low productivity employment or low-paid work; that is, the oppositive as what is know as a decent job: sufficient in quality and quantity, stable jobs, with decent wages (CINTERFOR/OIT 2001). These are issues social concern as well as social challenge.

Working on training for improving disabled people's basic skills or key competencies is important for giving them the opportunity to gain access to spheres of society and make their active participation happen.

If we consider labour as a key social context for becoming full citizens, access to vocational education and training is crucial. As authors suchs as Wagner and Davis (2006) or Eisenman (2007) claim, the integration of workplace behaviours, occupational skills and careers awareness is critical, as well as providing work exploration opportunities to help people with disability identify their social roles and be proactive in developing their social participation and self-determination and auntonomy.

Achieving this is possible through VET due to the fact VET can offer people with disability the opportunity to learn in a combined approach where training-based and work-based approaches are developed. This fact makes possible people with disability interact into workplace communities where interrelationship with others is possible and where they can be responsible and autonomous; they can take decisions and they can transfer their knowledge, skills, abilities and attitudes in order to develop their own social role as full citizens.

In this event, VET can contribute to disabled people's personal and social growth and this requires training based on self-determination, self-comprehension, acquiring social skills linked to responsible citizenship therefore VET develops a crucial role into their social participation and self-determination.

In the light of this reflection, we can conclude VET can support people with disability to be aware of their different and multiple opportunities in order to become full citizens in the current changing society. Nevertheless, maybe the lack of opportunities, limited range of VET options and poor access to vocational education and training that, nowadays, people with disability still encounter for accessing to VET as well as the direct consequences that are derived due to this fact (ILO 2008; Nagle 2001) should make us reflect on the necessity of rethinking the VET curriculum in order to make VET more accessible for people with disability. Here is opened the framework for future researches and some tips have been suggested for its development.

References

Acar, E. 2011. Effects of social capital on academic success: A narrative synthesis. Educational Research and Reviews, 6(6): 456–461.

Algozzine, B., Browder, D., Karvonen, M., Test, D. W., and Wood, W. M. 2001. Effects of interventions to promote self-determination for individuals with disabilities. Review of Educational Research, 71(2): 219–277.

Bourdieu, P. 1986. The forms of capital. In J. Richardson (ed.), Handbook of Theory and Research for the Sociology of Education. New York, Greenwood.

Callado, J. A. 2008. La formación del discapacitado necesaria para su inserción laboral. Innovación y experiencas educatives, 9. [retrieved from: <http://www.csi-csif.es/andalucia/modules/mod_ense/revista/pdf/Numero_9/JUAN_A_CALLADO_1.pdf> – March, 10th 2016].

Cavallaro, T., Foley, P., Saunders, J., and Bowman, K. 2005. People with a disability in vocational education and training A statistical compendium. Melbourne, NVEAC.

CEDEFOP. 2003. Beating the odds Integrating people with disabilities into lifelong learning and the world of work. Policy, Practice and Partnership: Getting to work on Lifelong Learning, 2 and 3 June 2003 at Cedefop Thessaloniki Lifelong learning: thematic workshop report.

CEDEFOP. 2011. Vocational education and training is good for you. The social benefits of VET for individuals. Luxembourg, Publications Office of the European Union.

CINTERFOR/ILO 2001. Training for decent work. Montevideo, Cinterfor.

Coleman, J. 1988. Social Capital in the Creation of Human Capital. The American Journal of Sociology, 94, Supplement Organizations and

Institutions: Sociological and Economic Approaches to the Analysis of Social Structure, S95–S120.

Colley, H. 2003. Engagement mentoring for 'disaffected' youth: A new model of mentoring for social inclusion. British Educational Research Journal, 29(4): 521–542.

Colley, H., Hodkinson, P., and Malcolm, J. 2002. Non-formal learning: mapping the conceptual terrain. A Consultation Report. Leeds: University of Leeds Lifelong Learning Institute. [retrieved from: <http://www.infed.org/archives/e-texts/colley_informal_learning. htm> – March, 10th 2016].

Comisión Europea. 2000. Establecer políticas activas de empleo. Principales enseñanzas derivadas de las iniciativas de recursos humanos. Luxembourg, Oficina de Publicaciones Oficiales de las Comunidades Europeas.

Côté, J. E. 2002. The Role of Identity Capital in the Transition to Adulthood: The Individualization Thesis Examined. Journal of Youth Studies, 5(2): 117–134.

Côté, J. E. 2005. Identity capital, social capital and the wider benefits of learning: generating resources facilitative of social cohesion. London Review of Education, 3(3): 221–237.

Côté, J. E. and Schwartz, S. J. 2002. Comparing psychological and sociological approaches to identity: Identity status, identity capital, and the individualization process. Journal of Adolescence 25: 571−586.

Descy, P. and Tessaring, M. 2002. Formar y aprender para la competencia profesional. Segundo Informe de la Investigación sobre formación profesional en Europa: Resumen ejecutivo. Luxemburgo, Cedefop, EUR-OP.

Eisenman, L. T. 2007. Self-determination interventions: Building a foundation for school completion. Remedial and Special Education, 28(1): 2–8.

European Agency for Development in Special Needs Education. 2012. Vocational Education and Training: Policy and Practice in the field of Special Needs Education – Literature Review. Odense, Denmark, European Agency for Development in Special Needs Education.

European Commission. 2010. European Disability Strategy 2010–2020: A renewed commitment to a barrier-free Europe. COM(2010) 636 Final.

Ferragina, E. 2009. Social Capital and Equality: Tocqueville's Legacy. Working Paper No. 515. Luxembourg, Income Study (LIS), asbl.

Field, J. and Malcolm, I. 2010. Learning in emotional labour and emotion work. In, L. Cooper and S.Walters (eds.), Learning/work: turning work and learning inside out (pp. 169–181). Cape Town, Human Sciences Research Council Press.

Field, S., Sarver, M. D., and Shaw, S. F. 2003. Self-determination: A key to success in post-secondary education for students with learning disabilities. Remedial and Special Education, 24(6): 339–349.

Forbes, J. and Mccartney, E. 2010. Social capital theory: A cross-cutting analytic for teacher/therapist work in integrating children's services? Child Language Teaching and Therapy, 26(3): 321–334.

Guile, D. and Griffiths, T. 2010. Learning Through Work Experience. Journal of Education and Work, 14(1): 113–131.

Helve, H. and Bynner, J. 2007. Youth and Social Capital. London, Tufnell Press.

Hyland, T. 2003. Work-based learning programmes and social capital. Journal of In-Service Education, 29(1): 49–60.

ILO. 2000. Training for employment: Social inclusion, productivity and youth employment Human resources training and d evelopment: Vocational guidance and vocational training International Labour Conference. 88th Session, 30 May–15 June 2000. Report 5.

ILO. 2008. Skills for improved productivity, employment growth and development. International Labour Conference, 97th Session.

Jochum, V. 2003. Social capital: beyond the theory. London, National Council for Voluntary Organizations.

Jones, M., Latreille, P., and Sloane, P. 2006. Disability, gender and the British labour market. Oxford Economic Papers 58: 407–449.

Kidd, M., Sloane, P., and Ferko, I. 2000. Disability and the labour market: an analysis of British males. Journal of Human Resources 19: 961–981.

Luyckx, K. and Hans De Witte, L. G. 2011. Perceived instability in emerging adulthood: The protective role of identity capital. Journal of Applied Developmental Psychology 32: 137–145.

Martin, J. E., Van Dycke, J., D'Ottavio, M., and Nickerson, K. 2007. The student-directed summary of performance: Increasing student and family involvement in the transition planning process. Career Development for Exceptional Individuals, 30(1): 13–26.

Mavromaras, K. and Polidano, C. 2011. Improving the Employment Rates of People with Disabilities through Vocational Education. IZA Discussion Paper No. 5548.

McMahon, W. 2009. Higher learning, greater good: the private and social benefits of higher education. Washington DC, John Hopkins University Press.

Meuronen, T., Moon, J., and Patecka, A. 2014. Social Inclusion through VET – New Opportunities for NEETs. Solidar Foundation. [retrieved from: <http://www.solidar.org/IMG/pdf/69_solidar_briefing.pdf> – March, 10th 2016].

Millán, R. and Gordon, S. 2004. Capital social: una lectura de tres perspectivas clásicas. Revista Mexicana de Sociología, 66(4): 711–747.

Nagle K. 2001. Transition to employment and community life for youths with visual impairments: Current status and future directions. Journal of Visual Impairment and Blindness, 95(12): 725–738.

Nechvoglod, L. and Griffin, T. 2011. The attitudes of people with a disability to undertaking VET training. Melbourne, NVEAC.

Nietupski, J. A. 2008. Connecting students to careers. Techniques: Connecting Education and Careers, 83(2): 26–29.

Olmos, P. 2009. Empleabilidad y adaptabilidad de los jóvenes con inteligencia límite y sus procesos de integración laboral: hacia un modelo de formación y de orientación para su inserción en el mundo del trabajo. [retrieved from: <http://hdl.handle.net/2072/41959> – March, 10th 2016].

Olmos, P. 2011. Orientación y formación para la integración laboral del colectivo de jóvenes vulnerables: la inserción laboral mediante estrategias de empleabilidad [thesis]. [retrieved from: <http://www.tdx.cat/handle/10803/51432> – March, 10th 2016].

Olmos, P. 2013a. Entender un modelo para la integración educativolaboral desde la perspectiva histórico-cultural. Nuances: estudos sobre Educação, 24(1): 147–162.

Olmos, P. 2013b. Los desafíos de la formación con el colectivo funcionamiento intelectual límite. In, C. Ruiz, A. Navío, M. Fandos, and P. Olmos (coord.), Formación para el Trabajo en tiempos de crisi. Balance y prospectiva (pp.197–206). Madrid, Tornapunta Ediciones.

Olmos, P. 2014. Competencias básicas y procesos perceptivos: factores claves en la formación y orientación de los jóvenes en riesgo de exclusión educativa y sociolaboral. Revista de investigación educativa, 32(2): 531–546.

Preston, J. and Green, A. 2008. The role of vocational education and training in enhancing social inclusion and cohesion. In, P. Descy and M. Tessaring (eds.), Modernising vocational education and training: fourth report on vocational training research in Europe: background report, Volume 1. Luxembourg, Publications Office of the European Union.

Putnam, R. D. 2000. Bowling alone: The collapse and revival of American community. New York, Simon & Schuster.

Rothman, S., Shah, Ch., Underwood, C., McMillan, J., Brown, J., and McKenzie, P. 2013. National Report on Social Equity in VET 2013. Melbourne, NVEAC.

Salvà, F. and Nicolau, I. 2000. Formación e inserción laboral. Conceptos básicos, políticas, programas y recursos para la intervención. Madrid, Pirámide.

Schalock, R. 2009. La Nueva Definición de Discapacidad Intelectual, los Apoyos Individuales y los Resultados Personales. En M. A. Verdugo, T. Nieto, B. Jordán de Urríes, and M. Crespo, Mejorando Resultados Personales para una Vida de Calidad (pp. 69–88). Salamanca, Amarú.

Schalock, R. and Verdugo, M. A. 2003. Calidad de vida. Manual para profesionales de la educación, salud y servicios sociales. Madrid, Alianza.

Schalock, R. and Verdugo, M. A. 2007. El concepto de calidad de vida en los servicios y apoyos para personas con discapacidad intelectual. Revista Española sobre discapacidad intel·lectual, vol 38(4), n. 224, 21–36.

Schuller, T., Brassett-Grundy, A., Green, A., Hammond, C., and Preston, J. 2002. Learning, continuity and change in adult life. Wider Benefits of Learning Research Report No 3. London, Institute of Education. Centre for Research on Wider Benefits of Learning.

Smith, D. I. 2009. Changes in transitions: the role of mobility, class and gender. Journal of Education and Work, 22(5): 369–390.

Schmidt, M. A. and Smith, D. L. 2007. Individuals with disabilities' perceptions on preparedness for the workforce and factors that limit employment. Work: A Journal of Prevention, Assessment and Rehabilitation, 28(1): 13–21.

Schwartz, S. J., Côté, J. E., and Jensen, J. (2005). Identity and Agency in Emerging Adulthood: Two Developmental Routes in the Individualization Process. Youth & Society, 37(2): 201–229.

UNESCO. 2004. Normative instruments concerning technical and vocational education. Revised recommendation concerning technical and vocational education (2001) and Convention on technical and vocational education (1989). [retrieved from: <http://unesdoc.unesco.org/images/0014/001406/140603e.pdf> – March, 10th 2016].

UNESCO. 2000. Charter of Fundamental Rights of the European Union. OJ C 364, 18.12.2000. Official Journal of the European Union.

United Nations. 1996. Programa de acción mundial par alas personas con discapacidad y Normas uniformes sobre la igualdad de oportunidades para las personas con discapacidad. Madrid, Artegraf.

Wagner, M. and Davis, M. A. 2006. How are we preparing students with emotional disturbances for the transition to young adulthood? Findings from the National Longitudinal Transition Study-2. Journal of Emotional & Behavioral Disorders, 14(2): 86–98.

Weller, S. 2009. Young people's social capital: complex identities, dynamic networks. Ethnic and Racial Studies, 33(5): 872–888.

Woolcock, M. 2001. The Place of Social Capital in Understanding Social and Economic Outcomes. ISUMA Canadian Journal of Policy Research, 2(1): 11–17.

Woolcock, M. and Narayan, D. 2000. Social capital: implications for development theory, research and policy. World Bank Research Observer, 15(2): 225–250.

World Health Organisation. 2011. World report on disability. [retrieved from: <http://www.who.int/disabilities/world_report/2011/report. pdf> – March, 10th 2016].

Katerina Arkoudi-Vafea

Students of Vocational Training Centers in Greece and Financial Crisis

1. Introduction

In Greece one of the structural elements of Lifelong Learning are the Vocational Training Centers (VTCs) which are mostly private. They were established in the late 1990s during the 3rd Community Support Framework from the European Union and they are supervised and certified by the National Organization for the Certification of Qualifications & Vocational Guidance (EOPPEP). Their main projects are co-financed by the European Union and the Greek state and they cater for the acquisition of skills for different groups of people. Some skills that are being taught in VTCs are Information and Communications Technology (ICT) skills, Language skills, Hygiene and Safety in the Workplace, Basic Principles of Labor Law, Job Search Techniques, Environmental Studies, and Finance. Nowadays VTCs work mainly with unemployed who, through European Union (EU) programs, are trained in VTCs in order to be more competitive by acquiring new skills and find employment.

At the beginning of their creation, VTCs attracted a target group which is quite different than today. Few people – compared to these days – were unemployed and it was quite easy to get a job even without many skills. But the last few years the reality is quite different: Greece is in deep recession and has a great unemployment rate of 26.5% in February 2014 – about double the average level of unemployment in the euro zone, which was 12.1% in October 2013 (Stamouli 2014). Economic crisis has even driven people with experience and great careers to unemployment and thus to seek further training in VTCs. Also there have been differences between rural and urban areas regarding, for example, the educational level of the students and their incentives for studying in VTCs.

This research explores the profile of the students of Vocational Training Centers in Greece in 2004 and 2014 and the effect of the economic crisis on them. Economic crisis has cause big changes in Greek society. By applying the human capital theory, the study contextualizes and analyzes the similarities and differences and determines how the global economic crisis affects the students' profile in all the three research sites: urban, rural and island. Choosing 2004 and 2014 as a year to compare is not random. In Greece, in 2004, there was an illusion of prosperity as, among others, the Olympic Games were held and it gave the impression of a strong economy and of progression on many levels. Consequently, people had the possibility, among others, to study, to build or buy a house, to start a business, to earn easy money, to live with high-living standards even though many of those were substantiated with long term bank loans, which were thought then that would be easy to repay. Few people – compared to these days – were unemployed and it was quite easy to get a job even for the less skilled. The research was conducted in 2014, therefore the ten-year span is indicative of the change that has taken place.

In the past, there has been some small scale research about the profile of the VTC student in Greece and most of them have been within the framework of larger studies. This study is thus a contribution to the academic field because it explores in a ten-year timeframe the demographics, the motives and obstacles of the VTC students, which is an area that has not been addressed sufficiently yet.

2. VTCs

In Greece one of the structural elements of Lifelong Learning are the Vocational Training Centers (VTCs) which are mostly private. They were established in the late 1990s during the 3rd Community Support Framework from the European Union. Their main projects are co-financed by the European Union and the Greek state and they cater for the acquisition of skills for different groups of people.

VTCs train adults and implement training programs addressed to the adult population of the country. They belong to the non-formal education. They offer short term education: from 1 week up to six months programs. The schooling is free, and most of the times it is sponsored. If the program is a sponsored one the students of the VTCs are getting about 5€ per hour of training upon the completion of program of education. The educational level of VTC students varies from persons that have not finished primary school to persons with postgraduate studies. The level of education in the VTCs also varies according to the program: There are programs of high educational level who address to students with higher education in order to specialize them in a specific skill, for example "Executives of software applications development – education in programming language ABAP-SAP" and programs that address to students with low educational level like "Wood processing". Some skills that are being taught in VTCs are Information and Communications Technology (ICT) skills, Language skills, Hygiene and Safety in the Workplace, Basic Principles of Labor Law, Job Search Techniques, Environmental Studies, and Finance. Nowadays VTCs work mainly with unemployed who, through European Union (EU) programs, are trained in VTCs in order to be more competitive by acquiring new skills and find employment.

3. Research aim – research questions

The aim of the research is to explore how the students of VTCs have changed during the last 10 years in Greece and therefore the following research questions were stated:

- What was and what is VTC student's profile of the academic year 2003–2004 and 2013–2014 respectively and what are their differences?

• Has the economic crisis affected the change of VTC student's profile from 2004 to 2014?

4. Methods & methodology

Through the literature review of international and Greek literature it
became clear that the research of motives and obstacles involves many
factors that makes it difficult to imprint an accurate image of adults'
participation in the learning procedure and also to compare with findings reported in similar researches of the past. Those factors are associated on one hand with the analysis of parameters and documentation of
the adults' participation in education (for example age range) and on the
other hand, with the ways that social subjects give meaning to critical
terms such as adult education or participation.

The research was quantitative and was based into two different data
sources: To analyze the student of 2003–2004, secondary data were
used from three different VTCs. To analyze the student of 2013–2014 a
web based self-completion questionnaire was used in the above VTCs
to be responded by students that were educated this academic year.

The secondary data were asked from the above three VTCs. An
email was sent to them explaining about the research, the data needed,
the way data would be processed under the view of confidentiality and
anonymity. The data were provided back through email, had info about
the year and month of the educational program, the name of the education program, the student's sex, employment status, and length of unemployment if unemployed.

In addition to the analysis of the secondary data, a questionnaire
was developed to obtain information directly from the VTC students for
the academic year 2014. The questionnaire was designed in the English
language and then was translated in Greek in order for the participants
to fill it in. It was then digitized with the use of Google Forms and
hosted in the following webpage (<http://erevnakek.weebly.com>). It
contained both closed-ended and open-ended questions with most of
them being closed-ended. The participants were asked to add an answer

of their own in the closed-ended questions. Thus, the open-ended questions were only used as part of the closed ended ones. As an example after answering the close-ended question of the importance of several obstacles for learning, the next question was an open-ended one where they were asked if they have another obstacle that was not stated in the above question.

The original data records (population) of secondary data were 7000. After the removal of duplicates and inadequate data the sampling frame was reduced to 1807. With the use of stratified random sampling and by using as strata the VTC's site (urban, rural or island) the final probability sample was formed to 170 records, equal to the responders of the questionnaire. Stratified random sample data was selected as a sampling method because it ensures that the final sample will represent the initial distribution in the sampling frame in terms of the stratifying criterion (Bryman 2012).

In order to get a representative sample of VTC students to answer the questionnaire the following actions were taken. The sample frame was selected: The sample frame includes all the VTC students of the academic year 2013–2014. The representative sample was selected: From all the 400 VTCs of Greece, three of them were selected. Next step was to select the students that would complete the questionnaire. The sampling size was decided to be 180. Each educational program has about 15 participants. So, the students of four educational programs from each VTC were eligible to complete the questionnaire. From each VTC a list of the current educational programs was retrieved and using the method of systematic sample, 4 educational programs were selected. The non-response rate was 5.55%. 10 individuals decided not to complete the questionnaire for various reasons. The total number of answered questionnaires was 170.

5. Findings

As a result of the processing of the questionnaires and the evaluation of the most important data the results obtained were as follows:

In Figure 1 the significant change of the percentage of males attending educational programs in VTCs is shown. In 2004 the percentage of females was 82.4% and of the males 17.6%. In 2014 the percentage of males doubled and became 34.7% for males and 65.3% for females. The 2004 figure are almost identical to Mpelias' (2011) research who examines the quality of the offered training in the VTCs of a certain prefecture of Greece in 2008–2009. In Mpelias' research the percentages of the participants were 82.3% for females and 17.7% for males. In his research Mpelias concludes that the larger participation of women evidences their high unemployment rate. If we take into account the high rise of the unemployment rate during the last years in Greece this can also explain the doubling of the percentage of male participants. This will be analyzed further on.

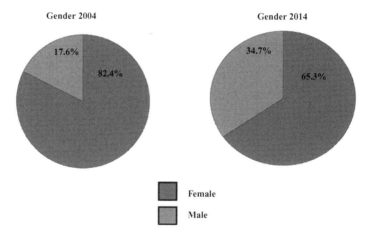

Figure 1: Percentage of Male & Female participants in 2004 and 2014.

This research took place in three contexts: an urban area, a rural area and an island. The male to female ratio in 2004 is exactly the same for rural and island (0.15) and there is a small rise in urban sites (0.34). In 2014, it is observed firstly, that the percentage of the male students doubled in comparison to 2014 and secondly, that although the ratios in the island and rural area are close (0.36 and 0.42) in the urban site the male students almost equal arithmetically to the female ones: the ratio is 0.93 (Figure 2). VTCs students are mostly unemployed as it will be presented below according to this research and as it is described by Zontiros (2006).

The rise in the percentage of the male students can be explained with the rise of male unemployment in 2014. In 2004 the unemployment percentages were 7.7% for males and 14% for females while in the first quarter of 2014 the male unemployment reached 24.1% and the female reached 31.1%. Also in 2004 the unemployment percentage in urban area, rural area and island were 15.8%, 9.3% and 7.3% respectively whereas in 2014 28.1%, 24.5% and 20.3% respectively (Hellenic Statistical Authority 2014, Loukas 2011).

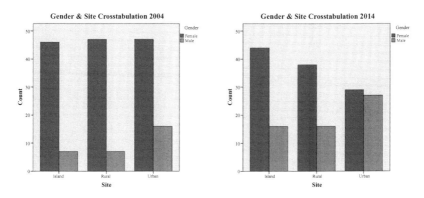

Figure 2: Number of males and females at the three different research sites.

Only a small percentage of the participants were employed; both in 2004 and 2014. The majority of the current educational programs at VTCs are offered to unemployed people. This is also affirmed by the findings. VTCs' educational programs are co-financed by the private sector and the European Union, which participates as a stakeholder on VTCs programs for unemployed in order to help them enter the labor market (Ministry of Labor 2014).

The educational level of the participants has changed considerably. There is a shift to post-secondary education. The question is whether this is happening because of a general uplift of the educational level in Greece, or that in 2014 the unemployment of the ones with higher educational level has increased. According to OECD's (2013) statistics for 2011, 31% attends Vocational programs (Tertiary-type B – Vocational

Training Institutes) and 40% University programs (Tertiary-type A –
Technological Education Institute & Universities). In 2000 the corresponding values were 21% and 30%. So there is a greater upturn at the
educational level.

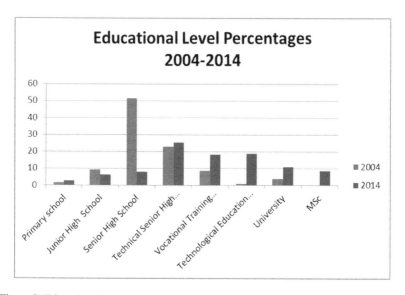

Figure 3: Educational Level Percentages 2004–2014.

However, the percentage of unemployed who have tertiary education
both of type A and B reaches 18.2% for 2014 while it was 2.8% in 2004
(Loukas 2011). This shows that, the answer to the question is that the
educational level of Greeks has increased, but the unemployment of the
educated ones has risen as well. A result of this fact is that more people
who are higher educated turn to VTCs.

The age of the participants has changed as well. The participants of
2004 were older in comparison to the participants of 2014.

It is characteristic that there were no participants of the age group
18–25 in 2004 in comparison to the 2014 that the same age group had the
higher percentage of participants, that is, 34.7%. The participants' ages
follow the unemployment rates as well: in 2004 the unemployment rates
were 47.3% for ages 15–29, 51.7% for ages 30–44 and 9.9% for ages 45

and up. In 2014 it is 64.9% for ages 15–29, 37.7% for ages 30–44 and 14% for ages 45 and up (Hellenic Statistical Authority 2014, Loukas 2011).

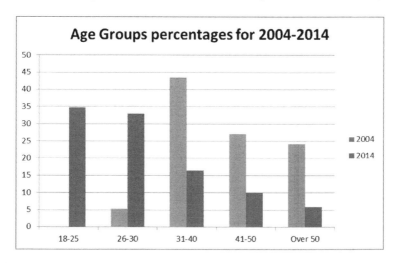

Figure 4: Age groups percentages of participants 2004–2014.

The very high unemployment rate in 2014 of people up to 30 years and the relatively low of people of 45 and up, explains the high participation of the age groups 18–25 & 26–30 (34.7% and 32.9%) and the low participation of age groups 41–50 & over 50 (10% and 5.9%). Also, according to OECD (2007), the older ones are the ones who need more training in order to cope with the rapid changes occurring at the work-places but they are the least likely to get trained.

Motives in 2004 and 2014

The participants' motives have changed considerably before financial crisis and 2014. Before financial crisis participants were motivated to "learn new things" and "To improve knowledge, skills, and abilities". In 2014 those more specific motives have been transformed to "Because education should last throughout our lives". Those three motives can be classified as cognitive motives according to Boshier's (1971) regions of motivation. Bearing in mind the European Union's policies about Lifelong Learning (European Union 2009) and how they are integrated into Greek state policies by the various stakeholders like the Ministry

of Education and the Ministry of Labor it can be assumed that the scope
and aims of EU's policies have been met, as people get to understand
the importance of Lifelong Learning.

Table 1: The five most important motives before financial crisis and 2014.

Motives before financial crisis		Motives in 2014	
Motive	Percentage of "Very Important"	Motive	Percentage of "Very Important"
To get a better work position	72.7%	To find a job	87.1%
To improve knowledge. skills. abilities	68.2%	To get the subsidy for the program	79.4%
I like learning new things	62.7%	To get the participation certificate	65.9%
To get the participation certificate	59.1%	Because education should last throughout our lives	57.6%
To facilitate access to the employment through internships	58.2%	To be more productive at work	52.9%

It is interesting to see that the only motive from before financial crisis
present in 2014 list is "To get the participation certificate". We can consider that although this is an extrinsic and external expectation motive
the need for participants to prove their presence in an educational program and to document their skills is diachronic.

There is a slight shift of people that were joining the educational
programs because they had a continuous thirst for knowledge and
improvement to people who are joining them because they want to
reach explicit targets.

In Tough's research (1968), the average student had six reasons
to begin an educational program and seven to continue it. Among the
most important reasons in this research were enjoyment from receiving the content, pleasure from learning activities and satisfaction from
possession of knowledge. If we map 2004's motives to those reasons,
they are linked to "To improve knowledge, skills, abilities" and "I like
learning new things". In 2014 motives only "Because education should

last throughout our lives" can link to those reasons but only to a limited extent – the same goes with "To improve knowledge, skills, abilities" of before financial crisis. It does not confer any feelings of pleasure or satisfaction like the reasons in Tough's research (1968).

We can consider that the feelings of pleasure from learning have declined. The reasons may vary as from that participants have been in a way "forced" to attend the educational programs to that they are generally more depressed and it is more difficult to feel positive feelings or feelings of joy and happiness. If we associate that with the high percentage of the participants who attend the program for the subsidy, students are in a way forced to attend the programs in order to be able to have some income through the subsidy.

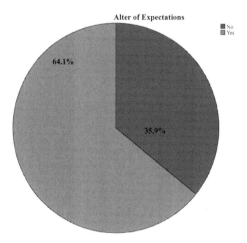

Figure 5: Do you think that financial crisis has altered your expectations from educational programs in VTCs?

This is reinforced by the high percentage of the participants who attend the educational programs for the subsidy and have attended more than three educational programs as this is a way to have a regular income. Also a significant association was recorded between major depression and economic hardship. The depression rates almost tripled since the beginning of the crisis – 3.3% in 2008 in comparison to 8.2% in 2011 (Economou *et al.* 2013). That can explain the absence of positive feelings about learning.

Shift of expectations from VTCs

The last question in the questionnaire was whether the financial crisis altered the expectations of the participants from educational programs in VTCs; 64.1% of the participants answered that their expectations have changed. This result was expected as the socio-economic situation has changed during the last ten years. This can be detected from the change in motives. Educational structures should follow that change, but this is not easy.

Programs 2004 and 2014

The programs that took place in 2004 were different from 2014. This is expected, as VTCs offer Vocational Training and the needs of the labor market have changed since then. In 2004 there is a plurality of course subjects (43) that includes computer related courses – both basic and quite advanced, tourism, shipping industry, food production, catering services, constructions, traditional construction, graphic design, Greek language and different machines' operation. In 2014 the educational programs are more oriented towards employability: Basic ICT skills, Management related courses, training of electrician contractors. The most interesting of all is the program "Voucher for entrance in the work market for the unemployed". It was the most widespread program in this research: the participants that were attending it were the 64% of the sample, in all the three sites of research. This program does not have a major object of training. The students are educated in different sectors like computer use, basic economics & management, construction of curriculum vitae, techniques of finding a job and safety and hygiene at work (Ministry of Labor 2014).

6. Findings – human capital

Surprisingly, what is deduced from the findings of the research is contrary to the fundamentals of the theory of human capital. Human Capital theory supports that the better education one has, the better job he can acquire. Also, it supports that countries with educated citizens have a faster economic growth and an increase in the rate of economic growth (Psacharopoulos 1999).

As can be derived from the findings of the research, the students of VTCs in Greece in 2014 are younger and more educated than they were in 2004 in all the three research sites. Therefore ideally there should be a growth in the Greek economy and plenty of jobs. But situation in Greece is quite different. The rate of economic growth in 2004 was 5% while in 2014 has fallen in -2.3% (National Statistical Service of Greece 2014, Reuters 2011). The huge difference between human capital theory and reality is due to the global recession that followed the global economic crisis. The effects of the global crisis are more discernible in Greek economy and society because of the pathogeneses that existed before.

After World War II the Greek economy was destroyed. The recovery of the economy started without any long-range planning and even short-term planning was perfunctory. There was no planning on what were the best possible sectors to be developed based on the country's natural resources and therefore there was an unregulated development (Fragiadakis 2007).

Until the beginning of 1980s Greek economy was in a good state (Kasimati & Dawson 2009, Dritsakis & Adamopoulos 2004). There was an industrial sector where many people were working at. Greek products were competitive in comparison to the imported ones due to state protectionism and the imposition of duties on the imported goods. When Greece joined the European Community with the liberation of the imports, Greek goods were not competitive anymore, and the Greek industries closed down. After deindustrialization the workforce turned to trade business.

Greek public sector also had several pathogens during this time: instead of a small, flexible public sector with high quality employees there were a huge, cumbersome, public sector with most of the employees to be hired through favors. The high quality workforce did not have any chance of being hired in the state, except if they knew someone that could hire them directly – a politician or someone in a high position. That, along with the high corruption rate – Greece has among the highest corruption rates globally (Smith 2012) – led to a public sector without any vision for the future and therefore no future planning for the economic growth of the country. The sectors that could make use of the highly educated citizens such as research and industrial sector were not developed. Also there was no planning on post-secondary education: the students could study in different faculties without any design on whether when they finish their studies, there would be available jobs for their profession. This led to a high unemployment rate of highly educated personnel (Magoula & Psacharopoulos 1999).

This highly educated personnel was the main source of VTCs students both in 2004 and 2014. Young and recently graduated without any future prospect of finding a job (especially in 2014) they turned to VTCs to get some more skills and the potential of getting a job.

Normally those students would be able to find a job after studying in VTCs because most of the programs in 2014 and especially voucher programs include few months of internships.

But still, the reality is quite different now. In 2004 the VTC programs were more skill-oriented and focused on the needs of the local economy. This according to human capital theory would raise their employability. As a matter of fact most of the students of 2004 were able to get a job after finishing the educational program (GSEE, 2013). 2014 VTC students are being trained in very broad programs without getting any specialization or they are trained in programs that focus on specializations that are very difficult to be used in Greece due to the absence of industrial sector. An example of this is the educational program "Executives of software applications development – education in programming language ABAP-SAP" when there are only six companies in Greece who use the SAP ERP (SAP 2014).

Moreover, as referred above, most of the 2014 programs include internships. Employers use this option in a very large scale and hire the VTC graduates for about 5 months as interns. Employers pay a very small amount of the employee wage; the bigger part is a contribution of EU as it is a stakeholder of those programs. The internship lasts for about five months; the intern is insured only for health issues and is uninsured for pension. The intern gets about the half of the lowest wage of the unskilled worker. But as presented earlier according to the findings of this research, the average VTC student has more skills and knowledge than the average unskilled worker. This has turned into an infinite loop for Greek economy as employers use only VTC graduates as expendable personnel and that hinders the evolution of the economy (GSEE 2013).

Human Capital theory is a theory which explains the economic growth that takes place in a healthy economy due to the human asset. But as the Greek economy is not a healthy one – and has not been healthy since the foundation of the Modern Greek state, this theory cannot be applied to the total of the economy, but only to smaller parts. For example the impact of the formal education graduates into the human capital of the country or how the vocational educational and training students may raise the economic growth of their workplace or of the industry they are working at.

As Melampianakis (2007) stated the human capital of a training program can be measured by the degree of its usefulness. There are quite a few examples of programs that are not adding anything to the human capital of Greece. For example the very specialized programs that the skills acquired cannot be applied in the Greek labor market or the voucher programs that don't actually offer any skills and only lead to a postponed unemployment, does not seem to add anything to the human capital of Greece. Other programs that offer skills and knowledge that lead to more permanent forms of employment boost the human capital and the high economic efficiency on both the individual and social levels (Magoula & Psacharopoulos 1999). By being on a more permanent form of employment the employees receive more training and have a higher incentive to invest in human capital. Also, in contrast to temporary jobs that allow employees to gain general-purpose human capital, more permanent forms of employment offer the employees the chance to develop themselves on skills that are more useful and on the spot and therefore can help them be more productive at work and consequently to boost the economic growth of the company for which they work (Berton *et al.* 2011).

Although this seems as an infinite loop, the production of high skilled workforce is the only way to break it. Vocational education and training is considered an investment and a production good (Friedman 1948, Kindleberger 1977, Schultz 1972). By investing in those the future consumption levels are to rise up according to the theory of human capital. It will take some time for the global and consequently Greek economy to get back in an equilibrium that will allow for economic growth, but when this happens it is crucial for Greece to have the suitable workforce – trained through VTCs to exploit the chances. Therefore, it can be argued, VTCs should adapt their educational programs to fit not only to today's needs, but to those of the future too. In other words, it is necessary to strategically plan in the long run.

References

Berton, F., Devicienti, F., & Pacelli, L. 2011. Are temporary jobs a port of entry into permanent employment?: Evidence from matched employer-employee. International Journal of Manpower, 32(8): 879–899. <http://doi.org/10.1108/01437721111181651>.

Boshier, R. 1971. Motivational orientations of adult education participants: A factor analytic exploration of Houle's typology. Adult Education Quarterly, 21(2): 3–26.

Bryman, A. 2012. Social research methods. Oxford, Oxford University Press.

Dritsakis, N., & Adamopoulos, A. 2004. A causal relationship between government spending and economic development: an empirical examination of the Greek economy. Applied Economics, 36(5): 457–464.

Economou, M., Madianos, M., Peppou, L. E., Patelakis, A., & Stefanis, C. N. 2013. Major depression in the Era of economic crisis: A replication of a cross-sectional study across Greece. Journal of Affective Disorders, 145(3): 308–314. <http://doi.org/10.1016/j.jad.2012.08.008>.

European Union. 2009, January 29. Lifelong Learning Programme 2007–13 [retrieved from: <http://europa.eu/legislation_summaries/education_training_youth/general_framework/c11082_en.htm> – May 18th 2014].

Fragiadakis, A. 2007. O psixros polemos kai to elliniko "oikonomiko thavma" – Cold war and Greek "Financial miracle." Athens, Nefeli.

Friedman, M. 1948. A monetary and fiscal framework for economic stability. The American Economic Review, 245–264.

GSEE. 2013. Ιδιωτική Εκπαίδευση στην Ελλάδα: Πολύ χαμηλή η απορρόφηση αποφοίτων ΙΕΚ και ΚΕΚ στην απασχόληση. [retrieved from: <http://private-education-in-greece.blogspot.gr/2013/11/blog-post.html> – May 18th 2014].

Hellenic Statistical Authority. 2014. Έρευνα Απασχόλησης Εργατικού Δυναμικού (Α` Τρίμηνο 2014 ) – Érevna Apaschólisis Ergatikoú Dynamikoú ( A`Trímino 2014) -Manpower Research (First Quarter 2014). Hellenic Statistical Authority.

Kasimati, E., & Dawson, P. (2009). Assessing the impact of the 2004 Olympic Games on the Greek economy: A small macroeconometric model.Economic Modelling, 26(1): 139–146.

Kindleberger, C. 1977. Herrick, Bruce. Economic Development. Tokyo, McGraw-Hill Kogakusha Limited.

Loukas, V. 2011. Η ανεργία στην Ελλάδα από το *1980* έως σήμερα – I anergía stin Elláda apó to 1980 éos símera – Unemployment in Greece from 1980 to today. TEI of Crete, Irakleio. [retrieved from: <http://nefeli.lib.teicrete.gr/browse2/sdo/log/2011/LoukasVasilis/attached-document-1297154080-295822-27214/Loukas2011.pdf> – May 18th 2014].

Magoula,T.,& Psacharopoulos,G. 1999. Schooling and monetary rewards in Greece: an over-education false alarm? Applied Economics, 31(12): 1589–1597. <http://doi.org/10.1080/000368499323111>.

Melampianakis, E. 2007. Διερεύνηση του μορφωτικού επιπέδου και της ποιότητας του ανθρώπινου κεφαλαίου των ανέργων (εν δυνάμει εργαζομένων) και των δύο φύλων, που συμμετέχουν σε προγράμματα κατάρτισης, ως προοπτικές απασχόλησης και απασχολησιμότητας στην Κοινωνία της Πληροφορίας και της Γνώσης. – Dierevnisi tou morfotikou epipedou ki tis poiotitas tou anthrwpinou kefalaiou kai twn dyo fylwn pou simmetexoun se programmaata apasxolisis kai apasxolisimotitas stin koinwnia tis pliroforias kai tis gnwsis Investigation of educational level and the quality of human capital of the unemployed (potential workers) of both genders, participating in training programs, as job prospects and employability in the Society of Information and Knowledge. Rhodes, University of Aegean.

Ministry of Labor. 2014. VOUCHER FOR ENTRANCE IN THE WORK MARKET FOR UNEMPLOYED. [retrieved from: <http://voucher.gov.gr/project> – May 18th 2014].

Mpelias, D. 2011. Διερευνηση των απόψεων των εκπαιδευομένων του ΚΕΚ της νομαρχιακής αυτοδιοίκησης νομού Τρικάλων αναφορικά με το πρόγραμμα επαγγελματικής κατάρτισης που τους παρέχεται. – Dierevnisi ton apópseon ton ekpaideyoménon tou KEK tis nomarchiakís aftodioíkisis nomoú Trikálon anaforiká me to prógramma epangelmatikís katártisis pou tous paréchetai. [Research of the opinion of students of VTCs of Trikala prefecture regarding the training program they attend]. Patras, Greek Open University.

National Statistical Service of Greece. 2014. Greece GDP Annual Growth Rate | Actual Data | Forecasts | Calendar. [retrieved from: <http://www.tradingeconomics.com/greece/gdp-growth-annual> – May 27th 2014].

OECD. 2007. OECD Insights Summary: How what you know shapes your life. OECD Publishing.

OECD. 2013. Education at a Glance 2013 – Greece. OECD Publishing. [retrieved from: <http://www.oecd.org/edu/Greece_EAG2013%20Country%20Note.pdf> – May 18th 2014].

Psacharopoulos, G. 1999. Οικονομική της Εκπαίδευσης – Oikonomikí tis Ekpaídefsis – Economics of Education. Athens, Papazisis.

Reuters, T. 2011. GDP Growth Since 2000 – Graphic of the Day | The Knowledge Effect. [retrieved from: <http://blog.thomsonreuters.com/index.php/gdp-growth-since-2000-graphic-of-the-day/> – May 29th 2014].

SAP. 2014. SAP Solutions. [retrieved from: <http://portal.singularlogic.eu/solution/91/sap> – May 29th 2014].

Schultz, T. W. 1972. Human capital: policy issues and research opportunities. In Economic Research: Retrospect and Prospect Vol 6: Human Resources (1–84). UMI.

Smith, H. 2012. Greece slips to 94th in corruption index as austerity makes it EU's weakest link | World news | The Guardian.

[retrieved from: <http://www.theguardian.com/world/2012/dec/05/ greece-analysis-corruption-index-austerity> – May 29th 2014].

Stamouli, N. (2014, January 9). Greece's Unemployment Rate Continues to Rise in October. The Wall Street Journal.

Tough, A. M. 1968. Why Adults Learn; A Study of the Major Reasons for Beginning and Continuing a Learning Project. [retrieved from: <http://eric.ed.gov/?id=ED025688%20> – May 18th 2014].

Zontiros, D. 2006. Τα κινητρα συμμετοχης των ενηλικων εκπαιδευομενων σε προγραμματα εκπαιδευσης που προσφερονται απο εργαστηρια ελευθερων σπουδων – Ta kinitra symmetochis ton enilikon ekpaideyomenon se programmata ekpaidefsis pou prosferontai apo ergastiria eleftheron spoudon [Motives of edult learners at programs offered at VTCs]. Patras, Greek Open University.

TÂNIA SUELY ANTONELLI MARCELINO BRABO

The Recent History of Vocational Education in Brazil: The Qualification of the Workforce and its Empowerment through Criticism and Mobilization

1. Vocational education in Brazil

Vocational education in Brazil begins in 1909 with the creation of 19 schools of arts and crafts by the State. These schools were intended to promote actions with the poor population, removing of the streets the excluded, orphans and destitute to give them moral education. The creation of these schools had no relation to the process of production and industrialization was, at that moment, almost nonexistent. (Aranha 1996 *apud* Silva 2010).

Education of workers was, throughout the twentieth century, an option for the poor in Brazil. The children of the economic elite had primary school warranty, followed by secondary, with the goal of access to the University. This duality, namely the direction of elite for upper secondary level nd the direction of the poor segment of the population for vocational education, marked the separation of those who would perform intellectual or instrumental functions. In addressing this duality, Kuenzer says:

> To these two functions of the production system corresponded different educational trajectories and schools. For the firsts, the academic education, intellectualized and detached of instrumental actions; for workers, vocational training in specialized institutions or in their own work, with emphasis on learning, almost exclusively, of ways to track the development of psychophysical skills (Kuenzer 2002, p.27, our translation).

The 1930s marked a significant urban-industrial growth in Brazil. Nevertheless, despite the changes that the Brazilian economy passed through, the educational system remained deeply late and ineffective.

According to Aranha (1996, p. 198), after the First Great War, with industrialization and urbanization, the new urban bourgeoisie was formed, and emerging strata of the petty bourgeoisie require access to education. Returning, however, the values of the oligarchy, these segments aspire to academic and elitist education and despise technical training, which was considered inferior. The working class requires a minimum of schooling, and the pressures for the expansion of educational opportunities start.

In this context, emerged the ideals known as New School who defended, among other things, compulsory and free education as a duty of the State and the fight against the duality of the education system. Several social groups will understand at this moment, the education as an instrument of emancipation of society and the seeking of citizenship. In order to provide professional education to the poor part of the population, were developed actions of both private initiative and public sector aimed at developing this type of education.

According to Romanelli (1982 *apud* Silva 2010), the expansion of technical education in Brazil begins in the 1940s, through the Decree-Law no. 4073, January, 30th, 1942, which organized the industrial education; Decree-Law no. 6141 establishing the Organic Law of Commercial Education, of December 28th, 1943 and Decree-Law no. 9613 of August 20th, 1946 establishing the Organic Law of Agricultural Education.

In accordance with Silva (2010), the first two laws were published in the Estado Novo (1937–1945) and in the context of the Second World War. It was precisely in this period that started in Brazil, the phase of import substitution, which was a result of the war's necessities. This process is justified by the fact that it was necessary to satisfy the desire for consumption, at a time when imports of industrial products were affected by the already mentioned conflict. The solution was to expand the Brazilian industrial sector and it depended, of course, of the hand labor's growth.

The SENAI (National Service of Industrial Learning) creation in 1942, and in 1946, of the National Service Commercial Apprenticeship

– SENAC, sought to provide technical training to the worker, a consistent need with the industrial development of half of the twentieth century. In this context, the creation of SENAI represents the decision of the industries of participate in the labor-work training. The courses offered by SENAI, under the administration of the National Confederation of Industries, multiplied by the country in the mid-twentieth century and survived the subsequent educational policy reforms.

The national project of industrialization of President Getulio Vargas government began to include concern for the worker's preparation for the market. This preparation will happen to the effective participation of entrepreneurs who will manage, together with the government, the financial resources captured on a compulsory way (often through payroll discount). According to Pochmann (2000), beyond the short and medium term training courses presented by sectoral institutions (SENAI and SENAC, for example), it was up to the government the diffusion of technical courses of long duration (federal schools, and state universities). The author points out that, with this, the country now has a vocational training model anchored on organizational and financial bases, which tend to operate with very different characteristics.

The vocational education offering is currently divided into three major groups, as mentioned above: "S" system, public education and private education institution. The "S" system is formed by the following organizations: SENAI – National Service of Industrial Learning, SESI – Industry Social Service, SENAC – National Service Commercial Apprenticeship, SESC – Social Service of Commerce, SEBRAE – Brazilian Support Service for Micro and Small Business, Airway Fund – Linked Fund to the Ministry of Aeronautics, SENAR – National Service of Rural Learning, SEST – Social Transport Service, SENAT – National Service for Transport Training, SESCOOP – National Service of Learning Cooperativism.

Are considered public education institutions (Federal, State and Municipal) those maintained with public funds, in the three legal and administrative spheres: Federal, State or Municipal. The private educational institutions are incumbency of private rights, and can be communal, philanthropic, religious or private, as entities of free professional teaching and organizations of civil society, trade unions of workers, of entrepreneurs, non-governmental organizations (NGOs), lay community associations or confessional (churches, cooperatives etc.).

The Law of Guidelines and Bases of National Education of 1961 brought significant changes in national education, with the integration of professional teaching and regular education system. But we cannot affirm that the duality was overcome, once the different types of training continued to have different clienteles.

Despite the Law No. 5.692 / 1971 (BRAZIL 1971) try to implement compulsory professionalization in secondary level school during the military dictatorship, this initiative was not successful due to difficulties on implementation of the new model and also due to the economic crisis that the period known as "economic miracle" was facing. According to Kuenzer (2002, p.30, our translation), in this way, "[…] returns to the scene the old structural duality, even because, originated in the class structure, cannot be resolved within the school pedagogical political project".

The structure of the Brazilian educational system complies with the demands of the Taylor-Fordist production model, serving the social division of labour (when each social class must occupy a certain pre-established function) and the technical division (separation of the production process into small parts).

To Kuenzer (2002), the educational principle that determined the pedagogical project of vocational education in the Taylor-Fordist organization is based on the concept of vocational training as an individual process, to the learning of ways of doing, defined by occupation which needs to be exercised. The author also points out that:

> In this conception, which founded the training courses of business, professional qualification of the agencies that are responsible for training and professionalizing the middle school, the development of higher intellectual skills and mastery of technological scientific knowledge has not been presented as a necessity for workers. For them, the concept of professional competence was understood as a few years of schooling, training for the occupation and a lot of experience, the combination resulted in dexterity and speed as a result of repetition and memorization of well-defined tasks with reduced complexity […]. (Kuenzer 2002, p. 31).

Still according to the author, with the changes in the labour market resulting from the productive restructuring phenomenon, a new educational project was adopted by the government. One of the main expressions of this new project was the Reform of Technical Education of 1996. The changes brought about by the reforms are preceded by Guidelines and Framework Law – LDB (Lei de Diretrizes e Bases), n.9394 (BRAZIL 1996).

In the LDB / 96, when they defined up the high school purposes, seek to overcome the socially established duality between general education and professional education. The article, which deals with the issue, said that the high school purposes are:

I – the consolidation and deepening of the knowledge acquired in primary education, enabling further study;

II – the basic preparation for work and citizenship of the student to continue learning in order to be able to adapt flexibly to new conditions of employment or further training;

III – the improvement of the student as a human person, including ethics education and the development of intellectual autonomy and critical thinking;

IV – understanding of scientific and technological foundations of productive processes, linking theory with practice, in the teaching of each discipline (our translation).

Although the legislation presents a formal unification, in practice still exists two school systems aimed at different audiences, as happened in the whole history of Brazilian education.

The Reform of Technical Education is a measure that is part of a broader policy: the proposal of the National System of Technological Education. Such system is justified by the defense that, in order to achieve economic development, it is necessary to use modern technologies that, in turn, demand qualified human resources. Thus, based on the main object, according to the government, of improvement of the educational offer and its adaptation to the new economic reality, they seek an articulation between the Federal Centers for Technological Education – CEFETs (now called Federal Institutes of Technological Education), SENAI, SENAC, universities and other institutions involved in technical education.

Kuenzer (2002) affirms that the Reform of Technical Education follows the logic of educational policies, being ruled by the financial rationality. Moreover, such policies repose no longer on the acknowledgment of the universality of the right to education at all levels, but on the principle of equity, which means different treatment according to the demands of the economy. Investment in state-education is subject to the development project and the idea of providing the costs that result in economic returns to the country. According to Moraes, as the right to education is guaranteed constitutionally, the expansion and elevation of schooling should have been goals not for employment, "[…] but as a requirement of expansion of citizenship rights, as a precondition to the implementation and consolidation of the democratic process in the country" (Moraes 1999, p.26, our translation).

The author also criticizes the implementation process of the said reform, because although the Ministry of Labour have held broad debate on reforms that should have been implemented in the Brazilian professional education, such discussions were ignored in the draft bill presented by the Ministry of Education and Culture – MEC. In this process, the text of the draft was mainly built by experts from the Ministry, having the influence of international financial organizations, particularly the World Bank, without the participation of the various actors involved in the reform. Moraes (1999 p. 76) relates to the fact that

> Historically, the productive sector appealed few times to the State for the qualification of its workers in the face of the productive processes specificity, of the industrial secrecy, the competitiveness, the speed and the market dynamics. For this constituted its own network, funding it with public funds, but that are presented as coming from the private sector (our translation).

In the new conformation of the vocational education process, we realized that with the process of productive restructuring, the worker no longer acquires a professional skill as the Fordist / Taylorist model of production, when it was acquired during their education and exercised throughout life. Now, the worker is in a constant process of training and preparation for work. The author questions whether this fact is really a new characteristic of the mode of production originated from the current economic changes or if it is more like a justification for the exclusion of workers from a production model where there are no jobs for everyone.

The impact of technological modernization in the field of work, as well as, the productive restructuring of the last decades, both are issues that are not yet exhausted and that raise many controversies. Moreover, it must remember that the impacts of these changes are felt in varying intensities from one country to another and even within the same country. There are countries, like Brazil, which have both companies working with the most advanced cutting-edge technology and companies that deal with obsolete technologies. Further, according to Kuenzer and Grabowski (2006, p. 312).

> The management of professional education in Brazil is under responsibility of several federal agencies. The network of technical schools is under the responsibility of the Ministry of Education and Culture (MEC); the workers education, the National Qualification Program (PNQ), is under the aegis of the Ministry of Labor and Employment (MTE); education in the field is divided between MEC and the Ministry of Agrarian Development (MDA) through PRONERA; to the Ministry of Science and Technology is attributed the technological training policy of the country and the nine systems 'S' are attached to the Ministry of Agriculture (SENAR), Ministry of Industry and Commerce (SEBRAE), Ministry of Social Action (SESI and SESC), Ministry of Labour (SENAI and SENAC), and the Pro-young, which is linked to the General Secretary of the Government (our translation).

As the other authors expose, these government agencies that have specific responsibilities at the federal level, "coordinating policies, programs, actions, networks of schools, education centers and professional education systems, they require internal articulation". They also claim that you can see that there is fragmentation in the very government agencies responsible for professional education, which demands, according to Kuenzer and Grabowski (2006, p. 312) a level of organization, articulation, coordination and public management of policies and professional education programs in national scale. By considering strategic for the country the formulation and implementation of public policies of professional education, it is up to the government to define the spheres of relative competency for the coordination, articulation and supervision of the various initiatives, demands, networks, programs and existing actions in country, seeking to build organicity between the various professional education activities, currently dispersed through programs that are carried out by a plurality of public agencies, private institutions and non-governmental organizations in order to assume the State as a regulator in this area.

1.1 *Brief look on vocational education initiatives of Trade Unions and the Landless Workers Movement, MST*

In the early twentieth century, in Brazil, it was created several class associations such as the Union of Longshoremen Workers Union and the Society of Stokers in 1903; the Union of Workers in Factory in 1917, among others. Although not possessing union character already showed interest in the social significance of trade unionism and the importance of labor movements.

In the 1930s, with mobilizations of civil society as the Modern Art Week, a different proposal of education through the Manifesto of the Pioneers, with the mobilization of women the right to vote and the Constitutionalist Revolution, it was drawn up the Democratic Charter of 1934 then replaced the 1937 Constitution by, totalitarian nature. Thereafter, this was repealed by the 1946 Federal Constitution, despite its liberal nature, preserved in relation to trade union organization and on the principle of unity, this principle has remained unchanged in the Constitutions of 1967 and 1969 and even causing great strangeness remained unscathed in the 1988 Federal Constitution, according to the order expressed in Article 8, II:

> It is free professional or trade association, noted:
> [...]
> II – it is forbidden to create more than one trade union organization, in any degree, representative of economic professional category in the same territorial base, which will be defined by the workers or employers concerned may not be less than the area of a Municipality;
> [...] (BRAZIL 1988, our translation).

Despite advances in the Constituent process of 1988, which aimed to establish a system of effective trade union democracy, by proclaiming the freedom of association; by prohibiting the State intervention in the granting of prior authorization for the establishment of trade unions; by ensuring the autonomy of professional associations; by granting to the trade union a broad power of representation; and so on, it is necessary, however, to show that the 1988 Law comes up against two obsolete rules adopted under the aegis of the lobby of the official trade unions, which confront the trade union democracy established by Article 8 of the Federal Constitution of 1988, which are:

a) unity trade union, provided for Article 8, II of the Federal Constitution of 1988;
b) trade union contribution provided for Article 8, IV of the Federal Constitution of 1988, as well as being set in Articles 578 and following of the Consolidated Laws of Labour, which despite not being imposed is accepted by the Constituent Assembly. (BRAZIL 1988, our translation).

At this point of this study it is absolutely necessary to point out that although the totalitarian regime adopted by the Consolidation of Labour Laws, arising of the orientation of the previous Constitutional Law, where there was no legal probability for the creation of trade unions centers, these however were organized and so they were born Workers' Unique Central (CUT); the General Confederation of Workers (CGT) and Trade Union' Strength, which are currently the three most important centrals in operation in the country.

With the neoliberal model, it was affected directly the lives of workers, because this economic model entails a deregulation of social rights, informality, precarious employment contracts and flexible working. "Arises in this context a multipurpose worker, the one who is called upon to perform several functions at the same time working with the same salary as a result of the downsizing of the company staff [...]". (Iamamoto 2010, p.32, our translation). Moreover, unemployment worsened due to the increase of new technologies that have replaced human labor, causes feelings of insecurity in the workers. In accordance to Iamamoto (2010, p. 33) "In the current context recessive of world economic production, the trade unions struggles are weakened and the work defense is hampered on the growth of unemployment" (Iamamoto 2010, p. 33, our translation).

This economic model has also influenced the structure of the trade unions, which makes that these did not have the same force because, as exposes Giroletti (2007, p. 310) neoliberalism brings as a consequence further deregulation of labour laws, mass unemployment, precariousness in contract job. "These structural and superstructural changes are ongoing teasing, among other consequences, a higher trade union's weakness at national and international level" (our translation).

The current structure of trade union organization is based on the trade union that may join a federation and confederation or any entity. Regardless of your membership the trade union must, above all, defend the collective or individual interests, including in legal and administrative issues. According to Queiroz (2007, p 39), the main operating standards of trade union today are:

> Autonomy and interference: the constitution says that is free the professional association or trade union, but the PEC (amendment proposal to the Constitution) prohibits the interference and the intervention in the trade union organization, the same for the Government / State.
> Representation of union framework: This framework is given by a specific category in which this category will frame into a specific trade union, which will cover a certain area, such as its city.
> [...]
> Democracy and participation: the trade union must make it clear to the category that it is a democratic space with the knowledge of their rights and access to ineducation inside of the trade union, which is responsible to found the trade union citizenship.
> [...]
> Outsourcing: Today is a big problem for the trade union, because the boss of the outsourced employee does not belong to the same company to which the employee works. (our translation).

In this short overview of education and changes in Brazilian trade unions, we note another concern, according to Siqueira (2003), which is the issue of education, workers' professional qualifications so that they can be better prepared in the pursuit of an opportunity in the business market. Some trade unions also offer medical assistance, legal assistance, life insurance and even funeral assistance. Considering its character of set of claims, it is observed that their work, over this last decade, have changed the target, means and purposes.

For example, in the State of São Paulo, in the Center of Professional Education of the Metalworkers Trade Union, among the courses offered, referring to those up to two years duration there are: technician in industrial automation, electronics technician, technician in logistics, technical in automotive maintenance, technician in mechatronics. They offered also courses of Initial and Continuing Education up to four months duration. In the case of the Trade Union of Commerce, Courses: Visual Mechadising and Brazilian Sign Language. Registration Rural

Trade Union (SP): Pesticide Application Course with spray Costal, Electrician-installations in Low Voltage, handmade Processing of Pork, among others.

Another example, the Integrate Program – Education and Qualification for Work – a national educational education program with elementary school certification, responsibility and management of the National Confederation of Metalworkers of Workers' Unique Central (CUT); financed with public funds from the Fund of Assistance for Workers (FAT) and destinated to those who are employed and unemployed of the metal-mechanical complex.

In a society that is very present social inequalities between antagonistic classes, it is constantly a lag in labour struggles, thus causing a weakening in the achievements of labour rights, leaving workers at the mercy of Capital. From 1980, trade unionism was at the apex of the social movements. The workers were more present in social struggles and claim their rights without fear of being reprimanded by the police force and their oppressors, in the workplace by their employers. With the new syndicalist structure in Brazil (New Trade Unionism), social movements proved to be stronger, emphasizing the CUT, the Landless Workers Movement (MST) and other trade union movements.

In relation to MST, as we read in the website of the movement:

> In the early 1980s, Brazil was living a situation of workers mobilizations in cities and struggle to end the dictatorship. In this context, in 1984, it was held the 1st National Meeting of the Landless in Cascavel, Paraná. This meeting marked the starting point for its construction bringing together 80 rural workers who helped organize land occupations in the states of Rio Grande do Sul, Santa Catarina, Paraná, São Paulo, Mato Grosso do Sul, Espírito Santo, Bahia, Pará, Goiás, Rondônia, Acre and Roraima, also attended by representatives of ABRA (Brazilian Association for Agrarian Reform, CUT (Single Workers Central), CIMI (Indigenous Missionary Council) and Pastoral Workers of São Paulo (MST 2016, our translation).

Concluding that the occupation of the land was a fundamental and legitimate tool of rural workers in the struggle for the democratization of land, after this meeting, initiated a project to build an organic movement at the national level, having as objectives: the struggle for land, the struggle for agrarian reform and a new agricultural model, the struggle for education, as well as a national project of development with social justice.

Thus, in 1985, amid the climate of the *Direct Elections Now* campaign, the MST held its first National Congress in Curitiba, Paraná, with the slogan: "Occupation is the only solution". That same year, the government of José Sarney approved the National Agrarian Reform Plan (NARP), which was only on paper, for it was pressured by the interests of the landowners, thus only 6% of the targets set out in NARP were met. (MST 2016, our translation).

One of the struggles of the movement in the camps and settlements is an adequate education for the reality in which they live. With more than 2000 public schools built in camps and settlements; 200000 children, adolescents, youth and adults with guaranteed access to education; 50000 adult literacy; 2000 students in technical courses and superior as well as more than 100 undergraduate courses in partnership with Brazilian universities (MST 2016).

Another initiative of the movement is the Itinerant School to guarantee the right to education of children, adolescents, youth and adults in itinerant situation, when they are camped, fighting for expropriation of unproductive lands and when they are implementing the landless settlement.

According to Lima, Guhur, Tona and Noma (2011, p. 212), the educational practices of professional education in agroecology developed by the Landless Workers' Movement of the State of Paraná (MST/PR) are based on the MST's Pedagogy, and they articulate "[…] political action in the struggle for land and changes in society with the struggle for school education and education in its broadest sense, as formative processes aimed at human emancipation".

Since 2002, the MST/PR has initiated actions to consolidate educational practices in agroecology aimed at political and technical education of the landless subjects. Throughout this period, the centers and schools of the MST/PR have faced the challenge of building pedagogical strategies that dealing the specificity of the education in agroecology.

Courses are held in partnership with public educational institutions, with funds from the National Education Program in Agrarian Reform (Pronera), certified by the Federal Institute of Paraná (IFPR) and by the National Institute of Colonization and Agrarian Reform (Incra).

The Centres / Education schools MST / PR are: School Iraci Salette Strozak (Cantagalo); School Ireno Alves dos Santos (in Rio Bonito do Iguaçu) – both linked to the Sustainable Development Center and Training in Agroecology (CEAGRO), school José Gomes da Silva (in São Miguel do Iguaçu); School Milton Santos (in Maringa) and the Latin American School of Agroecology (in Lapa). More than 300 students graduated in these schools, and currently there are four classes in progress totaling about 140 students (Santos 2014; Pires 2016).

In the case of settlement Contestado, we find all educational levels, from the Children's Education through high school. In 2015 began an undergraduate degree, the Earth Sciences. In this settlement is hosting the Latin American School of Agroecology, the ELAA, which promotes numerous courses to its members, including continuing education courses for teachers in their schools around the country. The movement, in partnership with several universities, provides to its members Courses of Graduation, through the Pedagogy of Alternation and others.

As expose Lima, Guhur, Tona and Noma (2011, p.204), the Centers/ Schools of education are not part of the official school system, act as Centers of Education in Rural Education, having officially recognized courses through partnerships with Universities and Federal Technical Institutes, among others.

In the Centers/Schools are also made non-formal courses offered to members and Movement supporters, which encompass broader issues related to the education of society, agrarian reform, politics, cooperatives, agro-ecology, education, labor, class conflict, meetings and seminars of MST.

Based on the MST/PR document (2004) cited by Lima *et al* (2011, p 87) the main objectives of the Centers /Schools of Education of the Movement in the State of Paraná are:

- To be an education space for the organizations of the working class;
- To be a space for the Landless Movement meetings and other organizations seeking the same goals of social transeducation;
- To be a reference in the development of experiences in agroecological production area, with concrete results for farmers;
- To be a development space of socialist humanist values, developed through the collective life;

–   Improve the technical training method and political education from elementary school, but also in High School and higher education;
–   To be developing area of scientific and technological experiments, focused on peasant reality;
–   To be an incentive space and experience of popular culture, rescuing especially peasant culture;
–   To be a space where people can live, teaching themselves, working, having fun and building future prospects (our translation).

Lima *et al* (2011, p. 194) argues that the Centers/Schools of the Movement "represent: a) an important place, in development, in the education of militant framework; b) the socialization of historical and scientific knowledge produced by humanity; c) the approach of workers in the countryside and the city, supporting the construction of collective actions of common interest" (our translation).

Another conclusion of the authors is that there is, in the legislation of the Brazilian state, the constitutional or legal responsibility for education funding, that is, unlike the various levels of education that have inherent features, or maintenance and development funds, education remains professional unsecured and available own resources needed to achieve them, depending on annual budgetary allocations or special programs financed by international organizations, such as the World Bank.

2. The current state of discussion on the qualifications of the workforce in Brazil

During the 1980s and early 1990s – in which the economic agenda is permeated by inflation, strikes and demands for wage increases, rising unemployment, it is observed failed stabilization attempts. The necessary economic and institutional reforms are not operated except with regard to the opening to international trade (1990–1992). In that decade, it should be noted the creation in 1986 of unemployment insurance, a consolidated policy in European capitalism in the post-World War II.

If major economic changes are not operated during this period, some institutional reforms of certain depth occurred after the promulgation of the Constitution of the Federative Republic of Brazil, 1988, which allowed expansion of the set of policies and social programs in Brazil over the 1990's and 2000: rural retirement; Support Fund for Workers (FAT); Continuous Cash Benefit (BPC); Child Labor Eradication Program (Peti); Bolsa Escola and thereafter Bolsa Família – among others, both of them are federal programs of income transfer to those who need financial help for school (Bolsa Escola) and for their family (Bolsa Família).

FAT propitiated what is considered the third vector of professional qualifications: National Plan for Professional Qualification (Planfor), initiated in 1995 as part of what came to be called the Public System of Employment and Income, which included active and passive policies for the labour market (programs of generation of employment and income, professional qualification, intermediary of workforce, unemployment insurance, these two latter encompass the preexisting National Employment System – (SINE).

As the literature indicates, the issue of qualification is placed (or re-placed) today by the conjunction of two factors: the acceleration of economic growth and the changes resulting from the diffusion of the new paradigm of production, both as regards to the spread of new automation technologies as new forms of management. The following we will point out the main findings on the subject, which constitute in challenges for education and qualification that really meets the needs of workers in the current configuration of the capitalist mode of production.

2.1 The heterogeneity of the labour market

The first concerns the heterogeneity of the labour market and of the occupational structure, resulting in different demands for qualification. The Brazilian productive structure is quite heterogeneous. Here, still live typical occupations of the Fordist paradigm, bounded in positions and tasks, with occupation structures based in new techniques of automation and management, which have greater autonomy at work and they take decisions nearer to the factory floor. This does not occur only in different production units, but often within the same establishment.

In the automotive industry, for example, there are several ways of working and living in the same work space. But in general, they begin to demand workers' capacity for decision making and for a number of new attitudes and skills that are associated immediately to the specific professional education, but also require more solid basic training. On the other hand, some companies seek in the least developed countries, workers in occupations that disappeared in the most technologically advanced countries or who no longer arouse more interest in their workers. An emblematic case is that of call centers, a sector that expands based on this model. It is one of the sectors that employ more women and which finds a greater exploitation of labor, as research has indicated. In this regard, Hirata (2001) argues that with the rapid development of new technologies, there is a "feminization" of work with an increase in women in the computer sector. However, especially in peripheral countries, these jobs have increased in the context of flexible, insecure and vulnerable working relationships, especially in women's employment.

In the banking sector, Segnini (2001, cited by Cordeiro 2011) found that 88% of the services provided via telemarketing were done by women. The occupations that experienced the greatest changes in the most automated companies are occupations that are in the core of the occupational hierarchy. They are neither skilled occupations neither those requiring little qualification. The most affected was the core composed by employees of more traditional part of the industrial production structure, such as a lathe operator. In the services sector, staff of public services such as, for example, the functions of bank teller, large magazines sellers. In offices, in general, computerization has rendered obsolete a huge range of functions, resulting in a significant reduction in jobs and the need for more highly qualified professionals who occupy the remaining positions.

In this scenario, according to Hirata (2009), the intensification of women's inclusion was the key feature in the last two decades, however, this presence occurs most of all in the space of precarious jobs where exploitation is sharper.

The coexistence of different production processes leads to professional qualification demands very different from each other. The needs are of the most different orders throughout the whole occupational gradient and at different levels. Companies miss engineers, technologists, technicians in the industrial informatics line, also in the area of services. There is a fairly widespread need of skilled workforce in all sectors of the economy and in several levels of qualification. In the context of the specific professional qualification, from what is called basic qualification of workers, the former professional education basic level, passing through technical professional education of mid-level, the technological education courses and the bachelor's degree programs in general.

2.2 Educational demands

However, regardless of the production process model, it seems that there is, in common, the demand for workers with the education and general quality. In the last ten years there has been an increase in hiring needs. Today, the educational requirements are higher for all functions, in contrast to the low qualification of much of the workforce. However, not the greatest education of the workforce nor the requirement of higher qualifications by the labor market, ensured the availability of workers with vocational training to respond to market requirements recognized.

The education of the workforce has become an important aspect, regardless of function. The data from the RAIS (Annual Social Ineducation), made available by the Ministry of Labour and Social Security recently show that for those who have completed primary education, the largest employment opportunity was in office as a truck driver or maintenance buildings. For those who have completed high school, there are the guard positions, office clerk and retail seller.

The greater demand for education can be explained in part by unemployment, although smaller, is still high in some segments of the population, especially among young people. Added to this is the fact that a large number of workers have completed high school. With the labor supply of abundant labor, research shows that going to require the average level for less skilled occupations.

While, about ten years ago, the privileged competitive factors by foreign investors were given mainly by infrastructure conditions (roads, airports, energy etc.), today, increasingly, they focus on the workforce qualification characteristics. In addition to training, the ability to communicate in foreign languages and cultural aspects, such as the ability to work in environments with cultural diversity, are also considered essential. The critical areas are mainly those involving ineducation technologies, both in industry and in services.

Companies have invested in the training of their staff, both in training in their specific areas and in other skills such as foreign languages. However, it is also worth noting that Brazil has a segment familiar with the latest technology, with training and performance that leave nothing to be desired in relation to developed countries. Relevant, yet, is the fact that these professionals are mostly formed in educational institutions in their own country and not abroad, as often occurs in developing countries. This highlights the country's ability to train highly qualified professionals in post graduate level, technological and technical, although restricted in quantitative terms.

2.3 *Expansion of vocational education offer*

Formal education quality, besides being a constitutionally guaranteed right is a central issue in the new economic context. In the field of vocational education, some characteristics are considered essential for the expansion of labor supply: the diversification and flexibility of courses, adherence to the real requirements of the market, for which it is necessary to involve companies. In recent years, there has been a diversification and a very large expertise in the market beyond the demand for professional education.

Taking for example the Paula Souza Center, which is a profissinal Education institution of the State of São Paulo, linked to the Department of Economic Development, Science, Technology and Innovation (SDECTI). It is responsible for the offer of education courses and mid-level technology. Ten years ago, offered 37 technical skills. In 2008, it offered more than 90. The agricultural sector provides a good example. Traditionally, this area formed agricultural technicians. The current profile of the courses is much more diversified, including, for example, agro-ecology and poultry. In the health area, beyond nursing and nutrition by request of the Hospital of Clinicas in Sao Paulo, is being organized a course in orthosis and prosthesis. At the same time, the Center keeps the traditional technical courses of mechanical, electrical engineering, of buildings, accounting, though reworded whenever necessary. The institution manages 219 State Technical Schools (Etecs) and 66 Colleges of Technology (Fatecs), gathering more than 290,000 students in technical courses of medium and higher technological level, in more than 300 cities.

> The Etecs serve 213,000 students in Technical Teaching, Hish School and Integrated Technical to the High School, with 138 technical courses for industrial sector, agricultural and services, including qualifications in semipresential modality, Youth and Adult Education (EJA) and technical expertise (São Paulo 2015, our translation).

Another action, this from the Government of the State of Ceará, is the e-Jovem program. Through the Department of Education (SEDUC), aims to provide training in Ineducation and Communication Technology (TIC) with emphasis on youth participation, to the students of elementary and high school and egresses of public schools. The Ceará Secretariat Education-SEDUC, states that since 2008, achieved the following results "[…] it means an intemship opportunity for students, ensuring professional experience for their first job and generating algernative of economic and technological development of Ceará." (SEDUC 2015, our translation).

According to SEDUC, the overall objective of the e-Jovem is to articulate the average level education with professional teaching and the world of work, through the youth qualification in informatics, ineducation and communication technologies, entrepreneurship and cooperatives, increasing the chances of entering the market and also providing employment generation and income in the poorest regions of the State of Ceará (SEDUC 2007, p.2). It provides training in web development areas, network, hardware and programming, functions that are present in these Brazilian Cadastre of Occupations[1] (CBO), watching free software policies, through universalization of the digital culture.

---

1   Brazilian Cadastre of Occupations: 2624–10 Designer of pages of internet-web designer and 3171–10, Programmer of Ineducation Systems (BRAZIL, CBO, 2013).

Moreover, as exposes Calou (2015), from reports of SEDUC (2007), it aims to develop social entrepreneurship projects in communities and schools entered in the scope of e-Jovem. It is intended to create a culture of social responsibility, qualified workforce to correspond to the demand of the software industry in Ceará, and might be distributed in the cities, together with Cearense companies of ineducation and communication technology as well as promote cooperation with other knowledge areas.

Another action is the National Program for Access to Technical Education and Employment (Pronatec) that was created by the Federal Government in 2011 over the Law no.12,513 / 2011 in order to expand, internalize and democratize the offer of professional education courses and technology in the country. The Pronatec seeks to expand educational opportunities and qualified professional education to young people, workers and beneficiaries of income transfer programs. According to data provided by the Ministry of Education and Culture, "From 2011 to 2014, through Pronatec, there were made more than 8.1 million registrations, between technical courses and professional training in more than 4,300 cities. In 2015, there were 1.3 million registrations".

3. Final considerations

According to Alves (2014, p. 107), in the 2000s,

> called the 'inclusive decade' in the statement 155 of the Applied Economic Research Institute (IPEA), released in September 2012, Brazil showed significant improvements in social indicators with the reduction of poverty and social inequality through income transfer policies (IPEA, 2012). Nevertheless, Brazil remains one of the twelve unequal countries in the world. In fact, the 2000s, the boom decade of the global economy and also the decade of its financial crash in 2008, was for Brazil, a decade of growth of the capitalist economy, with the country skirting the global financial crisis that hit the organic core of the global system of Capital (US, EU and Japan).

At the same time, according to the author, the labour market in the "inclusive decade" followed the trend of good social indicators, with the fall of unemployment in the metropolitan areas and the increased rate of formality in the labour market, reducing, significantly, labour informality in Brazil (OIT 2012 *apud* Alves 2014).

It must be added, yet, according to Alves (2014, p. 111) that in capitalist countries with a high level of social misery as Brazil, the improvement of social indicators is a positive factor because it allows a certain quality of life for poorest people, of men and women living in situations of extreme precariousness because millions of Brazilians are excluded from a decent standard of living with access to education and health quality. According to the author, in this new capitalist order, "[…] the idea of 'inclusion' presupposes layer of poor workers excluded from social progress and human development linked to the inclusion in the consumer society" (our translation). As further argues Alves (2014, p. 111),

> […] the logic of human development and quality of life as inclusion in the formal labour market and access to minimum rent is sharply limited and shortsighted. In fact, it hides new ways of degradation of social work towards new forms of subtle and destructive alienation in workers' health plan and quality of life of men and women who work (our translation).

Regarding professional education courses or qualifications, they need to have adherence to local demands that change frequently, which requires flexibility. It's hard to keep up with this dynamic of occupational needs. The dialogue between school and enterprise, with the commitment of both parties, is the best way to solve the mismatch between offer and demand for education in professional level. It must be stressed that such dialogue is not always simple, since differences persist among perspectives, concepts, and timing. The latter is related to the speed with which the demands appear, especially in the informatics area. Hardly strategies can be agile enough to connect in time the course offerings to several demands. This problem is not Brazil's exclusivity; some European countries can achieve a rapid recycling, but not always in the quantities which are required.

In our case, on the issue of quality of basic education, it puts an additional challenge to professional education: that the courses do not be guided exclusively on technical content and, for they can incorporate ways to overcome previous deficiencies in general content.

In this period the trade unionism found itself extenuating also began to emerge economic trends, political and ideological focused on productive restructuring and the emergency of neoliberal adjustment. Nowadays, since the neoliberal adjustment has influence since the 1990s, this gives the idea of a multi-purpose worker, with deregulation of the laws of social, civil and political rights. With the retraction of the state in social policies, comes precariousness both in worker life and in society.

We realize that, beyond the economic, social and political changes, there is also a change in social relations and especially in the lives of workers, which passes through an ideological transeducation and its way of working. Even with these changes in trade unionism, this continues to be a mediator between classes.

So they are not extinct, the trade unions are driving their actions in the area of social responsibility, so propagated. As examples, we can mention the Trade Union of Bank Workers of São Paulo, which takes care of street children; the Trade Union of the ABC Metalworkers leading a campaign against illiteracy and the education of workers in cooperatives to manage bankrupt factories; the Trade Union Strength created the Social Solidarity Center and forwards unemployed for new job opportunities or professional training (Grinbaum 2002).

The labour market leads to inequalities and discrimination due to the concentration of income in the hands of a few who can get better working conditions, while a considerable portion is unemployed and submissive to precarious jobs, with no prospect of social mobility and permanence in the labour market.

According to Pochmann (2004), the dynamics of the labour market is extremely exclusive and damages the contributions that education offers, increasing therefore social inequalities in the country. Unemployment rates have been increasing for the most educated population, which ultimately exceed workforce to the market, in this social segment. Thus the rise in education levels – in economic stagnation framework, low investment in technology and precariousness of labour market – turns out to be insufficient to enhance the generation of work.

It can be noticed that the best jobs end up with the wealthiest, the poor and those with higher scholarity are unemployed and they suffer prejudice of race, gender and class. It must occur an expansion of education, not only the productive point of view, but also as citizenship.

References

Alves. G. 2014. Brasil nos anos 2000: "Década Inclusiva" e a precarização do homem-que-trabalha [Notas críticas]. In T.S.A.M. Brabo (org.). Direitos humanos, ética, trabalho e educação. São Paulo, Icone Editora.

Aranha, M. L. de A. 1996. História da Educação. São Paulo, Moderna.

Araujo, T. P.; Lima, R. A. 2014. Formação profissional no Brasil: revisão crítica, estágio atual e perspectivas. Estudos Avançados, 28, 81 SãoPaulo May/Aug. [retrieved from: <http://dx.doi.org/10.1590/S0103-40142014000200012> February, 26th 2016].

BRASIL 2009. Pesquisa Nacional por Amostra de Domicílios. Aspectos complementares da Educação de Jovens e Adultos e Educação Profissional-2007. Ministério do Planejamento, Orçamento e Gestão; Instituto Brasileiro de Geografia e Estatística; Diretoria de Pesquisas; Coordenação de Trabalho e Rendimento, Rio de Janeiro.

BRASIL 1996. Lei de Diretrizes e Bases da Educação Nacional. MEC.

BRASIL. 1988. Constituição da República Federativa do Brasil.

Caldart, R. S. 2004. Pedagogia do Movimento Sem Terra. São Paulo, Expressão Popular.

Calou, C.R.B. 2014. Projeto E-Jovem: a política pública de formação profissional de jovens no Estado do Ceará. Texto de qualificação de Doutorado, Programa de Pós-Graduação em Educação, Universidade Estadual Paulista. (*mimeo*)

Cordeiro, B.K. 2011. O trabalho em Call Center: a saúde do trabalhador e sua relação com a atividade. Mestrado em Psicologia. Universidade Federal Fluminense. [retrieved from: <http://www.slab.uff.br/images/Aqruivos/dissertacoes/2011/Bruna.pdf.> February, 26th 2016].

Ficher, M.C. 1999. Os sindicatos e a formação profissional nos anos
    90 – contribuições da sociedade civil para uma educação inte-
    gral do ser humano, ANPED. [retrieved from: <http://www.port
    alanpedsul.com.br/admin/uploads/1999/Educacao_E_Trabalho/
    Trabalho/08_34_05_OS_SINDICATOS_E_A_FORMACAO_
    PROFISSIONAL_NOS_ANOS_90___CONTRIBUICOES_
    DA_SOCIEDADE_CIVIL_PARA_UMA_EDUCACAO_INTEG
    RAL_DO_SER_HUMANO.pdf> February, 26th 2016].
Guimarães, G. 1996. Sindicalismo e Cooperativismo – A economia
    solidária em debate. Transformações no mundo do trabalho. São
    Paulo, Unitrabalho.
Giroletti, D. 2007. Os desafios do sindicalismo no século XXI. In
    Inácio, J.R. (Org.). Sindicalismo no Brasil: os primeiros 100 anos.
    Belo Horizonte, Crisálida.
Grimbaun, R. 2002. Trabalho: Sindicalismo sai da ressaca dos anos 90.
    [retrieved from: <http://www.pessoal.bridge.com.br/sindicalismo>
    February, 26th 2016].
Hirata, H. 2001. Globalização e divisão sexual do Trabalho. [retrieved
    from: <http://www.scielo.br/pdf/cpa/n17-18/n17a06.pdf> Febru-
    ary, 26th 2016].
Hirata, H. 2009. A precarização e a divisão internacional e sexual do
    trabalho. Sociologias. Porto-Alegre, 21: 24–41.
Iamamoto, M. V. 2010. O serviço social na contemporaneidade: tra-
    balho e formação profissional. São Paulo, Cortez.
Kuenzer, A.Z.; Grabowski, G. 2006. Educação Profissional: desafios
    para a construção de um projeto para os que vivem do trabalho. Flo-
    rianópolis, Perspectiva, 24(1): 297–318. [retrieved from: <http://
    www.perspectiva.ufsc.br> February, 26th 2016].
Kuenzer, A.Z. 2002 *Ensino Médio* – construindo uma proposta para os
    que vivem do trabalho. São Paulo, Cortez.
Leite, M. de P., Rizek, C.S. 1997. Projeto: reestruturação produtiva e
    qualificação. Educação & Sociedade, Campinas, 18(58): 178–198.
Lima, A.C.; Guhur, D. M. P.; Toná, N.; Noma, A. K. 2011. Reflexões
    sobre a Educação Profissional em Agroecologia no MST: desafios
    nos cursos técnicos do Paraná. In H.T. Novaes (org.) Movimentos

sociais, trabalho associado e educação para além do capital. São Paulo, Outras Expressões.

Manfredi, S.M., Bastos, S. 1997 Experiências e projetos de formação profissional entre trabalhadores brasileiros. Educação & Sociedade, ano XVIII(60): 117–143.

Moraes, C.S.V. (coord.) 1999. Diagnóstico da formação profissional: o ramo metalúrgico. São Paulo, Artchip Editora.

Pochmann, M. 2000. Mudanças na ocupação e a formação profissional. Trabalho & Educação. Belo Horizonte, 6: 48–71.

Queiroz, A.A. 2007. Movimento Sindical: passado, presente e futuro. In J.R. Inácio, (org.). Sindicalismo no Brasil: os primeiros 100 anos. Belo Horizonte, Crisálida.

Segnini, L. R.P. 2001. Entre le chômage et l'engrenage dês emplois precaries. Revue Internationale de Psychopatologie et de Psychodynamique du Travail. Paris, Martins Media.

SENAI 2005. Departamento Nacional. Relatório Anual 2005. Brasília, SENAI/DN.

Siqueira, W. 2003. O sindicalismo para o século XXI. [retrieved from: <http://wagnersiqueira.com.br/opiniao/sindixxi.htm> February, 26th 2016].

Silva, L.P. 2010. Formação profissional no Brasil: o papel do Serviço Nacional de Aprendizagem Industrial – SENAI. História, 29, 1, Franca. [retrieved from: <http://dx.doi.org/10.1590/S0101-90742010000100022>.

Steinke, A.L.O sindicalismo no Brasil. [retrieved from: <http://www.sintet.ufu.br/sindicalismo.htm> February, 26th 2016].

Toaldo, C.J. 2002. Sindicalismo. [retrieved from: <http://www.toaldo.hpg.ig.com.br/sindicalismo.htm> February, 26th 2016].

VICENTE PALOP-ESTEBAN

VET Challenges in Local Development: The UDATMA Case in Ecuador[1]

This chapter is based on the fieldwork performed in 2014 for the completion of a PhD. The thesis title is "Vocational Education and Training and its Focus on Local Development" (Palop Esteban, 2015). During my PhD, I conducted qualitative fieldwork in six different places in Ecuador. One of these observations was the Unit of Agricultural Development, Tourism and Environment (UDATMA) and its link to the Marcabelí municipality in Ecuador, South America. UDATMA and Marcabelí were elected for fieldwork because we found several indicators that it could provide significant data for the social development, (e. g. minimum rates of Unsatisfied Basic Needs – UBN) as well as highlighting the local initiative for creating an ecological international market from the local municipally.

The UDATMA choice is a significant accomplishment, and Marcabelí exemplifies social and economic work from the public authority, involving both institutions (municipality and UDATMA), and answering questions about the inclusion of people in the employment. The municipality is proposing a training program according to the demand of the working environment and the choices of the students (such as new local markets and production). The objective is to offer opportunities to the students for production at the end of their education, through the construction of a trade exhibition where students display products they've developed in the educative environment. (GAD Marcabelí 2012).

---

1   I would like to thank the contributions from Professor Fernando Marhuenda to this chapter, his reviews, knowledge and proximity have been, without a doubt, irreplaceable.

1. The context: Marcabelí, the municipality and its educational offer

The Marcabelí municipality is in the south of Ecuador. It is located in a coastal area but extends into an interior area called "Montubia" region. This area was populated by settlers only twenty five years ago. In the province, there are seven-thousand people: two-thousand are in the urban area. The majority are Mestizos[2] from the coast, mostly Manabí and Guayas. They are looking for fields to grow crops.

The people make their living from agriculture and animal breeding. They also grow sugar cane and other short-cycle plants, like coffee, corn, rice, soy and bean. There is also a refinery for the processing of *panela*[3] sugar cane and the liqueur of sugar cane, all of these based on the cooperative model.

The cooperative work that is happening in recent years consists of small producer groups that belong to the association searching for economic alternatives (often from abroad) and defense against larger farms in the area. This circumstance is promoted by smallholders but also by the municipality of Marcabelí. In fact, the birth of training initiatives and the promotion of the association of farmers is part of the community strategy for the local economy.

The urban area is quite modern because it was planned in the Seventies. The structure is typical from the construction models of the "liberal" countries. Each corner and sidewalk belongs to a different designer with different criteria.

In the town center, local trade is typical, although this kind of diversity is not as prevalent as the "invasion"[4] zones or homeless areas. In contrast to this circumstance, an important citizen movement is making significant changes. For instance, the population has a selective collection of rubbish, and there are penalties if someone doesn't separate their

---

2   Mixed aboriginal and European
3   Unrefined whole cane sugar.
4   The "invasion" zones are population areas in the frontier of the city areas or areas very near to the town. These areas are occupied by the population illegally. Usually, the people of these invasion zones are coming from rural areas with troubles meeting their basic needs.

rubbish in material-specific containers. The town also has a recycling plant (which is unique in the province). In addition, there is an incipient movement for work in communal agricultural fields. This circumstance is not common in non-indigenous zones, namely in zones where there is a colonist population like Marcabelí.

The area of Marcabelí, as already mentioned, is populated by settlers from coast, which have brought a negative impact on the environment. The settlers tend to think that the length of their stay in the new territory will be temporary, extracting the most benefits at the expense of their land (at least in the first years of their settlement). Typically, these settlers do not use traditional forms of farming in the area, nor the agricultural products of the local culture because, among other reasons, they are not acquainted with them – or choose not to. In the case of indigenous populations, this phenomenon is completely the contrary: information is transmitted by previous generations, and in addition, they have a community responsibility and respect for the earth and their environment – an important distinction.

This circumstance favors dynamic ecological exploitation and community land use. However, Marcabelí, despite having no indigenous population, refuses colonial development models. An explanation for this refusal can be found in the work of awareness-raising efforts and the promotion of the municipality in recent years.

The space has been utilized to the maximum and the earth has been re-cultivated from the harm caused by the use of chemical fertilizing. This re-cultivation can be observed from old aerial photographs of the zone. Only ten years ago, there were extensive barren lands, but at this moment, the earth is gradually regenerating.

Also, as a result of the municipal plans, informal living places are decreasing greatly, including in the peripheral areas. Although we can still find poor living places, many of the houses are now built with permanent structural materials (*e.g.*, bricks and concrete), with basic services (*e.g.*, water, sewerage, and electricity), thanks to municipal intervention.

In summary, Marcabelí can be seen as a rural zone with an interesting productive movement in cooperative work. Also, it has the help of the government in economical vocational training. Basically, we are speaking about a zone where governmental and productive involvement for development exists. We see that this fact has a capital importance, not only in Marcabelí. We can find in the bibliography about the local development other examples that demonstrate the importance that it has the link between Government – productive world – context and vocational training (Geerlings 1999) for example is the case of Mondragon in the Basque Country (Greenwood & Santos 1989), where the combined performance of the factors above generate synergies of highly profitable economical product but also in social development. The advance in this sense, can have relationship with a particular culture collaborative that we should study to know how can it is generating.

In relation to the quantitative data, the aggregated value rate per person in the locality is $3.47USD[5] per person. This indicator is very near to the Gross Domestic Product, GDP. While that data is not too high, but it reveals significant local growth.

We can see that Social Indicators System of Ecuador (SIISE) and Marcabelí have a positive mark in the Unsatisfied Basic Needs (UBN) indicator, of 52%. That data is important because Marcabelí has a rural population, where more difficulties exist for certain infrastructural aspects, like drainage systems or water by pipeline. In fact, in these cases, the data shows 70 to 80% of UBN, according to the SIISE, in which case, this is quite good. We think, based on this data, that the region has been able to maintain its development rate despite the outbreak of the *roya* plague[6]. Perhaps the key has been the successful exploitation of resources (in reference the SIISE data).

The indicator UBN is a very common indicator in Latin America, recommended by CEPAL (United Nations Economic Commission for Latin America and the Caribbean) since the 1970s (Gómez, Alvarez, Lucarini, & Olmos 1994), despite being an indicator with some biases, it is still used as a matrix for the design of social policies. The methodology used was defined by the Andean Community of Nations (CAN). The UBN is defined from the lack of at least, one of the following circumstances (Equipo SIISE 2014): inadequate physical characteristics (walls of fabric, cardboard, or cane, etc.), or are natural or urban

---

5   In Quito, the capital of Ecuador, the aggregated value rate is $5.80USD per person.

6   Insect that kills the coffee plant: the plague affected all small farmers of this zone (Redacción Economía 2014).

shelters; inadequate services (without water or drains); high economic dependence (more than three household members depend on a person with incomplete primary education); the existence of children without school-based education (at least one between six to twelve years); and critical overcrowding (more than three people per room).

Another influence can be in the context of structural changes. Ecuador has had a continuous historical context of inequity in recent decades (or even centuries, depending on perspective), which, as the rest of Latin America, has passed from systems of supply of raw material for the North, to models of development by import substitution, generating an unpayable debt throughout recent history. This circumstance generated impoverishment and highly-inefficient government systems in areas such as the care of the environment and democratic participation.

The arrival of the current constitution of 2008 is coining a new model of *Sumak kawsay* (good living) relations, meaning living harmoniously with the people, but also with the environment and with economic growth. This philosophical-political contribution, without having achieved its goal yet, makes us intuit some changes in the collective work. In this sense, it is possible to see in Ecuador certain methodological contributions and identity models, which have to do with the transformation and growth of the public apparatus as a guarantor of rights, efforts for redistribution of wealth, the return to the population of the infrastructures in the propriety of the oligarchy, etc. Although it is necessary to acknowledge that these advances are still considered very questionable by sectors of the population, especially from the democratic point of view that "good living" needs "imposing" in order to carry out the mentioned structural reforms.

For the *Sumak kawsay*, on one hand, the technical training is inclusive and open to all people, while on the other hand, it works for a new consideration of secondary studies, dignifying the technical training, integrated it into the mandatory training and giving it the same rights as a Bachelor's degree. It is one of the reasons for the development of unified systems of the middle schools, where all of the students pass along the same track (unified system) avoiding the segregation that technical training produces in some countries. Additionally, the change of the production matrix requires an adequate education that allows a flexible learning, based in life skills and helping face the challenges of society and changing jobs.

Therefore, we can consider Marcabelí as a territory with growth (by economic indicators) and development (the observed evidence regarding the scope of the common welfare). Upon this context, our research has seeked to determine whether and how the contribution of UDATMA has been key to the positive process of the area.

Apart from UDATMA, like non-formal educational offer coordinated with the municipality for the training and integration of people, as already described, we can find the Technical College where technical baccalaureate is provided. The school is a formal entity under the law of the Ministry of Education, therefore, its capacity for local articulation is quite limited; however, thanks to UDATMA, the students of the school have opportunities to practice in the fields of the city council and receive first-hand experience from the adult students from the UDATMA. It should take into account that students of the UDATMA is mostly a group of students expert in practical issues because many of them have years in the crops of own propriety or the others, it can teach technical expertise in adolescent students but also a human formation, in relation to the relations and the labor climate in the world of agricultural.

2. Research questions and methodology

As already mentioned, this work is part of the doctoral thesis about the contributions from the VET to the local development. In this work we can find connections in the educational technical world and local productive initiatives. One of the experiences that is marked like a successful experience, was the municipal school of the UDATMA, where the involvement of the different stakeholders (productive, educational and Government) are getting good results, for instance in professional integration, promotion of local markets, indicators of well-being, I mean local development.

The methodology for the extraction of information is based on qualitative analysis of semi-structured interviews according to the Grounded Theory in its constructivist version (Charmaz 2000). The inquiry took significant amounts of participants and testimonies, and then the investigation extracted the data. The interviews took place in one week during the month of November 2013, and at all times, the researcher worked to create a climate of trust, openness, and collaboration.

The questions were written, but the researcher allowed the respondents to go in the direction that the persons considered. The research was intended to create a conversational atmosphere where questions and answers happened in a spontaneous way (Goode & Hatt 1979). To strengthen the dialogue, the same questions were asked in different ways to procure the most accurate information (de Souza Martins 2013), especially in cases of unclear or conflicting answers or reports.

The interviews and the observations were made in the surroundings of the school of UDATMA. The school is included by the technical studies and its consequent relationship with the productive environment. The UDATMA is a non-formal vocational training institute for adults; however, the Marcabelí Technical School is a formal technical school. It is interesting to note that the VET in Ecuador has now been inserted into the school since the last educational reform of 2013. This trend is following the Nordic model of the Unified System (Stenström & Lasonen 2005).

In the central ideas of the conversations, there emerged some recurring concepts: the most frequent was the ways and possibilities of the local production for improving the development. Other important observation was the set of ideas relating to the preservation of the environment and the responsibility for its care. These ideas were very significant because they provided information about the development and care of the common good. These concepts were complemented by similar ideas in the narration. For instance, it was very often that the people in the interviews used the words "association", "credit", "cooperative" and "city." We can see the emergence in a significant number of interviews of the word "city". It would mean that the municipal action is present and encourages the local development. However, in this concrete case, we must bear in mind that the UDATMA is a municipal organization, so it is normal to have these links in the narrative map.

Also, we can find that, in the "environmental" concept, this fact seems linked to development and production. In addition, we find testimonies that connect with the field of education.

3. UDATMA's VET contribution to the development model in Marcabelí

3.1 The educational model of the UDATMA

During the fieldwork, the informants used a recurring formation concept for local development, e.g it was very common to find in the interviews continuous references to the possibilities of opening small businesses (even by children interviewed), and in many cases they have mentioned the importance of the work in a cooperative form. On the other hand, we can see the use of projects as a method of work with background values. This is one of the scenarios of my doctoral thesis. In my thesis, I'm defending that the educative inclusion has tendency for work in values; in particular, we can find the importance of work in values that intersect with the other subjects as a possibility for the creation of environments for local development, (Barretto Ghione 2007, Palop Esteban 2015) in the Technical School and as well as the non-formal organizations, like in the UDATMA.

In the area of educative inclusion, it is interesting to visualize as the UDATMA push for methodological resources of importance, as the priority inclusion of the weak people, or the collective construction of knowledge among others. This push leads us to think about the quality of the educative offer, as well as if the UDATMA can be a good element for the promotion of the development, where the work in inclusive education is a work for the social and the equitable development, as already mentioned.

3.2 The development view

In the root of the interviews in relation with the notion of development, we can observe a widespread concern. This fact is according to the trend where the development is not only a mere economic aspect for growth; it's also the capacity for the redistribution of resources and investment in the well-being of the community. For instance, in basic services such as education and health; or in the desire of productive resources, such as access to the ownership of the land (Sen 1999). We can think that, in this case, development is a much debated topic, and perhaps with guidelines and good criteria, we could collect some testimonies with not very conclusive evidence in this tendency.

There are aspects with relevance like the existence of a model for free trade, which hindered small producers, or the weak legal regulation to protect the small entrepreneurs and workers. These circumstances can be promoting a scenario beneficial to large-scale production, and it can be poor for the small producer. Therefore, these elements should be considered for the analysis.

We can perceive two opposing trends. On one hand, we can observe a tendency in local action by the municipal government and the small producer's organizations. In the other hand, we see the centralist state legislation support the large-scale production. In fact, it is generating good indicators of development for the nation, but this development is not always for the people, as small production is excluded. Despite these two opposing trends, according to the quantitative indicators, Marcabelí seems to have gained traction among local trends, determined by the good economic indicators observed in the area. For example, the recovery of the ground productivity by cultivation without chemists has been a work realized in the last decade. This effort has allowed smaller owners to obtain certain profitability from agricultural work.

Regarding the environmentalist view of development, we observe a significant glut of evidence in the vision of the organic agriculture as a source of future development. In this sense, it is no coincidence that most of the local producers work on their own promotion and dissemination, mostly in the production and the consumption. This fact is the difference between large-scale producers. Larger production is based in productivity by the use of agrochemicals, so the cultural change in relation to the use of organic products would benefit smaller production. This could be one of the reasons for this trend.

3.3 The configuration of the relationships of the people

Through the relation between educational institutions and their environments, we can perceive a very clear trend towards the multidisciplinary and dynamic relations with the different stakeholders of the territory, with the relations appearing to work very well. Also, the relations of the institution with its environment seems to help foster local development scenarios. This fact is an optimal circumstance when the VET Center is configured as a local node[7]. The local node could be a strategy for planning efforts from civil society[8] for aiding processes of local development, like coordinating the productive apparatus with governmental institutions and other stakeholders present in the context. It is possible that the suggested way allows to create new aspects for deepening the democracy, as the scenario is based on the horizontality and the participation of the people, as opposed to the "entrepreneurial leadership" of only one person or a dominant group. So, the node could diagnose the productive ways, provide ways to take into account the reality of the territory and therefore propose training alternatives.

We can see structures resembling a participative model, like the association of the producers and cooperatives, among others. One circumstance that can contribute to the social constructions are the *mingas*. Part of the local heritage and tradition of the area, a *minga* is a voluntary act of communitarian work for the population's benefit. *Mingas* can be found in rural areas of the Andine region. The communitarian work is very useful, for instance, for repairing a road, or painting the school of the community. In addition, the *mingas* improve the social cohesion in the community.

But there exists another trend in the way of the neo-liberal political model: low wages and poor protection of the workers. We can observe

---

7   In the thesis, it mentioned the local node development (Rodríguez 2007).
8   Small producers, representatives of the structure of government, representatives of cultural, political and religious groups, community leaders and all those interested in providing cooperation.

the low protection to the small producers by the central state. This situation may be related to practices of the past, where the large-scale productions have always belonged to the oligarchies, mostly by people that have operated from outside of the country. This trend is now decreasing, but the culture and the forms are still active.

In the present case, we see that relations are good between the stakeholders, except for the big producers. Jonny Cueva (director of UDATMA) recognizes this fact. This testimony must be taken into account as Jonny is one of the most qualified authorities of the territory. Mr. Cueva has demonstrated aptitude to carry forward the educational task of the municipality, being involved in all the phases of the teaching process. Also, he has demonstrated an interpretation of the events during the interviews conducted. He is linking wide-reaching ideas, as he has served as the head of one of the most important precursors to Marcabelí local development. In this sense, we can find that the large-scale producers can create opportunities for growth, but this circumstance doesn't always appear to extend to the local development. For instance, while the large-scale producers can provide salaries to a large portion of the local population, strengthening the community, this is not always the case, as this salary may not always be sufficient or permanent. An additional problem is created: people leave their traditional practices, which produces a weakening of the local economic structure; the people, no longer dependent on their agricultural work, now depend on a salary of poor quality. Finally, the loss of local production could weaken relationships that, in many cases, feed the social capital, reducing the ways to foster relationships and enhance the lives of the community.

Bigger companies can bring an unstable economy because the people depend on the capital (Navarro 2014). Because of this, the populations can lose development. These cases are described in the economic literature of the same Ecuador which mentions "anchor companies" (Chiriboga 2010). At first glance, these companies are called by the government for job creation and associated productions, but the results do not always conform to the expectations detailed above.

The growth, in this case, is not equitable because better methods of economic redistribution are missing, especially as already described, if the wages are quite precarious (Navarro 2014). The idea of the

UDATMA (and the municipality) is to resist the described tendency in relation to the dominance of the great capital. The plan could be creating a network of local production relatively independent from the big producers, with the aim to establish the basis for a joint municipal economic policy, and in this way, the municipality could work to make the population more equitable. Also, it would be interesting because it would guarantee the protection of the land for sustainable production in the following years. Additionally, this strategy would be an incentive for trade because we are speaking about an organic product and therefore of better quality.

Therefore, the target would be increasing the productive volume of the small associate farmers to at least 50% of the entire productive volume of the area to be able to determine proper productive politics. The commercialization could serve two purposes, (1) the exportation of ecological products (like coffee) in the fair trade markets (in contrast to big producer, who haven't explored this market); (2) and the progressive sensitization of the domestic consumers towards the national product and, in this sense, the small producers can meet the demand for the national product that the Ecuadoran government is trying to stimulate.

Concerning the urban model, we can observe the care of the urban space and certain proximity between the public resources and its possibilities for building personal relations. So, we can confirm that the relations in the communitarian field are working also in the organization of the city. As an example, we can find communitarian spaces in the urban fabric for relaxation, conversation, and playing sports, which permit interdisciplinary communication.

4. Contributions of the UDATMA to local development through vocational education

In relation to the interviews and the observations conducted, we can consider that the UDATMA is a resource that is working for the development community with special circumstances, like involving in the work of the municipality and its educational resources as part of the strategy for the community growth. This scenario makes the UDATMA an excellent stakeholder for coordinating actions for local development, where education is an important line of work.

We can observe important work for creative learning that is implementing an educational strategy by participative projects. We could see how this line has permitted the inclusion of people with difficulties for social integration. This circumstance has been thanks to the adapted projects, permitting the regulation of the goal to the particular interest of the student.

We can appreciate working within this trend towards personal development, as it has been realized in the activities that the institution is responsible for. This strategy is programed and contextualized in the offered curriculum. For example, during studies in UDATMA there are activities along with the courses offered, these activities have to do with the exhibitions or with the production offered by UDATMA during the courses. Students can even offer their products commercially even before finishing their studies. The organization of the fairs and the channels of distribution has been, for the majority of the time, the responsibility of the pupils. Also, it is important to note that the students are those who introduce products are experienced in part from the school curriculum, i.e. it is the own students which proposes that species or crops are of particular interest. These plantations are experienced in the spaces of the UDATMA from a point of view of production, taking care to be within organic agriculture. Therefore most of the programming of the course depends on the proper student and its implication with the realized investigation.

It is convenient to say that there is a certain culture of values for local development, ie, participation, citizenship, the common good, etc., these values are perceived as part of the construction for a better future in the territory. We are not talking about a specific subject in the curriculum, but we can see a cross-cutting dimension of the studies where the experience of the academic life is imbued with democracy, environmentalism and mutual collaboration.

Perhaps the reason for working in this trend is building multidisciplinary interactions between the resources of the community, creating a local development model that fosters the formation and growth in the capacities of the people. It is maybe one of the advantages that non-formal studies offer, as the formation offered by the UDATMA has the capacity to be very close to all interests. In contrast, the technical school of Marcabelí, where the structure is formal with a much less professional outlook, the relation between studies and context is one of the keys for an academic promotion for the local development.

Another interesting aspect is the perspective of the institution. UDATMA has international connections from around the world. UDATMA has close relations with the Marcabelí Coffee Producers Association (APECAM), mutually benefiting through projects for the promotion of the local agriculture. One of these projects is the internationalization and promotion of organic agriculture and fair trade, since APECAM has very good relations in its international relations; in fact, governments like Holland and Germany are giving economic support with the international cooperation for commercialization projects. We can talk about how our organization has first-hand experience in a "g-lo-cal"[9] work model, because it creates a *glo*bal change through *local* interventions.

This development model of the municipality, with the closer collaboration of the UDATMA created in 2010, is based on the vision for the preservation of the environment, by teaching non-aggressive techniques for cultivating the land. As an example, the promotion of natural products for plagues and fertilizing for producers.

Essentially, we can speak about a strategy with different lines of work but with a confluent vision for local development by educational strategies.

5. Conclusions

Our analysis offers us a territory that, in few years, has experienced economic growth combined with local development, exceeding expectations according to economic and the social development indicators.

---

9   We find the term in the local movements with international links, where the global changes always have a local actuation (Robertson, 2012).

We can observe in this way, through the growth of the local trade and the small production, that Marcabelí has an endogenous plan with economic identity. This is a relevant circumstance, because the previous trend has been that the concentration of trade in large-scale producers existed with a minimal return in regards to the welfare of the local populations. This is typical according with the colonial model, as shown in agricultural exploitations like the Marcabelí area. In the already mentioned doctoral thesis where this work is gathered, we can find other territories in Ecuador where we can certify that this relation between economic colonialism and poverty is present, for which, we can say that Marcabelí municipality has been able to oppose a strong tendency for the poverty of the area, where the production is extensive and harmful to the ground, and on the other hand, to the dictation of the international markets (without local strategy).

In addition, the municipality has opened some strategies for productive linkages with small producers and environmental strategic policies, such as waste collection services or the commitment to organic farming. Therefore, in Marcabelí we can highlight crucial indicators:

– From the municipality, there is a trend to promote and coordinate producers and vocational training, although it is true that this articulation is done mostly by individual interests and not in a fully-institutionalized strategy. Primarily responsible for this work is the UDATMA, by the hand of its director. Also, we can highlight that all agricultural products proposed by the pupils for investigating its productive possibilities are from the Marcabelí area, at least from the existence of settlers, and it is investigated by the students. It seems that they have an endogenous development and allows some productive independence from international markets, ensuring opportunities for local development.

– We can consider that there exists a high degree of participation between most of the farmers, although not all. We must remember that the Marcabelí area is also a large agricultural production and these are not in the local participatory dynamic. Small and medium producers are quite organized, and thanks to the confidence of the municipality and some international organizations, they are moving to cooperative productive models. It is based on regulation and mutual trust. These factors result in the creation of a climate of cooperation that can ensure growth and development scenarios.

– We can find places and gardens equipped for sports and recreation, with these infrastructures being provided by the city council, confirming the social trend to create a community partnership.

– We can assert that the UDATMA has the capacity to agglutinate synergies in a participatory manner, which is the idea of the local development node. Technical School of Marcabelí and UDATMA work with common programs so they can establish strategies with the association of producers, undertaking placement and vocational training promotion.

– The model of teaching of the school is rather traditional: vertical education, little participatory teaching, contents and methodology rarely discussed; up until now, it has been creating new lines of working with practical experimentations with students. Instead, the UDATMA can be considered a center where teaching and learning is significant. In other words, the contents are marked by the needs of students (they are adults and, in many cases, with agricultural experience), they have experience with the research-productive products. Finally, cooperatives and other associated workers are working with the employment of the students. Perhaps these are due to the productive movement being associative in a good part of the study area.

The UDATMA is providing a very interesting productive coordination between producers and educational dynamics. Embedded in the social context, it is seeking to prepare alliances for strengthening the development of producers. Also, it has a special significance in the teaching, researching, and personalized work, so it is unique in its class.

In discussions with Jonny Cueva and Fabio Apolo (responsible APECAM) about the possibilities for improvement, some ideas emerged, such as the urgent need for the protection of the small producer in front of the large company, perhaps by reducing taxes for small production, at least in municipal environments. Similarly, it would be good to create a strategy for how the large producers can be involved in the local development work that is taking place in the area. Perhaps if all small producers are able to provide a unique option, maybe we can establish another horizon where the large production cannot be.

In this case, the UDATMA is one institution of the VET which coordinates the area, with producers and local authorities. In fact, the UDATMA also has the favor of the council for local promotion, managing the relationships of all stakeholders through meetings and planning participatory strategies. Also, this coordination could be carried out by educational institutions associated with the municipality and other stakeholders, like the producers.

In this scenario, VET is revealed as a key player in the strategies for the development processes from the people. These strategies can come from the local government for the local development, and the key, it seems to be, is the educational component of the curriculum, or that is to say, how the educational process is building on behalf of development for the people.

In other words, training is revealed as a factor for development only if there is a link with the growth of the person, where the educational inclusion is a key for the construction of the community. We could see this indicator in the low levels of educative attrition in enrollment. Without these contributions, technical education has the risk to contribute to the promotion of inequalities in the communities. This fact we could see in Guayaquil, in the Labor Initiation Center (CIL). In the CIL, the dropout rates are very severe. In addition, we detected that the graduates are incorporated into the informal work market in very small productions. Also, the CIL students don't have the trend to open associated productive alternatives or cooperative work. According to this data, the interviews revealed high levels of distrust. Maybe for these reasons, the CIL is operating in a very poor zone with strong indicators of underdevelopment.

But the link between development and vocational training, as well as the educational dimension, must suggest the participation of technical training institutions in the territory in a local development node with perspective to coordinate their operations like a territorial node. This would coordinate with the productive sector, the government, and other stakeholders of the context.

Such centers, with vocation for local development work, could hypothesize production alternatives, present a formation from the context and propose educational alternatives, and other possibilities. In addition, we could propose that nodes could have the ability to manage

other processes, like cultural activities, activities for community education, or non-formal education. It is possible that the suggested way can
be a way to reveal new aspects for the deepening of democracy from the
participation of the people based on horizontality and, as opposed to the
"entrepreneurial leadership" with a more individualistic character.

In this sense, it is necessary to mention some models of anti-de-
velopment or questionable development (*e.g.*, sweatshops in Latin
America), where people and even institutions propose and implement
external models with bad consequences for the territory. This strategy
usually generates dependency and little capacity to generate endogenous development because it is focused on specific individuals or institutions, in spite of the community. These "development" models usually
do not prepare for creative alternatives and offer undemocratic models,
with little (or without) representation (Barrios Hernández & Santiago
Hernández 2004).

References

Barretto Ghione, H. 2007. Formación profesional en el diálogo social.
    Formación profesional en el diálogo social. Montevideo, Cinterfor/
    OIT.
Barrios Hernández, M. A., & Santiago Hernández, R. 2004. Tehuacán:
    del calzón de manta a los blue jeans.
Charmaz, K. 2000. Grounded theory: Objectivist and constructivist
    methods. In N. Denzin & Y. Lincoln (eds.), Handbook of qualita-
    tive research. Thousand Oaks, CA, Sage.
Chiriboga, A. (coord) 2010. Agenda de la Política Económica para el
    Buen Vivir 2011–2013. Quito.
de Souza Martins, J. 2013. O artesanato intelectual na sociologia.
    Revista Brasileira de Sociologia, 1(2), 36.
Equipo SIISE 2014. Sistema Integrado de Indicadores Sociales del
    Ecuador. [retrieved from: <http://www.siise.gob.ec/> – May, 1st
    2014].

GAD Marcabelí 2012. Plan de Desarrollo y Ordenamiento Territorial. Marcabelí.

Geerlings, J. 1999. Design of Responsive. Vocational Education and Training. Gouda, Eburon Publishers.

Gómez, A., Alvarez, G., Lucarini, A., & Olmos, F. 1994. Las Necesidades Básicas Insatisfechas: Sus deficiencias técnicas y su impacto en la definición de Políticas Sociales. INDEC – Argentina.

Goode, W. J., & Hatt, P. J. 1979. Métodos em pesquisa social. Sao Paulo, Companhia Editora Nacional.

Greenwood, D., & Santos, J. 1989. Culturas de Fagor: estudio antropológico de las cooperativas de Mondragón. Txertoa.

Navarro, V. 2014. Las causas del enorme desempleo y la baja ocupación en la Unión Europea. Nueva Tribuna.

Palop Esteban, V.R. 2015. La Formación Profesional y su incidencia en el desarrollo local. Universidad de Valencia (España). [retrieved from: <http://roderic.uv.es/handle/10550/44641> – March, 14th 2016].

Redacción Economía 2014. 85.000 hectáreas de café arábigo afectadas con roya. El Telégrafo, 26 junio: 6–7.

Robertson, R. 2012. Globalisation or glocalisation? Journal of International Communication, 18(2), 191–208. http://doi.org/10.1080/132 16597.2012.709925.

Rodríguez, F. 2007. Desarrollo local. Elementos conceptuales básicos. Oviedo.

Sen, A. 1999. Development as freedom. New York, Anchor Books.

Stenström, M.-L., & Lasonen, J. 2005. Strategies for reforming workforce preparation programs in Europe. The Journal of Technology Studies, 38–43.

Section 3.
Tensions Between the Global and the Local:
Adoptions, Rejections and Reactions to
Standardization of VET Traditions

Lea Zehnder and Philipp Gonon

Civic and Market Convention as Driving Forces of the Development of Swiss VET[1]

As in most countries, the trigger for establishing educational systems in the 19th century was the aim to build up nations. Such efforts did not only focus on primary schooling but were extended to all forms of education, from kindergarten to university. Thus, also post-elementary enrolment experienced a considerable growth. The "liberal legacy", as Andy Green puts it, also included, besides ideological hegemony, openness towards industrial needs (Green 1992, p. 308). Exactly this setting is also the starting point of our contribution in this volume and the line of depicting the development of the Swiss educational system and its vocational education and training (VET). Our arguments are based on a sociological theory of conventions, that the establishment of local and federal amendments and legislations which supported VET had a strong civic notion, but also included the option of a well-organised industrial society. Within such a setting the educated worker is nowadays able to pursue a professional career. Thus, the development of Swiss VET ended up in a compromise of different claims related to the state, the industry and the market, hybridizing the educational system.

1   This contribution was written as part of the research project 'From the Former Master Apprenticeship to Modern Dual Vocational Education' of the Chair of Vocational Education and Training (Prof. Dr. Philipp Gonon) at the University of Zurich. The project was funded by the Swiss National Science Foundation.

1. Historical premises

In this first section we want to sketch a short historical trajectory of vocational education in Switzerland before the beginning of the 20th century.

At that time, like in a lot of countries in Central Europe, education was a local affair, often limited to a smaller group and not a national project. However, at the beginning of the 19th century an educational reform project was launched by the Helvetic government to raise the standards of education and to boost the further dispersion of popular education. The Enlightenment idea of making all citizens capable of participating in society and being a member of a productive nation was supported by most educators, who themselves established new forms of education and training. A renowned educator was e.g. Johann Heinrich Pestalozzi, who urged authorities in his pamphlet Über *Volksbildung und Industrie* (About Popular Education and Industry) to foster on a broad but also hands-on education already at the beginning of the 19th century, in order of making not just the underprivileged youth but all inhabitants fit for society. Elementary education for industry was also a contribution to civic and personal development (Pestalozzi 2005 [1806]). The possibility of enlarging the traditional apprenticeships was interestingly not seen as an alternative, due to its limited presence in the economy in those days.

Furthermore, at the beginning of the 19th century the traditional apprenticeship model[2] experienced a crisis, due to technological innovations and economic pressure from neighbouring countries, stemming from the growing industrial production there. Christoph Bernoulli, a university professor situated in Basel, urged to abandon this kind of

---

2   Since the Middle Ages, the responsibility for the traditional apprenticeship model was in the hands of the guilds. They set several general conditions regarding apprenticeship with the master (e.g. regarding pre-conditions, period of the apprenticeship, apprentice wage and graduation), but all in all it was still a very limited formalized learning process. With the growing industry at the beginning of the 19th century, the training of industrial job activities was extremely shortened in time, which put heavy pressure on the traditional master apprenticeship model (Gonon 2002a).

education and to transfer these tasks to schools. The lawyer Johann Jakob Vest, on the other hand, argued for still relying on this apprenticeship system in order to keep the balance between different social classes. If the industrial regime takes over, he argued in this controversy taking place in the year 1823, the middle class will vanish and there will remain only a small elite and poor servants (Gonon 2002b). This controversy was one of the debates which focused on the future of the economic system, which some saw in a free trade system without restrictions, whereas others pleaded for a closed or only partly opened economic space. However, this important aspect also included the question of an adequate vocational education and training system.

Heinrich Zschokke, an influential Swiss education reformer of the first half of the 19th century and writer, coined the expression "crafts have a golden basis", which should be the basis of economy and society. He said that one should enlarge "hands-on work" with "head work" and establish vocationally oriented schools in order to be competitive also against products coming from abroad, like the English textiles (Zschokke 1893). Beside economics, also social implications were discussed related to the education system. Especially at the end of the 19th century the so-called "social question" and the aim of integrating the working class were a hot issue not only in Switzerland but in different continental countries as well. In Switzerland e.g. the ETH-Professor Victor Boehmert argued for the establishment of a well-developed educational system, in order to reconcile class differences (Boehmert 1873).

Developing the VET system was also pushed by the reports about the world exhibitions. In the context of the first amendment on vocational education in 1884, which made it possible to subsidize institutions offering vocational education, a lot of reformers referred to the world exhibitions in Paris (1878 and again 1900), Vienna (1873), Philadelphia (1876) and other exhibitions to underscore their arguments for establishing and reforming a national VET system. These exhibitions offered insights into social, economic and industrial progress in other countries and were a trigger for putting the VET system in a global perspective. It was clearly stated that nations with a developed technical education like France had a big competitive advantage, as education reformers could easily observe (Dumreicher 1879). One of the aims

was also to overcome a local *régime corporatif* through a national legislation (Brizon 1909).

All these different claims were supported by several actors like
the *Schweizerischer Gewerbeverband* (Swiss trade association), the
Schweizerische Gemeinnützige Gesellschaft (Swiss welfare organization), teachers associations and union-forerunners (e.g. *Grütliverein*)
which at that time began forming their interests regarding vocational
training.

2. Thesis: The VET system as a result of different actor-driven claims

Based on this short historical sketch of the intentions connected to the
development of Swiss VET, we deduce that, being a compromise of
different actor driven claims, the VET system incorporates more than
one institutional setting. On the one hand, vocational education tries to
provide access to the workplace. If people do not find a job after graduation from a VET programme, the system obviously fails. Furthermore – from today's perspective – vocational education is also a kind
of a foundation for a career step. Incorporating different claims (from
the perspective of the state, the economy as well as from an individual
perspective) and institutional settings then become important objects
of a federal framework legislation[3] that gives some kind of structure to
vocational education, while being flexible enough to take the needs and
conditions of all regions and cantons of Switzerland into consideration.

We assume that the establishment of a new federal legislation
framework and a new scheme is very much related to very particular
modes of justification by the political and governmental establishment.
For this contribution we are looking for exactly these modes of justification that are reflected in terms of the educational policy discourse as
well. We therefore are guided by the following theses:

---

3   The first national Federal Vocational and Professional Education and Training Act
     came into force in 1933.

(1) Establishing a new law requires civic justification beyond pure qualification of the workforce (section 4).

(2) Today, establishing a new law and a new scheme requires the opening of a career path beyond the workplace which is linked to the educational system (section 5).

Following these two theses, we divide our contribution into two sections: by a first step, we are looking at the starting point of the Swiss vocation educational system, the promulgation of the first Federal Vocational and Professional Education and Training Act in 1930. We are going to argue that this first Federal Vocational and Professional Education and Training Act can be understood as a compromise of different modes of justification – meanwhile respecting and integrating a civic as well as a market justification is of overriding importance. By a second step, we are looking at the establishment of the federal vocational baccalaureate in 1993 as a new scheme of the VET pathway. This hybrid qualification (by providing vocational training and extended general education with access to higher education) indicates a significant milestone within the development from a former master apprenticeship model to a modern vocational education system in Switzerland. Over the past fifty years a professional career was more and more linked to extended general education as well as to extended technical expertise. Increasing investments in appropriate formal learning settings like the so called *Berufsmittelschulen* (vocational upper secondary schools) and institutions, which offered extended general education within the VET system, is a very characteristic element of these developments (Wettstein & Gonon 2009). And these developments were as well continuously incorporated into the corresponding federal framework legislation and the corresponding regulations, respecting again a civic justification (section 5). The establishment of the federal vocational baccalaureate as a federal certificate offered by the *Berufsmaturitätsschulen (federal vocational baccalaureate schools)*[4], as they are now called, was closely linked to the development of the universities of applied sciences, and together they stand for a complete new vocational career path up to the tertiary level.

---

4   With the establishment of the Federal Vocational Baccalaureate, the *Berufsmittelschulen* have been renamed and are now called *Berufsmaturitätsschulen*.

From a theoretical point of view, our considerations regarding modes of justification and related conventions do refer to the framework of French pragmatic sociology, the economy of conventions, presented by Luc Boltanski and Laurent Thévenot in 1991. The analysis of conventions, principles of coordination and quality claims within the above mentioned contexts will therefore be the content of the following section.

3. Theoretical approach

From a historical perspective, the development of the vocational education system in Switzerland can be understood as an ongoing process of compromises. Civic and market, but also industrial arguments play a prominent role in the field of VET policy, when it comes to reforms. As a result, we identify these compromises, for instance, in the form of the vertical and horizontal hybridisation of the system (Gonon & Zehnder 2016). Looking at the assimilation of different – often enough conflicting – interests within the Federal Act on Vocational and Professional Education and Training, we do refer to the French économie *des conventions* (economy of conventions) approach as part of the pragmatic social sciences. This transdisciplinary approach draws attention to negotiation processes exactly like those we do observe within the development of a new law or segments of an existing law. This approach incorporates the different actors, their interests and value positions, while emphasizing that situative decision-making processes call for justification. The justification of decisions towards third parties requires the actors to coordinate their actions, although, using a specific mode of justification and referring to the corresponding convention, actors are aiming for common welfare as a rule. And that again "can lead to permanent and therefor objective 'solutions' which are called conventions" (Diaz-Bone 2009a, p. 7[5]). Therefore, the concept of convention allows to mutually question other frames of reference and to reject them

---

5   Translation by the authors.

or to agree with and accept a kind of compromise (Diaz-Bone 2009b; Boltanski & Thévenot 1991). With the économie *des conventions* we are able to visualize contexts of reasoning that could push through other modes of justification. This leads to a kind of order of justification (as a cognitive format) and makes actors and objects comparable.

Boltanski und Thévenot in their seminal book *De La Justification* (On Justification) – first time published in 1991 – identified six conventions by help of which "a majority of justifications raised in everyday situations" (Boltanski & Thévenot 2011, p. 57[6]) can be described. The following table gives some basic information about these six conventions – complemented by a seventh convention that was introduced by Boltanski and Chiapello in 1999. We present these conventions with the related principles of coordination and actor-applied quality claims. The field of vocational education and training is characterised mainly by a tension between claims on the part of the economy (as employers' engagement) as on the part of the state (as strategic and organizational management at federal level and cantonal level). The contribution focuses on the civic as well on the market, crafts and industry conventions, which is what actors in the field of VET are mostly referring to. Thus, we refrain from paying more attention to the other three conventions which did not play a prominent role in the analysed documentations.

Table 1: Justifications based on conventions & actor-applied claims.

Convention	Coordination	Quality Claim
Market	Price, Exchange	Competitiveness
Industry	Practicability	Efficiency
Craft (Domestic)	Trust *(Community)*	Reputation, Dexterity
Civic	Principles of Equality Participation	Collective Claims, Legal Protection
Inspiration	Free Circulation	Creativity
Public Opinion	Mediation	Visibility, Popularity
Project	Network	Flexibility, Openness

Source: Gonon & Zehnder (2016) following Boltanski & Thévenot (1991) and Boltanski & Chiapello (1999).

6   Translation by the authors.

We identify the analytical power of the concept of conventions in the way in which it allows to reconstruct how actors coordinate and deal with the uncertainty of social situations. However, usually uncertainty increases in situations of conflict that herewith are described as cases of clashing conventions: Opposing actors are questioning lines of argumentation and frames of reference. To finally bring a negotiation to an end, Boltanski and Thévenot (2011) introduce two possible ways. First, there is the possibility to come back to one single convention or frame of reference. The second way is – as mentioned above – to accept a kind of compromise without clarifying the principle. However, without agreement and referring just to a single convention compromises stay fragile and open the door to broad criticism (Boltanski & Thévenot 1991). Finding a common form is crucial for stabilizing this compromise. Furthermore, for a better understanding of the upcoming considerations it is important to point out that compromises are able to integrate different claims in an 'at the same time' sense on the one hand as well as in an 'as well as' sense on the other hand.

In terms of our theses, we describe a national framework legislation like the Federal Vocational and Professional Education and Training Act as a compromise that is able to incorporate very different interests, value concepts and claims (see section 4). A compromise that is able to emphasize relevant 'things' from different conventions in terms of the authors we are directly referring to (Boltanski & Thévenot 2011). But a compromise has as well to be open to further developments and adjustments. How stable this compromise was and how it could be maintained became obvious when the establishment of new schemes like the federal vocational baccalaureate took place (see section 5).

4. Legal development: The origin of the Swiss Federal Act on Vocational and Professional Education and Training (1880–1930)

One of the starting points for the reform and extension of vocational training was criticism of the results produced by the elementary schools which had been fully established in the 19th century. It was said that they prepared only insufficiently for the world of work and that they were too "bookish" anyway. Already in the early 1880s France had declared so called "handicraft teaching" to be mandatory at elementary school. French elementary schools were equipped with workshops including carpenter´s benches, lathes, vices, but also with equipment for house-hold economy and health (Gonon 2012). Since the 1880s the *Pionier* (Pioneer) magazine, with progressive educationalist and Social Demo-crat member of the Swiss parliament Robert Seidel contributing, prop-agated the introduction of an appropriate kind of practical teaching in Switzerland as well (Gonon 2002c). In 1890 at the latest, by the first classes on handicraft teaching for school teachers in Basel, these efforts towards rooting handicraft teaching at elementary school became obvi-ous. The thus established handicrafts in school were meant to get the children used to work with tools and to develop their manual skills.

However, the complete transformation of elementary schools into anticipating institutions of vocational training was not possible. Thus, the establishment of vocational schools after elementary schooling and a reform of apprenticeships was envisaged. That is why local examina-tions of the apprentices and the continuing schools, which were sup-posed to complete learning at the workplace, became more important. Heinrich Bendel, director of an arts and crafts museum in St. Gallen, played an important role in arguing for an enhancement of quality by extending these elements. He conceived a comprehensive system of vocational education on a national level (Bendel 1899). Besides these local efforts, which were supposed to strengthen the education of the youth through an occupational focus, also the legal activities on a can-tonal and national level were important.

The decision by the Federal Government in 1884 was mostly in line with these premises, and it established a guarantee that subsidies for educational institutions dedicated to vocational education in the trade and industrial sectors would rise continuously.

Nevertheless, cantonal laws for the protection of apprentices were established in the 1890s. In this context the Cantons of Neuchâtel (1890), Genève (1892), Fribourg (1895), Vaud (1896) and Valais (1903) were pioneers. Law-making at cantonal level referred to two demands, which were on the one hand a regulation of vocational skills and capabilities in the fields of trade, commerce and industry, which had to be fixed by a written apprenticeship contract. On the other hand it was the issue of youth protection, which was supposed to protect apprentices from being exploited and to support them with finding the right vocation. Already the first regulation of this kind, the Neuchâtel *Loi sur la protection des apprentis* (law on the protection of apprentices) from 1890, stipulated that all apprenticeships in the Canton were under supervision of the (municipal) authorities or a *commission special des apprentissages* (special committee of apprenticeship), where instructors and workers had to be represented (Gonon & Maurer 2012).

At the turn of the century the big crafts associations, as well as the unions and the employers entered a debate for creating a national legal basis for vocational education and training. The establishment of a VET system itself was a compromise between civic, industry and market conventions. A qualified workforce was seen as an important factor for the Swiss political system, an argument supported by the unions. Highly qualified workers would on the other hand help to make small and medium enterprises more competitive, as the big crafts associations argued.

It was stated that for the whole country and for the growing industry a strong VET would be important. Vocational education was a common ground for most actors. Despite all visible measures and improvements, the *Vereinigung Schweizerischer Lehrlingspatronate* (Association of Swiss Apprenticeship Instructors), the *Schweizerischer Arbeiterbund* (Swiss Workers Union) and the *Schweizerische Gewerkschaftsbund* (Swiss Trade Union Association) demanded a "Swiss Apprenticeship Law" (SGB 1913) as a comprehensive nationwide law to support vocational education at the national level and to standardise the different regulations of the cantons. In 1918 the *Schweizerischer Gewerbeverband* (Swiss Trade Association) presented an even more comprehensive bill. The small and medium enterprises and the trade associations argued for support of the former, referring to the market value. The unions on the other hand saw an opportunity for workers to get a better position in society. Collective protection and a legislation which offered the possibility of high-quality training was crucial for them. Thus, also participation in society was connected to a well-educated workforce.

The big industry, as a third dominant player, learned to see the advantages of vocationally educated workers and believed in a massif support for industrialization through VET (Gonon & Zehnder 2016). These different interests were equilibrated in a debate for establishing the first national law in 1930. When the Federal Council argued that there was progressing rationalisation and a growing need of economic coordination resulting from international pressure of competition, even sceptics acknowledged that there was a demand for "quality work" based on a support of vocational education and thus finally supported the draft of a law which was also to include subject examinations at upper secondary level. As emphasized by two expert statements in view of the constitutional article, the term "trade" included also factories and commerce (Schweizerischer Bundesrat 1928, p. 737). In this context, the *Federal Assembly of the Swiss Confederation* would only set guidelines, whereas implementation would be left to the cantons. Consequently, the law was passed by the Assembly of the Swiss Confederation in 1930 and came into force in 1933. It proved to be a good basis for the support of vocational education in Switzerland, precisely because of the balanced distribution of tasks among the Federal Government, the cantons and the professional associations as well as because private initiative and the responsibility of company owners were maintained.

The result was a legislation which offered quite an open framework with a lot of possibilities for local and branch-specific implementation. This law, providing rough guidelines, developed as the main feature of this VET approach and has been kept alive until today. Succeeding framework legislations followed in 1964, 1978 and in 2002. They amplified the existing law and enlarged some aspects without changing the character of this VET legislation at all.

5. The hybridization of vocational education since the 1990s

The most recent revision of the Federal Vocational and Professional Education and Training Act in 2002 expressed a declared belief in the future of VET and especially in the dual character of Swiss vocational education. The third article emphasizes several fields of tension in which a vocational education system ranges: "economy and society, individual and community. In the context of vocational education, the education of an individual, its integration into the working environment and the competitiveness of the companies have to be coordinated likewise" (Schweizerischer Bundesrat 2000, p. 5748[7]). This contextualization indicates – regarding our hybridisation argument – an essential demand on the Swiss vocational education system to bring together and hybridize different quality claims, i.e. conventions of state, industry and market. Vocational education and training should be able to promote the vocational as well as the personal development of the people. The integration of young people into the world of economy is one claim, like emphasising individual interests and the promotion of socio-political and cultural participation. The validation of the quality claims regarding vocational dexterity and the acquisition of civic competencies – that were defined already by the first Federal Vocational and Professional Education and Training Act from 1930 – stabilizes this conventional foundation (Diaz-Bone & Salais 2011). Referring to the civic convention, among the requests regarding the development of vocational flexibility we also find "true gender equality" and the "balancing of education and training opportunities in social and regional terms" (BBG 2002, Art. 3 a and c). The contextualisation of this third article emphasizes at the same time the consideration of the efficiency and competitiveness of training companies. From this perspective, apprentices are defined as specific members of the workforce who have to execute their tasks within a prospering economy referring to the market convention. Thus, the hybridisation of vocational education is able to incorporate very different – and at first sight even divergent – quality claims and to integrate them in a corresponding framework legislation in an 'at the same time' sense.

At the beginning of the 1990s the Swiss vocational education system was changed fundamentally. The crucial reform was indicated by a strong declaration of intent by all significant actors to strengthen general education within the vocational education and training (VET) system. Until the late 1980s the educational system in Switzerland was more or less divided into two systems: On the one hand we had the

---

7   Translation by the authors.

VET system with progression routes of further professional education and on the other hand we had the general education system followed by studies at a university or the Federal Institute of Technology level. Since the late 1960s new schools with additional general subjects, the so-called *Berufsmittelschulen (vocational upper secondary schools),* offered extended general education for talented apprentices in a dual track VET program. But the idea to create a smooth transition from VET programs to further professional education and training at engineering and business administration colleges did not push through. A majority of the colleges mentioned stuck to their own selection and admission processes (Feierabend 1975). The intention of strengthening general education within the VET system in the 1990s then attempts exactly to overcome this uncertainty about the added value of extended general education as offered by the *Berufsmittelschulen* (Ochsenbein 1991).

In its first expert report on Swiss educational policy, the OECD criticized in the early 1990s that the existing model of vocational training was a dead end model. The OECD thus demanded an increased accessibility to further education and better cooperation between the responsible departments (OECD 1990, p. 177). It was stated that, on the one hand, a rapid development – particularly in polytechnic education – was occurring and that currently Switzerland was in the danger of falling back. Consequently, the lacking options for further qualification at the tertiary level for people with completed vocational training remained in the focus of further considerations. Against the background of the European Community becoming stronger, the necessity to maintain international competitiveness was gradually, however then clearly recognized (op. cit., p. 193), and the report on vocational training from 1996, which was presented by the Federal Government, put the improvement of the "permeability of vocational and general education" (Schweizerischer Bundesrat 1996, p. 21[8]) on the education policy agenda. As stated in the introduction, vertical permeability was increased through structural adjustments of the educational system: coordinated by federal responsibilities, an advanced general education program for the VET pathway was designed. Graduates of this new programme were

8   Translation by the authors.

supposed to be certified with a federal vocational baccalaureate and to have access to further professional education and training colleges. At the same time, the colleges of further professional education and training were pushed to the tertiary level and became Universities of Applied Sciences. This shift was quite in line with making "diplomas fit for Europe" (Schweizerischer Bundesrat 1996). Thus, the introduction of the federal vocational baccalaureate has to be understood as a new scheme and a precondition for a new level of tertiary education (Kiener & Gonon 1998). As a result, both educational systems – vocational and general education – have been linked and integrated into one common system. The law on Universities of Applied Sciences (1995) embedded the federal vocational baccalaureate, which had been introduced two years earlier, into this legal framework, finally realizing the permeability postulate. Thus, by creating a degree at the end of the *Berufsmittelschule* and by regulating direct access to universities the debate was steered away from the criticized support of the elites towards more favoured permeability.

The organization of the transition from the *Berufsmittelschule* to the colleges of further professional education and training was under discussion since 1984 (Kiener & Gonon 1998). A small group of cantonal ministers of education and representatives of the *Berufsmittelschulen* as well as of the technical colleges of further professional education and training laid the foundation for the content and amount of lessons for a new qualification – the federal vocational baccalaureate. The proposal of this group went through a consultation process: a very typical political process of asking all relevant interest groups (VET schools and colleges, political parties, branch associations and unions) to give written feedbacks. Finally the federal administration reviewed the proposal while reflecting on and respecting the feedbacks of the interest groups.

This federal vocational baccalaureate as a qualification for the workplace and at the same time as an entrance qualification to Universities of Applied Sciences was very much in the interest of the principals committee of the schools offering extended general education within the VET system. They emphasized the upgrading of their schools and therefore as well an added value for their graduates. Political authorities supported these efforts by referring to the permeability argument. They noted that an efficient and permeably structured educational system should help to strengthen the competitiveness of the national economy in an international context. This argumentation refers especially to the market convention. Professional and branch associations (technical industry played a dominant role) pointed out to the international argument as well. But from their perspective it was not the efficiency of the system they referred to but the mobility and competitiveness of qualified workforce that is in line with the market convention. By taking this international perspective the associations also intended to support the engineering schools with their 3-year full time courses to strengthen their position in comparison to the Federal Institutes of Technology (ETH Zurich and Lausanne) at tertiary level. They expected equal classification of the courses or rather a revaluation of the engineering schools. Claiming for legal protection by help of stating the argument of principles of equality refers again to the civic convention (Gonon & Zehnder 2016). The power of the civic convention for the development of the Swiss vocational education and training system is getting apparent.

Especially former engineering schools also argued with strong requirements in subjects like mathematics and (descriptive) geometry, which justified an upgrading of their institutions (EVD 1992). Therefore, an efficient and effective pre-qualification was at the heart of their argumentation. Highlighting a smooth and effective transition to the future Universities of Applied Sciences then refers to the industrial convention. Although this branch-orientation is somewhat inconsistent with the idea of general education, it stands for successful transitions to and finally graduation at the corresponding University of Applied Sciences (Kaiser, Grütter & Fitzli 2013).

With the introduction of the federal vocational baccalaureate the extended general education within the VET system got its own certification and met the appropriate admission criteria for the new Universities of Applied Sciences. In this context we speak of both a horizontal and vertical hybridisation of the vocational education system. The horizontal perspective emphasizes the introduction of a 'dual qualification' in terms of extended general education and personal development on the one hand and a vocational qualification on the other hand. The vertical perspective introduces the federal vocational baccalaureate as a branch-oriented professional pre-qualification that allows for direct access to the Universities of Applied Sciences (Gonon & Zehnder 2016).

The discussion shows that while the horizontal hybridisation is able to integrate divergent quality claims in an 'at the same time' sense, the vertical hybridisation integrates both direct access to universities as well as being a branch-oriented and professional pre-qualification in an 'as well as' sense. With the introduction of the federal vocational baccalaureate, a true added value for general education within the VET system has been achieved. It has been linked with the goal of making the VET pathway more attractive and also to provide practically talented adolescents with good academic ability with an appropriate alternative to the general education pathway (Gonon 2013). From today's perspective, it can be said that the introduction of the federal vocational baccalaureate was a significant innovation and is an established element of today's vocational education system in Switzerland. Providing smooth transitions and permeability between the vocational and general education pathways, the new scheme of federal vocational baccalaureate and Universities of Applied Sciences stands for an opening and diversification of career paths in every sector. Respecting that as well the combination of the terms 'vocational' and 'baccalaureate' refers to a compromise about background conventions (especially the civic and the market convention), the newly introduced scheme can be seen as an identity-giving form and therefore a stabilizing element for Swiss VET.

6. Conclusion

This contribution characterizes the historical (1930) and the most recent Swiss Federal Vocational and Professional Education and Training Act (2002) as a compromise between very different aspects. The perspective of an education which meets societal, industrial and market needs was an important driving force for developing VET in Switzerland. Historically seen, this vision of a well-equipped and educated citizen who knows a lot of useful things for everyday and work life was an important starting point for Swiss society, the trades and the emerging industry. This process of unification and progressive systematization on a national level is quite in line with Margret Archers' pattern of the development of educational systems (Archer 1979).

The debate regarding the introduction of the first federal framework legislation in the 1930s was oscillating between quality claims regarding vocational dexterity, socio-political requests and educational efforts from the industry. A very important point to mention herewith is the emphasis on the dual character dominating the Swiss VET system until today, which itself brings together different quality claims. Respecting a broad variety of aspects, the development of the Swiss VET system ended up in a compromise and its hybridization of the corresponding institutional settings. On the one hand, we see this hybridization within the intention of vocational and professional education and training to provide access to workplace. And on the other hand within the ambition to create, by help of VET, a foundation for a career step. With the growing differentiation of the VET system (development of two to four years VET programs, possibility to attend extended general education, increasing and broader offer of professional education courses) and with the latest reforms, particularisms could be decreased and more permeability between vocational and general educational system was introduced. The integration of the vocational and the general educational system into a common educational system can therefore be interpreted as a kind of opening more career paths in industry, society and the market itself. Within all depicted development steps we find a lot of evidence regarding the power of the civic, market and the industry conventions. From today's perspective it can be added that strengthening general education within the VET system and increased emphasis on the role of individual responsibility regarding personal development will modify the quality claims and compromises of conventions for future reforms. This would fit with the explored "new spirit of capitalism" (Boltanski & Chiapello 1999) and the upcoming convention of project oriented modes of justification.

References

Archer, M. 1979. Social Origins of Educational Systems. London, Sage Publications.

Bendel, H. 1899. Winke und Anregungen für das gewerbliche und industrielle Bildungswesen der Schweiz. Bern, Haupt.

Boehmert, V. 1873. Der Einfluss der Wiener Weltausstellung auf die Arbeit des Volkes. Wien, Athenäum.

Boltanski, L. & Chiapello, E. 1999. Le nouvel ésprit du capitalisme. Paris, Gallimard.

Boltanski, L. & Thévenot, L. 1991. De la justification: les économies de la grandeur. Paris, Gallimard.

Boltanski, L. & Thévenot, L. 2011. Die Soziologie der kritischen Kompetenzen. In R. Diaz-Bone (eds.), Soziologie der Konventionen. Grundlagen einer pragmatischen Antrhopologie. Frankfurt/New York, Campus.

Brizon, P. 1909. L'apprentissage. Hier – aujourd'hui – demain. Paris, Librairie de Pages Libres.

Bundesgesetz über die Berufsbildung (BBG) vom 13. Dezember 2002 (SR 412.10) [retrieved from: <https://www.admin.ch/opc/de/class ified-compilation/20001860/index.html> – March, 15th 2016].

Bundesgesetz über die Fachhochschulen (FHSG) vom 6. Oktober 1995 (SR 414.71) [retrieved from: <https://www.admin.ch/opc/de/class ified-compilation/19950279/index.html> – March, 15th 2016].

Diaz-Bone, R. 2009a. Die „Économie des conventions" – ein neuer insitutionalistischer Ansatz in der Wirtschaftssoziologie (Working Paper No 02/09). [retrieved from University of Lucerne website: <https://www.unilu.ch/fileadmin/shared/Publika-tionen/diaz-bone_die-economie-des-conventions_workingpaper_2-09.pdf> – April, 29th 2016].

Diaz-Bone, R. 2009b. Konvention, Organisation und Institution. Der institutionalistische Beitrag der „Economice des conventions". History Social Research 37(2): 235–264.

Diaz-Bone, R. & Salais, R. 2011. Economics of Convention and the History of Economies. Towards a Transdisciplinary Approach in Economic History. Historical Social Research, 36(04): 7–39.

Dumreicher, A. F. v. 1879. Über den französischen National-Wohlstand als Werk der Erziehung. Wien, Athenaeum.

EVD (Eidgenössisches Volkswirtschaftsdepartement) 1992. Vernehmlassung Technische Berufsmaturität – Auswertung. Schweizerisches Bundesarchiv Bern, Bestand BAR E3375-2002/208–346.

Feierabend, U. J. 1975. Die Berufsmittelschule – mit besonderer Berücksichtigung der Verhältnisse im Kanton Solothurn. Ein Beitrag zur Berufsbildungsforschung. Aarau, Sauerländer.

Gonon, P. 2002a. Zur Berufsbildung und Bildung durch Arbeit in der Schweiz: eine historische Perspektive. In P. Gonon & S. Stolz (eds.), Arbeit, Beruf und Bildung. Bern, hep.

Gonon, P. 2002b. Berufliche Bildung zwischen Zunft, Handelsfreiheit und Demokratie. In P. Gonon & S. Stolz (eds.), Arbeit, Beruf und Bildung. Bern, hep.

Gonon, P. 2002c. Von der Berufsvorbereitung zur Kultur der Arbeit in der Schule: Handfertigkeitsbewerung und Reformpädagogik in der Schweiz um die Jahrhundertwende. In P. Gonon & S. Stolz (eds.), Arbeit, Beruf und Bildung. Bern, hep.

Gonon, P. 2012. Policy Borrowing and the Rise of Vocational and Education System – The Case of Switzerland. In G. Steiner-Khamsi & F. Waldow (eds.), World Year Book of Education 2012 – Policy Borrowing and Lending in Education. Oxon, New York, Routledge.

Gonon, P. 2013. Berufsmaturität als Reform – Hybris oder Erfolgstory? In M. Maurer & P. Gonon (eds.), Herausforderungen für die Berufsbildung in der Schweiz. Bestandesaufnahme und Perspektiven. Bern, hep.

Gonon, P. & Maurer, M. 2012. Education Policy Actors as Stakeholders in the Development of the Collective Skill System: The Case of Switzerland. In M. R. Busemeyer & C. Trampusch (eds.), The Political Economy of Collective Skill Formation. Oxford, University Press.

Gonon, P. & Zehnder, L. 2016. Die Berufsbildung der Schweiz als per-
    manenter Kompromissbildungsprozess. In J. Seifried, S. Seeber &
    B. Ziegler (eds.), Jahrbuch der berufs- und wirtschaftspädagogis-
    chen Forschung 2016. Leverkusen, Verlag Barbara Budrich.
Green, A. 1992. Education and State Formation. The Rise of Educa-
    tion Systems in England, France and the USA. London, MacMillan
    Press.
Kaiser, N., Grütter, M. & Fitzli, D. 2013. Evaluation der Studierfähig-
    keit von Be-rufsmaturitäts-Absolventen/innen an den Fachhoch-
    schulen. Analyse der Statistischen Daten. Bericht zum Teilprojekt
    1. Zürich, econcept.
Kiener, U. & Gonon, P. 1998. Die Berufsmatur. Ein Fallbeispiel schweiz-
    erischer Berufsbildungspolitik. Chur / Zürich, Rüegger.
Ochsenbein, H. 1991. Zum Übertritt von der gewerblich-industriellen
    Berufsbildung an die Ingenieurschulen. Schweizerische Blätter für
    beruflichen Unterricht, 5: 206–209.
OECD 1991. Berufsbildungspolitik in der Schweiz. Expertenbericht.
    Paris, OECD.
Pestalozzi, J.H. 2005 [1806]. Über Volksbildung und Industrie. In:
    P. Gonon (ed.), J.H. Pestalozzi – Sozialpädagogische Schriften.
    Zürich, Pestalozzianum.
Schweizerischer Bundesrat 1928. Botschaft des Bundesrates an die
    Bundesversammlung zum Entwurf eines Bundesgesetzes über die
    berufliche Ausbildung vom 9. November 1928. In: Bundesblatt
    1928 (2): 725–780.
Schweizerischer Bundesrat 1996. Bericht des Bundesrates über die
    Berufsbildung (Bundesgesetz über die Berufsbildung). Bern.
Schweizerischer Bundesrat 2000. Botschaft zu einem neuen Bundes-
    gesetz über die Berufsbildung. Bundesblatt, 47: 5686–5774.
SGB (Schweizerischer Gewerkschaftsbund) 1913. Das Bundeskomitee
    des Schweiz. Gewerkschaftsbundes an das Industriedepartement.
    Eingabe betreffend ein Eidgenössisches Lehrlingsgesetz. Bern,
    SGB.

Wettstein, E. & Gonon, P. 2009. Berufsbildung in der Schweiz. Bern, hep.

Zschokke, H. 1893. Meister Jordan oder Handwerk hat goldenen Boden: Ein Feierabend-Büchlein für Lehrlinge, verständige Gesellen und Meister. Zürich, Verein für Verbreitung guter Schriften.

THOMAS DEISSINGER AND DANIELA GREMM

The Status of VET in Canada: Evidence from Literature and Qualitative Research

1. Introduction

There is currently ample interest in both educational research and politics that "well-working" VET systems might or should be transferred to other national and cultural contexts. One of the most observed "models" hereby seems to be the German dual system of apprenticeship training (Deissinger 2010). One of the arguments mostly referred to is the function of VET to combat youth unemployment. On the other hand, literature suggests that transfers are problematic even if the governments involved develop a clear strategy for their respective countries to change and/or improve their VET systems (Euler 2013; Gonon 2013; Pilz and Li 2014; Deissinger 2015). It is without any doubt that apprenticeship systems, although this model of skill formation exists all over the world, function in various ways – which means: (i) they differ in their status and recognition within society and (ii) they do not necessarily work in the sense of a regulated and therefore trustworthy approach for initial training. Comparative research shows that cultural patterns and specific historical developments make for "individual" solution patterns for the problem of integrating young people into training and work by giving them a foundation on which they can build up their personal and professional life courses. The German-English comparison is a good example for these different cultural imprints of VET systems although both countries have a strong apprenticeship tradition (Deissinger 1994). In the German case, two parameters seem to be the most relevant shaping forces of the VET system as it developed and further developed in the 20th century: (i) the "vocational principle" with its strong implications for "holistic" training courses, law-based regulations, and the vocational part-time school as the educational though junior partner alongside training in companies (*ibid.* 1998); (ii) the role of chambers, employer organizations, and trade unions, which are responsible for various functions in the apprenticeship system beyond the narrow sphere of governmental regulation, above all when it comes to the establishment and ongoing modernization of training courses (Deissinger and Gonon 2016). Both aspects are linked up and explain why it might be difficult to simply transplant them to another national, social and cultural context. In the Canadian case, which is the core topic of this article, apprenticeships play an important role in the formal structure of the VET system even though their reputation is rather weak in both international terms and in terms of their standing against higher education (in the meaning of undergraduate studies/degrees). After looking at these structural and social issues we will also shortly touch upon the transfer aspect. Our insights are based on the few available sources on the Canadian VET system and on interviews that were carried out in September and October 2015.

2. Vocational Education in Canada

2.1 The structure of Canada's education system

Canada is a parliamentary federation with ten provinces and three territories. The country has no nationwide uniform education system with a coordinating federal ministry of education. Instead, each province/territory has its own educational jurisdiction and provides one to two departments or ministries of education, accountable for delivery, organization, and assessment of education in elementary and secondary schools, as well as for post-secondary and vocational education (Bohlinger 2011, p. 37; Council of Ministers of Education 2016; Lehmann 2012, p. 26; Miller 2013, p. 57). Even though regional educational systems across Canada share many similarities, there are some aspects, such as compulsory schooling age, assessment or curriculum where system structures differ. These differences are due to local history, geography, language, culture, and specific requirements of the respective provinces and territories (CICIC 2016a; Council of Ministers of Education 2016; Lehmann 2012, p. 26). In case of switching over to another provincial jurisdiction, recognition of qualifications is necessary (Bohlinger 2011, p. 37; Council of Ministers of Education 2016). Figure 1 shows the education system in Canada in a simplified form.

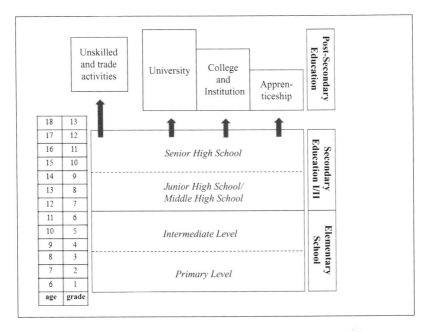

Figure 1: Canada's Education System – Source: Council of Ministers of Education 2016; Government of Canada 2016; Lehmann 2012, pp. 25f; Schaub and Zenke 2000, p. 313.

Children enter *primary* or *elementary school* at the age of six years, in some provinces already at an age of five. By law, pupils have a compulsory education until the age of 16 to 18, depending on the province or territory (CICIC 2016a; Government of Canada 2016; Lehmann 2012, p. 26; Taylor, Watt-Malcolm and Wimmer 2013, p. 170). After passing elementary school, which is divided into *primary level* (grade 1–3) and *intermediate level* (grade 4–6/7), Canadian pupils (normally 12 years old) enter *high school (secondary education)*. In all Canadian provinces and territories, high schools are organized as comprehensive schools and are free of charge (Lehmann 2012, p. 25). In contrast to other European countries, Canada's education systems are character-ized by a relatively great openness (Taylor, Watt-Malcolm and Wimmer 2013, p. 170). "Single-stream schools" are exceptional and most of the high schools confer "the same general credential to graduates regard-less of course stream" (*ibid.*). High schools are structured into *junior high school* or *middle school* and *senior high school* and cover a period of time of four to six years, depending on the jurisdiction. In the first years of secondary education most of the courses are compulsory, with-out many options for students to choose a specialization. In the years before graduation, choices for students increase, so pupils have the pos-sibility to take specialized academic and vocational programs "to pre-pare for the job market or to meet the differing entrance requirements of post-secondary institutions" (Council of Ministers of Education 2016). When graduating from senior high school, the students, being 17 to 18 years old, are awarded a high school diploma which qualifies for uni-versity entrance (Government of Canada 2016; Lehmann 2012, p. 25).

The secondary education system prepares students for labour market entry as well as for *post-secondary education* (PSE). Canada's PSE system consists, besides apprenticeships, of 163 public and private universities (including theological schools), 183 recognized public col-leges, as well as of 68 university-level institutions and 51 college-level ones (Council of Ministers of Education 2016). These institutions charge fees and offer academic and vocational degrees, diplomas and certificates, depending on the type of the institution and the duration of the program (CICIC 2016a; Council of Ministers of Education 2016)[1]. It is certainly a major trait of the Canadian system that the boundaries between higher education (in the sense of academic studies) and col-lege-based PSE appear to be somewhat blurred. This is also a point of interest which we will pick up later in this article.

---

1   For more information see CICIC 2016b and 2016c. – Diplomas are the more valued qualifications.

2.2 The structure of Vocational Education and Training

In Canada, Vocational Education and Training (VET) is offered as *workplace based apprenticeship* and as *school-based VET in colleges and institutes*. Apprenticeships hereby resemble a kind of dual system as they include quite a large amount of systematic training in colleges. However, compared to other countries, apprenticeships are not the most important segment of the Canadian VET system.

The *Canadian Apprenticeship Forum*[2] defines apprenticeship as "a workplace-based training program that teaches people the skills they need in the trades to achieve competencies and perform tasks to the industry standard" (Canadian Apprenticeship Forum 2016b). Each province and territory has its own government apprenticeship authority office, so the offer of designated trades as well as the curriculum, assessment, and certification differ across Canada (Bohlinger 2011, p. 39; Canadian Apprenticeship Forum 2016b; Miller 2013, pp. 52f., 57). However, there are nationwide standards: The *Red Seal Program* is meant to be the "Canadian standard of excellence for skilled trades" (Red Seal Program 2016a) as it sets uniform standards in currently 56 Red Seal trades which are laid down to evaluate the skills of tradespersons across Canada. By passing the inter-provincial Red seal examination, apprentices get a Red Seal Endorsement (RSE) on their provincial/territorial trade certificates. The RSE enables them to exercise their trade without having to complete additional examinations in another province or territory, and ensures professional and social mobility within the country (Miller 2013, pp. 53f, 59; Munro, MacLaine and Stuckey 2014, p. 80; Red Seal Program 2016a and 2016b).

In Canada, students who want to start an apprenticeship have to find an employer who acts as a "sponsor" and offers them a workplace (Canadian Apprenticeship Forum 2016c; Miller 2013, p. 52; Sharpe and Gibson 2005, p. 14). Apprenticeships also can be carried out by doing the first year in college. Apprenticeship training lasts between two to

---

2   The Canadian Apprenticeship Forum is a non-profit organization which connects Canada's apprenticeship community. Due to research, discussion and collaboration the organization, often called as "national voice" for the apprenticeship community, has an influence on apprenticeship strategies in Canada (Canadian Apprenticeship Forum 2016a).

five years, depending on the trade program and jurisdiction. It consists of two periods, of work "in-the-job" and of "in-class" introduction also called "academic release" (Miller 2013, p. 52). Roughly 80 per cent of the vocational training takes place in the company, for the remaining time (four to ten weeks per year) apprentices obtain technical training "off-the-job" in colleges, union training centers, online or with a private trainer (Canadian Apprenticeship Forum 2016b). In most of the provinces and territories, the two periods alternate. Apprentices complete their vocational training with a trade qualification (TQ) (Miller 2013, p. 52; Sharpe and Gibson 2005, p. 14). The majority of apprentices are adults – which clearly differs from, *e.g.*, Germany, Switzerland or Austria (Deissinger 2010).

The majority of VET courses in Canada is offered school-based in colleges and in university undergraduate courses (Lehmann 2012, pp. 26f.). It is Canada's *college and institutes system* which plays an important part in the field of professional and technical training and education, consisting of a range of institutional types: *community colleges, technical institutions, polytechnics, and collèges d'enseignement général et professionnel (Cégeps) in Quebec* (Bohlinger 2011, p. 38; Munro, MacLaine and Stuckey 2014, pp. 53f.). Due to their diversity, practical orientation, and easier accessibility in comparison to universities, colleges and institutes are very attractive. They respond to the requirements of a wide variety of individuals with regard to their age, income, and geographical and social background (Munro, MacLaine and Stuckey 2014, pp. 64, 74).

It is interesting to note that Canada's college system overlaps with universities as colleges may also offer academic programs to students. In 2014, 209 bachelor's degree programs were registered in 34 Canadian colleges and institutes, which now have an increasing focus on technology and trades (Colleges and Institutes Canada 2014; Munro, MacLaine and Stuckey 2014, pp. 57f.). Canada's college sector is well connected to industry and has "advisory committees" which are required to have representatives from community or regional employers to ensure that education and training programs are developed and updated in accordance with employers' needs (Association of Canadian Community Colleges 2004, p. 4). Community colleges are hybrid institutions, also called "applied universities" (Lehmann 2012, p. 27), where students not only gain academic skills like numeracy or literacy, but also professional and job-ready skills for many professions (Lehmann 2012, p. 27; Munro, MacLaine and Stuckey 2014, p. 54). It needs to be emphasized that Canada's understanding of hibridity differs from hybrid courses in Germany, which formally link up general and vocational qualifications in the VET segment of upper secondary education (Taylor, Watt-Malcolm and Wimmer 2013, pp. 165ff.). In Canada, in contrast, hybridity exists as a form of pre-vocational education within the secondary school system (high schools) – which clearly resembles approaches in Australia, *e.g.* in Victoria, where the Victorian Certificate of Applied Learning (VCAL) also comes up with an explicit denomination for the vocational character of such a qualification that aims at "practical work-related experience, as well as literary and numeracy skills and the opportunity to build personal skills that are important for life and work" (Victorian Curriculum and Assessment Authority 2007, p. 14; Deissinger 2016; Polesel 2016).

Half of the 100 bachelor's degree programs in the college system are offered in polytechnic institutes, playing an essential role in the VET sector (Colleges and Institutes Canada 2014; Munro, MacLaine and Stuckey 2014, pp. 57f.). Polytechnic institutes combine the practical part of college education with the depth of study content, and, in contrast to colleges, have a strong focus on advanced technical and technological education (Polytechnics Canada 2016, p. 4). They provide "highly qualified and skilled talent for Canadian employers of all sizes, in all sectors" (*ibid.*) to almost 300,000 full- and part-time students, as well as to 45,000 apprentices (Polytechnics Canada 2015). College and institutes education programs are also an opportunity for university graduates who want to obtain a "further, career-oriented-training" (Munro, MacLaine and Stuckey 2014, p. 65). Experts found out, that the "reverse-transfers" of university students and graduates to the college sector have increased over the last couple of years (Birchard 2010).

According to experts, it has become "increasingly difficult" these days to draw a line between Canada's universities and colleges, "as many colleges now offer degrees and engage in applied research, while universities increasingly complement their academic focus with experiential and practical learning opportunities" (Council of Ministers of Education 2016; Munro, MacLaine and Stuckey 2014, pp. 54f.). Taylor,

Watt-Malcolm and Wimmer (2013) refer to a "blurring of boundaries" between colleges and universities, as well as between colleges and schools (Taylor, Watt-Malcolm and Wimmer 2013, p. 174). The government in Alberta, for example, constructed a PSE (post-secondary education) system, which combines general and technical education in the same institution ("university colleges") and enables transfers between different natures of PSE (*ibid.*, p. 172). However, in most Canadian provinces and territories, moving "from college certificate and diploma programs to university" still turns out as challenging for young people, as real permeability between apprenticeship training and college or university programs is weak (*ibid.*, p. 174). If we understand "academic drift" also in these institutional terms, the Canadian system seems to be a typical example for "a process in which non-university institutions aspire to operate like universities", while individuals (traditionally) seek "to obtain the highest possible level of formal qualification, which draws them into tertiary education" (Kopatz and Pilz 2015, p. 310).

2.3 Canada's VET problem? Evidence from literature

In Canada, apprenticeship training has always been an incidental type of VET (Lehmann 2012, p. 25). However, in contrast to school-based VET in colleges and institutes, apprenticeships, covering only 50 trades, predominantly in craft and technical occupations, have low importance for Canada's school leavers (Bohlinger 2011, p. 38; Munro, MacLaine and Stuckey 2014, p. 77; Sharpe and Gibson 2005, p. 14). Less than one per cent of high school graduates immediately start an apprenticeship (Lehmann 2012, p. 25; Ménard, Chan and Walker 2008, pp. 12ff.), unlike in Germany, where still more than half of each school leaving cohort take the pathway into the trades, but also into attractive commercial occupations (Statistisches Bundesamt 2013, p. 22; Lehmann, Taylor and Wright 2014, p. 572; Deissinger 2010 and 2015). Canada's apprenticeships seem to be much more a pathway for "upskilling" adults who have already worked as unskilled trade workers for some years than for high school graduates (Lehmann 2012, p. 29; Sharpe and Gibson 2005, pp. 6ff.). In 2011, less than 7 per cent of Canada's apprentices were 20 years or younger, which is the lowest proportion of registration in the G20 countries, whereas 40 per cent of new registrants were 30 years or older (Munro, MacLaine and Stuckey 2014, p. 105; Sharpe and Gibson 2005, pp. 6ff.; Statistics Canada 2015b). As a matter of fact, however, apprenticeship participation has increased significantly, *e.g.* from 199,000 in 2000 to 359,000 in 2007 (Kopatz and Pilz 2015, p. 319). In 2013, 469,680 apprentices were recorded in Canada, 15 per cent more than in 2009 (Statistics Canada 2015a), but still, completion rates remain low (Lehmann, Taylor and Wright 2014, pp. 572f.). According to a national apprenticeship survey in 2011, only 12 per cent of Canada's workforce held trades certificates (Munro, MacLaine and Stuckey 2014, p. 17; Statistics Canada 2013, p. 8).

Canada's apprenticeship sector has the reputation of being a pathway for people who are "stupid", "not smart", or "less ambitious or talented" (Lehmann 2012, p. 34; Lehmann, Taylor and Wright 2014, pp. 572f.; Taylor 2010, pp. 504f.). Many Canadians associate apprenticeship training with dirty, black collar work, offering poor working conditions and little pay (Lehmann 2012, p. 34) and therefore consider trades as "lower-class type jobs" (*ibid.*). This "dirty hands attitude" is reinforced by the fact that Canada's population generally has a comparatively high level of formal education – the highest among OECD countries (Statistics Canada 2016, pp. 12, 22, 25) – and that Canadians completing higher education are less likely to become unemployed than those without (Munro, MacLaine and Stuckey 2014, pp. 13f.; Sharpe and Gibson 2005, p. 44; Statistics Canada 2015c; Statistics Canada 2016, p. 41). Since education is considered a status symbol, demand for higher education has increased in the country over the years (CICIC 2016a; Statistics Canada 2016, p. 12). University education is still perceived as the "king's way" into employment, whereas tradespeople still have the reputation "not going to make anything out of [...] [their] life" (Lehmann 2012, p. 34). Because of the negative stereotype attached to apprenticeships, vocational programs have moved into PSE institutions over time (Taylor, Watt-Malcolm and Wimmer 2013, p. 171). These facts underline that "meritocratic thinking" (Goldthorpe 1996) is paramount within the Canadian society. According to this principle, which rules the social attributes given to education and educational decisions, the main function of certificates, qualifications, and underlying pathways by no means derives from the benefit of the contents of the respective qualification, but rather from its formalized result. Paradoxically, shifts in the education system towards university studies can currently also be observed in Germany, although traditionally this country has always been categorized, together with Switzerland, as *the* "model apprenticeship country" (Deissinger 2010 and 2015; Deissinger and Gonon 2016; Deissinger and Ott 2016).

Against this background, interest and support from the side of Canadian employers for apprenticeship training is very tentative (Lehmann 2012, p. 29; Munro, MacLaine and Stuckey 2014, p. 102; Sharpe and Gibson 2005, p. 7). There are often tensions between apprentices' learning demands and employers' organizational needs as a consequence of insufficient structures and rules for the training process. A stronger regulating framework seems necessary to combine academic and applied types of learning in a more powerful way and to raise the status and perceived benefit of apprenticeship training (Lehmann 2012, pp. 35, 38f.). According to Lehmann (2012), weak involvement can also be associated with companies' fear of poaching (this is similar for the English VET system) (Deissinger and Greuling 1994; see also Smith 2010): "if only few employers invest in the training of their workforce, this investment can easily be lost if the trained employee leaves to assume employment with a different employer, likely one that did not invest in training" (Lehmann 2012, p. 29). Hence, there is often little motivation among companies to invest in the skill formation of their own labour force (*ibid.*).

In order to increase the attractiveness of apprenticeships and careers in trades, some provinces have already taken steps by introducing *high school-based youth apprenticeship programs* (Lehmann, Taylor and Wright 2014, p. 572; Taylor, Watt-Malcolm and Wimmer 2013, p. 171). This means that at least parts of an apprenticeship can be an element of secondary school education. Alberta, for example, provides, in addition to mandatory courses in mathematics, English language arts, science, and social studies, optional "off-campus education programs" for secondary school students, such as the *Registered Apprenticeship Program* (RAP), the *Green Certificate Program* (related to the agriculture sector), *Career Internship*, and *Work Experience* in grades 10 to 12 (Alberta Education 2010, pp. 1, 20, 207; Lehmann 2012, pp. 30ff.). Alberta's senior high school students can now obtain practical experience, and, in the case of RAP, also have the possibility to combine school education with an apprenticeship and get two types of qualifications (Alberta Education 2010, p. 21; for more information about each program see Alberta Education 2010, pp. 2ff.). The combination between school and work seems to be appealing especially for young people whose needs often disagree with the "academic-abstract demand of the education system" (Lehmann 2012, p. 30), and who "are bored with school" and "want to do anything" (*ibid.*, p. 37). However, according to Smaller (2003), vocational programs in Canada's secondary education system have actually decreased since the 1970s due to several reasons, such as concerns about "streaming students too early" (Taylor, Watt-Malcolm and Wimmer 2013, p. 170). Lehmann (2012) found that many high school students only start an RAP in the hope of evading the "perceived drudgery of academic learning" (Lehmann 2012, p. 38).

Against this background, research from literature seems to reveal the precarious state of VET in Canada and its obvious subnormality in contrast with academic pathways. In the following, two interviews will be referred to which are meant to widen our understanding of "Canada's VET problem". They also are bound to have a heuristic function for further research.

3. Comparative issues

3.1 The relevance and status of apprenticeships in Canada: Evidence from two interviews

The insights from the two interviews which we now refer to in this chapter have an illustrating function and do not claim to be representative, although the colleges involved are more or less typical examples for Canadian post-secondary institutions. The two interviews (one in a college located near Toronto/Ontario and the other one on Vancouver Island/British Columbia) were carried out in autumn 2015. They may help to improve our general understanding of what is taught in the post-secondary VET sector in Canada and, in particular, to understand how VET and apprenticeships work in the country in relation to academic pathways[3]. We will therefore stress those statements from the interviews which seem appropriate to work out the problem of "meritocracy" explicitly, besides the stream of arguments which underline the pretension of being a vocational institution for "applied learning"[4], and therefore also want to throw light onto the ambivalence in the character of these institutions. The interviewees reported on these issues by referring to four general and twelve specific questions focusing the apprenticeship system:

Interview 1:

This college on Vancouver Island is described by the interviewee as a "comprehensive college" in that it is a polytechnic as well as an "academic upgrade college". Besides academic degrees, the college gives away about 2,000 trade certificates (out of 9,000 full-time students completing in a given year), which are subject to standards developed by the *Industry Training Authority* (ITA)[5], which also pays for vocational courses the college offers. This vocational part of the business of colleges was extended in the 1990s when some Canadian colleges developed into university colleges offering degrees from established universities (such as Simon Fraser University, *e.g.*). After 2005, these colleges became known as teaching universities, in contrast to research universities. Currently, the college dishes out some 3,000 certificates

3   Interview 1 was carried out on September 29, 2015, at Camosun College, Victoria (British Columbia) with the Vice President for Strategic Development. Interview 2 took place on October 6, 2015, at Sheridan College, Oakville (Ontario) with the coordinator of the Industrial Mechanical Millwright program. Both interviews lasted roughly 40 minutes each. The interviews were transliterated and we carried out a content analysis (according to Mayring 2010) from which we are quoting the most striking arguments.
4   However, differences between the two interviewees have to be mentioned here: While the BC interviewee represents his institution as a vice president (and therefore also the partial academic character of the college), the Ontario interviewee outed himself as firmly rooted in the vocational sphere of the apprenticeship courses his college offers.
5   The ITA is responsible for the coordination of the skilled trades system in British Columbia, and cooperates with industry, labour, government, training providers, employers and employees (Industry Training Authority 2015).

and diplomas and some 1,500 bachelor's degrees. This fact underlines the hybrid character of the institution.

The interviewee reports that apprenticeships are normally confined to technical trades, such as carpentry, sheet metal, horticulture, pipe fitting etc., while business profiles are more or less academic and require a diploma or certificate issued by the college. Apprenticeships in the college normally last for four years and follow a general pattern which applies to all provinces. Apprenticeships are offered on three levels, with the last one after four years indicating the *Red Seal* quality tag (see above).

The interviewee mentions that there has been a tentative change in public attention of apprenticeships, i.e. away from their traditionally reduced perception as "low-level and dirty". This was due to the boom in the oil and gas industry in Canada starting in 2005. People obviously have realized *"that the careers in the trades are much more flexible, pay much better money and have an immediate chance of employment whereas a lot of university careers, especially in the liberal arts fields, lead to unemployment or to underpaid employment"*. Nevertheless, when listening to the parents of high school students, they still would love their child to be a doctor or a lawyer. Skilled trades have lost a little bit their stigma, and they are now more recognized as an option – but maybe not as the most desirable option. There still seems to exist a kind of academic-vocational divide in the minds of people. *"Yes, it's definitely that parents still think that applied education is one step below university education"*.

With respect to government policy, the interviewee stated that it appears to be *"on the right track"*, although university representatives still may argue that in *"our skills obsessed world we will all be dumbing down and we need more thinkers and less workers"*. The interviewee says that *"the universities are firing back and you hear some very [...] insulting comments"*. The surprising other side of the story, however, seems to be the shift in income opportunities in favor of VET, even if this may not be a long-term perspective considering the economic environment, which is prone to unexpected changes:

> *[...] what helped a lot with it was Canada's oil industry [...] where young apprentices were making 140–150–180,000 $ a year and they came home with a big car,*

*and the friend next door who had gone to university was making 60,000$. And
they loved it and they spoke highly of it. So this is when people realized.*

In the interview, there was also the point brought forward by the interviewee that a "dual system", such as the German one, would be difficult
to introduce in the Canadian context. The Canadians indeed like *"the
idea that apprenticeships should not be limited to just the trades [...]"*.
However, compared to Germany, British Columbia does not have the
industrial infrastructure and is less densely populated. This fact makes
it difficult to establish a VET system which has the potential to include
e.g. business qualifications, which are now more or less academic
degrees in the Canadian context.

Interview 2:

This college near Toronto, which was founded in 1967, is one of Ontario's leading post-secondary institutions, and offers various programs
in the fields of arts, business, community service, health, technology,
and the skilled trades. Here 21,000 full-time and 17,000 continuing and
part-time students, from Canada and all over the world, are educated.
The interviewee mentions a "mass of diversity of programs" right across
his college, stretching from general ones to more specific vocational
ones and also degrees. The current background is one of transition as
the college is expected to become a university, while at the same time
continuing as a college.

    In the apprenticeship courses that take place in Ontario, appren-
tices go to school for three time periods during the time of their apprenticeship, as mandated by the government. During the training they
have to pass three levels, whereby students are just allowed to go to
the next level after the preceding one is successfully completed. After
finishing level three the apprentices receive a "certificate of apprenticeship". Metal cutting, electricity and millwrighting come up for the most
chosen occupational fields.

    The interviewee states that companies and colleges are not sepa-
rated from each other. The theoretical training content, which is taught
in colleges, is mainly determined in cooperation with the industry,
which has a large say. In Ontario, the government has so called "pack

committees". These consist of representatives of industry and of colleges, who

> *sit down together and [...] figure out what the best way would be for an individual program. So every few years [...] [these representatives] will refocus where the curriculum is going from a ministry level, because some aspects become redundant due to technology changes.*

It is interesting that this college does not offer specialized apprenticeship training for individual companies since apprenticeships are meant to be more general vocational programs. Siemens is mentioned as an example for a German company in the region offering apprenticeships around Toronto, sending its apprentices to the college.

The general reputation of apprenticeships in Canada *"overall would be accepted"*. In the opinion of the interviewee, every person with a certificate of apprenticeship would have *"a foot in a company's door"*. He points out that

> *if somebody comes into [a company] with a piece of paper and says that [...] [he/ she is] a qualified electrician, plumber, carpenter or whatever it might be, [...] the person who is running the company they gonna know very quick if this person is walking the walk and talking the talk.*

Nevertheless, as pointed out by the interviewee, there still seems to exist a strong academic-vocational divide in Canada between higher education on the one side and the vocational system and other pathways on the other. In his view a lot of parents are

> *trying to encourage their children to start a higher education in colleges or universities, but often this may not be the right pathway for these individuals. [...] People think just because they have a degree that they are better than a tradesperson. [...] There is a little bit of snobbery involved with higher education because the reality is if we don't have trades the world that we live in is going to stop functioning.*

In the opinion of the interviewee vocational qualifications, including apprenticeship qualifications and courses, should also be considered "degrees" and be given more attention by industry and government. There should be done more on a political level, also because the population of Ontario and across Canada is getting older. The companies need young employees to fill the gap, which occurs when several work-ers retire. Companies have to be proactive in such situations, because

> *if you have a tradesperson who retires on a Friday and they have 35 years of expe-rience or 40 years of experience in a particular company or a particular trade and then they leave and then the wealth of that knowledge is just gone forever [...] you need people to be chaperoned and taken under the wings of these individuals where they can pass on the wealth of experience.*

Another interesting aspect is put forward by the interviewee saying that in Canada trade unions try to restrict the ratio of apprentices to tradespersons, and there are discussions at the moment in Ontario about trying to change this ratio. He calls this tradition "shortsighted" with respect to the future.

Apart from the classical apprenticeship model, young people in the college are also given the opportunity to progress to higher edu-cation. If a student wants to go to university to study engineering *e.g.*, an evaluator, or a committee, would check what he/she has done over the years and the student would get credits for competence units he/she has passed in the past. Also, in this college the post-secondary courses outside apprenticeships are classified in two- and three-year programs. *E.g.*, the mechanical technician takes two years whereas the mechanical technologist takes three years. The three-year program includes a one-year work placement: Here the students go to school for one year before they go to work (also for one year). Finally they go back to college and finish off their studies. The last year is a one-year program correspond-ing to a two-semester program. After the students have completed the whole three-year program their certificate is a diploma.

We can see from these statements that full-time VET and part-time VET are the two basic models, although the first one also includes one third of the training time as a work placement. Obviously, this college places strong emphasis on the traditional notion of an apprenticeship setting where the young person learns with a master or experienced journeyman, thus "cultivating" and "preserving" the wealth of knowl-edge and skills needed for the respective occupation (Smith 2010, p. 313). However, apprenticeship programs do not include general edu-cation, quite contrary to the German model. Another difference is the fact that apprentices have to pay for their schooling, although they can get back up to 4,000 $ from the government. In Ontario, the average age for starting an apprenticeship is 27 years. Day release models instead of sandwich courses here resemble the structure of a kind of dual system. According to the interviewee, this is reported to be especially interesting for smaller companies. Finally, the interviewee pleads for more financial support for apprentices who come to college a couple of hours per week, and for more incentives for companies to offer training.

All in all, the interviewee generally believes that the overall climate for vocational education and training in Canada is a main issue at the moment and underlines that it ought to remain on the political agenda.

3.2 Is there a need to learn from Germany as an "apprenticeship country"?

We may conclude from the interviews and from literature that VET in Canada has many faces. Although research generally shows that income, social status and prestige seem to be the most significant contributory factors to its comparatively low status (Kopatz and Pilz 2015, p. 320), the VET system is firmly established in the colleges and polytechnics. Here, apprenticeships play a visible role when it comes to delivering skills to young people who want to work in the trades. Therefore, a kind of ambivalence remains towards the end of this paper. What we have seen here is a "national solution in progress", which, however, has to tackle the problem of "over-education" (Vahey 2000) within a "top-heavy system" (Raffe 1993) which has also been mentioned by our two interviewees.

The German dual system has attracted some considerable attention in recent years, with a number of countries trying to introduce similar concepts of structured apprenticeships leading to initial vocational qualifications (Deissinger 2015). Quite manifestly, there is expectation in particular among politicians that such a system might help cope with integration problems of school leavers into the VET sector and support combatting youth unemployment. However, with respect to what we have learnt from the Canadian situation, we dare not recommend any kind of transfer from a more developed system to the one we have briefly discussed here. Moreover, the argument should lead us to the conclusion that "learning from each other" would be a sensible way of dealing with the assumption that there are "best practices" which could be copied, other than pretending that "whole systems" and their specific culture and logic could be transplanted (*ibid.*; Stockmann 1999).

In fact, with respect to transferring a German-type dual system to the Canadian context, several factors would have to be taken into account. According to Euler (2013) the *cultural setting* is a key prerequisite for importing VET into another country. If social acceptance is missing, the consequence would be a

> risk of a self-reinforcing downward trend: there are no stakeholders with political power; the political decision-makers see no need to promote vocational training since there is no lobby pressure; and vocational training is neglected, causing its acceptance to decrease further (Euler 2013, p. 62).

In the minds of many Canadian people university education is just the one way into employment, so it is necessary to sensitize them that vocational training pathways can be successful. A basic esteem for practical learning and its standing against academic learning needs to be generated in the Canadian society, and a kind of "occupational logic" should find its place besides "meritocracy" (Deissinger 1998; Euler 2013, p. 32). Furthermore, companies need to understand even more what benefits they could get when training young people and building up their future workforce with apprenticeship qualifications.

The *institutional aspect* seems to be another relevant factor which has to be considered. The VET system needs to be recognizable as such, and it should represent good quality teaching and learning opportunities. In order to guarantee the quality of VET it is necessary to include a "practical learning route" in work orientation. In addition, a close collaboration between government and business is needed, so in the case of Canada the state has to be involved and Canadian employers need to become committed in the VET system as training institutions as well as in financial terms (Deissinger 2015, pp. 561ff.; Euler 2013, pp. 36, 42ff.). Moreover, standardisation, also across provinces, seems to be an issue. The Red Seal label mentioned above is clearly limited to the trades. Although there are around 3,000 standards in existence, most of them have a voluntary character or differ between sectors, regions and provinces (Allais 2016, p. 441).

Finally, *education system implications* have to be observed. The VET system has to be organized in a way which enables students to develop their different talents. According to Euler (2013) vocational training should be perceived and used as a chance for young people "to share their own life, develop their full potential, and increase their self-efficacy and motivation to learn" (Euler 2013, p. 21). If the aspiration of many colleges to become universities is the right way to bring VET into the focus as a viable alternative to degree studies seems at least doubtful. Furthermore, it may be stated that it is indispensable to grant teachers in VET a similar kind of training and status as teachers in general education (Euler 2013, p. 53).

Against the background of these aspects it has to be said that Canada's politicians and stakeholders are currently discussing the VET system and with it the value of practical and applied learning. It seems that a stronger VET system has to be developed within the existing framework, and it is the Canadian colleges and polytechnics that seem to have the potential to become an even tighter bond between academic and vocational traditions and mindsets. It becomes clear from the interviews that in Canada there is in fact a strong economic argument behind the proposition to raise the status and quality of vocational training in general, and of apprenticeships in particular. Lehmann's statement that apprenticeships can be looked at as "an alternative pathway into fulfilling and rewarding employment for young people [...] who are generally more interested in applied, rather than academic learning" (Lehmann 2012, p. 25) underlines the pedagogical logic behind any policy aiming at making the VET system stronger in order to avoid "over-education". Further research steps with respect to the Canadian VET context should therefore consist in looking more deeply and systematically into the "frame of mind" of companies in Canada and raise the question whether economic pressure – namely the awareness of companies of skill mismatches and serious skill shortages – alone is really strong enough to consolidate an already existing vocational culture in the college system and strengthen apprenticeships. At the moment, in Canada, financial returns from academic education no longer seem to be an argument *against* VET (Kopatz and Pilz 2015). This aspect once again highlights the relevance of "meritocracy" and socio-cultural factors when it comes to the attractiveness of different educational options underlying career pathways. By now, Canada still is the country with the highest share of holders of "tertiary qualifications" among all OECD countries, and 20% of adults (OECD average = 16%) hold a bachelor's degree (notwithstanding that college diplomas and certificates, as VET qualifications, are also tertiary or post-secondary) (OECD 2016). Critical commentators state – by looking at Germany – that "perhaps the most important lesson, however, is that a successful economy doesn't require everyone to have a university degree hanging on their wall" (Sorensen 2014). However, more systematic research is required to understand the political and cultural environment of VET in Canada more profoundly and its obvious dependency from meritocratic thinking – above all when it comes to appraising the importance of pathways from VET, and apprenticeships in particular, into higher education. We hope that this article has set up a kind of framework of arguments, and open issues, for such further research activities.

References

Alberta Education 2010. Off-campus Education Handbook. Edmonton, Government of Alberta.

Allais, St. 2016. Occupational standards in the English-speaking world: A dysfunctional product for export? In S. Bohlinger, T.K.A. Dang and M. Glatt (eds.), Education Policy: mapping the landscape and scope. Frankfurt a.M., Peter Lang.

Association of Canadian Community Colleges 2004. Consultation with Canadian Colleges and Institutes. [retrieved from: <http://www.accc.ca/wp-content/uploads/archive/briefs-memoires/200410-shrc_consultation.pdf> June, 26th 2016].

Birchard, K. 2010. Canadian University Graduates Are Going Back to the Classroom for Vocational Training. The Chronicle of Higher Education. [retrieved from: <http://chronicle.com/article/Canad ian-University-Graduates/66078/> June, 20th 2016].

Bohlinger, S. 2011. Leistungsfeststellung in Kanadas Berufsbildung. Berufsbildung in Wissenschaft und Praxis 40(5): 37–40.

Canadian Apprenticeship Forum 2016a. About CAF-FCA. [retrieved from: <http://caf-fca.org/about-caf-fca/> September, 26th 2016].

Canadian Apprenticeship Forum 2016b. Apprenticeship in Canada. [retrieved from: <http://caf-fca.org/apprenticeship-in-canada/> June, 28th 2016].

Canadian Apprenticeship Forum 2016c. Apprenticeship 101. [retrieved from: <http://caf-fca.org/apprenticeship-in-canada/apprenticeship-101/> June, 27th 2016].

CICIC The Canadian Information Centre for International Credentials 2016. Postsecondary education systems in Canada – postsecondary institutions. [retrieved from: <http://www.cicic.ca/1243/Postseco ndary-institutions/index.canada> June, 23rd 2016].

CICIC The Canadian Information Centre for International Credentials 2016b. Postsecondary education systems in Canada – degree-granting institutions. [retrieved from: <http://www.cicic.ca/1244/ Degree-granting-institutions/index.canada> June, 23rd 2016].

CICIC The Canadian Information Centre for International Credentials 2016c. Postsecondary education systems in Canada – non-degree-granting institutions. [retrieved from: <http://www.cicic.ca/1245/ Non-degree-granting-institutions/index.canada> June, 23rd 2016].

Colleges and Institutes Canada 2014. Listing of Degrees Awarded by Colleges, Institutes, Polytechnics and Universities with a College Mandate. [retrieved from: <http://docplayer.net/1614669-Listing-of-degrees-awarded-by-colleges-institutes-polytechnics-and-universit ies-with-a-college-mandate.html> June, 27th 2016].

Council of Ministers of Education 2016. Education in Canada: An Overview. [retrieved from: <http://www.cmec.ca/299/Educat ion-in-Canada-An-Overview/index.html#02> June, 23rd 2016].

Deissinger, Th. 1994. The Evolution of the Modern Vocational Training Systems in England and Germany: A Comparative View. Compare. A Journal of Comparative Education 24:17–36.

Deissinger, Th. 1998. Beruflichkeit als „organisierendes Prinzip" der deutschen Berufsausbildung. Markt Schwaben, Eusl-Verlag.

Deissinger, Th. 2010. Dual System. In P. Peterson, E. Baker and B. McGaw (eds.), International Encyclopedia of Education, 3rd Edition, Vol. 8, 448–454. Oxford, Elsevier.

Deissinger, Th. 2015. The German dual vocational and education system as "good practice"? Local Economy 30(5): 557–567.

Deissinger, Th. 2016. Vollzeitschulische Berufsbildung und berufsorientierte schulische Bildung in Australien im Kontext eines kompetenzorientierten Berufsbildungssystems. In B. Greimel-Fuhrmann and R. Fortmüller (eds.), Facetten der Entrepreneurship Education. Festschrift für Josef Aff anlässlich seiner Emeritierung. Wien, Manz.

Deissinger, Th. and Gonon, Ph. 2016. Stakeholders in the German and Swiss vocational educational and training system: Their role in innovating apprenticeships against the background of academisation. Education and Training 58(6): 568–577.

Deissinger, Th. and Greuling, O. 1994. Die englische Berufsbildungspolitik der achtziger Jahre im Zeichen der Krise eines „Ausbildungssystems": Historische Hintergründe und aktuelle Problemlagen. Zeitschrift für Berufs- und Wirtschaftspädagogik 90: 127–146.

Deissinger, Th. and Ott, M. 2016. Tertiarisation of Vocational Education and Training and its implications – problems and issues in Germany and France. In S. Bohlinger, T.K.A. Dang and M. Glatt (eds.), Education Policy: mapping the landscape and scope. Frankfurt a.M., Peter Lang.

Euler, D. 2013. Germany's dual vocational training system: a model for other countries? Gütersloh, Bertelsmann Stiftung.

Goldthorpe, J.H. 1996. Problems of "Meritocracy". In R. Erikson and J.O. Jonsson (eds.), Can Education be Equalized?. Boulder, Westview Press Inc.

Gonon, Ph. 2013. What makes the Dual System to a Dual System? A new Attempt to Define VET through a Governance Approach. bwp@ 25. [retrieved from: <http://www.bwpat.de/ausgabe25/gonon_bwpat25.pdf> July, 28th 2016].

Government of Canada 2016. Elementary and secondary education. [retrieved from: <http://www.cic.gc.ca/english/newcomers/before-education-schools.asp> June, 24th 2016].

Industry Training Authority (ITA) 2015. Overview. [retrieved from: <http://www.itabc.ca/overview/about-ita> September, 27th 2016].

Kopatz, S. and Pilz, M. 2015. The Academic Takes it All? A Comparison of Returns to Investment in Education between Graduates and Apprentices in Canada. International Journal for Research in Vocational Education and Training 2(4): 308–325.

Lehmann, W. 2012. Youth apprenticeships in Canada: context, structures and apprentice' experiences. In M. Pilz (ed.), The Future of Vocational Education and Training in a Changing World. Wiesbaden, Springer VS.

Lehmann, W., Taylor, A. and Wright, L. 2014. Youth apprenticeships in Canada: on their inferior status despite skilled labour shortages. Journal of Vocational Education & Training 66(4): 572–589.

Mayring, Ph. 2010. Qualitative Inhaltsanalyse. Grundlagen und Techniken. Weinheim, Beltz.

Ménard, M., Chan, C. and Walker, M. 2008. National Apprenticeship Survey. Canada Overview Report 2007. Ottawa, Statistics Canada (Research paper).

Miller, L. 2013. Canada. In E. Smith and R. Brennan Kemmis (eds.), Towards a model apprenticeship framework: a comparative analysis of national apprenticeship systems. New Delhi, International Labour Office.

Munro, D., MacLaine, C. and Stuckey, J. 2014. Skills – Where are we today? The state of skills and PSE in Canada. Ottawa, The Conference Board of Canada.

OECD 2016. Education at a Glance. Paris, OECD.

Pilz, M. and Li, J. 2014. Tracing Teutonic footprints in VET around the world? The skills development strategies of German companies in the USA, China and India. European Journal of Training and Development 38(8): 745–763.

Polesel, J. 2016. Separating the sheep and the goats – vocational programs in Victorian schools. In S. Bohlinger, T.K.A. Dang and M. Glatt (eds.), Education Policy: mapping the landscape and scope. Frankfurt a.M., Peter Lang.

Polytechnics Canada 2015. About Us. [retrieved from: <http://www.polytechnicscanada.ca/about-us> June, 28th 2016].

Polytechnics Canada 2016. Canada's Polytechnics: Contributing solutions for federal priorities. Ottawa, Polytechnics Canada.

Raffe, D. 1993. The Changing Scottish Scene: Implications for South of the Border. In W. Richardson, J. Woolhouse and D. Finegold (eds.), The Reform of Post-16 Education and Training in England and Wales. Harlow, Longman.

Red Seal Program 2016a. Red Seal Program. [retrieved from: <http://www.red-seal.ca/about/pr.4gr.1m-eng.html> June, 14th 2016].

Red Seal Program 2016b. Information for students. [retrieved from: <http://www.red-seal.ca/information/st.5d.2nts-eng.html> June, 14th 2016].

Schaub, H. and Zenke, K. G. 2000. Wörterbuch Pädagogik, 4. Aufl. München, Deutscher Taschenbuch Verlag.

Sharpe, A. and Gibson, J. 2005. The Apprenticeship System in Canada: Trends and Issues. CSLS Research report 2005–04. [retrieved from: <http://www.csls.ca/reports/csls2005-04.PDF> June, 14th 2016].

Smaller, H. 2003. Vocational education in Ontario secondary schools. In H. Schuetze and R. Sweet (eds.), Integrating school and workplace learning in Canada. Principles and Practices of Alternation Education and Training. Montreal, McGill-Queen's University Press.

Smith, E. 2010. Apprenticeships. In P. Peterson, E. Baker and B. McGaw (eds.), International Encyclopedia of Education, 3rd Edition, Vol. 8. Oxford, Elsevier.

Sorensen, Chr. 2014. How the German style of apprenticeships could be a model for Canada. Would the German way really work here? [retrieved from: <http://www.macleans.ca/work/how-the-german-style-of-apprenticeships-could-be-a-model-for-canada> November, 15th 2016].

Statistics Canada 2013. Education in Canada: Attainment, Field of Study and Location of Study. National Household Survey 2011. Ottawa, Statistics Canada.

Statistics Canada 2015a. Registered apprenticeship training, registrations, byagegroups,sexandmajortradegroups. [retrieved from: <http://www5.statcan.gc.ca/cansim/a26?lang=eng&retrLang=eng&id=4770053&&pattern=&stByVal=1&p1=1&p2=-1&tabMode=dataTable&csid=> June, 29th 2016].

Statistics Canada 2015b. Registered apprenticeship or trade qualifier certificates, by age groups, sex, major trade groups and Red Seal or non-Red seal indicator. [retrieved from: <http://www5.statcan.gc.ca/cansim/a26> June, 29th 2016].

Statistics Canada 2015c. Unemployment rates of population aged 15 and over, by educational attainment, Canada, 1990 to 2011. [retrieved from: <http://www.statcan.gc.ca/pub/81-582-x/2012001/tbl/tble3.1-eng.htm> June, 28th 2016].

Statistics Canada 2016. Education Indicators in Canada: An International Perspective 2015. Ottawa, Statistics Canada.

Statistisches Bundesamt 2013. Berufsbildung auf einen Blick. Wiesbaden, Statistisches Bundesamt.

Stockmann, R. 1999. Duale Berufsbildungsmodelle in Entwicklungsländern – Typologie der Implementationsversuche und ihrer Strategien. Zeitschrift für internationale erziehungs- und sozialwissenschaftliche Forschung 16(1/2): 253–286.

Taylor, A. 2010. The contradictory location of high school apprenticeship in Canada, Journal of Education Policy. Journal of Vocational Education & Training 25(4): 503–517.

Taylor, A., Watt-Malcolm, B. and Wimmer, R. 2013. "Hybridity" in two Canadian provinces: Blurring institutional boundaries. In T. Deissinger, J. Aff, A. Fuller and H. Jorgensen (eds.), Hybrid Qualifications: Structures and Problems in the Context of European VET Policy. Bern, Lang.

Vahey, S.P. 2000. The great Canadian training robbery: evidence on the returns to educational mismatch. Economics of Education Review 19(2): 219–227.

Victorian Curriculum and Assessment Authority 2007. Guide to the VCE, VCAL and Apprenticeships and Traineeships for 2008. Melbourne, VCAA.

María José Chisvert-Tarazona and Ana I. Córdoba-Iñesta

Validation and Accreditation of Qualifications and Citizenship: a Method to Guarantee Social Equity in Spain[1]

1. Introduction

A healthy citizenry makes political decisions as a practice of autonomy in the public context, which assumes the benefits of the greater good (Clarke 2010). This is seen as a possible horizon of citizenship with roots going beyond a middle-class, white, adult and worship male citizen (Macedo 2009). Christian, cosmopolitan and organized by the State (Stoer and Magalhaes 2005), to include differentiated groups and individuals like men or women. This is based on a democratic view, appreciated by Western thought ever since ancient times, and refers to both the benefit of individual freedom (Freire 2009), and the adhesion of members of society to common projects (Cortina 1997).

Some approaches reject human rights as a theoretical founding principle of citizenship, arguing that citizenship rights are particularistic and dynamic, and based on a person's political design, while human rights have a "universalist" nature and responsibilities held in an ethical design (Kirwan 2005). This chapter nevertheless refers to the intersection between human rights and citizenship, investing in political

---

1   This text stems from the precompetitive research project funded by the University of Valencia (UV-INV-PRECOMP13-115340): "Mapa de ocupaciones acreditables desde el Sistema Nacional de las Cualificaciones y de la formación Profesional en empresas de inserción" (Map of accreditable occupations from the National System for Professional Qualifications and Vocational and Training Education in Work Integration Social Enterprises) directed by Dr María José Chisvert Tarazona (University of Valencia).

participation (Macedo 2012), and in the recognition of training and labour, and citizens' human rights.

In Adult Education (AE) we should remember the personal history of those accessing this, their actions, their opportunities to assert their rights, to build their legitimacy. The education they received, the teaching-learning process in which they participated, will clearly be one of the key aspects in building a citizen, but not the only one. The relationships between the right to education and the right to work also have to be taken into account as elements which influence the development of citizenship. This conceptualisation opens a path to the possibility of strengthening educational citizenship through participation in the development and construction of knowledge (Macedo 2012).

The Presidency's Conclusions at the Lisbon European Council held on 24th and 25th March 2000 specifically referred to the recognition and accreditation of work experience and non-formal training. At that meeting a goal was set for the EU countries for the next 10 years: to become the most competitive and dynamic economy in the world based on knowledge and capable of sustainable economic growth with more and better jobs and with greater social cohesion. This goal may also be linked to the milestone reached in 2002 by the National System for Qualifications and Vocational Education and Training, which focused on the promotion of social cohesion.

The National System for Professional Qualifications in Spain offered the opportunity for the recognition of adult learning and particularly the accreditation of skills, and also made us wonder whether this situation is possible in Spain. The goal of this chapter is to provide a comprehensive view of the assessment of skills and learning outcomes recently launched in the Spanish context. The focus is on where this approach based on learning outcomes is going, and whether it will be beneficial for the most vulnerable groups.

In this context, we should firstly explain what we understand about certification and accreditation of professional skills. We use the definition of the term proposed by the European Centre for the Development of Vocational Training (CEDEFOP 2012). They define it as official and formal certification throughout a period of proven working performance capacity. It requires the recognition of skills in relation to a standard rather than relying on prior completion of an educational process.

What is subject to accreditation would be professional skills. According to Navío (2005), professional skills are knowledge, procedures and attitudes that help to solve different situations in different working scenarios. Professional skills are also defined by Rodríguez-Moreno (2006) as the skills which transfer higher levels of engagement, motivation and joint accountability.

Vulnerable groups do not usually have accreditable professional skills, and professional experience and training acquired in non-formal settings become an opportunity to vouch for their knowhow. So, what are the potential opportunities for accreditation of work experience and non-formal training paths amongst the most vulnerable groups?

To answer to this question, our objective is to review the appropriateness of the National Catalogue of Professional Qualifications (CNCP) for assessing the qualifications, occupations and skill sets held by integration workers (IW) in Work Integration Social Enterprises (WISEs) and to draw a map of occupations that may be subject to accreditation by these enterprises.

Our research sheds light on opportunities for accreditation from the reference standard curriculum of vulnerable people or those at social risk of exclusion who receive training during professional experience in a labour context (Chisvert-Tarazona, Ros-Garrido, Córdoba-Iñesta and Marhuenda-Fluixà 2015). Learning the proximity or distance between occupations performed by IW and CNCP allows accurate knowledge to be obtained about the possibilities of accreditation of groups at risk of social exclusion and enables a map of accreditable qualifications to be drawn up.

It is also relevant to provide managers, WISE support and production workers with valuable information regarding the procedures for qualification of the accreditation, and to develop an area for discussion in academia and at work with environments connected with the accreditation of the work experience of vulnerable groups.

To sum up, this chapter arises from the study of occupations, qualifications and skill sets taught by and learnt from WISEs and their accreditation opportunities in relation to the CNCP.

We are concerned that most occupations to which integration workers have access through WISEs are subject to accreditation as qualifications of level 1. At WISEs the most significant learning-teaching processes tend to focus on key learning skills. These skills are not however expressed as such under the CNCP, and they are not therefore subject to accreditation. This also happens with occupations/qualifications at level 1 undertaken by WISEs that are not included in the CNCP yet, meaning that vulnerable groups would have greater difficulties in terms of access and accreditation under the Spanish National System for Professional Qualifications.

2. WISEs and the integration process

In today's increasingly forceful labour market liberalisation there is a difference in the role of these social economy undertakings in combining both training for those workers likely to be excluded and their progressive inclusion in the ordinary labour market. The WISE scheme is an intermediate step between training programmes and access to the ordinary market.

Further to former regulations in autonomous regions in Spain, the enactment of Spanish Act 44/2007, of December 13th, for the regulation of the governance of such work integration social enterprises defines WISE in its Article 4 as a legally constituted cooperative society, qualified by the competent regional organizations, which performs any economic activity of producing goods and services, with the social purpose of socio-labour training and the integration of people at risk of social exclusion into the regular market. These enterprises must therefore provide workers with customized processes of paid work, training in the workplace, and labour and social habituation to improve socio-labour integration to the regular workplace.

Article 5 establishes the requirements which need to be met by these enterprises:

–   They have to be promoted by one or several promoting entities: this participation has to be at least fifty-one percent of the share capital for corporations. In the case of Cooperative Societies and labour companies, such participation shall be within the limits.

- Premises included in the different legislations applicable to the collaborating partners or associates.
- They have to be registered in the corresponding Register according to its legal form, as well as in the Administrative Register of Work Integration Enterprises of the Autonomous Community.
- They have to maintain on an annual basis a percentage of integration workers in the insertion process, under any type of contract: at least thirty percent during the first three years of activity and at least fifty percent of the total workforce from the fourth year, with at least two integration workers.
- They cannot carry out economic activities outside their corporate purposes.
- They have to allocate at least eighty percent of the results or available surplus obtained each year to the improvement or expansion of their production and integration structures.
- They must annually submit a Corporate Balance Sheet of the company's activity, including an economic and social report, the degree of integration in the regular labour market and the composition of the workforce, information on the integration tasks performed and forecasts for the next financial year.
- They must guarantee the means to meet commitments under the itineraries of socio-labour integration.

This regulation came out with overall all-party support as regards the meaning of integration worker. Hence, integration workers are people who are socially excluded or at serious risk of being socially excluded, unemployed and facing difficulties to enter the ordinary job market.

There is a great variety of integration workers that can enter these enterprises: some receive low-income benefits, some are long-term unemployed, young people who have not finished their mandatory schooling; others are people with drug abuse problems or who suffer from other addictions, while some are under rehabilitation, or in prison, ex-convicts; and finally other groups are ethnic minorities, immigrants or single caregivers with dependants. According to the Ministry of Employment and Social Security, WISEs in Spain employed around 4,111 people (García 2014).

The Spanish Federation of Entrepreneurial Associations (Faedei) and the Spanish Association of Social and Solidarity Economy Recuperators (Aeress) define the support given by these enterprises as a social integration process in a pedagogical relationship with one main objective: the achievement of personal autonomy, independence or emancipation of the integration worker in personal, socio-labour and professional dimensions (Faedei-Aeress 2014).

These enterprises provide a rehabilitation roadmap in three stages: the first stage consists of a personalised work plan detailing a pathway designed along with support workers. According to the Faedei-Aeress handbook (2014), the WISE implements a process of selection and access in which it is essential to define the workplace properly and to plan this process to incorporate new social integration workers in the company. After selection comes the initial diagnosis of the selected person. The enterprise gives the person all the information he/she needs about characteristics, conditions and requirements of the job, and at the same time it asks about their expectations and goals. Finally it ends with a joint commitment through the design of a custom integration itinerary. This work plan is reviewed throughout the second stage, the performance period. In this second phase the company gives a chance to learn, become qualified in professional skills, in order to achieve labour market integration by the end of the process. The third stage is to develop guidance and mediation to prepare transition into the ordinary labour market. It is during this stage when integration workers could get the accreditation of the learning acquired from their employment at such enterprises.

3. Methods and data

In this study we present the results of the project "Map of accreditable occupations from the National System for Professional Qualifications and Vocational and Training Education in Work Integration Social Enterprises". The state of the art of the recognition and accreditation of work experience and non-formal training are analysed in three phases:

- Documentary phase. This stage includes the review of all references looked at and aims to enrich the discussion from academic sources, studies made by international organisations such as the CEDEFOP, CIDEC, OECD or the ILO, regulatory documentation concerning the accreditation of knowledge in informal and non-formal learning environments and specialist texts, Europe-wide, but mostly at Spanish level. Such sources of information met certain needs allowing a review of the literature by context, text and method analysis.
- Experimental phase. We carried out 15 comprehensive interviews with experts in accreditation from academia (University of Bath, University of Valencia) and with work professionals (directors from the national and regional qualifications institutes, trainers of assessors and advisors in the process, and an advisor, an assessor, director of a national observatory of qualifications); and lastly, with 2 experts in integration enterprises and vulnerable groups. These people contributed practical and procedural keys that allowed us to establish the link between the accreditation of qualifications through work experience and vulnerable groups.
- Analysis and interpretation of results. This chapter gives some of the most significant results.

The methodology used to complete the *Map of occupations for accreditation of professional experience in work integration enterprises* stems from a quantitative analysis.

One of the first issues we focused on in the experimental phase was to develop a map of occupations that can be accredited in WISEs. To do so, we made phone interviews to the responsible staff of the whole WISEs universe. We usually made several calls to each company to guarantee that we were talking to the key staff and to offer them both general information about the project and specific information about the closest qualifications of the jobs done by integration workers at that company. This information was supported by written documentation sent by e-mail. After that, we contacted the company again by phone to get the final information about the qualifications and units of competency and the number of integration workers for any occupation in the company. The objective was to find out the proximity/distance between the CNCP and the jobs currently done by integration workers at these companies.

Subsequently the research group conducted a seminar in five parts of Spain: Zaragoza, Valencia, Madrid, Bilbao and Seville, selected according to the number of WISEs. These seminars addressed the professionals working on training relations with integration workers. The curricular contents of the seminars involved institutional discourse as regards accreditation of competencies, accreditation protocols and the specific assessment criteria about the recognised qualifications in the map of occupations. These seminars meant that the results of the map of occupations could be refined.

Data bases available on FAEDEI were used in order to draw the map of the occupations that can be accredited from the Spanish National System of Qualifications in WISE. We regularly updated these databases in view of the contributions of different business associations of all the regions in Spain. There is a close coincidence between the universe and the companies contacted in the sample: 199.

It is relevant to emphasize the large number of companies that have closed during the research process; basically 11 in the last year. Companies found coping with the crisis particularly hard. We got corroborated results from 144 companies from every Spanish region except Murcia, La Rioja and Ceuta and Melilla. The number of integration workers concerned was 1,566.

4. Four areas of analysis

We include four types of outcomes. One generic outcome is related to the analysis of western socio-political reality and its relation to accreditation of qualifications. The other three concern: (1) learning outcomes; (2) agents involved in accreditation systems; (3) the pedagogical and evaluation dimension of the system. These points are then linked to citizenship.

The analysis of western socio-political reality and its relation to the accreditation of qualifications force us to take into account the complexity of life nowadays. This is confirmed by the high rates of unemployment, the high rate of early school leavers and the increasingly poor transition between education and work, as well as the large numbers of unskilled workers, a context connected with the deterioration of citizenship.

The institutionalisation of free and mandatory schooling is acknowledged as being insufficient and a broad learning fabric that may help address the challenges posed by a post-industrial society is required. Long-life learning is considered to be fundamental by the EU in addressing these new challenges.

The accreditation of qualifications seems to have its effects attenuated by the recognition of knowledge brought about by new learning spaces, so this recognition may be effective if the National System for Qualifications in Spain introduces a system for the accreditation of skills aimed at the assessment and certification of such new expertise. This will require its recognition in the labour market led by an understanding amongst trade unions and confederation of industries (social agents).

The emergence of this change is favoured by a new educational narrative that prioritises results. The important issue is *what* one learned and not *where* or *how* one had access to such knowledge, although this could seem paradoxical for citizens. On the one hand, individuals will be able to benefit from the assessment of their abilities without questioning whether they have been acquired in an academic educational context or not; on the other, citizens finally become the sole parties responsible for their learning, obviating any responsibility of the State or enterprise organizations.

The first main interpretation and theoretical analysis refer to the relevance of the learning outcomes already mentioned, which are clearly represented by the accreditation of qualifications.

According to Bjornavold (2000), this is a matter of viewing the knowledge acquired in different contexts and the recognition of the power of non-formal and informal spaces to generate skills and capabilities equivalent to the ones produced with formal education systems.

Amongst its supporters we may mention Raffe (2009), who asserts that the differences offered by the various teaching-learning contexts are institutional in nature, referring to social constructs, but not to epistemological ones.

We find direct pros and cons in the learning outcomes from this perspective. Amongst the *pros* we could highlight:

−   The recognition of learning prevents overlapping. For example, in Spain we still have ambulance drivers with 15 years' professional experience who go through a standardised and recognised vocational course in order to guarantee their jobs because it recently became a regulated profession. It is nevertheless true that this situation did not occur in some autonomous communities which prioritized the accreditation of regulated professions.
−   It generates transparency in the job market, making it possible to acknowledge the skills developed in the workplace as regards industrial relations. This certainly represents a benefit for citizens who can demonstrate the skills developed in the workplace and even review their professional status.
−   It favours the adoption of second opportunities for those groups that left school early. The proximity between validations and recognition of skills and training is great. In many cases it represents an opportunity to access specific training. Moreover, motivation or empowerment significantly expands confidence in the education system and in the opportunities for citizens to access this successfully. We could perhaps learn from the example of the Portuguese accreditation system, which even calls the places for skill accreditation *Second Chance Centres*, although the goal of these centres is also to accredit school abilities in order to enable access to certification and validation of the compulsory schooling stage.
−   If we cannot know where the learning has occurred, the most vulnerable groups (those excluded from commercialised access to knowledge) may benefit. A good example would be the access to certification from learning processes produced in labour contexts by individuals who could not afford the learning acquired in the formal educational context.

Some of the *cons* of such concern for learning outcomes are:

−   It transfers the responsibility to those who (or who do not) finally access learning, to the weakest link in the chain. The most vulnerable groups are subjected to a new control, a new system that could also leave them "out". In this case, the individuality that legitimizes the proposal requires citizens to assume all the responsibility.

– Its instrumental exchange value adds to the list of properties to be accumulated by people and states. The polarisation of the level of qualifications in Spain shows the dearth of recognised qualifications, supervised through international rankings. The recognition and accreditation system becomes an enabler of quick transitions towards qualification through recognition of learning. In the words of one of the academic experts in the interview: "It can be a path, should we say, to increase positive figures".

– We must also note how close it is to the goal-focussed approach to learning. The learning objectives and outcomes show what the students are capable of, but they do not specify purpose or targeted content that the teachers can see. Most abstract issues, such as the acquisition of transversal skills, are difficult to assess in fast processes of skill validation, while in training contexts it is easier to identify whether the individual achieved those skills.

– Vocational qualification systems deploy their recognition and accreditation systems for professional skills under this approach focused on the learning outcomes. As it obviates the teaching processes, citizens' place continues to be subject to an account of available individual skills. This is a market of knowledge, tending to credentialism.

Young (2008) refers to powerful knowledge, theoretical knowledge which is easily conveyed in schools and colleges, but which is hard to access from work experience. This is knowledge which gives theoretical sense to "know how".

The *second main interpretation* and *theoretical analysis* refers to the agents involved in accreditation systems. Mertens (1996) talks about different models of qualification and vocational training systems depending on the agents concerned in their development:

– Run by government, as it is the case in the United Kingdom, Australia, South Africa, Portugal and New Zealand. In those countries the law requires there to be a national authority for qualifications in charge of running and managing the system.

-   Run by the socio-economic and professional sectors based on the demand of the labour market, as is the case in the U.S.
-   Run by trade unions and confederation of industries (social agents), as is the case in Germany, France or Canada.

The Spanish model is run by the government, but it also has the involvement of the autonomous regional governments and the trade unions and confederation of industries (social agents).

The analysis of the context of states and their institutions is illustrated by the different forms of adherence to, and implementation of, the National Qualifications Framework (NQF). The interpretation and recontextualising processes carried out by either individual states or by different actors and non-governmental groups inside these illustrates the unenforceability of a linear process of implementation of European guidelines.

Audits conducted by government agencies become a new form of control and regulatory assessment of the learning outcomes in non-formal and informal environments, validated by such principles as confidentiality, impartiality, credibility and reliability.

The third aspect, the pedagogical and evaluation dimension of the system, highlights some relevant questions. The accreditation system fragments evaluation into units of competence and this thus enables partial certification of professional qualification as expressed in the regulation (Royal Decree 1224/2009), as stated in academic publications (Bernad and Marhuenda 2008; Chisvert-Tarazona 2013).

This Royal Decree guarantees the recognition of professional skills and explicitly states the requirement for proven non-mainstream training and/or proven work experience. This legislation introduces an exception for those over 25 who may not have documentary evidence. These people may go through an interim registration and produce some evidence allowed by law of their work experience or non-formal learning. The assessors and advisors in the interviews conducted in the study about accreditation of professional qualifications were not aware of this possibility which would entail the inclusion of the activities carried out by a significant portion of the population such as privately-undertaken activities or work in the black economy, etc. The lack of awareness of this opportunity to demonstrate their skills is linked to impoverished counselling where learning contexts are avoided because of the difficulties in demonstrate learning.

There are some companies which organise their own call for the accreditation of their own employees. There is no political will for the provision of necessary resources to allow the procedure to fulfil its function, the accreditation of those who have non-recognised professional skills. This is a process which all professionally competent individuals should be able to access, as it becomes a citizen's right.

The specialised language used in the procedure is obscure and not very accessible to applicants and even to companies. There is no common code accessible to citizens as a whole and especially to the most vulnerable groups.

The accreditation of competences starts from an educational approach that favours learning outcomes, and we therefore pay great attention to the pedagogical effects of this evaluation, as it does not enable the compensatory approach.

Finally, current assessment depends on the government rationality that controls learning inside and outside the education system.

5. The situation of work integration social enterprises: Map of accreditable qualifications

The National System of Qualifications and Vocational Training (SNCFP) in Spain was conceived to address comprehensive organization of vocational training, qualifications and accreditation, and to respond effectively and transparently to the social and economic demands through vocational training. In coordination with active employment policies and the free promotion of workers, it aims to promote training throughout life, and to respond to different expectations and personal and professional situations.

Its explicit aim is to improve the skills of the workforce, transparency of the labour market, the match between supply and demand, and the coherence of the vocational training system. To assure its accomplishment it proposes an inclusive and universalizing model, able to embrace learning obtained in various ways, as it addresses the entire working population, either unemployed or active.

The comparative study of different national realities is made by the Incual (2003), and displays the long gestation process required in any model of lifelong learning and equivalences between initial training systems, vocational and experiential learning.

The essential features of the National System of Professional Qualifications are defined by processes focused on integration in three areas: professional qualifications, various forms of acquisition of skills, and offers of vocational training.

The basic regulation of SNCFP seeks to articulate vocational training policies emanating from the General State Administration, Regional Authorities and social agents. The feeling of stagnation, of lack of progress in the final concretion of the system, stems not only from the complexity of its design, but because there are many different viewpoints that must be considered.

The National Catalogue of Professional Qualifications (CNCP) has until now been working on the concretion of qualifications. In recent years the catalogue has been improved as base and pillar of the system, to the extent that it defines qualifications through the general competence and the competence units (CU) of which it is composed, and it associates each CU training module to the two subsystems: Regulated Vocational Training and Training for Employment.

On the other hand, the offer of non-formal vocational training has been consolidated, and there are now multiple aspects working in favour of integration of vulnerable groups, paying attention to the training needs of organizations at the same time.

Regarding the most relevant results on the Map of occupations from the study of accreditation of professional qualifications covered by this chapter, the qualifications which can be accredited in WISEs belong to the professional families of Security and Environment and Sociocultural and community services. No WISEs working in such families as the Maritime industry and Fisheries, Chemistry, Personal image or Energy and water were found.

It is interesting to observe that 47.9% of WISEs participating in this study undertaken in Spain are located in two or more professional families: their introduction in the market does not aim for specialization, but mostly for performing low-skilled activities. WISEs value diversification in order to enable the integration of these vulnerable groups.

The National Catalogue for Professional Qualifications and VET has prioritized qualifications of levels 2 and 3. If we compare the situation of WISEs, we will observe that both the number of qualifications and the frequency of these qualifications appear in the map of occupations on level 1. It can also be appreciated that in the map of level 2 occupations the tendency is to find a smaller number of units of competency that could be accredited.

Table 1: Distribution of levels of qualifications in CNCP and WISEs.

Level of Qualific.	Nº Qualific CNCP	Nº Qualific in WISE	Frequency IW in WISE	% IW in WISE
1	78	30	1.048	64.38%
2	286	23	473	29.06%
3	298	5	26	1.59%
With no qualification			81	4.97%
Totals	662	58	1.628	100%

Source: research project "Map of accreditable occupations from the National System for Professional Qualifications and Vocational and Training Education in Work Integration Social Enterprises".

We also found a significant number of occupations which cannot be accredited. Professional families such as Security and Environment or Mechanical manufacturing should be revised. Occupations provided by WISEs not included in CNCP refer to these three elements: (1) Ancillary or basic activities of qualification level 1; (2) Very specific occupations that could hardly be conveyed beyond the company where they are generated; and (3) Craft activities sparsely introduced in the labour market. In the first case we could mention: the management of urban and industrial waste; the handling and packaging of products; the performance of collection, recovery and triage activities (textiles, toys, appliances, etc.); recycling of computer resources, or parking booths. In the second case, we can find some activities covering the maintenance and repair of furniture and/or appliances. Among artisanal occupations they highlight craft displays, specialists in the production of lamps, or blacksmiths. All these are activities not likely to be accredited at present since the CNCP, *i.e.* the normative curriculum, did not include them.

The map of occupations evidences that in many of the qualifications eligible for accreditation some units of competence are not part of the tasks and/or functions performed by the IW even if the occupation might be subject to accreditation.

This option becomes an opportunity only if the procedure is able to accredit on a regular basis the IW who has the prerequisites and the level of qualification required. Whether conditions in the accreditation system are met or not, some WISEs considered that career guidance in the last phase in the company would relate two-way optimal inclusion for these groups: VET and accreditation of work experience, instruments that draw the IW closer to the ultimate goal of promoting their incorporation in the regular labour market. But the places available in the regional calls for accreditation of qualifications in 2014 did not include qualifications subject to accreditation by the most vulnerable groups.

In order to open to citizens, the Government could extend its willingness to enable accreditations of low levels, specifically regional governments in Spain. Moreover, the National Institute of Professional Qualifications could review the CNCP in order to incorporate occupations likely to be accredited from those levels.

From a meso level, and especially from the State and Regional Federations, WISEs could ask for a positive discrimination of the accreditation of these groups, requiring places in calls. From a micro level and during the labour contract, they could develop an assessment based on the professional learning and criteria of performance of professional qualifications as regards as their occupations. Similarly, in the last stage of the WISE career path they could facilitate the approach to the accreditation system of professional skills through professional orientation.

In the study "Map of accreditable occupations from the National System for Professional Qualifications and Vocational and Training Education in Work Integration Social Enterprises" in Spain as a whole the percentage of IW with the potential to accredit their professional qualification according to the regional calls for accreditation[2] in 2014

---

2   Educational and Employment Regional Governments propose these calls for accreditation.

was 39.31%. This fact could seem very positive; but there are no State, but only regional calls. In some calls, one of the selection criteria is to belong to the region. Moreover, hardly any vulnerable people would move to other communities to participate in accreditation processes because in many cases they have been far from the formal education system for too long and these evaluation processes would require proximity to encourage confidence in the system. This is the case of the call in the Basque Country regarding Cleaning Surfaces and Furniture, since it extends access opportunities to calls to 22.11%. The service sector is the one which has the greatest similarity to the requirements in calls as regards as the map of occupations subject to accreditation in IW. Seven communities announce places for the Services for pest control qualification. 0.25% of IW could have access to this call. In the Sociocultural and community services family, Homecare and Socio-health care qualifications for dependent people have been convened in twelve communities, as these are regulated professions; in this case 3.63% of IW could benefit from this call. However, the call in the Basque Country related to Surface Cleaning and Furniture in buildings and premises is the one which would benefit the IW most (21.11%). Furthermore, in the Hotel and Tourism sector IW could submit to qualifications on level 1 relating to Basic kitchen, restaurant and bar operations, and to flats for accommodation (6.76%); and to the Kitchen (0.74%) and Reception (0.68%) qualifications. In the professional family of Physical and Sports activities the qualification of Lifesaving in water facilities would benefit 0.06% of IW.

The primary sector fails to include any qualification of the Agrarian professional family. Only level 2 qualifications of the Installation and maintenance professional family had places in the Basque Country, Andalusia, Galicia and Aragon administrative regions. In this sector only 0.30% of IW could apply for calls.

We find similar results in the manufacturing sector. Galicia and the Basque Country offer Welding, from the Mechanical manufacturing professional family. In the professional family of Wood, Furniture and Cork, again Galicia offers Carpentry and Furniture. In this sector the accreditation process could benefit 0.30% of IW.

In the construction sector places in the qualification for Concrete work are only available in Aragon, which belongs to the professional family of Building and Civil Engineering. 0.12% of IW could apply for this call.

In the sector of distribution and transports in Murcia 50 places are for Auxiliary trade activities, on qualification level 1, which belongs to the professional family of Trade and Marketing. In this case, a larger volume of IW, 4.36%, could benefit from this.

Hence, by comparing the qualifications subject to accreditation by IW in 2014 in the regional calls, the opportunities for certification were scarce.

6. Conclusions and discussion

The Spanish Government proposed a procedure of recognition and accreditation of work experience and non-formal training that helps guarantee access to work, which is useful and enriching. According to a trainer of assessors and advisors interviewed in the study entitled "Map of accreditable occupations from the National System for Professional Qualifications and Vocational and Training Education in Work Integration Social Enterprises": "It improves the self-esteem of those who submit to the process and it improves their chances for integration. That is the greatest virtue and that is what generates great expectations regarding this procedure".

Social, economic and work factors converge in the existence of "text" for accreditation of skills, materialised under the drive for Europe, underpinned by Spanish legislation and developed by the National Institute for Professional Qualifications. However, there is no "context", and proof of this is that there are no explicit demands for this procedure: it has not become widespread, the mechanism is uncertain and there is no guarantee that there will be a call for accreditation of some qualifications or others, with the exception of regulated professions.

After analysing the results, the first postulation is confirmed: most IW have occupations in WISEs likely to be creditable as qualifications and/or units of competency of level 1 (63.38%). This result is worrying if we consider calls for accreditation of professional competences made in the regions in 2014. This result also evidences that the system has forgotten level 1 qualifications, as shown in the big five sectors (service, manufacturing, distribution and transports, construction and primary sector).

The second postulation is confirmed as well: there are level 1 occupations/qualifications covered by WISE not included in CNCP. Results show how some occupations carried out are not subject to accreditation at present.

The revision by the General Council of Vocational Training and by the Institute of Professional Qualifications about the possibility of including new qualifications such as Auxiliary activities in management of urban and industrial waste could be really useful. In addition, the possibility of accreditation of transversal competences such as autonomous learning, teamwork in problem-solving could also be considered.

Another key point that hinders vulnerable people's access is that calls have a limited number of participants; this means that people with the competences required by the professional qualification in response to the rule are not the ones accredited, but those who have a professional and educational history of higher quality. The vast majority of applicants are filtered out at the beginning of the process according to the number of places available.

Complementarily, one of the criteria used in the calls is the inclusion of qualifications of regulated professions: unfortunately, many of these qualifications are not on the WISE map of occupations.

Nonetheless, the relevance of certification of groups at risk of social exclusion was verified through the seminars with relevant actors from WISEs. At these, some WISEs mentioned that they are making efforts to enable the homologation of classrooms in their facilities or seeking centres of training for employment in order to facilitate access to qualification of IW. Giving certificates of professionalism at some of these institutions is becoming a tangible option, although it would be much more effective if the professional experience accumulated could be accredited. If access to the validation and accreditation of competences is guaranteed in these groups, WISE could direct their training efforts to enable certification of professional qualifications or at least of units of competence of the qualification which are not being developed in the workplace.

The improvement of the process of accreditation of professional skills in vulnerable groups would therefore require updating the CNCP, paying special attention to level 1 qualifications, and reviewing the elements and requirements of calls for accreditation of skills in order to benefit vulnerable groups. As regards this analysis, which call for qualifications would benefit these groups? Would a positive discrimination with specific places be required? Perhaps the answer may be to modify the procedure and ensure that any person with specific competences could participate without limited places, regardless of where these skills were acquired. Ensuring real access to all the professional qualifications in each administrative region in annual calls would certainly be a step towards the visibility of competences acquired in non-formal and informal contexts. If we want vulnerable people to be able to prove their expertise, the procedure needs to be constructed on a basis of social equity: we need to be aware of learning obtained in the underground economy or in private contexts, to make obtaining the qualification feasible on a local level, and to ensure the existence of qualifications, especially those of level 1.

The availability of a venue for training and vocational guidance in WISE makes accompaniment to certification of qualifications feasible. A plausible strategy in these companies would streamline the training effort, directing it towards units of competence of the particular qualification that are not being developed in their jobs. But this will only make sense if the accreditation system really enables the certification of skills acquired through professional experience.

We stated above that processes of evaluation and accreditation of professional competences help to measure the distance that a person must advance to achieve the professional qualification (or, if applicable, unit of competence). Knowing this distance from the beginning of the process in a WISE could substantially extend the opportunities for accreditation. However, if we plan what is evaluable to facilitate accreditation, training in these companies would approach the conception of the curriculum conceptualized by Pozuelos and Romero (2002). It is a curriculum characterized by its high defined regulation and little flexibility, since it depends on the learning outcomes that can be assessed by the accreditation system of professional skills. Moreover, the pressure of production in these enterprises is also involved in curriculum definition, questioning what should be taught, and it can sometimes become a determining factor which limits the opportunity to teach the specific competences of a qualification.

Our research not only reflects on accreditation processes in general, but focuses its attention on a particular context: vulnerable groups in WISE. It should be considered whether access to processes of accreditation is possible for these groups. The risks of the accreditation process are not only the lack of available resources from the authorities, but also that the opportunity for accreditation is not a real possibility for those who need it most because they lack the opportunity to access calls.

Indeed, the WISE arises "as a socio-educative functional resource for a configuration of the labour market linked to the concepts of flexibility and adaptability" (Martínez-Morales, Bernad and Navas 2011:84). But as the authors warn, these companies acquire a compensatory approach if they emphasize individual responsibility (Córdoba, Llinares and Zacarés 2013), which can become a demonstration of neoliberal policy that blames vulnerable people for their vulnerability.

This is a system that accredits and discredits at the same time, since it does not guarantee the opportunity to participate in the procedure for all people with accreditable professional skills. Vulnerable groups are therefore excluded from the process of accreditation at three points: (1) in the concretion of the qualifications in the CNCP; (2) in the selection of the qualifications offered in calls; and (3) in the final selection of participants in these calls.

References

Bernad, J.C. and Marhuenda, F. 2008. El sistema de cualificación profesional en España y los/as trabajadores/as escasamente cualificados/as, Revista Europea de Formación Profesional, 42–43: 91–102.

Bjornavold, J. 2000. Making learning visible: identification, assessment and recognition of non-formal and informal learning in Europe. Luxembourg, Office for Official Publications of the European Communities.

Cedefop 2012. Development of national qualifications frameworks in Europe. October 2011. Luxembourg, Publications Office of the European Communities.

Chisvert-Tarazona, M. J. 2013. Reconocimiento de saberes no escolares: acreditación desde el Sistema Nacional de las Cualificaciones y de la Formación Profesional. In M.J. Chisvert, A. Ros y V. Horcas, A propósito de la diversidad Educativa. Barcelona, Octaedro.

Chisvert-Tarazona, M.J., Ros-Garrido, A., Córdoba-Iñesta, A. and Marhuenda-Fluixà, F. 2015. Mapa de cualificaciones profesionales acreditables en las empresas de inserción. CertiUni, 1, 36–50.

Clarke, P. B. 2010. Ser ciudadano: Conciencia y praxis. Madrid, Sequitur.

Córdoba, A.I., Llinares, L.I. and Zacarés, J.J. 2013. Employability Assessment in Vocational Education and Transition to the Workplace. In J. Seifried, and E. Wuttke, (Eds.), Transitions in Vocational Education, Research in Vocational Education (Vol. 2). Opladen, Berlin, Farmington Hills, Budrich publisher.

Cortina, A. 1997. Ciudadanos del mundo: Hacia una teoría de la ciudadanía. Madrid, Alianza.

Faedei-Aeress 2014. El acompañamiento en las empresas de inserción. Madrid, Faedei-Aeres.

Freire, P. 2009. La educación como práctica de la libertad. Madrid, Siglo XXI.

García, M.A. 2014. La Economía Social: una respuesta eficaz y social en la salida de la crisis. Simposio sobre Economía Social en el I Congreso Internacional de Facultades y Escuelas de Trabajo Social. Universidad de Murcia.

INCUAL 2003. Sistemas Nacionales de Cualificaciones y Formación Profesional. Colección Informes. Madrid, INEM.

Kiwan, D. 2005. Human rights and citizenship: An unjustifiable conflation? Journal of Philosophy of Education, 39(1): 37–50.

Macedo, E. 2009. Cidadania em confronto: Educação de elites em tempo de globalização. Porto, CIIE/Livpsic.

Macedo, E. 2012. School rankings on the other hand… Possibilities of young adult citizenship in the tension of educational and social change. Tese (Doutorado) – Faculdade de Psicologia e de Ciências da Educação, Universidade do Porto, 2003, Portugal.

Martínez-Morales, I., Bernad, J.C. and Navas, A. 2011. ¿Itinerarios hacia una ciudadanía precaria? Crítica de la regulación de las empresas de inserción social. In A. Córdoba-Iñesta, A.I. and Martínez-Morales, I. (Coord.) Trabajo, empleabilidad y vulnerabilidad social: condicionantes y potencialidades de la integración a través de las Empresas de Inserción Social. Valencia, Servicio de Publicaciones de la Universidad de Valencia.

Mertens, L. 1996. Competencia laboral: Sistemas, Surgimiento y Modelos. Montevideo, Cinterfor.

Navío, A. 2005. Propuestas conceptuales en torno a la competencia profesional. Revista de Educación, 337: 213–234.

Pozuelos, F. J. and Romero, A. 2002. El ámbito político. Papel de la administración educativa en la definición del curriculum: el curriculum *básico*. *In* F. J. Pozuelos y A. Romero, Decidir sobre el curriculum: Distribución de competencias y responsabilidades. Sevilla, Morón.

Raffe, D. 2009. The Action Plan, Scotland and the Making of the Modern Educational World: The First Quarter Century, Scottish Educational Review, 41(1): 22–35.

Rodríguez-Moreno, M. L. 2006. Evaluación, balance y formación de competencias laborales transversales. Barcelona, Laertes.

Royal Decree 1224/2009, of 17th July, on recognition of professional skills acquired by job experience. State Gazette (BOE) 205, 25/08/2009.

Stoer, S. R. and Magalhães, A. 2005. A diferença somos nós: A gestão da mudança social e as políticas educativas e sociais. Porto, Afrontamento.

Young, M. 2008. Bringing knowledge back in: from social constructivism to social realism in the sociology of education. London, Routledge.

Míriam Abiétar-López, Fernando Marhuenda-Fluixá
and Almudena A. Navas-Saurin

The Ambiguous Role of Basic VET upon Social Inclusion: A Participatory Perspective on Social Justice

The connection between Vocational Education and Training (VET hereafter) and citizenship that we are presenting in this chapter is framed by a dimensional perspective of social justice. We have recently provided and discussed on data of registration in basic VET and related statistics on Early School Leaving in Spain in recent years (Abiétar López, M., Navas Saurin, A. A., and Marhuenda Fluixá, F. 2015; Marhuenda Fluixá, F., Salvà Mut, F., Navas Saurin, A. A., Abiétar López, M. 2015). As a conclusion from those contributions, we strongly believe that it is necessary to analyse connections between social justice and education that can help us understand the pedagogical identities (Bernstein 1998) produced in these programs. To assess education through social justice is particularly necessary if we take Fraser's (2005, 2008, 2013) approach on social justice. By doing so, our analysis will try to show the effects that the differential production of education at the end of compulsory schooling, and particularly at basic VET, may have in the participation of students in society, that is, in their performance of citizenship. From this standpoint, we aim to link our theoretical positioning of social justice (embedding both a consideration of participation and its contribution to citizenship) to the realm of practice that we specify in the educational context of basic VET in Spain, which is addressed to vulnerable people, but which might consist of a context reinforcing vulnerability instead of counteracting it.

The connection of educational practice and the dimensional perspective of social justice reveals tensions in different spheres: first of all, in the generation of educational policies. With regard to this process, it should be considered that the process of producing and enacting a law involves a convergence of agents that are differentially positioned in the political, economical, and in the social arena (Bernstein 1998) as a whole. Decisions taken in this sphere have a direct impact in the production of the norm that will be established as the dominant principles on the basis of the educational policies. That is, specifically in the field of education, the decisions taken to establish and/or reform the curricula arise from a struggle between different groups that aim to convert their inclinations into the norm and practice of the State. Thus, here comes into play the production of the official knowledge, that is, the process of selecting which knowledge and culture is going to be institutionalized as the official one and as the dominant reference in the State sphere (Apple 2000; Bernstein 1998).

> The means and ends involved in educational policy and practice are the results of struggles by powerful groups and social movements to make their knowledge legitimate, to defend or increase their patterns of social mobility, and to increase their power in the larger social arena (Apple 2000, p. 9).

In a second sphere, which in fact should be considered as a continuation of the previous one, there is tension between policies and practices, that is, between the generation of educational policies and their various realizations in specific educational contexts. In this chapter we will specifically focus on how basic VET programs are developed in Spain. In order to do so, we will describe their position and main characteristics and analyse to what extent they are connected with the global trends that the educational policies are assuming in a context situated under the scope of conservative modernization (Apple 2000, 2006; Ball 2013).

In this respect, we propose an approach to the connections and tensions between the global trends and the local developments by describing the main traits and effects of basic VET programs, which are developed in a conservative modernization frame outlined by current educational policies in Spain. We focus on the effects of the programs by considering the participation options that the students attending these programs will have in social life. We consider specifically the situation of those groups positioned in a vulnerable zone. Castel (2004) suggests that it is possible to recognise different social zones in society: the integration zone, which refers to those persons that have stability; the vulnerability zone, considering those groups that are in a situation of precariousness and instability; and, finally, an exclusion zone, where those integrated and those vulnerable may fall into depending on any contingency. Castel's proposal in relation to the exclusion zones has been applied to the field of education: Escudero (2005) applies them to the study of school failure and the educational exclusion. In the description of this continuum of possible zones from exclusion to inclusion, the author highlights the different situations in the field of education and how students may be positioned differently depending on their situation in the school and the support they may be receiving from the educational institution.

In this zones continuum, the author proposes that basic VET programs, as they are developed in Spain, are measures aimed at students at risk of failure in an area of educational vulnerability that may become educational exclusion. However, these programs become late performances since at the time of its implementation, the risk of exclusion has been made evident (Escudero 2005). In this regard, it should be born in mind that the access condition to basic VET is linked to a record of school failure, i.e. the failure to achieve the certificate for completion of compulsory education. That means, indeed, that previous failure and educational exclusion are effectively a requirement to access the program. This condition of access presupposes that in an exercise of a democratic and socially just education, one of the aims of the program should be enabling mobility of students from the exclusion zone into the area of inclusion. This will be our main contend this chapter.

On the basis of these same theoretical references, Garcia (2015) identifies several social zones and sub-zones of inclusion and exclusion in two moments: during schooling and at the end of schooling. The differentiation of these moments leads us to think not only of what happens in the educational process, i.e. in the development of the program itself; but also in the position of young people at the end of their training. We may only know the social position of the youngsters once they leave school, but we may trace their educational pathway and how it is being produced while they are trained at basic VET. Thus, we will focus our analysis on the expected position of the students once they leave the program.

Having these educational and social zones in mind, it is possible to think of the different citizenship that may be developed in terms of participation in each zone and in each program. That is, we consider that depending on how young people are situated in these zones (inclusion, vulnerability, or exclusion), their options of participating in society and performing citizenship will vary according to the content of the program and the position it enables in the social order. In this regard, our approach to basic VET aims to describe and analyse to what extent these programs may change the position of the students in the different zones and, consequently, reinforce or undermine their social participation.

1. A theoretical perspective of social justice

The approach to citizenship proposed in this chapter is based on a conception of social justice that holds upon two main theoretical pillars. First, we consider that social justice – and, accordingly, social injustice – is the result of institutional actions that may include, among others, the structure of the organization and the institutional culture (Young 1990, 2004). Secondly, we refer to the conceptualization of social justice following a dimensional model that has at its core parity of participation. On the basis of this framework of social justice, described below, we intend to analyse the programs considering the dimensional conception of Fraser (2008) and to what extent it can be specified in different educational stages.

1.1 An institutionalized and dimensional conception of social justice

Iris M. Young (1990, 2004) proposes a conception of social justice focused on the role that institutional conditions play in the reinforcement of social injustices, which are consolidated on the basis of two key concepts: oppression and domination. The first one is understood as a structural situation that results of the institutional organization, culture and rules, while the second refers to the conditions that undermine the options of participation of the subjects involved in the institution.

> Justice should refer not only to distribution, but also to the institutional conditions
> necessary for the development and exercise of individual capacities and collec-
> tive communication and cooperation. Under this conception of justice, injustice
> refers primarily to two forms of disabling constraints, oppression and domination
> (Young 2004, p. 37).

According to this theoretical framework, oppression[1] is a structural concept, which is differentiated from the traditional understanding of the
concept, more related to a direct domination of certain groups:

> Oppression in this sense is structural, rather than the result of a few people's
> choices or policies. Its causes are embedded in unquestioned norms, habits, and
> symbols, in the assumptions underlying institutional rules and the collective con-
> sequences of following those rules (*ibid.* p. 39).

Close to this definition of oppression, domination is described as those
"institutional conditions that inhibit or prevent people from participating in determining their actions of the conditions of their actions"
(Young 1990, p. 38). Thus, institutional conditions are the core of social
injustice that result in the lack of participation in society. This approach
to social injustice, complemented and extended with the model of
Nancy Fraser, is the basis of our conceptualization of social justice in
education.

Close to this standpoint in Young's conceptualization of social justice, Nancy Fraser deals with the concept of "institutionalized obstacles". Focusing on participatory parity as the main basis of social
justice, the author explains that these obstacles "arise from the constitution of society [...] and are grounded in a specifically political mode
of social ordering" (Fraser 2005, p. 76). This statement about social
justice highlights that institutions and their structural conditions and
organization have a significant effect on the development of socially just
or unjust practices. Therefore, it is essential to consider to what extent
institutions produce situations that restrain participation in society, so
that we can aim for an approach to practices that reinforce social justice: "Overcoming injustice means dismantling institutionalized obstacles that prevent some people from participating on a par with others,

1   The author describes the "five faces of oppression", which are: exploitation, mar-
     ginalization, powerlessness, cultural imperialism, and violence (Young 1990,
     2004).

as full partners in social interaction" (*ibid*. 2005, p. 73). In accordance with this first theoretical pillar, we assume that educational organizations produce practices that may undermine or reinforce social justice depending on the way the distribution of opportunities to participate in society is conducted. Our aim as researchers is to identify which educational practices may reinforce social justice.

Fraser (2005, 2013) defines social justice as a three-dimensional concept based on the parity of participation. From her theoretical standpoint, three structures define the social order: the economical, the cultural, and the political one. In each of them, it is possible to find institutionalized obstacles that undermine parity of participation for certain groups that are positioned as vulnerable. For a practice to be just, parity of participation should be reinforced in the three dimensions through redistribution for the economical structure, recognition for the cultural, and representation for the political one. It is important to highlight that representation has to encompass redistribution and recognition, as it is a necessary step towards the achievement of practices that may be define as socially just:

> It is now apparent that no claim for justice can avoid presupposing some notion of representation, implicit or explicit, insofar as none can avoid assuming a frame. Thus, representation is always already inherent in all claims for redistribution and recognition. The political dimension is implicit. Thus, no redistribution or recognition without representation (Fraser 2003, p. 199).

Having this definition on the basis of our approach to social justice, we assume that educational practices may be described as socially just when they reinforce the three dimensions through all the educational process. Only by including the three of them the educational practices will reinforce a real development of citizenship that may enable participation in several social processes.

We believe that this approach to social justice is applicable to different educational contexts in the educational system, since all of them share institutional conditions that may undermine or reinforce representation and participation. Thus, both the first pillar, concerning the definition of structural injustice; as well as the second, the three-dimensional conceptualization, serve as reference points for the analysis of educational contexts from a perspective of social justice. Regarding our focus of attention, i.e. basic VET, we consider these programs are positioned in a situation of oppression and domination in the educational structure: On the one hand, by being addressed to a population at risk of educational exclusion (that is, students who have not achieved the secondary certificate); on the other hand, by enabling limited options of participation, as we will describe in more depth throughout the chapter.

1.2 Social justice and its impact upon education

In a second level of specification of the relation between social justice and education, we consider how the three dimensions may be related to different educational moments, so that we specify criteria to assess educational practices. For this purpose, we propose a model of analysis of social justice in education (table 1) considering the dimensions presented by Nancy Fraser and the educational moment in which it could be possible to find justice-injustice to a large extent. We also propose a specification of social justice into more detailed items, so that we could think of an approach to an operationalization of the concept.

Table 1: Proposal for the analysis of social justice in education.

Dimension	Economical	Cultural	Political
Answer to injustice	Redistribution	Recognition	Representation
Educational moment	Access to resources (accessing the program, access to resources during the program, access to resources after leaving the program) Educational local practice Leaving the program (further education or access into the labour market)		
Social Justice specification	Resources distributed in the programs (physical, cultural, social). Official Knowledge (selection of the "official" culture and knowledge) Participation in social life (enabled paths)		

Source: Abiétar, Navas and Marhuenda 2015, p. 153.

In the model proposed, the connection between the dimensions and the different educational moments may not be considered as an exclusive relation. That is, the three of them (redistribution, recognition, and representation) may be visible in all the educational process. In this regard, throughout the process there is a distribution of official knowledge, with the subsequent distribution of possible paths and participation opportunities depending on the qualification accomplished. In the same way, recognition is not limited to the transmission of contents in the local pedagogical practice, but it is also possible to find cultural oppression and domination in the process of generation and recontextualization of the official discourse itself. Representation is also visible in several moments of the educational process: the process of generation, recontextualization, and transmission of the pedagogic discourse are not neutral; there are also specific social groups behind decision-making processes.

What we would like to emphasize with this model is precisely the relationship that exists between different moments of the educational process and the reinforcement or undermining of social justice within educational practices. In this regard, it is important to bear in mind that the three moments (access to the program, its development, and the moment of leaving it) are to be considered in order to reinforce social justice in education. The aim here is not to stay in the initial distribution of resources (that is, accessing the program) as the only exercise of social justice, something that is often suggested and that is not but a reduced conceptualisation of social justice. Beyond this simplification, for an educational practice to be socially just, it should recognize the situation and characteristics of the students – especially of those that are initially positioned in a zone of vulnerability – and promote their participation in social life.

In the light of this model and the aforementioned theoretical references, we will focus here specifically in the moment of leaving the programs analysing the way citizenship is developed through the differential options of participation provided to basic VET students by completion of the program. Therefore, the main questions raised are: In which social zone are positioned basic VET students once they finish these programs? Are these programs reinforcing integration or segregation of these students?

2. Breaking down into basic VET

In order to answer those questions arising from the framework described in the previous sections, we will now apply the above-explained theoretical framework for the description and analysis of the educational context of basic VET in Spain. First, we will take into account the ideas related to social justice. Secondly, we will broaden this analysis considering the possible transitions that enable this program within the educational system and into the labour market. In this regard, we will consider here the proposals related to the social zones (inclusion, exclusion, and vulnerability) and the options of participation the students have once they finish basic VET.

2.1 Application of the model of social justice

We have defined a socially just practice as the one able to promote social participation. As we set out in the model, there are different dimensions and moments to consider in the assessment of social justice in the programs. Focusing on the educational relationship in specific contexts, we will aim our assessment to the pedagogical identities produced there. We consider the pedagogical identity as the insertion of a professional career in a collective basis (Bernstein 1998). This definition leads us to focus not only in the educational local practices, but also on the result they have in the positioning of the people in the social order, highlighting the different stakes associated with the positions. Therefore, it is a useful term to apply our perspective of social justice. By applying this definition of pedagogical identity, we assume that one of the main results of the educational process is the positioning of young people in the social order. This position leads to differential possibilities of participation depending on the zones in which they can be located (as aforementioned: Inclusion, exclusion, or vulnerability). Taking into account this definition, we relate it to our proposal for the analysis of social justice with the aim of assessing basic VET programs.

In relation to the resources distributed in the program, we take into consideration the knowledge that supports the curriculum of these programs. It should be noted that the content selected for these programs is not but a situation of vulnerability due to its low level of conceptual demand (García 2015). Thus, the decrease of contents of academic and professional character limits both the formation of the students of basic VET as their possibilities to continue in subsequent training levels. In this aspect, the distribution of knowledge leads to a limited distribution of opportunities for personal development and the future professional and social development, with the consequences in the performance of citizenship.

This selection of knowledge refers to the above-mentioned tensions that are generated in the definition of "official knowledge" selected for this educational context. That is to say, the decision making of what content is taught in certain contexts has a direct impact upon the possibilities of participation that practice is offering. Therefore, we believe that the distribution goes beyond access to the programs and also include distribution of personal and social resources.

The third dimension of social justice refers to participation in the social life on the basis of the future itineraries provided in the programs. This aspect, which we analyse in more detail in the next section, brings together two elements of the programs: the official content of these educational contexts and the structure of the educational system. The first one can induce or reduce the options of continuation and progress into further educational levels on the basis of the conceptual requirement of the contents and the academic and professional level of the programs. The second one, which is related to the structure of the system, to the regulations on the qualifications obtained at the end of the programs, and to the conditions of access to other levels, constrains the paths of young people in the system. In this aspect, it is necessary to consider that what is possible and what is limited implies an exercise of social justice: It takes into account what resources and options are distributed to these learners, what knowledge is recognized as needed for their training and future citizenship, and what possibilities of participation and representation in society, i.e. what career development they will have.

2.2 Basic VET between zones: transitions provided by basic VET

In order to analyse the participation options that these programs enable, we will focus here on the expected situation of the students once they leave the program. Considering that they are addressed to students finishing compulsory education, we suggest here that it is situated within a process of transition to adulthood. In the conceptualization of transition, we follow the model proposed by the Group of Research in Education and Work (GRET), which has focused on youth transitions to adulthood on the basis of the biographical perspective considering the social changes that may influence this process as consequence of the contexts of the informational capitalism (Casal, Merino, García, and Quesada 2006a, 2006b). Two main elements of their proposal are important for the aim of our research. Firstly, situating youth and their transitions on the basis of a biographical perspective, according to which three main ideas have to be considered. First, transition is a complex joint of education and training processes, professional integration and family empowerment. Secondly, it is also socially constructed in a specific socio-political framework that configures a system of transition. Finally, the system is socio-historical and geopolitical (*ibid.* 2006a, p. 29). Therefore, transitions have to be situated in this system considering all the specificities that each context may have.

The second key element of the proposal of GRET is their conceptualisation of transitions considering the path done and the probable paths ahead (*ibid.* p. 31). Thus, the path previously done conditions the possibilities and options people will have to develop their future path. Moreover, all this process is to be done in the structural framework defined by educational policies, which delimit the options, connections and continuations in the educational system and, consequently, in the labour market. Therefore, it should be highlighted that the point, the moment, between the path done and the possible paths is where (and when) we situate basic VET. This is a key fact in our analysis from a perspective of social justice. In this regard, it should be born in mind that students have access to the program after a path in the school system from which they have obtained certain results. In the case of basic VET, these results have to be the non-graduation in compulsory education, so that students are already positioned in a zone of educational exclusion. During the development of the programs more or less paths may be provided depending on the resources distributed: contents, experiences, and qualification, among others. Regarding basic VET, the more reduced path would be the continuation in a zone of educational exclusion and social vulnerability (or even exclusion) if they do not obtain the Certificate in Compulsory Education and, moreover, if they do not have options to continue their education and training in other educational contexts and levels. On the contrary, the options of mobility into an inclusion zone would increase if the program enabled continuation in the educational system and/or a labour insertion with a better training and qualification. Therefore, it is also significant to consider the role that the programs may have in increasing the possible future paths of the students, something that would lead to socially just educational practices.

As above-mentioned, not only the decisions and actions of the individuals are relevant in the process of transition, but also the structures (social and educational policies, educational contexts, the educational system, the labour market) that may constrain the possible paths for students attending those specific programs. Thus, both the organization of the educational system and the current situation of the labour market are relevant by considering the situation of students once they leave education and training and the way their integration in society takes place. In this regard, we will briefly describe these structures (educational system and labour market), as they may turn into "institutionalized obstacles" (Fraser 2005) in the transitions of those students attending basic VET.

– Transitions to further education from basic VET

It is important to take into account the current traits of the Spanish education system: how it is structured, the different levels of qualification it helps obtaining, the links between levels and programs and, consequently, the paths it enables. It is significant to consider how this structure enables different positions after leaving the educational system. The qualifications obtained (or even leaving the system without qualification) situate the students in quite different positions, with quite different options and skills to participate in social life. As detailed and discussed below, this correlation between qualification and possible paths is a key fact in the analysis of basic VET and an example of the global trend of the conservative modernization, where the qualification is the main evidence of the value that a program may have in society. Therefore, it is not only the result of a path done, but also the key to the future path or paths provided. This points to the limitations for the students attending basic VET.

Basic VET is situated in a zone of educational vulnerability, due to its position in the educational system and the reduced linkages that it has with other educational contexts and levels. Possible educational transitions from these programs drive the students away from the academic track and direct them toward vocational training pathways. In this sense, the structure of the educational system and the conditions of access for post compulsory levels has positioned these programs in an area of "hidden inclusion" (García 2015, p.150), or what we could also call as outsourcing young people located in the category of school failure (Casal 1998), this being a covert outsourcing to segregate them in their own programs within the system. These programs are formally included in the structure of the educational system; yet, their factual possibilities positions them in the beginning of a professional career not always feasible due to the conditions in which the program develops (limited content, low level of conceptual demand, and prioritization of content related to behaviour). Therefore, the possible educational transitions from basic VET refer to the professional path, i.e. to the continuation in CFGM[2]; while existing data show that access and retention in this track is really complex for young people who have attended basic VET.

– Transitions to work from basic VET

The segmented structure of the labor market (Fernández-Huerga 2010) is the main trait that allows us to consider the differential positioning of the students once they leave their education and training. On the one hand, the segmentation influences the type of labour insertion, as the segments correlate mostly with the qualification obtained in the educational system. On the other hand, it should be born in mind that the working conditions in each segment are quite different, being the

---

2   CFGM is an acronym that in Spanish stands for *Ciclos Formativos de Grado Medio*, meaning Intermediate Level for Vocational Education and Training. It is equivalent to levels 4/5 following the European Qualifications Framework.

lower segment the one characterized by a greater risk of vulnerability, insecurity, and instability. Therefore, although in periods of crisis like the current one, precariousness is widespread in the labour market, the workers situated in the lower segment suffer more intensely of unemployment and temporality, as they are mostly linked to labour sectors that are more unstable and dependent on economic situation, i.e. tourism or the building industry.

Considering both structures (education and the labour market) lead us to think about the bond between educational vulnerability that may result from obtaining a low qualification or even the educational exclusion resulting from school failure; and the labour and social insertion options for students with such an educational path. The result of the educational paths may turn into a real risk of misrepresentation and, consequently, of a diminished citizenship. This leads us to state that basic VET does not alter significantly the situation of students from exclusion to inclusion either in educational terms or in social ones because "in fact [it] offer[s] only a partial inclusion, insufficient or incomplete" (Escudero 2005, p. 94). That is to say, they leave the students in a zone of vulnerability at risk of arrival (or return) to exclusion. The relevance of this immobility between areas is particularly relevant for the analysis of social justice in education if we take into account the relationship between educational exclusion and social exclusion. For this reason, on the basis of our approach of social justice, the return to the educational system would be the option that enables more participation in society: not only the qualification would be higher, but also their training and their options to develop a professional career, their knowledge in several realms, their personal development and, on balance, their options to perform a more active participation in society and, consequently, a more significant citizenship. Therefore, we consider as socially just those realizations of the programs that enable more participation.

3. Misrepresentation within and after basic VET: A vulnerable context for vulnerable people?

In this chapter we have attempted to carry out an analysis of basic VET from a position of social justice highlighting the opportunities for participation provided by basic VET, and its relationship with the zones of social life. It is important to note that social injustice derives from the institutionalized obstacles that have kept these young people with a prior path of school failure in a zone between exclusion and educational vulnerability that can drift into a misrepresentation in the social order, i.e., in positions of oppression (Young 1990) and a reduced performance of citizenship.

We have wondered in which social zone are positioned basic VET students once they finish their education and training. After considering both the position and zone of social life in which they are placed, we have no choice but stating that basic VET are educational policies developed in the framework of the conservative modernization (Apple 2006; Ball 2013). By positioning students differentially and by providing different options of participation, these educational contexts are also enabling different performances of citizenship. In this regard, the development of educational policies of neoliberal character has been materialized in processes of marketization, managerialism, performativity (Ball 2013), resulting in the assumption of competitiveness, and the accountability of the individual in its positioning. Although we have already seen that there are possible realizations of professional careers located in the normative framework, the institutional structure does not really provide all the conditions that are necessary for the subjects to move from one area to another.

Basic VET is an educational context located between the exclusion zone and the area of vulnerability, in zone of care, aid-providing services (Tezanos 2001) that reflects a connection (there is continuity rather than tension) between the generation of policies, their implementation and local practices, and the options of performing citizenship. On the basis of the conceptualization of social justice exposed, the situation and the characteristics of the programs in the Spanish context provides evidence of a socially unjust education. One of the main outcomes of this unjust situation results in the different possibilities of participation in society, both for the content of the programs as well as for the possibilities of further training at various levels provided. The structure and the possible path in the educational system is therefore a key element with implications in the process of transition and the expansion of possible itineraries to give young people more opportunities for vocational training, academic and personal development (Abiétar López 2016).

In the previous pages we have argued that transitions processes happen in a structural framework shaped and limited both by the education system as by the labour market. This framework constrains the possible pathways that vulnerable young people can take, and which is already highly determined by their previous trajectories. As Casal *et al.* (2006) show, transition finishes with the positioning and allocation of people to a social class. This is, it ends with the acquisition of a position in the social order. This positioning is constrained by the previous trajectory, and basic VET contributes to such trajectory in ways that may widen or restrain the future possibilities of young people, both in terms of access to the labour market as well as of full adult participation in society.

Turning attention to the second question raised (Are these programs reinforcing integration or segregation of these students?) we could say that the basic VET as currently organized and developed is an educational context that reinforces the differential positioning in the educational and social zones and does not facilitate the mobility toward inclusion. On the basis of what was commented throughout the chapter, we believe that in order to achieve this transition toward the inclusion, changes in the selected knowledge and distributed in these programs should be taken into account. Moreover, the conceptual demand should be increased and the continuity and maintenance in other educational contexts should be ensured. In the structural level, it is necessary to have a structure that does not hinder the continuity in the system and that enables real links between levels. If the basic VET were the beginning of the professional career, enabling the continuity in (at least) CFGM should be a requirement to promote the careers of these young people and reinforce their options to move to a zone of inclusion.

In a macro context in which competitiveness is highly valued, the worth of basic VET is very limited: it can only rarely bring young people out of the zone of educational vulnerability and even exclusion. We might consider it rather an insertion policy (Castel 2004). The features of basic VET and the pathways to which it is linked, hold young people between vulnerability and exclusion. The fact that it is addressed to a particular group of young people reinforces it limitations in terms of possible ways out of vulnerability and hinders their chances to become active citizens. Even if basic VET provides the population to which it is aimed with some form of education, it is hard to consider them as socially just educational practices. Even so, it seems a more reasonable alternative than others like apprenticeships and Dual VET (Marhuenda 2015, 2016) for the same population, and school-based programs in Spain are better options in terms of increasing participation.

References

Abiétar López, M. 2016. La producción social de itinerarios de inserción: análisis de la Formación Profesional de base desde una perspectiva de justicia social. Valencia, Universitat de València.

Abiétar López, M., Navas Saurin, A. A. and Marhuenda Fluixá, F. 2015. Aportaciones desde la Justicia Social para una Educación Justa. La Identidad Pedagógica en Formación Profesional Básica. Revista Internacional de Educación para la Justicia Social (RIEJS), 4(2): 145–161. DOI: <http://dx.doi.org/10.15366/riejs2015.4.2>.

Apple, M. W. 2000. Official Knowledge. Democratic Education in a Conservative Age. New York, Routledge.

Apple, M. W. 2006. Educating the 'Right' Way. Markets, Standards, God and Inequality. New York, Routledge.

Ball, S. J. 2013. The Education Debate. Chicago, The Policy Press.

Bernstein, B. 1998. Pedagogía, control simbólico e identidad. Teoría, investigación y crítica. Madrid, Ediciones Morata.

Casal Bataller, J., García Gracia, M. and Planas Coll, J. 1998. Escolarización plena y 'estagnación'. Cuadernos de Pedagogía (268): 38–41.

Casal, J., García, M., Merino, R. and Quesada, M. 2006a. Aportaciones teóricas y metodológicas a la sociología de la juventud desde la perspectiva de la transición. Papers, 79: 21–48.

Casal, J., García, M., Merino, R. and Quesada, M. 2006b. Changes in forms of transition in contexts of informational capitalism. Papers, 79: 195–223.

Castel, R. 2004. Encuadre de la exclusión. In S. Karsz (ed.). La exclusión: bordeando sus fronteras. Definiciones y matices. Barcelona, Gedisa.

Escudero Muñoz, J. M. 2005. El fracaso escolar: nuevas formas de exclusión educativa. In J. García Molina (ed.). Exclusión social / exclusión educativa. Lógicas contemporáneas. Xàtiva, Diálogos.

Fernández-Huerga, E. 2010. La teoría de la segmentación del mercado de trabajo: enfoques, situación actual y perspectivas de futuro. Investigación Económica, LXIX(273): 115–150.

Fraser, N. 2005. Reframing justice in a globalizing world. New Left Review, 36: 69–88.

Fraser, N. 2008. Escalas de justicia (A. M. Riu, Trans. S. L.). Barcelona, Herder.

Fraser, N. 2013. Fortunes of Feminism. From State-Managed Capitalism to Neoliberal Crisis. London-New York, Verso.

García Rubio, J. 2015. El fracaso escolar desde la perspectiva de la exclusión educativa. El PDC y el PCPI. Valencia, UVEG.

Marhuenda Fluixá, F. 2015. Vocational Education Abused: Precarisation Disguised as Dual System. In Heikkinnen, A. and Lassnig, L. (eds.) Myths and Brands in Vocational Education and Training (pp. 59–77). Newcastle, Cambridge Scholars Publishing.

Marhuenda Fluixá, F. 2016. La FPD en España y la perspectiva de los centros sobre el proceso de implantación por parte de las administraciones. Workshop La formació professional dual a Catalunya. Tarragona, 31 de mayo de 2016.

Marhuenda Fluixá, F., Salvà Mut, F., Navas Saurin, A. A. and Abiétar López, M. 2015. Twenty Years of Basic Vocational Education Provision in Spain: Changes and Trends. International Journal for Research in Vocational Education and Training, 2 (2): 137–151. DOI: 10.13152/IJRVET.2.2.8.

Tezanos, J.F. 2001. La sociedad dividida. Estructuras de clase y desigual-dades en las sociedades tecnológicas. Madrid, Biblioteca Nueva.

Young, I. M. 1990. Justice and the politics of difference. Princeton, New Jersey, Princeton University Press.

Young, I. M. 2004. Five Faces of Oppresion. In L. Heldke and P. O'Connor (eds.), Oppression, privilege, and resistance: theoretical perspectives on racism, sexism, and heterosexism. Boston, McGraw-Hill.

Liv Mjelde

Learning through Praxis and Cooperation: Lev Vygotsky and Vocational Pedagogy

1. Introduction

One of the main findings in my research in the vocational sector over the past decades is that students and apprentices in the vocational trades prospered and learned when they were in activity in the workshops in the vocational schools or in the workplaces, while at the same time they found no meaning or relevance to the many hours spent in classrooms for general education. They showed up for the workshop classes but they failed to show up for the academic classes. Empirical research conducted by myself and students of vocational pedagogy during the past decades, decades marked in Norway's upper secondary schooling by a decrease in workshop instruction and an increase in the more abstract general curriculum, shows that the contradictions between these types of learning have remained fierce and persistent during the present school reforms in vocational and adult education (Bodin, 2004, Bongo 1999, 2001, Grimestad 1993, Frøland 2004, Mjelde 1993, 2006, Velten 2004).[1]

Vocational education in schools and apprenticeship are in focus in Norway right now. The Minister of Knowledge introducing a parliamentary report on education in March 2013 emphasized that more

---

[1]   Masters and doctoral theses are important for new empirical knowledge in the field. I have been teaching vocational school teachers in writing their Masters Theses at Akershus University College in Oslo for the past decades. I have also developed a Master's Program in Vocational Pedagogy in Kampala, Uganda for vocational teachers from Uganda and South Sudan. Students at the Institute of Sociology, University of Bergen have also made important contributions in later years (see Flaten 1999; Vogt 2013; Olsen *et al.* 1998; Olsen 2013).

attention will be paid to vocational subjects. The government intends to reduce today's large drop-out problems. This Norwegian Official Report (NOU. No. 20 2012–2013) has reported that 30% of the students did not finish Upper Secondary School (16–19 year cohorts) on time. The highest rate of drop-out happens in the vocational streams. The report points out that if student completion increases from 70 to 80 per cent it will lead to a cost reduction for society of between 5.4 and 8.8 billion Norwegian kroner per cohort (*ibid.* p. 174).

We have also seen a greater interest in what is now called evidence-based research in vocational education and new attention is being paid to the fact that 13 years of schooling, remote from working life, has created a new set of problems (Bakken and Elstad 2012).

Drop-out rates have been substantial both from lower secondary and upper secondary schools for decades. What are the reasons that vocational students' and apprentices' experiences of learning and meaning in the workshop setting and working life have contrasted so sharply and so negatively with those of the school where learning is supposed to take place in classrooms? Simultaneously, while one poses such questions one also see the concepts of "cooperative learning," "work-based learning", "master/apprenticeship learning" and "situated learning" have become "hot" concepts in the academic discourse around the social organization of learning, both in schools and in workplaces (Ainley and Rainbird 1999; Billett 2000; Coy 1989; Grosjean 2001; Nielsen and Kvale 1999, 2003; Lave and Wenger 1991).[2] But these discussions are seldom connected with the contradictions found within vocational education itself which harbours a tradition historically divided between workshop learning, vocational theory and general theory in the school program, often in combination with learning at actual sites of working life. The contradictions experienced in this mixed learning situation are full of conundrums. (Mjelde 1997)

Little research focussing on working class experiences has been conducted in this field till now.[3] My aim here is to explore these

2   The concept "pedagogy of professions" has developed in relation to these contra-
      dictions in higher education.
3   Boel Berner said in 1989 (p.19) that school problematic in Sweden is being dis-
      cussed as if there were no difference between general education and vocational
      education and as if vocational education does not exist. We have found the same

contradictions in light of how vocational students and apprentices experience their everyday learning life in the light of scientific thinking that might shed light on the complexities in vocational pedagogy. First I outline recent developments and contradictions in the present educational reforms in Norway in light of traditions in vocational education.

2. The organization of teaching and learning in vocational education

There have been many different roads in Norway into the skilled/semi-skilled manual labour market during the past hundred years. A usual path after the Second World War was for youngster to attend a vocational school for six months to one year and to enter apprenticeship before they went on to get a craft certificate. Some factories had their own workshop schools. Many youngsters also entered directly into apprenticeship and attended the apprenticeship school one day a week or in the evenings to get their training in vocational theory. The only constant in this development has been change (Mjelde 1993, pp. 76–80). A parliamentary law on vocational schools for trade and industry was passed in 1940, but was not enacted till 1945 due to the occupation of Norway by the Germans from April 9th 1940 till May 8th 1945. However, vocational education in schools expanded during the war years. In 1939 28 craft and industrial workshop schools existed in Norway. In 1945 the number had risen to 42 (Mjelde1993, p. 72). An Apprenticeship Act was passed by passed and enacted by parliament in 1950.

Vocational education in the craft and industry branches has followed many different ways of organizing the three different components. Hands-on workshop learning, vocational theory connected to the specific craft and general subjects such as language and natural

---

situation in Norway during the past 30 years. Erling Kokkersvold and I called it in 1982. *"The Vocational school that disappeared"*. Research interest has increased during the past decade. But the history of vocational education in Norway is not written yet. Claude Grignon (1971) has written an excellent book on the topic in France. *"L'Ordre des Choses"*.

sciences. Cooperation with craft and industry organisations has been the central feature till the 1970s.

As an educational model, apprenticeship originated in the guild system which developed under feudalism. The guilds were organised in three ranks: master, journeymen and apprentices. Hands-on learning and strict discipline were the order of the day. Journeymen and apprentices in each craft were organised to best serve the master's interest. They were tied to the existing order through their wish to become master craftsmen (Marx and Engels 1985.70; Mjelde 1993.54–58). Vocational schooling for crafts and industry took traditions from the guild system as its model until the parliamentary Upper Secondary Schooling Act came into effect in 1976. Forty-two hours a week was common in the training for many trades. In the period between 1945 and 1976 the major model saw two-thirds of the teaching time devoted to workshop and vocational theory instruction and one-third to general subjects in the classroom. I have illustrated the learning sites in the following way:

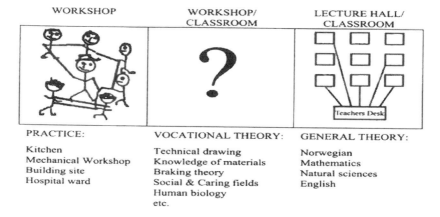

Figure 1: Arenas of learning in Vocational Education (Mjelde 2006: 80).

The above figure reflects two different learning traditions – *practice/ vocational theory* originated in the master/apprentice learning traditions and *general theory/ classroom traditions* developed from the Cathedral School traditions of the Middle Ages, In the workshop traditions the students are in hands-on activity making bread, repairing a car, building a house, cutting and styling hair or learning to lift patients in a hospital ward. Learning takes place amid the roar of machinery or the blast of hot ovens or equipment in a hospital. The students work together and consult one another while the teacher moves around the room advising the work process. Workshop practice and vocational theory are integrated and vocational theory might be taught in the workshop or in a separate classroom. The vocational teachers have a skilled trade in their background. General theory in vocational education is taught separately, away from the workshop and vocational theory portions of the syllabus. The general theory teachers have an academic background and the teaching takes place in traditional classrooms where students sit in rows. The general subjects are not connected to what is happening in the workshop or in vocational theory.

The School Commission of 1965 proposed that general and vocational education in upper secondary education (16–19 year olds) be administered by the same act and organized under the same roof. All learning should take place within a unitary school where vocational and academic studies should be integrated, in terms of both content and physical organisation. Apprenticeship was to be abolished. In 1974, the traditional gymnasia and the vocational schools came under one comprehensive law. The law was implemented from January 1st. 1976. One of the goals in social democratic Scandinavia in the post war period has been the elimination of class contradictions by means of creating "equality of opportunity regardless of class, gender or geographical origin" in the educational system. Another fundamental aim of the law of 1974 was to give equal status to practical and theoretical education. The former academic (gymnasiums) and vocational schools were now renamed; they became *Upper Secondary Schools* (KUF 1982, p. 19).

The integration of vocational and general education under one common law during the first decades after 1976 resulted in both vocational training and academic programmes continuing to perpetuate their respective traditions (Mjelde 1994, 1997, 2006). Vocational education in schools and working life has the specific complexity in being directly connected to the ebb and flow of the manual labour market. Competition over places, both in the vocational schools and over apprenticeships has been fierce. Before the reforms there were various points of entry into the semiskilled and skilled manual labour market. As mentioned before, youngsters entered apprenticeship directly from compulsory basic education and went to the apprenticeship schools in the evenings. The apprenticeship schools were often in the same locations as the vocational schools.

The last decades have seen reform after reform in relation to the whole educational system in Norway. Here I concentrate my comments on the reform in upper secondary education called Reform 94, which was instituted in the autumn of 1994.[4]

The main model for vocational education under the 1994 reform was two years spent in school followed by a two-year apprenticeship in working life. Compared to the period prior to 1976, the time in *workshops, in the bakery, in the technical engineering class or the car mechanics shop where hands-on learning* took place has decreased and general theory-based classroom training has increased. With Reform 94 all theory should be taken during the first two years in schools. The traditional apprenticeship schools were abolished overnight. All the roads were closed to craft-certificates by entering directly into an apprenticeship after compulsory school.

Research from the last decades shows that drop-out problems from a 13-year compulsory school have increased and the problems inside vocational education (16–19 year olds) also increased.[5] Follow-up research of Reform 94 has unveiled the problems. The research institutes FAFO and NIFU released the results of a 2011 study of the work and learning environment faced by apprentices. They interviewed 2,804 apprentices. 95 % were motivated to learn in the workplace, not in

---

4   Reform 94 was a reform specifically directed toward upper secondary education, vocational and general education for the age group 16–19. It is called Reform 94 because it was implemented in 1994. Kunnskapsløftet "The Knowledge Promotion Reform" was a reform introduced in all primary and secondary schools in Norway from 2006. The overall goal of that school reform was to increase the level of knowledge and of basic skills of all pupils. The reform of 2012–2013 was also directed to all levels of the educational system.

5   Drop-out problems have existed in Norway since the 1960's as elsewhere in the Western industrialised world. OECD point out in their report from 2016 the growing risk of social exclusion among early school leavers. Only lately has Norwegian authorities turned its attention to these problems. A reason for this attention might be that Norway is performing poorly in the Pisa-evaluations.

school (Bakken and Elstad 2012, see also the Country Report, Norway in VET in Europe 2013, Meld. no. 20. 2012–2013).

Many youngsters have rebelled against 13 years of compulsory school prior to being allowed to enter working life. A characteristic statement about the distance between learning in schools and learning in work life is. "School gives you no insight into the actual reality of work and how things develop. By and large school grinds you down with all its theoretical subjects". Apprentices also commented about difficulties with theoretical subjects and that schools fit neither the craftsman nor the academic (Mjelde 1993).

This in turn has led to new reforms. The reform of 2004 provided the possibility of entering directly from the elementary schools into apprenticeships and attending what is now called "coordinating school for theoretical training." Håkon Høst's (2013) empirical work among drop-outs from lower secondary school who are given a new chance in a combination between workplace and "coordinating school for theoretical training" show that this combination works. This is a return to the old apprenticeship school traditions.

The vocational school teacher Elisabet Frøland asked in 2004 why the old name "apprenticeship-school" could not be used. She says that the gap between "theory and practice" for vocational students has never been bigger (see also Høst 2013; Olsen 2013). The new name underlines the contradictions between decisions made in an academic bureaucracy and the everyday life of vocational teachers and students. One of the carpenter apprentices (16 years old) Frøland interviewed in 2002 said, "If I had not got an apprenticeship place, I would never have managed to be in the school." My own research among apprentices in the 1980's showed that eighty-nine per cent preferred being apprentices to sitting at a school desk. As one of them put it, "Going to school in today's society really takes it out of you." This apprentice, in Bergen, had experienced his everyday school life as a nightmare. "Being tired of school", or "sick of school" were expressions that came up again and again among the 1,617 apprentices in my study. What was the reason for the hostility the students had developed toward what they called "theory"? Citations from my apprenticeship study 1982–1984 (Mjelde 1993) shows the divisions very plainly. A graphics student said, "You learn more by working (in practice) than by sitting at a school desk with all that baloney about theory." The resistance against the hours spent in theory classrooms in Norwegian/Social Science and Chemistry was strong among the apprentices in the school where I did my participant observation. The apprentices were in discussions with the academic teachers over both the curriculum content and time spent in the classroom. They negotiated constantly with the chemistry teacher about leaving an hour earlier on Monday afternoon. All of the 17 apprentices in the mechanical engineering factory where I also did fieldwork expressed their contentment with their positions as apprentices in the factory. One of them said. "It was terrific to get away from sitting at that school desk where you're just supposed to accept stuff. Finally we could produce something ourselves. Working and earning money for three years suits me much better. And also, I was tired of school."

It is not a new phenomenon that students are tired of school learning, but it becomes even more serious as the length of obligatory schooling increases.[6] I present these examples as a background in order to pose questions about meaning and meaninglessness in the pedagogy that is pursued, whether it is in primary school, in vocational training or in higher education. Yet, the question of meaning is the basis for posing questions both about primary school and vocational training for the crafts and industry branches of the economy, particularly when as many as 89 % of the apprentices in my apprenticeship study of 1982–1984 found the learning arenas in school to be meaningless.

Lennart Nilsson (1981, 2004) is one of the few researchers in Scandinavia who has worked with the problems of learning and teaching in vocational education. He maintains that a prerequisite for the education of the future is that the teacher must find out how the students experiences are related to their activities and learning situations. Where are each individual in their learning process? Furthermore, one has to take these experiences seriously by taking up the teaching in such a way that

---

6   Paul Willis (1977) and Henry Giroux (1983) showed in their empirical work how the working class had a collective resistance against a system that had no relevance to their lives. Paulo Freire (1970) attacked the traditional school for having a "banking concept of education", in which the student was viewed as an empty account to be filled by the teacher. This is the pedagogy working class students rebel against. (See also Jarbas Novelino Barato 2011, 2016, Rose 2014).

it conveys what, from the perspective of the students, gives meaning to them in the learning activity. To experience education as something meaningful is a starting point for the development of competence and adjustment to the work situation. He points out that there has been little interest in researching how students in the vocational trades experience their learning conditions and possibilities.[7]

Back to the starting point. Why do vocational students thrive and learn in the workshops that are integral to vocational courses of study? What in particular is it about this learning situation that makes it different from the classroom tradition of education? What is it that creates an atmosphere for learning and cooperation? How can this be understood scientifically, from what we now know about learning? Learning is one of the basic social phenomena in the social sciences and the central one in pedagogy. Neurosciences as well as social sciences have been developing by leaps and bounds during the past decades and have opened renewed discussions about learning and teaching. But learning and teaching have been researched for a much longer time. The work of Lev Semenovich Vygotsky, Aleksei Nicolayvich Leontiev and Alexandr Romanovich Luria starting a century ago laid the groundwork for much of the discussions today.[8] Another Russian scientist from that period was Ivan Pavlov, a scientist they were inspired by and whom they also challenged. Here I will discuss specifically Vygotsky's scientific work in relation to the conundrums in vocational education today.[9] But first some words about the Cultural, Historical School of Moscow (CHAT).

---

7   Tove Lien (1984, 1995) has carried out empirical investigations concerning these questions in the context of adult education. Adult education and vocational education in crafts and industry trades are two sides of the same coin.

8   The Chicago School with John Dewey and his laboratory schools as a central figure, Georg Kerschensteiner with his activity schools in Munich, Celestin Freinet with his print schools in Vence worked in the same time period as Lev Vygotsky. I have discussed their work in other parts of my writings (Mjelde 2006, 2015 a, 2016.)

9   For a more general discussion see Mjelde 1993.33–47.

3. The Cultural Historical School of Moscow

The contribution of the Cultural-Historical Activity Theory, initiated by the Russian psychologists, Lev Semenovich Vygotsky, Aleksei Nicolayvich Leontiev and Alexander Romanovich Luria shed innovative light on the development and understanding of learning and teaching following the Russian Revolution. They sought to establish an approach to psychology that would enable them to "discover the way natural processes such as physical maturation and sensory mechanisms become intertwined with culturally determined processes to produce the psychological functions of adults". Vygotsky and his colleagues referred to this new approach variably as "cultural," "historical," and "instrumental" psychology. These three labels all index the centrality of cultural mediation in the constitution of specifically human psychological processes, and the role of the social environment in structuring the processes by which children appropriate the cultural tools of their society in the process of their ontogenetic development.

The three provided an historical and social analysis of the development of the higher mental functions of human beings. Lev Vygotsky was the leading scientist in this group in the 1920's. He is called "The Mozart of Psychology" (Toulmin 1978). A major feature of Lev Vygotsky's thinking is that a human being learns from the social context to the individual context and that the development of human speech, consciousness and thought must be understood in their concrete social and historical circumstances. People develop their mental and psychical activity inductively, by speaking to and communicating with other human beings. Thinking and language cannot profitably be studied by investigating individuals without their connections to others in society, but rather, they ought to be viewed interactively from a material and developmental perspective as members of a complex and living society. This point of view is of fundamental significance for all pedagogy. A. R. Luria and A. N. Leontiev further illuminated Vygotsky's findings by showing the variation in the development of consciousness in relation to geographical conditions and social background (Enerstvedt 1986).

Class and education have been discussed again and again in educational theory during the past century (Mjelde 1987, 2006, 2016).

Language development and forms of education and culture are some of the aspects that divide the middle class and the working class culture. Alexander Luria (1976, p. 28) expressed it in the following way. "The average middle class child begins her/his schooling with the attitude that problems are something you solve by first talking about them and then doing it, while the average working class child has learned that you solve the problem by acting and then talking about it." This lays the groundwork for an understanding of why many vocational schools students prefer to learn through activities in workshops and working life. The division between vocational and academic education is another class distinction in society. Lev Vygotsky's scientific work brings us further in understanding how the contradictions manifest themselves in the educational system today.

I was introduced to Lev Vygotsky's work through the writings of the US professor Jerome S. Bruner (1970, 1996) and what was referred to as "the Sputnik Shock." Vygotsky's theories gained currency in the West after the aerospace Sputnik developments of the late 1950s. In 1957, in the middle of the cold war between Soviet Union and the USA, a war that had both technological and political features, Sputnik, the first satellite to reach orbit, was launched in the Soviet Union.. The belief in the ultimate success of the American approach to everything was severely shaken by the Russians' success in starting and winning the initial "space race". This shocked the USA whose leaders believed in their country's technological superiority and led them to make a huge investment in education and a search for new approaches to learning and teaching – a new way to win or lose the Cold War (Portes and Salas 2011, p. 20). One might ask if the "space race" and Sputnik actually led to the translation to English of Lev Vygotsky's work. His book, *Thought and Language* was published by Harvard University Press in 1962. Lev Vygotsky's work *Mind in Society* appeared in USA in 1978.

Lev Vygotsky criticized traditional teaching based on his under- standing of the importance of societal *interaction* and *cooperation* in the learning processes. He argued that the learner's ongoing performance in interaction with the teacher and fellow students in the immediate social community of learners and the broader connections to society and cul- ture, was a far more precise index of learning than intelligence tests based upon a goal composed of pre-digested knowledge. Therefore the concept *Zone of Proximal Development* developed from his work can be viewed as directly addressing the workshop learning and master/ apprenticeship tradition, such as we can observe it in vocational education. He provided an historical analysis of the development of the higher mental functions of the socially situated human being in contrast to what has been called the school of "possessive individualism" and which is the focus of much of today's education.[10] A major feature of Vygotsky's thinking is that a human being learns in a certain definite direction; namely, *from the social to the individual.* People develop their mental and psychical activity through speech. Thinking and language are most profitably understood when viewed from a developmental perspective. The psychological development of the individual is dependent upon the historical epoch in which this development occurs. Luria and Leontiev's research have further illuminated this phenomenon by showing the variation in the development of consciousness in relation to geographical conditions and social background (Daly and Mjelde 2000; Mjelde 1987, 1990, 1993). This point of view is of fundamental significance for all pedagogy. It indicates that the child is not to be viewed first and foremost as a biological being to be socialized through norms and values so as to develop his or her cognition; rather, the child is a social being who develops her/himself through human interaction and language, through the internalization of the norms and the acquisition of whatever knowledge is particular to the time in history and the place on earth where that child is living. By so doing, she or he adds to the continuity and trajectory of the society and its culture.

Consequently, language and communication are fundamental both to human mental activity and to the development of each human generation in society. Human beings have developed language, thought and consciousness through work (activity) and cooperation. Vygotsky uses the concepts of *word* and *meaning* as basic tools for investigating the development of language and thought processes. A person does not learn a word's significance without the word being associated with its meaning (its socially created connotations [contextual meanings] and denotations [generalized or abstract meaning]). Individual experience

10   C.B. Macpherson (1962) provides an excellent analysis of "egocentric individualism" that has permeated modern western and political thinking in the last centuries and has come to be regarded as the "natural order of things".

can only be communicated beyond the experience of the individual when it is organized into categories that are confirmed and verified by other participants in society through established conventions and customs. Meaning is comprised of units of these implicitly common categories. The generalizations or denotations that are implicit in the categories simplify the complexities of experience. They enable science to develop and far-reaching plans and goals to be devised and implemented through time and across space.

Without simplifications and symbols to organize them, the higher forms of human interaction and cooperation would not be possible. Society needs systems of mediation for determining and categorizing what is rational and intentional in the actions and thoughts of its members. This system of mediation is language, the basic units of which are words and meanings. Thus, words and meanings are tools developed through verbal and written interactions between members of society. In the course of striving to understand one another and become members of good standing of society and its component parts we create new internal monologues in which our own experiences are measured against and contrasted with the conventions and generalizations of the society and culture. *Meaning* and *real life understanding* are core concepts for philosophers of language such as V. N. Voloshinov, M. Bakhtin and L. Wittgenstein. These philosophers of language argue that in normal everyday life, meaning is seldom denotative; it is not abstract or general; nor is it separated from a living social context. In a word, everyday meaning is always special, concrete, inductive and interactive (Mjelde 1993, p. 35).

To sum up: a major feature of Vygotsky's thinking is that human beings learn in a certain definite direction; from their *social milieu* to the development of the *individual*. Human knowledge and understanding are constituted by and arise from social relations and language, the key tools created by human kind for the organization of thinking. Mental activity is the result of social learning, of internalization of social signs, of social relationships and culture. Alexander Luria recalled that Lev Vygotsky referred to his psychology as instrumental, cultural and historical. As an epigraph to one of his works, Vygotsky quoted a citation inspired by Francis Bacon. "Neither the mind nor the hand can do much alone. The deed is brought to fruition through activity and cooperation." Another aspect of this way of thinking about teaching and learning is that by means of participating in practical activity one learns to develop one's mastery. The apprentice moves from one level to the next in the social medium of one's fellow practitioners under the guidance by the master and in cooperation with other learners. *No man is an island.* This talks to the traditions in workshop learning in vocational education.

4. Lev Vygotsky and vocational pedagogy

Lev Vygotsky, in his thought-provoking thinking now called *the zone of proximal development* speaks directly to the core of vocational pedagogy. Vygotsky's ideas have been known and utilized in the Western world in the last decades. But these ideas have not been brought forcefully into the realm of educational management and policies; nor are they well known in vocational education research. Lev Vygotsky's scientific work sheds light on the experiences that vocational students and apprentices have acquired from the learning arenas of present-day society, and also on their grasp of learning in the social relations of the school as compared to the social relations integral to the tradition of working life. In the school tradition, learning is separated from the real, local, concrete, contextualized understanding of life and of the concrete nature of everyday existence, namely the experience of working with others to make a living. This separation is neither as decisive nor as stark in the traditions of vocational training. On the other hand, one clearly sees how the development of vocational education at school, divided between the vocational trades on one side, and the general subjects on the other, is a development that has led to the impoverishment of broad and far-ranging education in the vocational trades. The hallmark of workshop learning in the field of vocational pedagogy is the relationship between concrete activities, whether they are in a kitchen or a mechanical workshop, beside a sickbed or an operating theatre in a hospital where learning and meaning are natural and concrete. Actions, words and meanings are integrated and stand together in the learning process. The learner has a distinct experience of meaningfulness and usefulness as she/he learns and expands hers/his zone of proximal development. A profound understanding of this interactive learning in the context of work is lacking among most policy makers.[11]

Vygotsky speaks to another aspect of vocational pedagogy, namely that learning occurs in the course of interacting and cooperating with others.[12] Vygotsky maintained that the thinking processes of any individual must be understood as a form of internal speech that has been transferred and internalized from its starting point in social interaction. His point of departure is that the learner moves dialectically between spontaneous self-reflective learning and a more scientific and logically-oriented form of learning. Concepts that children learn on their own, spontaneously by participating in physical and spoken interactions with other human beings, are what he refers to as everyday concepts. On the other hand, those ideas and concepts that the child acquires through an explicit and systematic assimilation of the material to be learned, into what s/he already knows, are called intellectual or scientific concepts, and are frequently defined theoretically with the help of other words. For example, an everyday term like "dog" can be put through a hierarchy of scientific concepts such as animal, vertebrate, mammal and canine. The learner's appropriation of a word's general and comparative meaning is extremely dependent upon being put into a special context. If the learner has not experienced a certain life situation, the learner's comprehension of the words that generalize experience remain incomplete until everyday life introduces experiences that give a greater depth of understanding to that particular generalizing word. This process takes place in the most immediate zone of development,

---

11   I am not saying that the relationship between meaning, meaninglessness and learning is solved in vocational education. *Far from it*, the deep split between workshop learning, vocational theory and general classroom teaching is just as destructive of vocational education now as it has been earlier in history. And the lack of real practice-based activities in classroom traditions are as destructive as in academic education. What I am stressing is that we now understand these contradictions to a greater degree than ever before. The content in the curriculum is another serious question far from solved. Technological change in the trades is another important problematic demanding new solutions.

12   We have been practising this in a Master course in vocational pedagogy at Kyambogo University, Kampala, Uganda with students from South Sudan and Uganda. 54 of 61 students finished their Masters theses on time (See Mjelde and Daly 2012, Mjelde 2015b).

in the necessary interplay between the learner's inductive experience (which gives rise to word sense) and the deductive, generalizing, teacher-directed instruction (which helps expand understanding of generalized word meanings). If one is lacking in rich experience with the multi-facetted nature of words and their significance, one does not learn to evaluate a word's full meaning in one's society, culture and historical moment (Daly and Mjelde 2000; Mjelde 2009). Lennart Nilsson's (2004) work in vocational pedagogy stresses the aspect of time in the learning processes and emphasizes how important it is for the learners themselves to have control of how much time they need for solving the task. When the task is formed in relation to the learners' own time perspective and the learner succeeds in finishing the task, this experience will lead to the mastering of new activities.

Vygotsky's scientific work and the concept *the zone of proximal development* address the workshop learning and master-apprenticeship tradition, such as we can observe in vocational training within the crafts and industry sector. A definition of this concept is found in Vygotsky's words (1978, p. 86) "It is the distance between the actual developmental level as determined by independent problem solving and the level of potential development as determined through problem solving under adult guidance or in collaboration with more capable peers". The concept of *scaffolding* is used to describe the supports and guidance involved in zones of proximal development (Wood, Bruner and Ross 1976). The concept is taken from the scaffolding in the construction site in the building trades. The scaffolding is the support that apprentices, be they children or adults, get when they are in the process of solving a task with which they can potentially cope. In the same sense that scaffolding at a building site is a temporary structure, a scaffolding of assistance for the learning student is equally provisional. It is there to help the student carry out the assigned task, and then to be taken away. The scaffolding can also be interpreted from the perspective, or the mentoring of the teacher who is involved in the learning process together with the students; that is, the teacher here sets definite goals for the students' learning activity. Stieg Mellin-Olsen and Reidar Solvang (1978) have developed this concept in relation to, among other things, mathematical instruction. They use the concept of *scaffold-building* for the process that a teacher sets into motion when he or she gives guidance in mathematics. The goal is to get the learning process underway so as to hand over the accomplishment to the learner and thereby tear down the scaffolding. Tony Irizar and Adita Chiappy's work (in Mjelde and Daly 2004) on applying these ideas in the teaching of English as a secondary language in Cuba is also an inspiration to further development.

Moll (1990, pp. 3–15) argues that it is the following aspects of Vygotsky's theory that have significance for understanding the zone of proximal development. Holistic teaching and the mediating and bringing about of learning and change.[13] By mediated learning he means that words and language are the tools that act as intermediaries and bring about internal human activity. Vygotsky criticized traditional teaching for having an atomistic view of learning. Among other things, he felt that both the splitting up of school subjects and the parcelling out of teaching content into individual subjects contributed to the elimination of the meaningfulness of the individual subjects. Knowledge, he argued, cannot be taken out of its natural context and passed on in isolation; it can only yield meaning and create motivation if it is taken up as a part of a whole. Another of his major principles is that learning occurs through the internalization of processes that, in the first place, the individual carries out together with others in her/his surroundings or habitat. As an alternative to traditional mediatory pedagogy, Vygotsky proposed a form of teaching that involved the development of higher psychological processes through an active cooperation between the teacher and the student collective, and which stimulates each individual to attain a new level of personal development, in relation to each other and to the teacher. Vygotsky (1962, p. 104) wrote "the only good kind of instruction is that which marches ahead of development and leads it; it must be aimed not so much at the ripe [functioning of ripeness] as at the ripening function".

---

13   I am not content with the concept *holistic*. Perhaps *integrated teaching and learning* is better.

I have described this process graphically in the following way:

Learning site workshop	The Adaptation of the Learning Processes	The Student/Apprentice Zone of Development
Learning as an integrated, cumulative process. The integration of hand, mind and heart. Learning and meaning created through goal oriented activity.	The goal is reached. The apprentices are mastering the task and have reached the next zone of proximal development. The new level is now the actual zone of development which creates the bases for further learning	*The next zone of development*
Lev Vygotsky. Neither hand nor mind can do much alone. The deed is brought to fruition with tools and cooperation	The master has developed his/her skills interaction with the learners and created a better basis for teaching the activity of building a boat or writing a thesis.	
Development through interaction and crisis. Mikail Bahktin. It is in the tensions and confrontations between different voices that new insight and understanding come into being.	The master + the apprentices decide on the next level of development The apprentices interact and negotiate Their understanding of the details and significance of the task. The master demonstrates, instructs and explains The apprentices train and repeat, assisting each other with the assistance of the master The apprentices perform the tasks without assistance	*The nearest zone of proximal development*
Learning by Doing. Luria . to move from the simple and concrete to the complex and general.	The master and the apprentices map and determine through tools and meditation what the learners are mastering in a field. This makes the basis for the adaptation of the teaching processes towards the nearest zone of proximal development.	*The actual zone of development*

Figure 2: The spiraling process of learning and teaching in apprenticeship traditions.
Liv Mjelde (1987, 1990, 2004, 2006, 2009, 2011, 2012, 2013).

I have described the learning processes as an escalation process. The learning site is the workshop and the master and the apprentices map and determine together through tools, cooperation and mediation what the learners are mastering in a field. This makes the basis for the adaptation of the teaching and learning processes towards the nearest zone of proximal development. The master and the apprentice decide on the next level of development. The apprentices interact with the master and each other about the details and significance of the task. The master demonstrates, instructs and explains. The apprentices train and repeat, assisting each other with the help of the master till they perform the tasks without assistance. They have then reached the nearest zone of proximal development. This is a process with learning through *praxis and cooperation*. The apprentice reaches a new level in the spiral which now becomes the actual zone of development; this in turn creates the basis for further learning. The novice moves through these stages: from *apprentice to journeyman to master*. The goal is being reached. The apprentice has become a master. These are similar processes whether you train to be a carpenter, a plumber, a medical doctor, a teacher, a nurse or a scientist. *The activity itself is the rotation point for learning.*

5. Conclusion

The development in vocational education is full of paradoxes and dilemmas, but many of today's concepts stem from the findings of Vygotsky and his followers. "Activity theory" is a concept coming out of this tradition (see Portes and Salas 2011). "The master-apprentice learning model", "learning through activity", "situated learning", "social learning" and "learning by doing" are now important conceptions in the academic debate about learning. The master apprenticeship model has been rehabilitated. (Kvale 1993; Nielsen and Kvale 1999). The anthology (Coy et al 1989) entitled *Apprenticeship. From Theory to Method and Back Again* is the result a group of social anthropologists taking up the theme of *learning by doing* and through *social relations*, as the contributors observed in many different learning situations around the

globe. A common feature of these works is their rootedness in the Cultural-Historical School of Moscow and Lev Vygotsky's work. These
ideas are seldom brought into the general debate concerning the problems of vocational education today.

Given the way the educational system has developed to the present,
we have a hegemonic situation where both general academic and vocational education separate knowledge from experience, theory from practice, thought from action. A course of studies that takes into account all
these factors and incorporates hands, heart and brain, conceptualization
processes and their practical exercise is necessary for a better education
for all. Similarly, a working life wherein one can advance with experience and maturity, where the mechanic can become an engineer, and the
caregiver with a craft certificate can, stone by stone, build her/himself
into a nurse, radiographer, or doctor, is essential if we are to achieve
a better life for all (see also Freire 1997,1998). Contradictions in the
present-day school show the limitations created by sectional interests in
society. This is strikingly evident when one tries to use one generalized
school and education system as an instrument for bringing about social
change across society. In other words, one comes up against the interests of the powerful and the conventional social boundaries, between
conceptual and practical knowledge, between individual-based conceptual learning and social learning and activities. This is particularly
evident when one tries to create both a common school and conformity
through education – especially in a society that is not nearly as equal
and united as the politicians assure us it is.

But to clarify the contradictions as they appear in the curricula of
the vocational trades in the upper secondary school is not to deny that
some are better than others. Flexibility and response to local conditions
are needed. But it is important to put forward an understanding of both
sides of this human activity, both the practical workshop tradition and
the scholarly general education route. They should both be taken up, but
in such a manner that they are encouraged to enrich one another. Contradictions can also be made fruitful when they are analyzed openly and
plainly, made conscious and comprehensible, and thus capable of contributing to wider democratization of the school and education in general through development of pedagogy for all. As Tor Halvorsen wrote
in 1994, p. 123). "Perhaps future research work in vocational education

and working life will establish knowledge that shows the ideal paradigm of the unified schools is atypical when seen in a historical light, despite the hegemony that this cultural inheritance has today."

References

Ainley, P. and Rainbird H. (eds.) 1999. Apprenticeship. Towards a New Paradigm of Learning. London, Kogan Page.

Bakhtin, M. 1981. The Dialogical Imagination. Four Essays. Austin, University of Texas Press.

Bakken, A and Elstad J.2012. For store forventninger. Kunnskapsløftet og ulikhetene i grunnskolekarakterer. Oslo. Nova Rapport no.7/12.

Barato, J.N. 2011. Saber do Trabalho, Aprendizagem Situado e Ensino Technico. Rio de Janeiro. Boletim Technico do Senac, 37, 3.

Barato J.N. 2016. Trabajo, conocimineto y formacion professional. Montevideo, OIT/Cinterfor.

Berner, B. 1989. Kunskapens väger. Teknik og lärande i skola och arbetsliv. Lund, Arkiv.

Billett, S. 2000. Coparticipation at Work. Knowing and Working Knowledge. In D. Boud and C. Symes (eds) Working Knowledge. Productive Learning at Work. Sydney, University of Technology.

Bodin, P. 2004. Det er nemlig her vi lærer. Hvordan opplever nautiske studenter læring på en visuell simulator. Masters thesis. Oslo, Høgskolen i Akershus.

Bongo, M.1999. Yrkesrettet voksenopplæring i en reformtid. Masters thesis. Oslo, Høgskolen i Akershus.

Bongo, M. 2001. Videregående opplæring. Møtestedet mellom to læringstradisjoner. Kan noen av reformproblemene tilskrives å ha grunnlaget i de grunnleggende motsetninger mellom ulike læringstradisjoner? Paper. Oslo, Høgskolen i Akershus.

Bruner, J.S. 1970. Om å lære. Oslo, Gyldendal.

Bruner, J.S. 1996. The Culture of Education. Cambridge, Harvard University Press.

Coy, M.W. (eds) 1989. Apprenticeship. From Theory to Method and Back Again. Albany, State University of New York Press.

Daly, R. and Mjelde, L. 2000. Learning at the Point of Production. New Challenges in the Social Divisions of Knowledge. In D. Boud and C. Symes (eds.), Working Knowledge. Productive Learning at Work. Sydney, University of Technology.

Enerstvedt, R. 1986. Hva er læring? Oslo, Falken forlag.

Flaten, S. V. 1999. Bedriften som arena for læring, opplæring og sosial-isering. En sosiologisk undersøkelse av fagopplæring ved Hydro Industripark. Masters Thesis. Bergen, University i Bergen.

Freire, P. 1970. Pedagogy of the Oppressed. New York, Continuum.

Freire, P. 1997. Mentoring the Mentor. A Critical dialogue with Paulo Freire. New York, Peter Lang.

Freire, P.1998. Pedagogy of the Heart. New York, Continuum.

Frøland, E.2004. Med rett til å velge. Gjennom avvik til full kom-petanse, om utviklingen av full opplæring i bedrift. Master's thesis. Oslo, Høgskolen i Akershus.

Giroux, H. 1983. Theory and Resistance in Education. Mass, Bergin and Garvey.

Grignon, C. 1971. L'Ordre des Choses. Paris, Les Edition de Minuit.

Grimestad, V.1993. Om bakgrunn og prestasjoner. Elever med grunnlag i forkurs mekaniske fags utvikling med hensyn til trivsel, moti-vasjon og sosial integrering i læremessig sammenheng. Master's Thesis. Oslo, SYH.

Grosjean, G. 2001. The Social Organization of Learning. Educational Provision, Process and Outcomes. Connecting it all. Linking Eco-nomics, Education and Policy. Paper. Vancouver, UBC.

Halvorsen, T. 1994. Forskning om yrkesutdanning og arbeidslivet. In J. Lauglo (ed.), Norsk forskning om utdanning. Perspektiver og velvalg Oslo, Ad Notam Gyldendal.

Høst, H. 2013. Kan arbeidslivet være et alternativ for skoletrøtte 16 åringer. In Søkelyset på arbeidslivet, 1 Oslo, Statistisk Sentralbyrå.

Irizar, T. and Chiappy A. 2006. The Concepts of "Working Knowledge" and "Zone of Proximal Development" as applied to the Teaching of English as a Secondary Language. In L. Mjelde and R. Daly (eds.),

Working Knowledge in a Globazing World. From Work to Learning. From Learning to Work. Bern, Peter Lang.

Kokkersvold, E. and Mjelde, L. 1982. Yrkesskolen som forsvant. Oslo, Gyldendal.

Kvale, S. 1993. En pedagogisk rehabilitering av mesterlæren? Dansk Pedagogisk tidsskrift 41.

Lave, J. and Wenger, E. 1991. Situated Learning. Cambridge, Cambridge University Press.

Lien, T. 1984. Kvalifisering til arbeid. En analyse av teori og praksis på to arbeidsmarkedskurs. Trondheim, Norsk voksenpedagogisk institutt.

Lien, T. 1995. Men helst vil jeg ha en jobb. Evaluering av AMO-kurs i Vestfold. Sandefjord, Fylkesarbeidskontoret i Vestfold.

Luria, A. 1976. Cognitive Development. Its Cultural and Social Foundations. Cambridge, Cambridge University Press.

Macpherson, C.B. 1962. The Political Theory of Possessive Individualism. London, Oxford University Press.

Marx, K. and Engels F. 1985. The German Ideology. New York, International Publishers.

Mellin Olsen, S. and Solvang R.1978. Matematikkundervisning som sosial prosess. Oslo, NKI forlaget

Mjelde, L. 1987. From Hand to Mind. In D. Livingstone (ed.), Critical Pedagogy and Cultural Power. Mass, Bergin and Garvey.

Mjelde, L. 1990. Labour and Learning. Toronto, Interchange 21(4).

Mjelde, L. 1993. Apprenticeship. From Practice to Theory and Back Again. PHD. Joensuu, University of Joensuu Press.

Mjelde, L. 1994.Will the Twain Meet? The Relationship between the World of Work and the World of Schools. In P. Heywood, K. Wain and J. Calleja (eds.), Research into Secondary School Curricula. Amsterdam, Swets and Zeitlinger.

Mjelde, L. 1997. The Apprenticeship Conundrum in Norwegian Vocational Education. In A. Heikkinen and R. Sultana (eds.), Vocational Education and Apprenticeships in Europe. Challenges for Practice and Research. Tampere, University of Tampere. Dep. of Education, Series B, No. 16.

Mjelde, L. 2006. The Magical Properties of Workshop Learning. Bern, Peter Lang.

Mjelde, L. 2009. Unity and Diversity in Vocational Didactics from the Standpoint of Different Vocations. In M. Weil, L. Koski and L. Mjelde (eds.), Knowing Work. The Social Relations of Working and Knowing. Bern, Peter Lang.

Mjelde, L. and Daly R. 2012. Aspects of Vocational Pedagogy as Practice. Decolonizing minds and negotiating local knowledge. International Journal of Training Research, 10, 1.

Mjelde, L. 2013. Challenges to the Dual Model in Norwegian and Adult Education Reforms. In M. Kattein and M. Vonken (eds.), Zeitbetractungen Bildung-Arbeit-Biografie. Festschrift für Rudolf Husemann. Frankfurt, Peter Lang.

Mjelde, L. 2015 (a). Workshop Learning and Georg Kerschensteiner in Nordic Countries. In A. Heikkinen and L. Lassnigg (eds.), Myths and Brands in Vocational Education, Cambridge, Cambridge Scholars Publishing.

Mjelde, L. 2015 (b). Mentoring Vocational Self-Reliance. Lessons from Uganda. In G. Molzberger and M. Wahle (eds.), Shaping the Futures of (Vocational) Education and Work. Bern, Peter Lang.

Mjelde, L. 2016. Las propiedades mágicas de la formación en el taller. Montevideo, OIT/Cinterfor.

Moll, L C. (ed.) 1990. Vygotskij and Education. Instructional Application and Applications of Sociohistorical Psychology. Cambridge, Cambridge University Press.

Nielsen, K. and. Kvale S. (eds) 1999. Mesterlære. Læring som sosial praksis. Oslo, Ad Notam Gyldendal.

Nielsen, K. and Kvale, S. 2003. Praktikkens læringslandskap. At lære gjennom arbeide. Copenhagen, Akademisk forlag.

Nilsson, L. 1981. Yrkesutbildning i nutidshistorisk perspektiv. PHD Gothenburg, University of Gothenburg.

Nilsson, L. 2004. Nordisk yrkespedagogikk i internationellt perspektiv. Den 19. Nordiske yrkespedagogiske konferanse. Reykjavik, Kennarahaskoli Islands.

Olsen, O. J et al (1998). Fagopplæring i omforming. Evaluering av Reform 94. Sluttrapport. AHS-serien. Bergen, University of Bergen.

Olsen, O. J. 2013. Challenges to Broadening and Specialization of Norwegian Vocational Education. In M. Kattein and M. Vonken (eds.), Zeitbetractungen Bildung-Arbeit-Biografie. Festschrift für Rudolf Husemann. Frankfurt, Peter Lang.

Portes, P. R. and Salas S. 2011. Vygotsky in 21st society. Advances in cultural historical theory and praxis with non-dominant communities. New York, Peter Lang.

Rose, M. 2014. The Mind at Work. Valuing the Intelligence of the American Worker. New York, Penguin

Toulmin, S.1978. The Mozart of Psychology. New York Review of Books September 28th.

Velten, K. 2004. Demokrati på grunnkurs helse og sosialfag. Masters thesis. Oslo, Høgskolen i Akershus.

Vogt, K. C. 2013. Approaches to work and education over the life course. A two-cohort study of men skilled in male-dominated manual occupations in Norway. PHD. Bergen, University of Bergen.

Vogt,K. C. 2016. Yrkesfagene. In Frønes, I and Kjølsrud, L. Det Norske samfunn. Oslo, Gyldendal.

Volosinov, V. N 1973. Marxism and philosophy of Language. New York, Seminar Press.

Vygotsky, L. 1962. Thought and Language. Cambridge, MIT press.

Vygotsky, L. 1978. Mind in Society. The Development of Higher Psychological Processes. Cambridge, Harvard University Press.

Wittgenstein, L. 2001. Philosophical Investigations. Oxford, Blackwell.

Willis, P. 1977. Learning to Labour. London, Collier Macmillan.

Wood, D., Bruner, J.S. and Ross, G. 1976. The Role of Tutoring in Problem-solving. Journal of Child Psychology and Psychiatry. 17, 2.

Norwegian public documents

Stortingsproposisjon (OT. Prop). Proposition to the Storting. Stortingsmelding (NOU). Norwegian Official Report. (White paper). Komiteer oppnevnt i statsråd. Royal Commissions. Lover. Parliamentary acts.

Acts and Proposals

1940 Lov om yrkeskoler for håndverk og industri. (Act on vocational schools for craft and industry). Oslo. (KUF) Ministry of Church and Education.

1950 Lov om Lærlinger I håndverk og industri, handel og kontor. (Act on apprenticeship in craft and industry, commerce and office work) Oslo. (KUD) Ministry of Church and Education.

1965 Skolekomiteen om videregående opplæring. (The school committee on Upper Secondary Education) Royal Commission. OT.Prop. Oslo. (KUD) Ministry of Church and Education.

1974 Lov om videregående opplæring av 21 juni 1974. (Act of June 21st 1974 on Upper Secondary Education.) Implemented January 1st. 1976. Oslo. (KUD) Ministry of Church and Education.

1982. Vocational Training in Norway. Oslo. (KUD) Ministry of Church and Education.

1991/1992 Kunnskap og kyndighet. Om visse sider ved videregående opplæring. (Knowledge and skills. Aspects of Upper Secondary Education). White paper No.33. Oslo. (KUF) Ministry of Education Research and Church Affairs. (Basis for Reform 94).

2004 Kultur for læring (Culture for Learning) White Paper no. 30 Oslo. (KUF) Ministry of Education and Research.

2006 Kunnskapsløftet. (The Knowledge Promotion Reform. Education reform introduced in 2006 in primary,lower secondary and upper secondary education and training.) White Paper (KUF) Ministry of Education and Research.

2012/2013 På rett vei. Kvalitet og mangfold i fellesskolen. (In the right direction. Quality and diversity in the comprehensive school). White Paper No. 20 Oslo. (KD) Ministry of Knowledge.

European Documents

OECD 2013. VET in Europe. Country Report, Norway. Paris, OECD.
OECD 2016. Society at a Glance 2016. Paris, OECD.

Anja Heikkinen, Perpetua Joseph Kalimasi, Elizabeth Opit and
Jesse Sjelvgren

Promoting Basic Social and Health Care Work through Education: Global North and Global South in Comparison

1. Introduction

In this chapter we discuss the function and recognition of basic social and healthcare work in the global context of 'the totality of societally recognized work' (Glucksman 1995) and the mainstream educational structures and hierarchies. It builds on lessons learnt during the ReWell Project (2014–2016) that focused on promoting regional wellbeing through adult and vocational education. The case studies in the course Vocational Education and Culture in University of Tampere, research theses of participant students and joint intensive seminars in Tanzania, between university staff, students and regional actors from Finland, Tanzania and Uganda were significant sources of information for this paper[1].

A pragmatic ground for the comparison is the joint project, but there is a more political and ethical reason. Although globalization is mainly considered as an industrial and commercial project, it also includes distinctive solutions in basic social and health care. Despite

---

[1]   Anja Heikkinen from Finland, Perpetua Kalimasi from Tanzania and Elizabeth Opit from Uganda were supervisors in the ReWell project. Jesse Sjelvgren participated in courses with ReWell teachers and students, and accomplished his MA thesis on development of competence-based curriculum for practical nurses in the Tampere Region Vocational College. Recruitment and qualification in basic social and health care hardly differ between youth and adults, we don't discuss them separately. More information about the project for example <http://mzumbe.ac.tz/rewell/>.

being a service, which is produced and consumed locally and simultaneously, basic social and health care is embedded in global industrial clusters and commodity chains. Still, minor attention is paid to the conceptual and practical diversity in organizing care work in different geo-economic and geo-political locations. The comparison between the global North and South, represented by Finland, Tanzania and Uganda remains fragmentary, but intends to raise discussion about the interrelatedness of local and global divisions of labour, and relations between local and global production and consumption (Narotzky 1997; Kerswell 2011). While Tanzania and Uganda share quite much with other countries in East-Africa, Finland can be considered rather similar with other Nordic countries.

In this chapter, basic social and health care is viewed from the perspective of the workers – the content of their work, the patterns of their education and recruitment to employment, and their work conditions – in the context of wider social and occupational structures and hierarchies. Instead of evaluating different solutions according to countries' rankings in economic development or corruption, we hope to understand better the challenges faced by globalization at so far ends of the globe. In the global North, prevailing neo-liberalist policies have opened up public welfare services to trans-national competition, increasing the power of multi-national care businesses to dictate the meaning and content of basic social and health care. In the global South, penetration of multi-nationals into national industries benefit from exploitation of traditional familial patterns of care. However, provision of care should be a fundamental duty of the nation-state and a fundamental right of its citizen. Workers in basic social and health care are in core position to identify and response to citizens' needs, but when welfare services become one industrial cluster serving the competitiveness of other industrial sectors, can they have ownership of their work and education anymore?

In questioning the global division of basic social work, health care work and education, we use provisory categories of occupational agency and social reproduction of the means of livelihood. The relation between subject and object, individual and society, free will and material conditions are traditionally in the core of philosophical, religious and social scientific debates. However, it has become extremely popular in contemporary psychological, sociological and educational research on occupational work and education. A powerful research stream has built on Margaret Archer's studies on culture and agency on an individuals' capacity to influence structural – economic, cultural societal – conditions of their actions. According to her, the opposition of agent and structural causality could be transcended through a historical perspective, which interprets structures as embodiments from individuals' intentional and non-intentional actions. They restrict and liberate individuals to exercise their wishes and wills, and indicate the complexity of prevailing power relations. (Archer 1996).

While the emphasis in agency-approach is on socio-cultural and individual formation of occupational identities, the means of livelihood-approach considers cultures as real experiences that engender reasons for action embodied in the production and reproduction of material life (Narotzky 1997). Following her, the global capitalism functions beyond wage-labour-capital relations, "irrespective of the actual 'ownership' status toward certain means of production" in labour, financial or product markets. While the complex logic of capitalism promotes celebration of cultural particularity, whether as political and economic, work-organizational or currently 'virtual/social media' communities, the challenge of mobilization of potential counter-hegemonic consciousness and action remains. In order to be more concrete about this, Kerswell (2011) reminds us about the 'global commodity chains', which constrain the ability of workers to consciously develop local or global alliances.

We subsequently make a short introduction to work and education in basic and social health care in Finland and the East-African regions of Tanzania and Uganda. We describe the context where negotiations about their education take place and discuss the options they have to participate in defining their work through educational reform. Discussions are related to occupational, educational and cultural factors, which are presumably relevant for understanding and changing existing practices in basic social and health care, both locally and in the global division of labour.

2. Basic social and health care work in Finland, Tanzania and Uganda

In Finland, the social welfare and health care acts oblige municipalities to organize common and special social and health care services to all citizens. The basic social and health care workers commonly known as *practical nurses* work in public, private and third sector (Non-Governmental Organisations). Currently, 70% of practical nurses work in the public sector and 91% of all the practitioners are female. The employment rate, a total of 85%, is higher than any other occupation in Finland (Superliitto, 2014). Practical nurses' work is rehabilitative, educative and caring. Their aim is to promote health, prevent problems and provide rehabilitation for the clients in social and health care services. Workers in basic social and health care consider themselves needed because they are "close to other people and usually our task is to be 'voice' for the weakest people in our society" (Female 1985, Lyamba *et al.* 2015).

Typical social work settings for practical nurses are early childhood education in kindergarten or family-setting, child welfare units, disability and mental health units, home care and institutional units for the elderly. For health care settings, there are wards, clinics, health care centres, dental care, emergency departments and home care. 65% of the qualified practical nurses work in social services while 35% serve in health care (Superliitto 2014; 2016). The practical nurses themselves consider requirements for basic social and health care to include

> basic knowledge, instruction skills, aseptic skills, skills of using different kinds of care instruments, rehabilitative skills, positive attitude towards every day, flexibility, acceptance of differences, respect for other people, encouragement of others and ability to throw oneself into 'situations' in work (Lyamba *et al.* 2015).

In Uganda and Tanzania, there are some categories of basic social and health care services. Formal qualifications are a pre-requisite for only in the case of 'nurses in hospitals and health centres'. They provide health care services such as health assessments, teaching about diseases and treatment, dressing changes, wound care, management, medication reconciliation, reports and administration. One becomes a nurse upon acquiring competence-based qualification of one, three or four years of a general nurses training course. The entry qualification for the course is the Ordinary Secondary School Leavers' Certificate with passes in science subjects, especially biology. The nurses are largely employed by the Ministry of Health, private health centres and medical stores.

Other categories of basic social and health care workers are recruited regardless of their educational background. They are generally domestic workers, working for private employers or families, and trained on the job. Basic social and health care workers have different names, such as 'house helps', 'house maids', 'house girls or boys' and 'house assistants' both in Tanzania and Uganda. Most of them are young girls between 16 and 25 years because in the East-African societies, domestic chores are primarily done by women while young boys are employed mostly by families engaged in activities such as poultry and animal keeping. The services offered by the indoor house maids in Uganda and Tanzania include "babysitting, cooking, washing clothes, buying groceries, housekeeping or caretaking, washing cars, attending to the sick and the aged, taking the children to and fetching them from school" (Tanzanian female University Teacher, June 2015). Recently in Tanzania, also energetic old women have been employed as house helps, but usually they undertake the activities during the day and return to their families in the evening.

In Tanzania, the job description of domestic workers varies from one household to another depending on the initial agreement and nature of the household. Some are permanently staying in the household and some come to the house in the morning and leave in the evening after finishing prescribed tasks. For the workers who are staying with their employers in the house, they do perform the prescribed tasks according to the context as well as any other emerging tasks at any time. For the workers who are not permanently staying with the employers, they are usually responsible for prescribed tasks during the day, then they go back to their homesteads after wards. In rare cases the employer can direct the house help to seek help from other family members, especially younger girls and boys. However, there are variations in the nature of tasks and activities in different households and to different employers. If the family is engaging in peasant agriculture, a worker may be obliged to join in agriculture or animal keeping. If the household is family with little children, the domestic worker may be obliged to babysit as well as to do cleaning, washing and cooking.

In Uganda, the term 'domestic engineer' is a recent invention coined for domestic workers by youth elites to acknowledge the "technical" and "professional" services they render to their clients. Ikiriza (2014) mentioned that "they do duties that their employers are unable to do for themselves in distinguished ways." Relatedly, Lubale (personal communication, October 13, 2015) observed that

> although some people think that domestic work is uncomplicated, it still remains real work just like other jobs. This work can be physically, emotionally, socially and psychologically challenging. This type of work demands long hours, from preparing children to go to school in the morning to finishing up when all others have gone to their beds. A domestic worker brings skills and experience into the home of her employer.

These excerpts connote that the work of house helps is specialized and valued by the clients and can be done only by persons of their calibre and training.

3. Ownership of basic social and health care education

In Finland social and health care work is strongly defined through education. The basic social and health care qualification for a 'practical nurse' is an upper secondary qualification which can be accomplished in vocational colleges or in vocational adult education institutes. It was developed in 1993 by merging previously separate lower social and health care qualifications. (Järvinen 1993). At polytechnic and university levels, social and health care is divided into different qualifications. Polytechnics offer bachelor level qualifications in social services and nursing, as well as a few master level degrees in social services and in health sciences. Universities offer Bachelors, Masters and Doctorates in social work and in health sciences.

Alongside the general reform of Finland's vocational education system, education for basic social and health care is competence-based.

Steps towards this were taken since 1993 through the performance-based qualification system for adults. The current reform builds on recommendations from the European Union for the member states in 2008, to use European Qualification Framework for lifelong learning (EQF) in their education systems. According to EU this would enable compatibility of vocational qualifications between European countries and therefore increase workers' mobility between European countries and facilitate their lifelong learning (European Commission 2008, p. 3). Finnish National Board of Education (FNBE) considers competence-based education as one solution for responding to the changing needs of the working life and educating labour force with market relevant skills (FNBE 2015, p. 7).

Jesse Sjelvgren used subjective-centred socio-cultural approach (Eteläpelto *et al.* 2013) for studying agency in the process of development of curriculum for practical nurses in Tampere Region Vocational College in 2015. At the end of the planning phase of the Curriculum Development (CD) process, six teachers (planners) and three program coordinators were interviewed. The study focused on the relation between structural – societal, communal and social – causes and participants' agency, from the side of the individuals (Moilanen 1999, p. 98). In Finland, vocational institutes form their own curriculum on the basis of the national core curriculum. It should be developed in cooperation with work-life representatives to ensure that actors in the field can influence the education of the future workers (FNBE 2013). However, study findings indicated the opposite. Cooperation between teachers and work-life representatives, such as the vocational advisory board, was very limited or absent. In practice, the board's role was to approve the final version of the curriculum. While teachers who worked as curriculum planners did not have time to cooperate with the practitioners, they trusted their previous experiences from the field, such as from supervision of students' on-the-job-learning periods (Sjelvgren 2016).

The study showed that teachers have much space for their own agency in the process. This enabled teachers to develop psychological ownership towards their planning work, and feel that the planned content was their own. Psychological ownership is formed through being in control, intimately knowing the target and investing the self into the target (*cf.* Pierce *et al.* 2001). Since the planning was not strictly guided, teachers had wide possibilities to interpret the core curriculum and use their own agency in the process. The content of the curriculum was linked to their professional expertise and experience from the field and intertwined to their identity and previous knowledge. However, when coordinators made modifications to these contents, teachers resisted the changes because they felt that the ownership of their work was being threatened. In light of these events, teachers acted as gate-keepers on what content was important in the curriculum and what kind of needs working life would have. However, due to teachers' powerful agency in the process, practitioners' experiences and voices are marginally heard and recognized in the development of their education. This signifies imbalanced power relations between educators and practitioners. It is reasonable to ask, should practitioners be empowered and therefore have more influence on developing their education?

The findings correspond to the Vocational education and culture-course interviews of local Finnish practical nurses who highlighted the importance of practical training and practical knowledge over theoretical knowledge in their education and practice.

There is much inequality in competence-based qualification. This means that the evaluation made by workers (work-place instructors) in on-the-job-learning places is very different when different students apply to show their skills in practice. Different things affect students' evaluation (how they like the person etc.) There are also difficulties in showing how students can show that they have learned theoretical knowledge (this is required in their vocational skills demonstration) and how they can use it in practice. It also feels that there is a pressure to increase the number of practical nurses which lowers the standard required for this work. Present education should be more compact, without too much theory and I would like to increase the amount of practical learning (on-the-job-learning + practical skills). (Female 1985, Lyamba *et al.* 2015).

They felt that the skills and theories they were taught in the vocational institute did not match with the skills they needed in their daily work. While vocational competencies should be based on the real needs of the occupation, it remains unclear who are the right persons to determine those needs?

In East-Africa, education for social and health care is not considered as vocational. Furthermore, education and certification of qualifications is only required from domestic workers who serve as home nurses. The other categories of domestic workers join the occupation without any certified formal qualifications or education. They learn their jobs through the informal training they receive from the employer and earlier socialization in their homes or work places. House helps who master the competences required for their work receive no certification but may receive a salary increment upon the employers' discretion.

The absence of certified qualifications in basic social and health care work disadvantages both the employers and the employees in various ways. On the one hand, in some instances, employers receive substandard work from unqualified house helps. The Head of Tanzanian National Resource Centre of Vocational Education and Training Authority supported this observation when he said: "there is no service satisfaction because they make many mistakes as their initial service delivery is so wanting while they learn on the job at your expense and some of them never learn" (Maro, personal communication, June 2015).

On the other hand, house helps are exploited by the employers based on a widely upheld view that domestic workers do not have certified qualifications. Arinaitwe (personal communication, October 20, 2015) noted that "employers feel it is okay to pay them anything, and they too have no bargaining power because they have no educational papers – the education they have was not paid for with tuition fees like the formal one, 'so why are you demanding for so much'… some employers have been known to argue like that".

4. Basic social and health care work in the orders of occupations and economy

4.1 Finnish context

In Finland, social and health care work is traditionally considered indispensable for the functioning of the economy and industries. It is financed through state and municipal taxes, insurance payments and employer or customer fees, and organized by municipalities in public, private or third sector organizations (NGOs). Practical nurses are mobilized into their own union (Super): the level of unionization is very high and they have a collective labour agreement on salaries and work conditions. The basic salary is under Finnish average, but because of shift, night and weekend work, their hourly wages may increase by 25–100%.

As indicated earlier, despite collective labour agreements practical nurses have minor opportunities to decide on education and development of their own occupation, on how their work is organized at societal level, which skills or competencies should be valued and how they should be practiced. The teachers of social or health care dominate the CD process, although their professional paradigm on necessary skills and competences differs from that of practical nurses. According to the Finnish National Board of Education (2015, p. 7) one reason for the delay in adoption of competence-based curriculum is the clinging of teachers to their science-based or subject-oriented profile, which may lead to resistance towards the reform. Although practical nurse qualification was established from separate basic social and health care qualifications in 1993, in polytechnics and universities the fields still have separate scientific basis, studies and professional aims. The study (Sjelvgren 2016) shows that the boundaries between social and health care in practical nurse qualification may not be transcended yet, because of the division among the teachers. For students the contest of paradigms shows as contents which are not relevant to occupational practice: "I think in practical nurse education there should be less learning of moral values and more time focused on teaching practical skills" (Female 1991, Lyamba *et al.* 2015).

While their work is so regulated through legislation, labour contracts, qualification control, salaries and requirements on work-conditions, most practitioners and educators hardly reflect on these controversies, especially while ageing population and rising standards of living increases rapidly employment in social and health care. However, the latest concerns among different social and health care professionals are about participation – through unions – in the current reforms in social and health care. For several years, leading politicians – both conservatives and the social democrats – have aimed at improving efficiency of basic social and health care through centralization, creation of large units, opening up services to trans-national markets, and – what is relevant here – lowering the occupational standards for distinctive social or health care qualifications. (*cf.* Kalliomaa-Puha *et al.* 2016.) Alongside with social and health care reforms, the government continues reforms in vocational education, challenging previous funding criteria, diversifying increasing workplace learning. (Grahn-Laasonen 2016, p. 34.) Both changes demand educators and practitioners in basic social and health care to find new ways to practice their agency and to negotiate their different paradigms of basic social and health care education.

4.2 Tanzanian and Ugandan context

In Uganda, the Employment Act (2006) states that there is no permit requirement for one to recruit a domestic servant for employment. Beyond this there is no other specific provision in the Constitution or in the labour laws regarding domestic workers. A similar scenario prevails in Tanzania. Consequently, the recruitment of basic social and health care workers in the South is privately and informally transacted in the following ways:

Direct negotiation with parents/guardians. Employers usually pick relatives as house helps from their homes after seeking their parents' or guardian's consent to employ them.

Go-between business agents (Recruitment bureaus): The bureaus outsource house helps from both rural and urban areas and link them to customers/employers at a fee. This is an increasing phenomenon in Kampala where the recruited house helps and their employers both need to pay the Recruitment bureau for networking them.

Advertisements: In Uganda, individual house helps and Recruitment bureaus are increasingly using advertising services. Also in big cities such as Dar-es-alaam, bloggers are use blogs or informal street companies to advertise posts of house helps. They act like middle persons for employers to get a house help as indicated in Advertising Dar (2016). Some adverts describe different house helps needed as follows:

"35 year old female is looking for a job as a housekeeper, maid, babysitter or office cleaner. I have 8 years working experience and I am fluent in English and Kiswahili. I am also willing to learn to pre-pare meals. Kindly call Ester 0716148583."Another post read; "I am 38 year old female. Looking for a job as a housekeeper, maid, babysitter or office cleaner. I have 14 years working experience and fluent in English and Kiswahili. Call Martha on 0783008225." A similar post was writ-ten that, "I am 28 year old female looking for a job as a housekeeper, maid, babysitter or office cleaner. I have 4 years working experience and fluent in Kiswahili. Call Fellen 0685743726."

Sometimes house helps use to walk around the street to look for jobs themselves. In many cases these encounter difficulties because some employers are afraid to hire them, because they do not know where they are coming from. If employed, some employers end up mis-treating or harming them, believing that since it was the employees who needed the job they have to tolerate any kind of treatment exposed to them by their respective employer. In this case, it was just a favour for them to be employed. Employers tend to pretend that they were not in need of them, but they just decide to employ them. However, in some situations, employers take this as an opportunity to get a house help with no cost, because at times it may require that the employer sends bus fare and small subsistence money to facilitate the trip from home to the employer. A slight difference is among domestic workers who are recruited to go abroad as migrant domestic workers especially in Arab countries. Apart from the previous ways of recruitment, migrant domes-tic workers may be recruited through Tanzania Agency for Employment Services, under the Ministry of Works, Labour and Employment (ILO 2014).

In response to the International Labour Organisation convention (ILO 2014), which Tanzania among other countries ratified in 2013, the government proposed a minimum salary of 60,000 Tshs for the house helps. However, there is no follow up of the proposed payment, and employers pay 30,000–50,000 Tshs or even less, depending on their agreement and the nature of tasks. Salary scale is a challenge, since some families pay in kind, with promises like taking them to school for further education or being given capital to start business over time. This depends on the age and decision of the house help's parents for minors. Some parents can even force the child to send the salary to them as payback of the work done by their child. In this way, they use their children as a labour force for capital gains. However, the payment rates by employers such as diplomats and experts working in different institutions are slightly higher, ranging between 90,000 and 200,000 Tshs (ILO 2014). In Uganda there is no fixed wage for a domestic worker and it depends on what the employer is willing to pay or the domestic worker is willing to accept. Consequently, the employer can set a very small pay for a worker, since there is no legal obligation.

Although domestic work is not regulated in Uganda and Tanzania, employees can report, like any other employee, to the District Labour Officer, who will call the employer to settle the matter. If the complaint is not resolved, it may be brought to the attention of the Labour Commissioner. In the cases of Tanzania, a house help may reach the social welfare office within the local area to complain against any form of mistreatment that cannot be tolerated. Furthermore, basic social and health care workers do not have employment contracts. Therefore, when they enter the labour market, they usually do not know their rights. The absence of employment contracts makes it easier for employers to terminate domestic staff at will without any notification. This is one of the reasons domestic staff do not have job security at their places of work. Such labour rights as annual leave and social security is still a huge challenge in the South. A recent study indicated that 70% of domestic workers in Tanzania have never been given chance to go for their annual leave (ILO 2014). In many cases, when the family goes for a holiday, a domestic worker is required to remain at home for security purposes. In addition, even though the laws in Uganda and Tanzania generally recognise a notice period for termination of services, domestic workers hardly receive it from their employers and vice versa. This is because it has been abused by the workers in a manner that disadvantages employers. Once served with a notice period, some domestic workers have been known to steal from their employers, become in-disciplined, abandon the job and begin to render poor quality services.

While domestic workers in East-Africa have no collective representative such as the union for practical nurses in Finland, their bargaining power depends on the value which individual employers attach to their services. The work is sometimes so valuable that employers are willing to put up with their limitations than dispense them off. Imoit (personal communication, October 21, 2015) mentioned that;

I have children… though I have always been sceptical about the conduct of domestic staff towards children, especially with the recent trend where some of them molest and abuse kids in the absence of the parents, I can't resist having one. I have decided to get one. The pressure from my place of work became too much and I became unable to bear the responsibility of giving my children the moral support they need…. I developed a means of relating with my house maid so that she would treat my children well… I buy clothes for her once in a while and I give her 'tips'… so far it has worked she takes care of my home and children properly when I am not around.

Agunyo (personal communication, June, 13, 2015) observed that "Employees may do away with a relative who is at loggerheads with a distinguished house help within a home." Acen (personal communication, October 22, 2015) concludes that some employees are even willing to employ and accommodate female house helps in their homes with pregnancies or children. Due to good behaviour and hard work, some house helps have pleased their employers and get opportunity to go to schools for academic education or vocational courses paid by their employers, employers give them property at their death, or sponsor their children and relatives' education. Some house helps start small businesses after accumulating enough money and start their own successful family life (Tanzanian University Teacher, personal communication, June 2015).

4.3 Comparative remarks

In their reflections the participants of the ReWell project assumed that in both locations, the traditional patterns of generational socialization are eroding and the familial solutions cannot provide qualified basic social and health care. In Finland, the reduction of the universalist, impersonal and public welfare, in the absence of familial patterns of care, is threatening the personal agency and citizenship of both providers and consumers of social and health care. In East-Africa, economization of care relations may threaten indigenous forms of life without systems of public recognition and protection. In the Table 1, a provisory comparison is suggested between agency in basic social and health care work, which is assumed to contribute to agency of individuals and collectives in the wider context of civic and occupational life.

Table 1: Comparing agency in basic social and health care between Finland and East-Africa.

Finland	East-Africa
Union of practical nurses, bargaining power. Societal recognition and occupational-ization of basic social and health care work. An important part of vocational educa-tion. Public, formal (legally controlled) responsibility and maintenance of occupation and education by taxes, i.e. universalist social security: economic and social independence of individuals from informal (family, relatives) struc-tures and networks. Formal, monetary, impersonal social relations: vulnerability during reduc-tion/deregulation of social and health services. Participation in CD processes at national, representative level, but HE graduates of social and health care dominate, especially at regional level as teachers, administrators and work-life representatives.	No mobilization of either employers or employees in basic social and health care, despite dissatisfaction. No formal recognition as certificates, tariff agreements, salary scales, labour contracts. Not part of "vocational education and training." Informally recognized: flexible adapta-tion among families, kinships and local communities to external economic and employment change and to informal division of work, to social and economic status between women. Private, non-monetary economic sphere – marginal public (tax-based) system for welfare. Socialization into house help work is controlled by families/kinship, employ-ees, and employers. Informal, sex-based division of health and social care is (also) an aspect of 'indigenous' ways to make a living, related to social and ethical values.

The apparent differences between the global North and the global South might still be functional for the global commodity chains, where local cultural particularities support the dominant geo-economic and politi-cal order, and promotes the competitiveness of local and national indus-tries. (Kerswell 2011; Moisio *et al.* 2013.) This includes subsumption or exploitation of traditional moral and religious practices for justification of division of work between and among sexes, whether it takes place in an occupationalized and monetized form as is the case in Finland or unstructured as in East Africa. (Narotzky 1997). Furthermore, differ-ent solutions may provide social and physical compensation in front of global economic imperatives, but they also indicate differences in the 'agency of regions' or countries in geo-economic competition.

On the surface, organization and practices in basic social health care work and education in Finland and East-Africa seem as if they would represent different planets: the one based on public and collectiveness, the other on familial and individual responsibility and recognition. On the other hand, the current policies in Finland supporting initiatives in the private sector, and proposed in the ReWell project for East-Africa, are strikingly similar. In the global North, globalization is used as a justification for reducing public responsibility, for promoting private provision and individual responsibility. In the global South, the lack of tradition and trust in public solutions and the growth of a wealthy middle-class justify the focus on private, individualized basic social and health care, hopefully leading to public, collective systems, guaranteed by legislation. In the hegemonic geo-economic and geopolitical agendas, places and people are valued differently depending on their capacities to operate in markets. Therefore, the social and health care policies in Finland support the creation of commercially efficient urban metropoles integrated to trans-national 'social and health commodity chains', however still building on public funding and regulations. In East-Africa the lack of public infrastructure and funding, in connection to corruption in governance and massive poverty, seems to justify hopes for more universal care through markets. (Moisio *et al.* 2013).

5. Concluding remarks

The practical nurse in Finland and the house help or domestic worker in East Africa might be called hybrid occupations, which are exemplary for global change in social and health care work. The first is an outcome of socio-political decision, where education is used for creation of a new occupation to bridge traditional division between social and health care work. This relates to long-term policy of improving vocational education through upgrading vocational teachers to higher education graduates, who do not represent the occupation of the students, and rather identify with their own educational and occupational background either in social or in health care. In this context, development of competence-based curriculum sounds paradoxical, while it should not reproduce previous occupational profiles any more. The second hybrid seems to be an extremely flexible reaction to diverse demands of labour markets and welfare needs, which are weakly regulated or publicly controlled. The lack of recognition and formal qualifications makes it almost impossible for workers to have agency and ownership of their occupation.

It is high time for public and private vocational education colleges in East-Africa to think about special courses for home nurses or house helps to expose them to various skills, knowledge about their rights and contracts. The social ties and needs are rapidly changing in Tanzanian and Ugandan societies. There are several homes full of old men and women who need help and support. In many cases, religious institutions are taking care of them with the support of informally educated helpers. Even with the affluent families in the society, it has almost become impossible for them to stay and survive without a house help because everyone is either studying or working in a public, private or self-employed job. They need someone to help children, disabled or elderly people in the house. Formal education is believed to be the weapon for their work to be recognized by relevant authorities and the entire community may change the current attitudes towards them.

Basic social and health care is indispensable for the general wellbeing, safety and democracy in any community and requires collective political decisions and solutions. Public authorities, such as ministries of social welfare, work, labour and employment and labour organizations should commit to international guidelines and conventions to guarantee equal rights to wellbeing. Governments should enforce all regulations and legal structure to enhance the status and rights of workers in basic social and health care. They should implement training policies and vocational education institutions for basic and social health care, fixed salary scales and laws against persons who employ minors as domestic workers. It may not be, however, possible or rational only to wait for policy-makers and public authorities to solve the challenges in the global South. Wealthy families may have more concerns about quality and willingness to pay for qualified basic social and health care providers. Educational institutes may be freer to develop programmes and qualifications for them.

Even in the global North, it is questionable whether current reforms are increasing the ownership and agency of practitioners in developing social and health care, when trans-national businesses can increasingly dictate its aims and content. The agency of practitioners in CD processes relates to their agency in wider society and labour markets. The practical nurses in Finland are highly and collectively organized, but how far are global labour associations interested in extending similar strategies and practices to opposite end of 'global commodity chains', although this would benefit some of the most vulnerable workers in the global division of labour? A step forward could be borrowing of some practices in the North, such as establishing a union, as a strategy for improving workers´ agency in basic social and health care.

What is the agency of educational institutions and actors, beside citizens, public authorities and workers themselves, in developing basic social and health care? One alternative could be to develop collaboration and dialogue between universities and teacher education institutes with practitioners, unions and policy-makers. Educators are key actors in raising continuous awareness among workers about their rights and responsibilities and among employers – whether private or public – to enable decent conditions for work.

References

Advertising Dar 2016. House Maid available in Dar-es-Salaam. [retrieved from: <http://www.advertisingdar.com/ads/house-maids-dar-es-sal aam/> – July, 28th 2016].

Archer, M. 1996. Culture and Agency. The Place of Culture in Social Theory. Cambridge, Cambridge University Press.

Employment Act 2006. [retrieved from: <http://mywage.ug/home/labour-laws/domestic-workers> – July, 28th 2016].

Eteläpelto, A., Vähäsantanen, K., Hökkä, P., & Paloniemi, S. 2013. What is agency? Conceptualizing professional agency at work. Educational Research Review 10: 45–65.

European Commission 2008. The European Qualification Framework for Lifelong Learning (EQF). [retrieved from: <http://www.ond.vlaan deren.be/hogeronderwijs/bologna/news/EQF_EN.pdf> – July, 28th 2016].

Finnish National Board of Education 2013. [retrieved from: <http://www.oph.fi/download/156393_Competencebased_qualification_guide_2.pdf> – July, 28th 2016].

Finnish National Board of Education 2015. Inspiring and Strengthening the Competence-Based Approach in all VET in Finland: Support material for implementation. [retrieved from: <http://www.oph.fi/download/167400_inspiring_and_strengthening_the_competence-based_approach_in_all_VET_in_finl.pdf> – July, 28th 2016].

Glucksman, M. (1995). Why work? Gender and the Total Social Organization of Labour. Gender, Work and Organization 2/1995.

Grahn-Laasonen, S. 2016. Skills and education. Action plan for the implementation of the key project and reforms defined in strategic government programme. Prime minister's office. [retrieved from: <http://valtioneuvosto.fi/documents/10616/1986338/Action+plan+for+the+implementation+Strategic+Government+Programme+EN.pdf/12f723ba-6f6b-4e6c-a636-4ad4175d7c4e> – July, 28th 2016].

Heikkinen, A., Kalimasi, P., & Opith, E. 2015. Regional Responsibility in Vocational Education – views from Global North and South. Presentation in Vocational Education and Citizenship-Conference, Valencia, 6.–8.7.2015.

ILO 2014. Domestic Workers in the United Republic of Tanzania: Summary of the Findings of a Situational Analysis. ILO, Dar es Salaam.

Ikiriza, K. E. 2014. (Presenter). 2014, January 15 Kick Start Radio Show. Kampala, Uganda. Power FM.

Järvinen, M. 1993. Koulutus hoivatyöhön: terveydenhuoltoalan koulutuksen muotoutuminen ja tulevaisuuden näkymät. Turku, Turun yliopisto.

Kalliomaa-Puha, L., Kangas, O. 2016. In-depth reform of the health-care system in Finland. ESPN Flash Report. 2016/34.

Kerswell, T. 2011. The Global Division of Labour and the Division in Global Labour. Doctoral Thesis. School of humanities and social services. Quensland, Queensland University of Technology.

Lyamba, N., Sjelvgren, J., Lee, Sang-A & Andresen, A. 2015. Analysis of Finnish Practical Nurse Education in the Context of Work Experiences, a field study. Unpublished Report. Tampere, University of Tampere.

Moilanen, P. 1999. Piilevä tieto ja reflektio. In H. Heikkinen, R. Huttunen & P. Moilanen (eds.), Siinä tutkija missä tekijä – toimintatutkimuksen perusteita ja näköaloja. Juva, Atena Kustannus.

Moisio, S., & Paasi, A. 2013. From Geopolitical to Geoeconomic? The Changing Political Rationalities of State Space. Geopolitics. DOI:10.1080/ 14650045.2012.723287.

Narotzky, S. (1997). New Directions in Economic Anthropology. London, Pluto Press.

Opetus- ja kulttuuriministeriö 2012. Koulutus ja tutkimus vuosina 2011–2016: kehittämissuunnitelma. [retrieved from: <http://www.minedu.fi/export/sites/default/OPM/Julkaisut/2012/liitteet/okm01.pdf?lang=fi> – July, 28th 2016].

Opetushallitus. 2010. Vocational qualification in social and health care: practical nurse. [retrieved from: <http://oph.fi/download/140436_vocational_qualification_in_social_and_healthcare_2010.pdf> – July, 28th 2016].

Pierce, J.L., Kostova, T. & Dirsk, K. T. 2001. Toward a Theory of Psychological Ownership in organizations. Academy of Management Review 2: 298–310.

Seppälä, T. & Pekurinen, M. (eds.) 2014. Sosiaali- ja terveydenhuollon keskeiset rahavirrat. THL. [retrieved from: <https://www.julkari.fi/bitstream/handle/10024/116653/THL_RAP022_2014verkko.pdf?sequence=1> – July, 28th 2016].

Sjelvgren, J. 2016. Vocational Teachers' Agency and Psychological Ownership in the Curriculum Development Process of Practical Nurse Qualification (in Finnish). Master's Thesis. Tampere, University of Tampere. [retrieved from: <https://tampub.uta.fi/bitstream/handle/10024/98598/GRADU-1455787401.pdf?sequence=1> – July, 28th 2016].

Superliitto 2014. Statistics about practical nurses in labour market. [retrieved from: <https://www.superliitto.fi/viestinta/ajankohtaista/lahihoitajat-tyomarkkinoilla/> – July, 28th 2016].

Superliitto 2016. Practical nurse training. [retrieved from: <https://www.superliitto.fi/in-english/practical-nursetraining/> – July, 28th 2016].

Tilastokeskus 2013. Total incomes according to occupation and sex (Kokonaisansiot ammatin ja sukupuolen mukaan). [retrieved from: <http://tilastokeskus.fi/tup/suoluk/suoluk_palkat.html#keskiansio-ammatti> – July, 28th 2016].

.

Lorenz Lassnigg and Stefan Vogtenhuber

VET Producing Second Class Citizens? Comparative Analyses of the VET and Tertiary Education Nexus

1. Introduction

In summer 2016 the Austrian conference about VET research was organised under the heading of a *"Renaissance of VET?"*.[1] Several facets of VET were mentioned in the outline of the conference: innovation, employment, participation, advancement, prosperity…; however an important aspect of education was missing: *citizenship and democracy*. In the Germanic tradition, VET has been situated at the secondary level and was always juxtaposed markedly against higher education, with VET having a highly instrumental and useful mission, whereas higher education, based on elitist academic secondary school (Gymnasium) has been related to the higher ranks of the society and polity, and to "real" education (Bildung). Consequently an old common saying in the social democratic policy discourse about the relationship of vocational and (elitist academic) general education has been that general education were the vocational education of those dominating society (die Berufsbildung der Herrschenden). A solution for these class divisions was seen in an extended amalgamation of general and vocational education by an enrichment of VET with general content.[2] In Germany the division between VET and higher education has been even called the *education-(Bildungs)-schism*, and vocational pedagogy has tried to reframe the education policy discourse by including a vocation as

---

1 See <http://www.bbfk.at/> Title: „Berufsbildung, eine Renaissance? Motor für Innovation, Beschäftigung, Teilhabe, Aufstieg, Wohlstand, […]".

2 The Swedish comprehensive upper secondary school can be seen as an attempt to realise this ideal, howsoever it works in practice.

constitutive element of *real* general education (Bildung). Higher education and VET has been strictly separated in this tradition, and the legal definition of higher education as part of VET is completely alien to it. However, if we accentuate the difference between higher education and VET in a more general sense, then the component of citizenship is a much more pronounced element in the understanding of higher education – thus VET has an ambivalent position in the Anglophone tradition, on the one hand it is part of higher education, institutionalised in the professional schools, on the other it is devalued as a second choice track at the secondary level.

These phenomena illustrate that the positioning of VET in the overall education and career structures is contested and ambivalent; the saying of *being different but of equal value* (gleichwertig, nicht gleichartig) is an expression of this ambivalence. A main message in this chapter is that because of various mostly incremental regroupings towards institutional diversity and hybridity, the clear division between VET and higher education is gradually vanishing. In terms of citizenship it must also been reminded that the accompanying school to apprenticeship had originally been devoted to civic purposes, however, much towards adaptation and integration of the young people into the state, and avoiding them to be seduced by socialist or revolutionary ideas of the time. Today VET has become defined rather practically, technically and instrumentally vis-a-vis higher education, with the ideal of a straightforward matching to the labour market demands in the foreground. Currently, the expansion of higher education by the widening access policies in the UK has been called even a threat to the economy.

In the international policy discourse VET did not have a particular good standing vs. higher education since the mid-20th century when the *vocational fallacy* (Foster 1965) was announced in the 1960s, saying that good careers were achieved by completers from general education, followed by results about low returns from VET by early world bank studies in the 1980s and later the problematisation of extensively high adaptation costs for school-based state-provided VET in the 1990s (Middleton, Ziderman and Van Adams 1993). The emphasis has been laid rather on higher education for a long time; however, the persistent and even worsening problems on the youth labour market, newly fired by the 2007 worldwide crisis, have guided the political emphasis back to VET, particularly to the German apprenticeship system.

This chapter tackles the questions related to citizenship in a rather indirect manner. Acquisition of educational credentials at a basic stage is today commonly agreed as a citizens' right, and we also know that the opportunity of access to these credentials that is unequally distributed everywhere, is also dependent to some degree on the institutional structure of education. Two major longer-term international shifts in the educational structure have emerged since the early 20th century. One major change has been a shift from organisationally tracked structures at the lower secondary level to comprehensive structures until the end of compulsory schooling, and this change has been motivated by the goal to increase equality of opportunity in access to educational credentials. The split between higher- and lower-level programmes according to more or less valuable credentials has been postponed to a stage after compulsory education by this change. Some countries, however, have not followed this change until recently, and among these countries we find some commonly known as comprising comparatively successful VET systems at upper secondary level, among them Austria, Germany, and Switzerland.

Another major structural change in education during recent decades has been that (part of) the more advanced VET institutions have been upgraded to the post-secondary or tertiary level, thus leading to more differentiated and broader higher education systems that include more vocationally or professionally oriented institutions besides traditional universities. This change conventionally called *mass higher education* is closely related to a change in the pattern of educational careers, as the access to the postponed VET-programmes or institutions shifted – at least to some degree – to the general (academic) programmes that previously worked as the pipeline towards the traditional universities. Historically, in the tracked structures of the past, these had been the more or less elitist higher-level academic schools in general education (some kinds of gymnasium, and the like), that have also broadened their access structure, or amalgamated with mass schools, and in several systems shifted the elitist track to the upper secondary level.

Taken together the two structural changes of comprehensiveness at the lower secondary level and mass higher education at the tertiary level, have given leeway for the stage of upper secondary education, where VET traditionally had been situated, and the relationship between vocational and general (academic) has become much more complex than before. The question arises of how VET is structurally positioned in these changes and dynamics, and further, which consequences might follow for the position in the stratification patterns in society.

This chapter explores the formal qualification structures in different countries in a comparative perspective and tries to interpret the positioning of VET in a more dynamic perspective of the expansion of tertiary education. The attempt is driven by the emphasis on a more neutral understanding of the changes, with a priory neither advocating superiority of higher education nor defending VET against the expansion of higher education. In the next section an argumentative framework is set up by summarizing some key concepts and developments in the discourse, which might contribute to a broader understanding of the dynamic. Then the structures of education based on statistical information are analysed, with a focus on the understanding of the positioning of VET in the overall structures.

2. Understandings and interpretations of structural changes in education: Massification, diversion, cooling out, de-occupationalisation and professionalization

In terms of standard careers and equality of opportunity these changes have been appraised quite ambiguously, and to some part controversial. The comprehensive structure of compulsory education seems widely established and is currently opposed and openly disputed only in a few – seemingly backward – countries, while influential players (e.g., European Commission or OECD) also expect it to increase equality of opportunity quite straightforward. It should be reminded also, that the justification of comprehensiveness was strongly driven by democratic ideals, not primarily by efficiency arguments. Ideas about an equity-efficiency trade-off were always prevalent, and also seem more recently undermine again the Nordic consensus about the common school.

Mass higher education, however, has always been perceived more contradictorily. On the one hand it expands access to education, as more young people prolong their education careers and earn additional credentials. On the other hand the expanded access towards higher education involves institutional differentiation and is spread across a wider spectre of programmes and/or institutions, which carry higher or lower levels of value and esteem. Two classical formulations, coined by famous (but somehow forgotten) publications, have characterised these ambiguities in case of the US Community Colleges, where these changes have occurred earlier than in most other countries. One is that of the *Diverted Dream* (Brint and Karabel 1989), and the other is that of *Cooling Out* (Clark 1960, 1980). The message is twofold: first that the broadening of higher education by vocationally oriented institutions would divert some part of the younger people, mostly from less privileged backgrounds, towards educational careers that are of lower value than those they would have accessed in the previous structure; second, that this allocation would be (seemingly) transferred from institutional selection procedures to the choice of individuals (the *diversion*), thus hiding the still working tracking mechanisms of the institutional structure behind individualisation. The cooling out mechanism includes as a decisive element the institutionalisation of guidance procedures as a (partly) substitute for selection procedures (which are a core part of today's policy devices promoted by the European or international institutions under headlines like lifelong guidance).

The two structural changes thus have shifted the main selection procedure from the lower secondary level in traditionally tracked structures to the stage of access to higher education, and have simultaneously changed the selection procedures by on the one hand expanding the pool of individuals potentially selected for higher education and on the other hand by shifting the focus of selection from external decisions predefined by structures towards internal decisions by the individuals in more permeable structures. Through the quantitative expansion towards mass higher education, access to this level has become much more of a successful standard career, which had previously been the acquisition of decent employment after secondary education, including kinds of vocational education and/or training. This shift towards differentiated higher education has also – overtly or silently – changed the structures and positioning of upper secondary education that increasingly became a transitional stage between compulsory education and higher education, and it also changed the position of compulsory education that increasingly received a preparatory role towards higher education.

An important aspect of understanding VET structures has always been its relationship to the occupational structure and its relationship to employment. This relationship is established in paradigmatic form with apprenticeship that defines the occupations and provides training and education at the workplace in combination with productive work. However, with economic and structural change the historical ideal of stable occupational structures increasingly has eroded (de-occupationalisation, Entberuflichung),[3] and processes of professionalization emerged in several fields that included the upgrading of education to tertiary or higher education level (*professionalization of everyone*). This dynamic of de-occupationalisation and professionalization was related to the combination of Fordist mass production in industry that needed un- or semiskilled workers and the expansion of the service sector that needed new kinds of personnel. Important examples of these upgrading processes are the caring and health professions or social work that have in parallel developed also their formalised knowledge bases. These upgrading processes create more ownership by the qualified personnel over the occupation, however, might also lead to new kinds of stratification within the field. Currently the caring professions are under a process of upgrading to the tertiary level in Austria; however, a new layer of helpers' occupations has been also formally established at a level of medium qualifications.

In terms of stratification and citizenship these changes might take different forms and configurations that also carry overlapping and competing concepts and discourses:

---

3   Following a saying in the 1970s in Germany, the biggest bakery was a well-known big plant of the automobile industry because it has employed the highest number of bakers at this time; ironically, the new technological developments lead to new production methods that indeed introduce baking of substantial parts of automobiles instead of mechanical assembling them.

– *Democracy, manpower demand, meritocracy, over education, skills matching.* The reforms towards increased equality of opportunity have increased the pool of applicants to higher education, however, that did not mean the same increase of access. Very different intentions can be found behind the expansion of higher education. One was a broadening of access and democratisation of the elite positions, another the provision of additional human capital, still another the increase of meritocratic competition for access to higher education; given the stratification in society and the relative scarcity of higher positions the quality of credentials as positional goods became clear and the question of containment came up, signified by the term over education, with skills matching as its positive formulation.

– *Elite-mass-universal higher education.* This discourse has taken different meaning and focus in the US vs. other regions; in the US the focus was on the differentiation of parallel and hierarchically ordered complementary sectors within higher education, whereas in Europe with its more homogenous universities – at least in some regions, e.g. Austria or Germany – the notion was more of a mass expansion of (formerly perceived) traditional elite institutions, or of a systemic change. However, quite different paths were found. In the Nordic countries comprehensive school was compatible with highly selective universities, whereas in Austria those who fought for democratisation demanded open access to university and also strongly objected differentiation of higher education; in Germany the concept of a comprehensive higher education institution (Gesamthochschule Kassel) was developed for democratisation. France and the UK have developed their own stratified structures. In practice the concept of mass higher education became increasingly understood as mediocre overcrowded institutions, and the elite institutions carry two different meanings that are difficult to reconcile: one of social exclusivity and elite reproduction, and another of outstanding research production. In terms of stratification these meanings go seldom hand in hand, as the researchers are not typically the social and political elites, they to some part act as their educators, and give the legitimation for the elite status. VET is in the US structure embedded in the professional schools in the different kinds of universities, and in the Community Colleges that provide wide arrays of diverse programmes.

– *Bologna process, qualifications frameworks, higher VET, vocationalization of higher education.* In Europe and beyond the Bologna process and the establishment of qualifications frameworks provide frameworks towards vocationalization of higher education, and the differentiation of teaching and research. This reinforces the different understanding and classification of higher education as part of vocational education in the EU vs. a wider understanding as general education in the US (and inspired by this structure also by the widely US-influenced economics of education). The understandings seem to differ particularly with respect to the bachelor level which is described mainly as aspiring preparatory general education in the US, whereas it should provide a step towards employability in the Bologna model. These new structures must be considered specifically to understand the future development of VET and higher education.

3. Identifying institutional structures of tracking and vocational education

The empirical structural positioning of vocational education is analysed here by using three comparative data-bases:[4] first participation at secondary level by the institutional classifications provided by the *OECD-Education-at-a-Glance-(EAG)* statistics, second more detailed tracking variables within schools at age 15 observed by the *Program for International Student Assessment (PISA)*[5] through surveying the principals,

---

4   This analysis builds on previous comparative work that tried to find structural and achievement relationships between primary, secondary and tertiary education; see Lassnigg 2009, 2011.

5   The wider analyses have used variables from the *PISA* 2009 and 2012 survey among the principals that indicate the proportion of 15-year old students experiencing different versions of grouping by achievement within class or within school. Three variables are available in 2009 across all subjects and in 2012 only in math:
     (1) proportion of students that undergo an exam for achievement-grouping,
     (2) proportion of students in different classes within school according to achievement (2009 named streaming, 2012 ability grouping between classes), (3) proportion of

and third the participation patterns of the population attended in initial education surveyed by the *PIAAC-data*.[6]

Taken together, these information bases allow to draw a more differentiated comparative picture of the patterns of initial education in various countries of the OECD and beyond than by the conventionally used single indicators. The following aspects can be combined on a cross-sectional country-by-country level:

–   age of first tracking by institutions/programmes in compulsory education (*PISA*).
–   early vocational education: proportion of VET at age 15 (*PISA*).
–   proportion of VET at upper secondary level (*EAG*).
–   participation in different tracks of tertiary education (*EAG*).
–   combinations of participation in education and employment, as well as affection of unemployment and non-employment by younger age groups 15–29 (*EAG*).
–   attention by levels and categories of initial education of the population (*PIAAC*)
–   participation in adult education (*PIAAC*)

The analysis of these data gives some more differentiated patterns of how vocational education is embedded in different countries in the overall institutional structures of education from compulsory to higher education. Two different perspectives are taken to classify the structures, first the *PIAAC data* describe a kind of longer term average structure that has produced the stock of qualifications owned by the current population, and second the *PISA* and *EAG data* describe the current structure of young cohorts.

According to the first wave of *PIAAC*, the participating countries can be described at a four-dimensional space by levels of education

---

students according to ability grouping within classes. The argument in this chapter uses the variable (2) about streaming.

6   24 countries and regions participated in the first round of the *PIAAC survey* in 2011–12, first published in OECD 2013; the cross-sectional analysis was performed using two groups of countries: all participants of the first wave, and a selection of advanced capitalist countries according to the Esping-Andersen welfare regimes (liberal Canada, UK-England, US; Nordic: Denmark, Finland, Sweden; Continental: Austria, Germany, Netherlands (partly Belgium-Flanders).

(tertiary, secondary, and less than secondary), and by additionally taking into account the proportion of vocational education (see fig.1).[7] Using these rough indicators, we can descriptively identify three quite clearly distinct clusters (1 *low education*, 2 *VET*, and 3 *tertiary*), two of which can be extended to more indistinct groups (2a *VET* and 2b *VET* extended; 3a *tertiary* and 3b *tertiary* extended), and Canada as an outstanding case with very high tertiary education:

Cluster 1: 1 *low education* cluster (ES, CY, IT): these countries are forming a clearly distinct group with more than one third of the population below secondary education, and all of them less than 40% owning secondary and less than 30% of the population owning tertiary education.

Cluster 2: 2a *VET* (CZ, AT, SK) and 2b *VET* extended (PL, DE, SE) clusters: Qualifications from vocational education are owned by a high proportion of the population only in this group of six countries, which can already be perceived as exceptions to the mainstream of the expansion of higher education, in this group secondary education is comparatively high and tertiary education comparatively low. In five of these countries more than half of the population own secondary education, and in four of these countries half to two thirds of secondary graduates also own vocational credentials (CZ, AT, PL, DE); the two further countries (SK with a lower proportion of VET, and SE as a special case that does not really fit into any cluster) show some similarities to this group. The proportion of tertiary education, however, despite comparatively low to the average of *PIAAC countries*, differs quite markedly in this group, between 15–20% (AT, CZ) and 30% (DE); in the conventional classification these proportions give the benchmarks for elite (15%) and mass (30%) higher education.

---

7   The three levels (tertiary, secondary and less than secondary sum up to 100%, so the oblique lines as a third dimension give the levels of low educated, resulting from the sum of tertiary and secondary education; the fourth dimension is given by the proportion of vocational education of secondary education, as indicated by the size of the bubble and the country labels (bold labels VET over 30%; regular labels VET 20–30%; + VET below 20%).

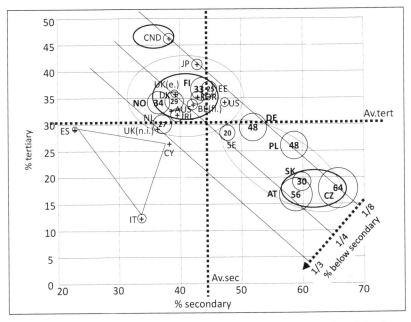

Figure 1: Comparison of education structures of populations in *PIAAC* participating countries.

Source: Own calculation and picture based on *PIAAC data* (Lassnigg and Vogtenhuber 2014).

Cluster 3: 3a *tertiary* (UK-e.-n.i., FI, EE, NO, DK, KOR, AUS, BE-fl., IRL) cluster, and three further countries (JP with more tertiary educated, US more secondary, and NL with both less tertiary and secondary and more low educated) in 3b *tertiary extended* cluster; in these clusters comprising together half of the *PIAAC* first wave countries, the proportion of secondary education among the adult population ranges mostly below average (35–45%), however, the proportion of VET among secondary graduates differs: the range lies between zero and one third, thus more tertiary education does not necessarily rule out vocational education; the VET proportion is higher (grossly 30–35%) in Nordic countries (NO, FI, DK), Estonia and the Netherlands (25–30%), compared to the Anglophone countries (UK, US, AUS, IRL), as well as the East-Asian countries (JP, KOR) and Belgium-Flanders (where it lies below 20%).

Canada is outstanding with the highest proportion of tertiary education (almost 50% which would indicate the benchmark of universal tertiary education), and an overall highly educated population.[8]

In comparing these clusters, we find three different structures with respect to the representation of secondary level vocational education in the educational attainment of the population. In the VET cluster(s), participation in vocational education seems to be an alternative pathway to higher education, with a proportion of VET in the total population between 25–40% (a: CZ, AT, SK, PL, DE, SE); in the TERTIARY cluster(s) vocational education seems to form two fairly distinct groups of countries, one which includes secondary vocational education as a distinct but more complementary pathway with participation in VET between 10–15% and some division of labour between secondary and tertiary institutions (b: FI, NO, DK, EE, NL), and another group of countries where tertiary education almost completely dominates and VET participation at secondary level is only very small (c: UK, US, AUS, IRL, JP, KOR, BE-fl) – in this third group vocational education seems to be embedded as a part in (differentiated) tertiary education structures (this structure seems most clearly pronounced in Canada).

Asking, how these attainment patterns are embedded in the wider institutional structures, analyses of the data from *PISA* and *EAG*[9] can be utilised, that give information about tracking structures at age 15 and participation at the overall upper secondary level. These data do not represent the population but only the young cohorts enrolled in education, and thus can indicate changes towards the current institutional structures (whereas the above structures based on *PIAAC* respondents represent a kind of longer term average qualifications structure of the population built up through the five to six decades since the 1940 and 1950s till the 2010s).

---

8   See also the chapter about Canada in the present volume that explains the structure more deeply.

9   The data sources differ from *PIAAC* that collects survey information from the respondents to the achievement testing, as *PISA* collects information from the school principals where the testing takes place, and *EAG* rests on mixed information bases, partly from surveys and partly from official national sources as the Statistical Offices and/or government agencies. Thus there might be inconsistencies between the information sources, from which robust typologies can be derived by triangulation and informed judgement based on further qualitative sources.

Fig 2 shows basic structures of how vocational education has been built into the education structures in the 2000s. Two observations must be mentioned: first that the broad variety between countries is distributed only gradually (not very distinctively), consequently countries can be grouped to some types that, however, are not very homogenous; second, an underlying expansionary dynamic of participation must be taken into account that makes the typology rather transient than stable.

	...combination with EAG 2006: proportion of VET at upper secondary level			
	1 early select low-medium VET upS (10-45%)	2 modest postp.sel. low-medium VET upS (5-45%)	3 early select high VET upS (60-80%)	4 late select medium high VET upS (35-65%)
PISA 2006: A first classification of VET structures 1: one programme, 1st selection 16, no VET at 15 — AUS, CND, [NZ], UK, US — DK, FIN, [IS], NO, SE — PL, ES, [LV]				AUS DK, FIN, NO, SE, [IS] PL, ES
2: 1st selection 13-15, low VET at 15 (below 20%) — [EL], IT, [PT, LUX], EE, [LT]		IT, [EL, PT]	[LUX]	
3: 1st selection 13-15, medium VET at 15 (20-40%) — IRL, JP, KOR, [RO]			IRL, JP, KOR	
3a: 1st selection 13-15, high VET at 15 (40%+) — [SI]				
4: 1st selection 10-12, low VET at 15 (below 20%) — CZ, [HU], SK, [BG, MEX, TR]	[HU, MEX, TR]		CZ, SK	
5: 1st selection 10-12, medium VET at 15 (20-40%) — BE*, GER, [CH]			BE*, DE, [CH]	
6: 1st selection 10-12, high VET at 15 (40%+) — AT, NL			AT, NL	

Figure 2: VET-typology based on combined *PISA* and *EAG* information.

Source: *PISA* 2006 (first selection between programmes; VET at age 15 = early VET), *EAG* 2006 (proportion of VET at upper secondary level = late VET); Explanation: all countries in *PISA* and *EAG*, VET-participation is missing in *EAG* for most Anglophone countries (CND, NZ, UK, US), and for some transition countries (LV, LT, RO, SI, BG); countries in [ ] not represented in *PIAAC* (NZ, IS, LV, PT, LUX, LT, RO, SI, HU, BG, MEX, TR, CH).

Three dimensions are basically combined:

Dimension 1: begin of tracking at lower secondary level that has been gradually postponed from age 10–12 (early tracked structures) to age 16 (comprehensive structures), with several countries lying in between).

Dimension 2: early starting of VET participation before age 15, that to some part overlays the early tracking structures, however, not all tracked structures also include an early start of vocational education.

Dimension 3: VET participation at the whole of upper secondary level, which includes early starting structures, and can also comprise quite extended age groups of young adults up to the mid-twenties within the upper secondary level (thus including structures where vocational education can take place in three parallel tracks, upper secondary, post-secondary, and tertiary/higher education, which might be difficult to distinguish and also might be not consistently classified in national and/or international perspectives).[10]

So we can find diverse structures between two extreme poles represented by a small minority of countries. One pole is represented by the traditional structure with a tracked lower secondary level, combined with early starting and high participation in VET at upper secondary level, and comparatively low participation in tertiary or higher education on the one extreme (represented most purely by Austria; only the Netherlands[11] fall in the same category with early selection, high early VET and high VET at upper secondary level); the other pole is represented by a comprehensive structure with mainly general education at upper secondary level, and VET postponed to the postsecondary or tertiary level on the other extreme (represented most purely by Canada and the US).

Tertiary education has a polarised positioning and sends oppositional signals in these extreme types of structures on the one end it is exceptional with low participation (resembling a traditional elite-structure with more or less dominating universities within the tertiary level), on the other end tertiary education is perceived as a predominating

10   The German structure, as an example, comprises (i) the large Dual apprenticeship system with participation well into the 20–25-age group including participants with abitur/university access credentials, (ii) post-secondary institutions like the *Berufsakademie*, (iii) two tracks of higher education, Fachhochschule which is more vocationally oriented, and university which is more academically oriented) – depending on what is classified as tertiary, the proportions might differ substantially.

11   This classification shows that the quite common grouping of the Germanic apprenticeship systems of Germany, Switzerland, and Austria do not fall in the same structure, if systematically classified by available indicators.

norm (resembling a universal structure) but is at the same time differentiated to levels with different value and a high degree of selection to the different levels within tertiary education.

Looking at the empirical structures, however, these extreme types are exceptions, and most countries lie in between, with less distinct and simple structures (whereas the political discourses might be influenced by the images of the extreme types, putting them against each other). Empirically these in-between-structures can be grouped to the following types:

– comprehensive structures at lower secondary level with late selection, providing VET in different ways at upper secondary level, in parallel to higher education (this structure can be found in the Nordic countries, in Australia, and in Spain and Poland).
– structures with moderately postponed first selection, providing VET to different but lesser degrees at upper secondary level (comprising the East-Asian countries Japan and Korea, together with Ireland, with higher VET participation, and some Mediterranean countries, Italy, Greece, and Portugal with lower VET participation).
– early tracked structures with low to medium proportions of early starting VET, gradually increasing to high participation in vocational education at upper secondary level, that also might provide access to tertiary education (this structure appears in Germany, Switzerland, and Belgium with more early starting VET, and in the Czech and Slovak Republics with less early starting VET).

The empirical description indicates much less clear-cut structures than the discourses about the positioning of VET often signify. The positioning of VET at upper secondary level and in the flow of careers is diverse, and can be interpreted on the background of a gradual movement of countries along *the expansion of tertiary education that simultaneously changes the basic missions of all sectors and levels of education.* This change is overseen or neglected, if the different educational structures are interpreted as a kind of a discrete shift from VET to higher education, implicitly assuming that both structures, VET and higher education, would remain the same – often this assumption is underlying the discourse. However, using quantitative information about participation the wider changes in VET and higher education either, according to their inner structures, qualities, missions, etc. cannot be seen. VET is very diverse in many terms, and its comparative statistical descriptors are reduced to whether instruction is combined with work or employment or not (and this descriptor is only valid to some part, when the real combination of instruction and employment is confronted with its institutionalised combination; see Lassnigg 2015). In higher education, differentiation has been observed since decades; however, its comparative statistical representation is also to some extent problematic. The OECD indicators have distinguished between the categories A (academic, main cycle), B (vocational, short courses), and C (academic, second cycle, doctorate), however, different layers of higher education have been classified differently in different countries (e.g., university and non-university institutions are sometimes in the same category, sometimes not, thus the real differentiation cannot be seen always in the statistical representations).

Another distinction, which is even more important and more overseen or neglected, concerns the tracking differentiation at lower secondary level. The structures are conventionally distinguished by comprehensive ones on the one hand and openly tracked ones that comprise different types of schools on the other. In the *PISA data*, the point of a first distinction between tracks by age of students, and the number of tracks at age 15 are observed at the structural level. At the process level, a further distinction is made concerning the schools in which the assessment is performed: questions to the principals are asked about what fraction of students are allocated in different kinds of tracks within school, or within class, or if individualised distinctions/adaptations in instruction are made. These variables give very important information about *practices within comprehensive schools*, however, at the same time the use of these variables can be misleading, if the school structures are not taken into account: if tracking occurs structurally between school types, distinctions within schools might be absent, and using these variables only would signify a comprehensive structure (of course, the structures are more complicated, as differentiation within schools might also additionally appear in combination with tracking between school types).

The use of these variables provides important information about linkages between tracking in compulsory school and VET structures at upper secondary level. A combination of *PIAAC data* with structural information from *PISA* was used for the further analysis of VET and higher education participation in *PIAAC countries*. Two main results follow from these analyses: First, the distinction between comprehensive and openly tracked structures is much less definitive than mostly assumed; second, the relationship between tracked structures and assessment results in terms of achievement levels and inequalities is much more blurred than expected.

4. A glance at structures and competence measures

Contemporary sociology uses two quantitative measurements of inequality, one concerning participation, the other – having gained more attention in recent decades – concerning competences. Competences are deemed even more important, because they should be the basis of progressing in life (this might be questioned of course by a perspective that focuses more on credentialism and doubts about the measurement of competences).

Nevertheless, it is interesting, how structural traits of education are related to the measurement of competences. *PIAAC* is an attempt to measure competences among the adult population in participating countries in literacy and numeracy, and allows comparison of the levels and the distributions of competences. A recent study (Lassnigg and Vogtenhuber 2014) has tried to explore these relationships more thoroughly. On a cross-sectional basis a set of comparisons between two groups of countries (all *PIAAC*-participants, and a selection of advanced capitalist countries based on the types of welfare regimes) was made:

– The proportion of tertiary education credentials was compared with the level and distribution of measured competences that against a widely held assumption (and against publications by the OECD) does not really indicate that expansion of tertiary education necessarily increases the stock of competences among all countries, and less so among the advanced group; the inequality of the distribution of competences is not related to tertiarisation in all countries, and by tendency increases in the advanced countries (more s in numeracy). In particular the three countries from the liberal welfare model (US, UK, CND), with a high proportion of tertiary education show in numeracy comparatively low levels and high inequality of competences.

– Concerning VET the analysis first looked at the achievement tracking structures at age 15 taken from *PISA data*, secondly related this structure to the proportion of VET and tertiary education alternatively, and thirdly compared two versions of tracking, one only considering the raw *PISA* variables of tracking within given schools, the other also considering the tracking between school types that goes hand in hand with a high proportion of VET in some typical countries. This analysis in first instance shows that comprehensive structures do not mean abolition of tracking by achievement, this takes only another form. At age 15 a differentiation of pupils to groups within class ranges typically between 30% and 70% of the cohort, whereas a streaming differentiation of grouping between classes within schools is much more widespread in the Anglophone countries and Korea (ranging between 80% and almost 100%), than in the Nordic or Continental countries. The latter groups overlap with the Continental countries ranging between 10% and 60%, and the Nordic countries in a range between 15% and 40% of a cohort in tracked classes within schools. Secondly, the correlation of the amount of tracking with the respective proportion of VET and higher education shows clearly a negative relationship between tracking within schools and VET (R^2=.47), and a positive relationship of the amount of tracking with higher education (R^2=.23). If tracking within schools is interpreted as an indicator for the selectivity of structures, then *this selectivity – against an intuitive assumption – is increasing with tertiarisation*. The third step confronts two measurements of tracking with the level and the inequality of the *PIAAC* achievement scores, one measurement taking only into account (covert) selectivity within schools, the second also adding the (open) selectivity between school types in the early tracked systems (with the *PISA* variable about the age of first tracking taken as the indicator). From widely held assumptions inequality of competences should increase with open selectivity, and – depending on opposing background ideologies about the role of achievement grouping – the level of achievement might increase or decrease. Reading levels show less or no relationship to tracking, numeracy shows by trend a negative relationship, the comparison of the two versions of tracking shows a decrease of the relationship in both domains of achievement; that means that stronger selectivity would have less influence on achievement levels. In terms of inequality by trend more selectivity is increasing inequality, however, the relationship is stronger if only covert tracking is considered; the additional consideration of open tracking by different school types reduces the correlation with inequality.

In sum, these results are clearly at odds with the widely held assumptions that an increase of tertiary participation would imply a decrease of educational inequality, and also indirectly corroborates the above result that tertiarisation does not necessarily increase the stock of competences, as the correlation of tertiarisation with the increasing selectivity might lessen the level of competences.

5. Conclusions: Diversity and gradual changes instead of classes, democracy and citizenship as challenges for VET

The analysis of educational structures using statistical figures cannot give a complete picture of the changes going on, however, can rule out some widely and persistently held assumptions about the social effects of educational structures. Overall the analysis indicates that the dynamic changes in participation cannot be reasonably described in terms of discrete distinctions any more. In particular two distinctions are much less definitive than assumed, first the distinction between comprehensive and tracked structures, and second the distinction between general and vocational education (which has particularly among human capital economists also a strong connotation with the higher education and VET distinction).

The analysis of the distinction between openly tracked structures including different school types and more hidden tracking practices within comprehensive structures indicates much less marked structural differences and consequences than is expected at a superficial first glance. In particular the Anglophone type comprehensive structures include a high degree of tracking in compulsory school that even reaches into the primary level (US).

Vocational education shows much more mixed and diverse structures than conventionally expected (and sometimes reified by defenders of strong secondary VET by pushing a discourse of whether "VET for dummies" vs. "VET not for dummies", and thus reinforcing a divide between good and bad VET structures, e.g., Switzerland vs. Anglophone structures). In particular a past distinction of two discretely separate worlds (if it ever has existed in such a sharp manner) between VET and higher education cannot be supported by the analysis. Studies of higher VET (CEDEFOP and Le Mouillour 2011) have already shown the blurring of these distinctions and the differentiation of levels and institutions in the studies and concepts of mass higher education, as well as the more inclusive concept of tertiary education also point to these gradual structural changes.

Thus a picture of the tertiarisation of education structures that assumes a discrete choice between persisting institutions in either secondary VET or alternatively in tertiary higher education (often understood synonymously with university education) is misleading in two respects: first, a choice of VET at secondary level is still related to somewhat different probabilities to continue in higher education, however, VET seems also much less separate from higher education than expected by the discrete view, as a high participation in VET is not related to a markedly lower participation in tertiary education at country level. Second tertiarisation does not only mean a shift in participation from one persistent institution to another persistent institution, but also means a change of institutions (which is not shown by the statistical indicators, but must also take into account additional qualitative information about the institutional structures). Paradigm cases are, e.g., the history of the US Community Colleges that have changed from general to vocational institutions (analysed by the seminal study of Brint and Karabel 1989, and augmented by the cooling out model of

Clark 1960) or the development of the various kinds of polytechnics or Fachhochschule institutions until very recent times that in most cases have changed vocational institutions into tertiary level institutions (e.g., in Finland and Switzerland in the 1990s, which often have posed new questions about the structuring of higher education, and about dynamics of *academic drift* attempting to make higher VET more similar to universities, which sets in motion new processes of differentiation and regrouping within universities and previous higher education institutions, as e.g., in the UK with the unification and differentiation dynamic).

On this background the question can be posed of how citizenship might be embedded in these manifold dynamics. First, citizenship concerns the right to education, and equal opportunities of access. From this perspective structural distinctions in participation are in need of legitimation, and the VET vs. higher education distinction is mostly legitimated by occupational, employment, and economic benefit vs. (only formal) educational benefits – here it has always been difficult to demonstrate clear and unambiguous preferences for VET. Second, the distinction has traditionally been related to issues of stratification in society, with higher education producing an elite responsible for the decisions about the course of society, and VET producing qualified people responsible for running the economy more or less dependent on the wider and higher level decisions. From this topic the (quite heavily) persisting discourse about VET producing second class citizens has emerged that is echoed (particularly in countries with strong VET systems in the past) by opposing discourses of better (short term) pragmatic opportunities on the labour market for VET completers and a futile overproduction from higher education leading to over education and mismatch.

Confronting these polarised discourses with the gradual empirical picture, this pattern rather points to a mismatch between the discourse level and the empirical representations, which calls for an explanation. A plausible line of thinking could be to interpret the defensive VET discourse as a shadow of the history of VET producing well-functioning workers but well-adapted second class citizens in terms of contributing to the elite-owned thinking and conceptualising about the broader development of society and about control of employment and the economy – the knowledge, skills and competences for the latter discourse is related to traditional universities whereas VET by and large draws a distinction to this discourse by orienting students towards the real things of instrumental and technical knowledge, skills and competences. This distinction might be related to the distinction of the two and three cultures of literature/philosophy, science/technology, and sociology/ social sciences drawn first by C.P.Snow (1959) and augmented later by W.Lepenies (1985). Originally VET was very much related to the *second culture*, with the upcoming of the sciences as part of the university and the emerging technological institutes within higher education. The culture of technocracy in the 20th century might be seen as a forerunner of the emerging third culture of the social sciences, with economics and business administration as a mediating force departing from the second culture. The growth of the service sector has contributed to the broadening of VET and a movement of professionalization in this field, that has been detected more or less in parallel with the two cultures' view in the 1960s (Wilensky 1964).

Based on this view of a cultural dynamic of the emergence of the three cultures (and of their various interrelations) the observed blurring in the institutional structures of VET on the one hand and general and higher education on the other, can be interpreted as complex processes of widening and re-groupings of perspectives, as well as of bodies of knowledge and knowing. The concrete structures are also influenced by the occupational structures outside education, and the more basic social, political and economic configurations. Tertiarisation of VET might in this vain be seen as a movement of gradually taking more command over an occupational field, and thus in an stylised way moving up from second class to more first class citizens – often being eyed distrustfully by the already established first class citizens. It must also be admitted that this movement is not a linear and very direct one, but might have many faces.

References

Brint, S. and Karabel, J. 1989. The Diverted Dream: Community Colleges and the Promise of Educational Opportunity in America 1900–1985. Oxford, New York, OUP.

CEDEFOP and Le Mouillour, I. 2011. Vocational education and training at higher qualification levels. Research paper No.15. Luxembourg, Publications Office of the European Union.

Clark, B. R. 1960. The "Cooling-Out" Function in Higher Education. American Journal of Sociology. 65(6): 569–576.

Clark, B.R. 1980. The "Cooling Out" Function Revisited. New Directions for Community Colleges, vol. 1980, (132): 15–31, DOI: 10.1002/cc.36819803204.

Foster, P.J. 1965. The Vocational School Fallacy in Development Planning. In C.A. Anderson and M.J. Bowman (eds.), Education and National Development. Chicago, Aldine.

Lassnigg, L. 2015. The Political Branding of Apprenticeship into the "Dual System": Reflections about Exporting the Myth of Employment Transition. In A. Heikkinen and L. Lassnigg (eds.), Myths and Brands in Vocational Education. Newcastle, Cambridge Scholars.

Lassnigg, L. and Vogtenhuber, S. 2014. Das österreichische Modell der Formation von Kompetenzen im Vergleich, in Schlüsselkompetenzen von Erwachsenen – Vertiefende Analysen der *PIAAC-Erhebung* 2011/12 ed. by Statistik Austria, Vienna: Statistik Austria (p. 49–79). [retrieved from: <http://www.equi.at/dateien/lassnigg-vogtenhuber_2014_ko.pdf> – October 19th 2016]. (German Version; detailed results in German: <http://www.equi.at/dateien/IHS-PIAAC.pdf>), see English Presentation at <http://www.equi.at/material/valencia-pdf.pdf>.

Lassnigg, L. 2009. Some insights about VET from Large-Scale-Assessments? Presentation at DECOWE CONFERENCE "Development of Competencies in the World of Work and Education", 24–26 September 2009, Ljubljana, paper. [retrieved from: <http://www.equi.at/dateien/Ljubljana-decowe-paper.pdf>; annex-data: <http://www.equi.at/dateien/ljubljana-decowe-annex.pdf>; presentation: <http://www.equi.at/dateien/ljubljana.pdf> – October 19th 2016].

Lassnigg, L. 2011. VET and Higher Education: two worlds, two frameworks? Presentation at International DEHEMS CONFERENCE
"Employability of Graduates & Higher Education Management
Systems", 22–23 September 2011, Vienna. [retrieved from: <http://
www.equi.at/dateien/Vienna-DEHEMS.pdf> – October 19th 2016].

Lepenies, W. 1985. Die drei Kulturen. Soziologie zwischen Literatur
und Wissenschaft. Munich, Hanser.

Middleton, J., Ziderman, A. and Van Adams, A. 1993. Skills for Productivity: Vocational Education and Training in Developing Countries.
Oxford, OUP. [retrieved from: <http://documents.worldbank.org/
curated/en/391781468782110321/pdf/multi-page.pdf>– October
19th 2016].

OECD. 2013. OECD Skills Outlook 2013: First Results from the Survey
of Adult Skills, OECD Publishing. [retrieved from: <http://dx.doi.
org/10.1787/9789264204256-en> – October 19th 2016].

Snow, C.P. 1959. The two cultures. The Rede Lecture. Cambridge, Cambridge University Press. [retrieved from: <http://s-f-walker.org.uk/
pubsebooks/2cultures/Rede-lecture-2-cultures.pdf > – October 19th
2016].

Wilensky, H.L. 1964. The Professionalization of Everyone? American
Journal of Sociology. 70(2): 137–158.

Notes on Contributors

Míriam Abiétar López. Research Personnel in Training at the University of Valencia (Spain). Her work is focused on the development of a conceptualization of social justice applied to the analysis of educational programs and to the role they play in the transitions of youth at risk of educational and social exclusion.

Aikaterini Arkoudi-Vafea IEK Lemnou, Greece. Aikaterini is the Director of Vocational Training Institute of Lemnos as well as Information and Communications Technology adult educator.

Esther Berner is a professor for education with focus on the history of ideas and discourse history at the Helmut-Schmidt-Universität in Hamburg. Her fields of research comprise the history of vocational education and training, history of science and philosophy of education.

Lorenzo Bonoli is Senior researcher and lecturer at the Swiss Federal Institute for Vocational Education and Training, in Lausanne. His research and teaching activities focus, on the one hand, on history and evolution of the Swiss VET system from the beginning of the XIX century until today and, on the other hand, on the current issues of the Swiss VET system in a national and international perspective.

Tânia Suely Antonelli Marcelino Brabo. Professor, Department of Management and Supervision School and the Graduate Program in Education of the Faculty of Philosophy and Sciences, Universidade Estadual Paulista, UNESP. Center Coordinator for Human Rights and Citizenship Marilia and Deputy Coordinator of the Centre of Education of UNESP Human Rights.

Ana I. Córdoba Iñesta is a Professor in the Department of Developmental and Educational Psychology at the University of Valencia. Her research interests include vulnerability and social exclusion, adult and adolescent development, resilience.

María José Chisvert-Tarazona is associate professor in the Department of Didactics and School Organization at the University of Valencia. Among her highlights research training and career guidance. She has been principal investigator of a project for the accreditation of professional skills.

Prof. Dr. Dr. h.c. Thomas Deissinger, University of Konstanz. Thomas Deissinger is a Professor of Business Education at the University of Konstanz. He graduated at the University of Mannheim, where he also did his Ph.D. and his habilitation. Since 1998 he holds the Chair of Business Education in Konstanz. His research interests include Vocational Education Systems, Vocational Education Policy, the History of Vocational Education and Full-time Vocational Education. He has published several papers on the VET systems in England and Australia. One of his major topics is the Dual System of VET in Germany. Recent research activities refer to the Canadian VET system and to VET Teacher Education in the context of an Erasmus plus project with Ukraine, Spain and Austria.

Germán Gil Rodríguez, M.A. of Contemporary History at the University of Valencia and Ph.Dr. in Philosophy and Sciences of Education. As a member of the research group AREA-EGRIS he has participated in research promoted by the European Commission: Families and transitions in Europe Contributors (FATE), Youth Policy an Participation (YOYO), "Youth – actor of social change, UP2YOUTH, Leonardo TVT: Tools of Trade for Teaching in Vet…".

Philipp Gonon is Professor of Vocational Education and Training at Zurich University, where he teaches vocational pedagogy, history and theory of (vocational) education, quality assurance and program evaluation at graduate and undergraduate level. From 1986 until 1992 he was research assistant and lecturer at the Institute of Pedagogy of the University of Bern. From 1999 until 2004 he served as a Full University Professor of Vocational Further Education at the University of Trier in Germany. Prof. Dr. Philipp Gonon, Universität Zürich, Institut für Erziehungswissenschaft.

Daniela Gremm, University of Konstanz. Daniela Gremm has been an academic staff member at the Chair of Business Education at the University of Konstanz since 2016. After receiving the general qualification for university entrance, she did an apprenticeship as a bank clerk. She then started her studies in Business and Economics Education at the Ludwig-Maximilians-University in Munich, where she gained a Bachelor of Science degree. In 2016 she completed her Master degree in Business Education at the University of Konstanz.

Anja Heikkinen is a professor of education in University of Tampere. Her research focus is on historical, philosophical and cultural aspects in adult and vocational education, often from perspectives of sex-distinctions and equality. She is chairing the research group Equality and Planetary Justice in Adult, Vocational and Higher Education, <https://equjust.wordpress.com>.

Ida Juul is an associated professor at Aarhus University in Denmark. She has written extensively on the Danish VET-system and especially on its development from the end of world war II till today. She has also written about the significance of gender in the VET system and has analyzed the choice of VET seen from a generational and narrative perspective. She is currently writing on a book on the history of the Danish apprenticeship system from the 15th. century when the guilds gained control over apprenticeship to 1937, when the influence of the social partners on the Danish VET system was institutionalised.

Dr. Perpetua J. Kalimasi. Lecturer and Head, Department of Educational Foundations and Teaching Management. Mzumbe University, Tanzania.

Prof. Dr. Werner Kuhlmeier Berufliche Bildung und Lebenslanges Lernen. Fakultät für Erziehungswissenschaft, Universität Hamburg.

Lorenz Lassnigg. Senior researcher and emerit. head of research group equi-employment-qualification-innovation (www.equi.at) at the Institute for Advanced Studies (IHS), Vienna.

Fernando Marhuenda-Fluixá is Professor in Didactics at the School of Philosophy and Education at the University of Valencia, Spain. His research interests focus on vocational education, workplace learning, transitions between education and work, and education and training in contexts of vulnerability. He is currently coordinating a Spanish research team on educational processes in Work Integration Companies, ref. EDU2013-45919-R.

Chiara Martinelli awarded her Phd in Contemporary History at the University of Florence with a thesis about the history of vocational education in Italy between 1861 and 1914.

Dr. philos. Liv Mjelde. Professor, Oslo and Akershus University College of applied sciences, Oslo, Norway. Professor Liv Mjelde is a sociologist specialised in the Sociology of Education. Her research interests focus on the changing relations between vocational and general education from psychological, didactic and sociological perspectives. One of her main research fields is gender division of labour.

Almudena A. Navas Saurin is Associate Professor at the University of Valencia (Spain); she teaches Curriculum Studies and Social Justice, and has participated in several research projects founded by the European Union related to youth transitions and identity construction. Her areas of interest include Pedagogical Practice as defined by Basil Bernstein in his Theory of Pedagogical Discourse. She has published her work in Revista de Educación, ILO (UNESCO International Labor Office), Tirant lo Blanch and the University of Valencia Press. She is currently the International Coordinator of Social Education Degree.

Patricia Olmos Rueda, Ph.D., professor postdoctoral researcher of the Applied Pedagogy Department in the Faculty of Education at the Universitat Autònoma de Barcelona (UAB). Her research interests and publications are mainly related to diversity; vulnerable groups at risk of exclusion; educational, social and labour inclusion; young people and early school leaving; guidance and training processes for improving employability and key competencies.

Elizabeth Opit is a lecturer of Sociology of Education at Kyambogo University in Uganda. Her research focus is on Social-cultural aspects in Education with specific reference to Gender and Education.

Vicente R. Palop Esteban. Popular educator with specialization in technical teachings. Manuel Castillo award for peace and social development. PhD in international development cooperation. Coordinator and trainer in educational programs for adults in employment and entrepreneurship (Fe y Alegría, Ecuador). Coordinator in VET of Social Integration (San José Schools, Valencia-Spain). Researcher fellow at the Interuniversity Institute for Local Development (University of Valencia-Spain).

Jesse Sjelvgren is Master of Arts (Education) from University of Tampere. He accomplished his MA thesis on development of competence-based curriculum for practical nurses in the Tampere Regional Vocational College. He is currently working as a project coordinator in the social care sector and interested in developing vocational education of social and health care professionals.

Kenneth Teitelbaum currently serves as Dean of the College of Education at Kutztown University in Pennsylvania. Prior to this appointment he was Dean and Professor of the Watson College of Education at the University of North Carolina Wilmington and the College of Education and Human Services at Southern Illinois University Carbondale. His research and teaching interests focus on school knowledge in current and historical contexts, school reform as it relates to democracy, social justice and diversity, and critical reflection in teacher education and teachers' work.

Stefan Vogtenhuber, researcher at equi-employment-qualification-innovation (www.equi.at), Institute for Advanced Studies (IHS) and University of Vienna.

PD. Dr. Burkhard Vollmers, Vertretungsprofessor Schulpädagogik, Sozialpädagogik, Behindertenpädagogik und Psychologie in Erziehung und Unterricht. Fakultät für Erziehungswissenschaft, Universität Hamburg.

Lea Zehnder, lic. phil. Research and Teaching Assistant, University of Zurich, Institute of Education – Department of Vocational Education and Training.

studies in vocational and continuing education

edited by
philipp gonon & anja heikkinen

The aim of this series is to present critical, historical and comparative research in the field of vocational and continuing education and human research development, seen from a pedagogical, organisational, economic and societal perspective. It discusses the implications of latest research to contemporary reform policies and practices. One central issue reflected in all publications is gender. A basic feature of all volumes is their cross-cultural approach.

The series has a firm basis in the international research network "VET and Culture" (Vocational Education and Training and Culture; www.peda.net/veraja/uta/vetculture) and the editors invite distinguished researchers from Europe and other continents to contribute to the series. Studies in vocational and continuing education include monographs, collected papers editions, and proceedings.

Vol.   1   Antony Lindgren & Anja Heikkinen (eds)
           Social Competences in Vocational and Continuing Education
           2004. 256 S. ISBN 3-03910-345-8 / US-ISBN 0-8204-7013-9

Vol.   2   Liv Mjelde
           The Magical Properties of Workshop Learning
           2006. 230 S. ISBN 3-03910-348-2 / US-ISBN 0-8204-7014-7

Vol.   3   Liv Mjelde & Richard Daly (eds)
           Working Knowledge in a Globalizing World
           From Work to Learning, from Learning to Work
           2006. 406 S. ISBN 3-03910-974-X / 0-8204-8364-8